Community in Modern Scottish Literature

Scottish Cultural Review of Language and Literature

VOLUME 25

The titles published in this series are listed at *brill.com/scrl*

Community in Modern
Scottish Literature

Edited by

Scott Lyall

BRILL

RODOPI

LEIDEN | BOSTON

Cover illustration: *The Baptism of Clyde*, 2013, Rachel Maclean. Commissioned and published by Edinburgh Printmakers; copyright Rachel Maclean.

Library of Congress Cataloging-in-Publication Data

Names: Lyall, Scott, editor.
Title: Community in modern Scottish literature / edited by Scott Lyall.
Description: Leiden ; Boston : Brill, [2016] | Series: Scottish cultural
   review of language and literature ; 25 | Includes bibliographical
   references and index.
Identifiers: LCCN 2016008959 (print) | LCCN 2016017580 (ebook) | ISBN
   9789004317444 (hardback : acid-free paper) | ISBN 9789004317451 (E-book)
Subjects: LCSH: English literature--Scottish authors--History and criticism.
   | Scottish literature--History and criticism. | Community life in
   literature. | Communities in literature. | Society in literature.
Classification: LCC PR8518 .C66 2016 (print) | LCC PR8518 (ebook) | DDC
   820.9/9411--dc23
LC record available at https://lccn.loc.gov/2016008959

Want or need Open Access? Brill Open offers you the choice to make your research freely accessible online in exchange for a publication charge. Review your various options on brill.com/brill-open.

Typeface for the Latin, Greek, and Cyrillic scripts: "Brill". See and download: brill.com/brill-typeface.

ISSN 1571-0734
ISBN 978-90-04-31744-4 (hardback)
ISBN 978-90-04-31745-1 (e-book)

This book is printed on acid-free paper and produced in a sustainable manner.

Printed by Printforce, the Netherlands

Contents

Preface: In Search of Community

Scott Lyall

> *Community* derives from the Latin root word *communis* (common),
> which itself breaks down into two possible derivations [...]. The first, *com*
> plus *munis* (what is indebted, bound, or obligated together), is thought to
> be more philologically accurate, while the second, *com* plus *unus* (what is
> together as one), carries the status of a folk-etymology.[1]

What is community? Is community a good thing, something to be aimed for?
Or is it exclusionary, a means of dividing people and keeping out the unwanted?
Indeed, does community, understood as a sense of togetherness and shared
values, a being in common, even exist in our time of capitalist individualism
and national borders? According to Gerard Delanty, 'the idea of community is
related to the search for belonging in the insecure conditions of modern
society'.[2] Delanty's terms are telling: *idea* is neither quite practice nor reality
(although of course it might necessarily inform these), and the *search* for the
sense of belonging that comes with community does not mean that that feeling or place will ever finally be reached. Seen in this light, 'community' might
now be more a metaphysics of striving for home, rather than the actuality, or
even the possibility, of arrival. In this spirit, *Community in Modern Scottish
Literature* is a search for what community means and how community is represented in Scottish literature from the late nineteenth to the early twenty-first
century.

Community is a highly pertinent contemporary issue, perhaps precisely
because the present age seems often to refute the possibility of community.
One of the first and most significant theorists of community, Ferdinand
Tönnies in *Gemeinschaft und Gesellschaft* (first published in 1887 and most
commonly translated into English as *Community and Society* or *Community
and Association*), considered community to consist of 'real and organic life',
whereas society should be understood as an 'imaginary and mechanical
structure'.[3] Tönnies conceived of 'community' and 'society' as typologies that
in practice somewhat blur into each other, but nonetheless he believed that in

---

1   Naomi E. Silver, 'The Politics of Sacrifice', in *The Politics of Community*, ed. by Michael Strysick
    (Aurora, CO: The Davies Group, 2002), pp. 201–19 (p. 204).
2   Gerard Delanty, *Community*, 2nd edn (Abingdon: Routledge, 2010), p. x.
3   Ferdinand Tönnies, *Community and Association*, trans. by Charles P. Loomis (London:
    Routledge & Kegan Paul, 1974), p. 37.

community people were 'essentially united', while in society, in spite of all civilisation's modes of bringing people together, they were 'essentially separated'.[4] *Gemeinschaft und Gesellschaft* traces community from the unified Middle Ages to the atomisation of the industrial epoch – a fragmentation that has arguably gone on apace into the globalised contemporary era. As Eric Hobsbawm writes of the twentieth century, especially post-1960s:

> The material advantages of a life in a world in which community and family declined were, and remain, undeniable. What few realized was how much of modern industrial society up to the mid-twentieth century had relied on a symbiosis between old community and family values and the new society, and therefore how dramatic the effects of their spectacularly rapid disintegration were likely to be. This became evident in the era of neo-liberal ideology [...].[5]

It is this perceived disintegration of community that has most exercised (post) modern theorists of the subject. Two strains can broadly be identified: a continental European theorising of community by such as Jean-Luc Nancy, Maurice Blanchot (both influenced by Georges Bataille), and Giorgio Agamben, and, at least in part inspired by those, university collectives in the US such as the Miami Theory Collective, responsible in 1991 for *Community at Loose Ends* (– significantly this collective emerged from the French and Italian departments at Miami University). While the likes of Nancy and Blanchot are more concerned with the ontology of community, the Miami Theory Collective and the contributors to *The Politics of Community* (2002) are generally troubled over the insecure place of community in a capitalist economy and a postmodern culture. However, the watershed crisis point for community-as-idea was reached with the collapse of communism as a viable alternative to global capitalism. This moment is a crossroads for community which for a Marxist such as David Harvey offers both hope and a warning: communities of resistance can align to achieve radical ends, yet equally the unifying 'spirit of community has long been held as an antidote to threats of social disorder, class war and revolutionary violence'.[6] We might blanch at the Marxist lexis of 'revolutionary violence', but Harvey's point remains valid that recourse to 'community' can serve to mask inequalities and conflict. A revivified interest in the idea of

---

4 Tönnies, *Community and Association*, p. 74.

5 Eric Hobsbawm, *The Age of Extremes: The Short Twentieth Century, 1914–1991* (London: Abacus, 1995), p. 340.

6 David Harvey, *Spaces of Hope* (Edinburgh: Edinburgh University Press, 2002), p. 170.

community during a period in which transnational capitalism appears to have defeated all economic alternatives and yet continues to suffer recurrent crises is telling, as for Jean-Luc Nancy community 'emerges at times of profound social transformation or of great turmoil including the destruction of the social order'.[7]

The nostalgia for community generated by Scottish Kailyard novelists of the late nineteenth century fits Nancy's diagnosis, with community remaining fundamental in the modern period to literary representations in and of Scotland. 'Community', as Timothy C. Baker tells us, 'is frequently viewed as a central theme in Scottish literature, and recognition of its position as such is a necessary prerequisite for any conceptualisation of Scottish literature as an identifiable whole'.[8] What Baker calls the 'predominant critical reading' of Scottish literature 'is regarded both as depicting real or imagined communities and as constituting community itself, in the sense of contributing to a national literary tradition'.[9] Community has not only been a key thematic concern in Scottish literary representations, in other words, it has also been a bulwark of the Scottish tradition, helping to form Scottish literature as a subject-area. In Scotland, as the Introduction makes clear, community has traditionally stood as a mythic signifier of commonality and communal resistance to Anglophone capital and perceived affectation, as well as white, normative, often working-class, traditionalism. Resistance to community in these mythic terms may suggest openness to a plurality of new forms of community, and many of the chapters in this volume examine representations of community that expose tensions in and posit oppositions to a normative conception of Scottish community, in turn troubling and broadening the limits of Scottish literature as a tradition and an academic discipline. For instance, Monica Germanà looks at the uncanny, claustrophobic nature of community as a Gothic realm in two contemporary novels, Louise Welsh's *The Cutting Room* and John Burnside's *The Devil's Footprints*, while Scott Hames examines the nature of voice in James Kelman's more recent work and finds characters who strain against a communal 'with-ness'. Carole Jones's chapter analyses the challenges that have been faced by gay and lesbian people in Scotland in forming communities at all, while suggesting that homonormative community might be just as restricting to gay liberation, and to a liberatory politics generally, as heteronormativity,

---

7   Jean-Luc Nancy, 'Communism, the Word', in *The Idea of Communism*, ed. by Costas Douzinas and Slavoj Žižek (London and New York: Verso, 2010), pp. 145–53 (p. 147).

8   Timothy C. Baker, *George Mackay Brown and the Philosophy of Community* (Edinburgh: Edinburgh University Press, 2009), p. 5.

9   Baker, *George Mackay Brown and the Philosophy of Community*, p. 5.

before examining queer depictions in Luke Sutherland's *Venus as a Boy* and Ali Smith's *Girl Meets Boy*. Reading against the grain of many previous interpretations of Janice Galloway's *The Trick is to Keep Breathing*, Alex Thomson claims that the novel's main character is not so much suffering from the breakdown of traditional community but is in existential rebellion against it; his analysis is salutary in its wariness of politicised readings that presuppose recovery of an antecedent 'community' to be the aim of (Scottish) literature.

Other chapters offer readings of community as places of restriction and release, such as Timothy C. Baker's on Scottish islands, from the Scots Renaissance to the present, as places of renewal and exile, and H. Gustav Klaus's survey of the individual (male) hero in relation to working-class community in fiction of the 1920–40s. The expectations, perhaps even burdens, of a rich communal cultural heritage form the background to Emma Dymock's analysis of the role of community for poets writing in Gaelic; yet, as she shows, the value of community has often been a spur to poetic innovation, especially for poets in Gaelic in the postmodern world. This is true too of Bashabi Fraser's chapter on the 'New Scots': poets from South Asian who have settled in Scotland and who reflect in their poetry on both the 'elsewhere' (as Fraser calls it) from which they and their families have come, and on their new homeland. These Scottish South Asian poets have created a new community of writers in Scotland, voicing new visions as well as reflecting back the sometimes racist views of the Scottish community about these 'New Scots'. But overwhelmingly, Fraser's chapter illustrates the manner in which communities, be they local, national or cultural, change and develop in rewarding ways due to migration. Immigration has, in every sense, *enlarged* the Scottish community and communities in Scotland; a static community, especially in a global age, is surely a dead or dying community.

The topic of immigration arises in my own chapter on Hugh MacDiarmid, which in part looks at the question of the poet's anti-Englishness, but also at the ways MacDiarmid reacted against the static and nostalgic community of the Kailyard, an important template of community for modern Scottish literature which is also examined in the Introduction. MacDiarmid, and his vision of Scottish culture and community, was a key antagonist for Hamish Henderson and Alexander Trocchi. Corey Gibson's chapter on Henderson examines the 'folk process' and the anonymous community of travelling people valorised by Henderson, while Gill Tasker points to the ways Trocchi concocted 'alternative communities' whose radical subjectivism and countercultural aims sought escape from the ideologies of the Cold War, and have continuing relevance today. While Hobsbawm is doubtless right to say '[t]he cultural revolution of the later twentieth century can [...] best be understood as the triumph of the individual over society' with all the challenges this brings to traditional community, he misses the ways in which this 'revolution' has sparked new oppositional communities of its own, from Trocchi's counterculture in the 1950s and '60s to, arguably, some of the virtual communities of our own time.[10]

The expansion of Scottish drama in both institutional practice, and in the depictions of largely male, working-class community to a wider, more inclusive purview, forms the basis of Trish Reid's chapter. Likewise, the growth and development of Scottish literature as a subject, alongside new readings of the meanings of community, particularly in postmodern terms, make this volume a necessary, though, as the first survey of its kind, clearly not exhaustive, intervention in these areas. As is hopefully clear from the preceding overview of the chapters, the 'community' examined in *Community in Modern Scottish Literature* covers a much wider terrain than solely that of national community, and the tenor of much of the analyses may be said to set itself against the striving for unity fundamental to nationalism.

The etymological definition of 'community' that opens this Preface – that of something held in common, an obligatory oneness – has been challenged by Michael Strysick as being troublingly polarising when translated into practice, precisely due to its totalising nature, which is often masked by the rhetoric of inclusivity.

> [C]ommunity, with its implicit sense of the common, is often conceived of in terms of those things that are merely common among people; or more specifically, through the *presence* of what is presumably mutual. In the process, a philosophy of community emerges which runs the risk of operating on the basis of convenient oppositions between same and other in which the bias of homogeneity is predominant. If, however, the common within community is reconceived on the basis of an *absence* of what is shared – our difference – then such convenient oppositions are seriously challenged; individuals must be conceived in terms of their potentially unregulatable differences.[11]

Strysick is right to point to the problems of a community of commonality, yet his own conception of community as based on absence, that which we do not share in common, arguably risks evacuating community of any meaning at all.

---

10   Hobsbawm, *The Age of Extremes*, p. 334.

11   Michael Strysick, 'The End of Community and the Politics of Grammar', in *The Politics of Community*, pp. 45–64 (p. 46). Italics in original.

Community might be better understood as interconnected dialectical space (see Figure 1). In this model, forces that might sometimes be seen as conflicting – the potential tensions between the individual and a larger group, the gap between the public self and the private self, the differences between local cultures in a globalised world – actually exist in relation to form the mainspring of a more fluid idea of community, one that is neither oppressively totalising or missing entirely. And while history and institutionality are important to the configurations of community, a model that promotes the overlapping realms of personal experience keeps open the importance of culture to the construction and deconstruction of community. Anthony P. Cohen argues that

> culture – the community as experienced by its members – does not consist in social structure or in 'the doing' of social behaviour. It inheres, rather, in 'the thinking' about it. It is in this sense that we can speak of community as a symbolic, rather than a structural, construct.[12]

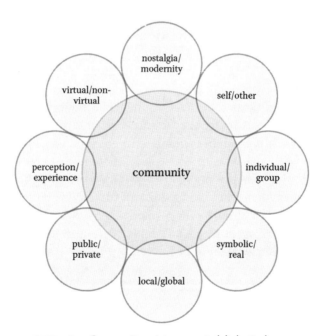

FIGURE 1   *Community as interconnected dialectical space*

---

12   Anthony P. Cohen, *The Symbolic Construction of Community* (Abingdon: Routledge, 2015), p. 98.

Thinking about community includes theorising on community and writing and examining literary representations of community. In each case the positionality of the thinker and writer is plainly of importance. If the archetypal Romantic 'genius' was paradigmatic in standing outside of the community, the position of today's artists is more complex, while the academic in UK universities is compelled to view communities outside of the university as mere instances of potential 'impact'.

Beginning in January 2016, a venture by the artist and art lecturer Ellie Harrison called 'The Glasgow Effect' illustrates many of the divisive and fascinating issues of relating art to the community in the present day. 'The Glasgow Effect' is described on its Facebook page as a 'year long "action research" project/durational performance, for which artist Ellie Harrison will not travel outside Greater Glasgow for a whole year [...]'.

> By setting this one simple restriction to her current lifestyle, she intends to test the limits of a 'sustainable practice' and to challenge the demand-to-travel placed upon the 'successful' artist/academic. The experiment will enable her to cut her carbon footprint and increase her sense of belonging, by encouraging her to seek out and create 'local opportunities' – testing what becomes possible when she invests all her ideas, time and energy within the city where she lives.[13]

Hostile social media response was unsurprisingly swift, with many native Glaswegians viewing the project as condescending, while there was added anger that the research was funded by Creative Scotland. 'The Glasgow Effect' illustrates, whether for serious or satirical purpose, the perceived loss of organic connection between art, artist and community, and raises questions as to how and to what extent art represents community at all. Rather than community finding expression through artistic representation, Harrison looks like an artist (and academic) trying to locate a community to represent. Our own positionality might determine whether we see this as farcical or laudable. But it reminds us that, in the atomisation of the present, the belonging promised by community may be found – or indeed lost – as much in the search for community as in its lived reality.

---

13   'The Glasgow Effect' <https://www.facebook.com/events/938052702945194/> [accessed 6 January, 2016].

Editor's Acknowledgements

The idea for this book emerged from a series of research seminars at Edinburgh Napier University. I'd like to thank my colleagues in the Centre for Literature and Writing there, especially Linda Dryden, for instigating and sustaining such a lively research community. Thank you to Sarah Dunnigan for her interest in translating concept into book, and to Masja Horn at Brill for her guidance and patience. Many thanks also to Rachel Maclean for allowing me to use her wonderful *The Baptism of Clyde* as a cover image. I'm particularly grateful for their help and support to Tim Baker, Scott Hames, Gill Tasker and Alex Thomson, and to all of the contributors for their enthusiasm for this project.

Notes on Contributors

Timothy C. Baker

is Senior Lecturer in Scottish and Contemporary Literature at the University of Aberdeen. He is author of *George Mackay Brown and the Philosophy of Community* and *Contemporary Scottish Gothic: Mourning, Authenticity, and Tradition*, and has published widely on Scottish fiction and poetry. Forthcoming projects include a monograph on the relation between animality, suffering, and language in contemporary fiction and another on gender and space in mid-twentieth-century women's fiction.

Emma Dymock

gained First Class Honours in Celtic at the University of Edinburgh in 2003, and has since completed an MSc on symbolism in twentieth-century Gaelic poetry and a PhD focussing on Sorley MacLean's long poem, 'An Cuilithionn'. She is a post-doctoral fellow at the University of Edinburgh, teaching classes in Celtic and Scottish Studies. She has co-edited two collections of essays on modern Scottish Gaelic and Scottish literature. In 2011 she co-edited, with Christopher Whyte, *Caoir Gheal Leumraich/White Leaping Flame: Sorley MacLean Collected Poems*. She is currently editing *Naething Dauntit: The Collected Poems of Douglas Young* and the Sorley MacLean – Douglas Young Correspondence, both due for publication in 2016.

Bashabi Fraser

is Professor of English and Creative Writing and co-founder and Director of the Scottish Centre of Tagore Studies at Edinburgh Napier University. A poet and academic, her recent publications include *Letters to my Mother and Other Mothers* (Luath Press, 2015), *Ragas & Reels* (2012), *Scots Beneath the Banyan Tree: Stories from Bengal* (2012), *From the Ganga to the Tay* (2009), *Bengal Partition Stories: An Unclosed Chapter* (2006; 2008), *A Meeting of Two Minds: The Geddes – Tagore Letters* (2005), and *Tartan & Turban* (2004). Currently she is co-editing an anthology of Scottish South Asian poetry and has been commissioned to write a critical biography of Rabindranath Tagore.

Monica Germanà

is Senior Lecturer in English Literature and Creative Writing at the University of Westminster. Her research interests include late twentieth- and twenty-first-century British literature, with a specific emphasis on Scottish fiction, the Gothic tradition and women's writing. She is author of *Scottish Women's Gothic and Fantastic Writing* (EUP, 2010) and editor of a special issue of *Gothic Studies* on Contemporary Scottish Gothic (2011). She has also co-edited *New Critical Perspectives: Ali Smith* (Bloomsbury, 2013) and has published articles and chapters on Iain Banks, James Kelman, Alasdair Gray, Janice Galloway, and A.L. Kennedy. She is currently co-editing *The Edinburgh Companion to Scottish Gothic* (2016), and working on a new monograph (*Bond Girls: Body, Dress, Gender*) exploring the sartorial appearance of dangerous women in Ian Fleming's novels and subsequent film adaptations.

Corey Gibson

lectures in Modern English Literature at the University of Groningen in the Netherlands. He is author of *The Voice of the People: Hamish Henderson and Scottish Cultural Politics* (EUP, 2015), which was shortlisted for the 2015 Saltire Society Research Book of the Year. He was awarded his PhD from the University of Edinburgh in 2012, and received the Ross Roy Medal for his research in Scottish literary studies in the same year. Between 2012 and 2013 he was a US–UK Fulbright Commission Scottish Studies Scholar at University of California, Berkeley. He has published on the politics of poetic production, folk culture, working-class literature, and nationalist and internationalist politics in modern literature.

Scott Hames

has published widely on contemporary Scottish literature and cultural politics. He edited *The Edinburgh Companion to James Kelman* and *Unstated: Writers on Scottish Independence*, and is completing a monograph on recent Scottish fiction and constitutional politics. He teaches at the University of Stirling.

Carole Jones

is lecturer in English and Scottish Literature at the University of Edinburgh and programme director of the MSc by Research in Gender and Culture. Her research interests span gender, sexuality and queering representations in Scottish fiction and beyond, and she has published various articles and book chapters on contemporary Scottish writers such as James Kelman, Irvine Welsh, Janice Galloway, and Laura Hird. She is author of *Disappearing Men: Gender Disorientation in Scottish Fiction 1979–1999* (Brill | Rodopi, 2009).

H. Gustav Klaus

is Emeritus Professor of the Literature of the British Isles at the University of Rostock, Germany. He has published widely on nineteenth- and twentieth-century working-class writing. His books include *The Literature of Labour*

(1985), *Factory Girl* (1998) and *James Kelman* (2005), as well as the edited collections *British Industrial Fictions* (2000), *'To Hell with Culture'* (2005) and *Ecology and the Literature of the British Left* (2012).

Scott Lyall

is Lecturer in Modern Literature and programme leader for English at Edinburgh Napier University, with research interests in Modernism and Scottish Literature, especially of the 1920s and '30s. His monograph *Hugh MacDiarmid's Poetry and Politics of Place: Imagining a Scottish Republic* (EUP, 2006) emerged from doctoral study at the University of St Andrews and a spell as postdoctoral research fellow in Scottish and Irish Studies at Trinity College Dublin. Co-editor of *The Edinburgh Companion to Hugh MacDiarmid* (2011) and editor of *The International Companion to Lewis Grassic Gibbon* (ASLS, 2015), he is working on a book on Modernism and religion.

Trish Reid

is Associate Dean Teaching and Learning in the Faculty of Arts and Social Sciences at Kingston University. Her research interests are primarily in contemporary Scottish theatre. Recent publications include 'Casanova' in *The Suspect Culture Book* (2013), *Theatre & Scotland* (Palgrave, 2013), 'Anthony Neilson' in *Modern British Playwriting: The 1990s* (2012), and 'Post-Devolutionary Drama' in *The Edinburgh Companion to Scottish Drama* (2011). She is currently working on a longer monograph for Palgrave on contemporary Scottish theatre and performance, and *The Theatre of Anthony Neilson* for Bloomsbury Methuen.

Gill Tasker

is former Joint Managing Director of the award-winning Glasgow-based independent publisher Cargo. She holds a doctorate in English Studies from the University of Strathclyde and her thesis, 'Cosmonaut of Inner Space: An Existential Enquiry into the writing of Alexander Trocchi', was shortlisted for the 2015 Universities Committee of Scottish Literature Ross Roy Medal. She currently lectures on the MLitt in Publishing Studies at the University of Stirling's International Centre for Publishing and Communication.

Alex Thomson

is Senior Lecturer in the School of Literatures, Languages and Cultures at the University of Edinburgh. His research is in modern literature, philosophy and political theory. He has published monographs on the work of Jacques Derrida and Theodor Adorno, and a critical edition of Robert Louis Stevenson's *Memories and Portraits* is forthcoming from Edinburgh University Press.

INTRODUCTION

'Tenshillingland': Community and Commerce, Myth and Madness in the Modern Scottish Novel

Scott Lyall

Abstract

While 'community' as a concept has come under increasing attack in a neoliberal era, it has remained in Scotland a mythic, though not unexamined, signifier of resistance to perceived threats to national identity. Community, central to the Scottish novel since the Kailyard, continues to be a prevalent theme in the many important novels of the twentieth and twenty-first centuries explored here. Yet, while often disturbingly oppressive in tenor, many of these representations of community actually attack the myth of Scottish communalism to critique, and often expose as forms of madness, the conventional values of social class, capitalism, patriarchy, and religion.

Keywords

Community – Scotland – myth – Kailyard – commercialism – *The House with the Green Shutters* – Calvinism – madness – class – *Sunset Song* – *Imagined Corners* – *The Prime of Miss Jean Brodie* – capitalism – *Lanark* – *Trainspotting* – *Tales from the Mall* – Scottish politics

The Myth of Scottish Communalism

If there is an American Dream, 'a narrative of considerable power which helps to define Americans to themselves, and they hope to other people', what, asks David McCrone, is the 'Scottish myth'?[1] McCrone makes clear that by myth he does not mean 'something which is manifestly false'.[2] While he acknowledges

---

1   David McCrone, *Understanding Scotland: The Sociology of a Nation*, 2nd edn (London and New York: Routledge, 2001), p. 90.
2   McCrone, *Understanding Scotland*, p. 91.

that myths 'represent a collection of symbolic elements assembled to account for and validate a set of social institutions', nonetheless neither is he using the term myth in entirely the same semiological sense as Barthes, who seeks the demythologisation of the everyday in order to expose as ideological what is often passed off as natural.[3] For McCrone, myths resemble traditions in having a complex connection with the past which also informs how we make sense of the present. As such, myths are neither true or false, refutable or irrefutable in any empirical sense, but rather provide tacit credence for certain aspects of self-definition and stereotype in relation to communal or national belonging. In this regard, as Gerard Carruthers points out, '[w]e find such active myths as the "fighting Scot", the "freedom-loving Scot", the "primitive Scot", the "puritanical Scot" and the "civilised Scot"'.[4] However, '[i]n the Scottish myth', according to McCrone, 'the central motif is the inherent egalitarianism of the Scots'.[5]

The importance of Scottish egalitarianism to Scottish identity, society and politics has distinct implications for an understanding of what community might mean in Scotland and in representations of community in Scottish literature, in the same mythic terms outlined above. McCrone has been influenced in his thinking here by Stephen Maxwell, who in an essay entitled 'Can Scotland's Political Myths Be Broken?' from 1976 – three years before the 'No' to Scottish devolution was returned in 1979 – argued that '[p]rovincial Scotland, denied the opportunity of defining its sense of national identity through the exercise of self-government, drugged itself with consoling myths'.[6] According to Maxwell,

> The idea that Scottish society is egalitarian is central to the myth of Scottish democracy. In its strong nationalist version, class division is held to be an alien importation from England. In the weaker version it describes the wider opportunity for social mobility in Scotland as illustrated in the 'lad o' pairts' tradition.[7]

Maxwell is suggesting that the Scots see themselves as an essentially classless and more democratic people than the English, with pernicious social stratification

---

3 McCrone, *Understanding Scotland*, p. 91. See Roland Barthes, *Mythologies*, trans. by Annette Lavers (London: Vintage, 2000), pp. 11–12.

4 Gerard Carruthers, *Scottish Literature* (Edinburgh: Edinburgh University Press, 2009), p. 2.

5 McCrone, *Understanding Scotland*, p. 91.

6 Stephen Maxwell, *The Case for Left Wing Nationalism: Essays and Articles* (Edinburgh: Luath Press, 2013), pp. 15–20 (p. 15).

7 Maxwell, *The Case for Left Wing Nationalism*, p. 17.

being introduced through union with England and the subsequent anglicisation of Scottish life. However, in spite of this, core areas of civic life in Scotland retain a uniquely Scottish egalitarian tradition, such as the education system, where talented students can succeed whatever their social background. McCrone takes these ideas forward in his own analysis, pointing out that it is contradictory to imagine Scotland as being at once a classless society and a place where class is no barrier to advancement for the lad o' pairts, who can only ever be a relatively select few. However, McCrone stresses that the nature of the egalitarian Scottish myth 'lends itself to conservative as well as to radical interpretations': if Scots are intrinsically equal, all 'Jock Tamson's bairns', then this can be construed as a call to radically reform the social system along equalitarian lines; yet it can also be seen as a symbol of spiritual equivalence that, in lived social reality, remains sublimely unperturbed by the continuance of a hierarchical status quo.[8] This second reading is key to what Maxwell means when he says that

> The historical accuracy of a myth is [...] less interesting than the political use to which it is put. The Left's favourite myth yields an obvious antinationalist conclusion. The only force which contains the Scotsman's Calvinist genius for social reaction is England's benign and progressive influence and the main obstacle to political reaction in Scotland is the united British labour movement.[9]

Maxwell's reference to Calvinism is echoed in McCrone's belief that the egalitarian myth has an 'almost mystical element'.[10] However, while Maxwell points to the perception of Scottish Calvinism as reactionary, McCrone links a democratic instinct to the centrality of the Kirk in Scottish community, a belief fostered by Kailyard representations (– as Ian Campbell points out, 'Churchgoing, decent rational practical Christianity, are the staples of kailyard society').[11] Ironically, the Kailyard, which has so often been characterised as aesthetically, culturally and politically backward-looking, a force inhibiting of radical progress towards Scottish self-determination, especially by writers for the revival of Scottish letters in the early twentieth century such as the nationalist Hugh MacDiarmid, has also been a keeper of communitarian values central to the

---

8   McCrone, *Understanding Scotland*, p. 91.
9   Maxwell, *The Case for Left Wing Nationalism*, p. 16.
10   McCrone, *Understanding Scotland*, p. 91.
11   Ian Campbell, *Kailyard: A New Assessment* (Edinburgh: The Ramsay Head Press, 1981), p. 14.

continuance of the equalitarian myth. If '[t]he Scottish myth of egalitarianism survived because it kept alive a sense of national identity', as McCrone argues, then the Kailyard played its own particular role in keeping the pulse ticking.[12]

The Kailyard Community

To the 'mythic structures' of 'tartanry' and the Kailyard that McCrone argues had for so long been the basis of debates on culture in Scotland can be added the category of community.[13] If McCrone is correct in his thesis that the Scottish myth supported a continuing sense of national identity this is because Scotland has had no independent national state community since the Union, and so community-as-myth and nation-as-class have acted as surrogates in the cultural imagination for nation-as-state. (This resounded in the manner in which the Yes movement was represented, and saw itself, as a social demo-cratic communal front during the run-up to the 2014 Scottish independence referendum, and the way in which many artists in Scotland have understood their role in political terms.[14]) 'Community', as Timothy C. Baker puts it, 'is both an idea located in a particular history and the replacement of that history'.[15] It is the Kailyard which has been foundational in the modern era in representing Scottish community in these mythic terms.

The Kailyard's centrality to ideas of community in modern Scottish literary culture creates certain paradoxes that find their focus around the figure of the lad o' pairts. The lad o' pairts – the gifted male pupil who, through the commu-nity's financial help, is enabled to go to university – occupies an ambivalent space in relation to the rest of the community not dissimilar to that of his author, the Kailyard writer. In supporting the lad o' pairts to get out of the community through education, the community illustrates at once its communitarian solidar-ity with one of its own and its understanding that the community's elite – 'the crème de la crème' proclaimed by Spark's Jean Brodie – should be released from the limits and ordinariness of community experience.[16] The Kailyard commu-nity thus shows its moral virtue as a place that recognises the value of education

---

12   McCrone, *Understanding Scotland*, p. 95.

13   McCrone, *Understanding Scotland*, p. 131.

14   For the latter, see *Unstated: Writers on Scottish Independence*, ed. by Scott Hames (Edinburgh: Word Power, 2012).

15   Timothy C. Baker, *George Mackay Brown and the Philosophy of Community* (Edinburgh: Edinburgh University Press, 2009), p. 9.

16   Muriel Spark, *The Prime of Miss Jean Brodie* (London: Penguin, 2000), p. 8.

and aspiration, and its material shortcomings as a place where such ambitions cannot be fulfilled. When in 1978 Francis Russell Hart wrote that '[t]rue community, for the Scottish imagination, is small', he meant that the representational focus of the modern Scottish novel had fallen largely upon the village and small-town community, something that was mostly to remain the case until the publication of Alasdair Gray's *Lanark* in 1981 and the increased popularity of urban writing from the 1980s onwards; but also that there has been what Hart calls an 'ironic anticosmopolitan impulse' pervading the Scottish novel that finds its homespun apotheosis in the Kailyard.[17] The Kailyard community is not only physically small but fundamentally limiting for the lad o' pairts, with the Kailyard as both mythic egalitarian community on the one hand and feeder for elite individualism (disguised as Calvinist meritocracy) on the other. This point is exemplified by the opening story of Ian Maclaren's Drumtochty tales, *Beside the Bonnie Brier Bush*, 'the quintessential work of the Kailyard'.[18] In 'Domsie', the lad o' pairts, George Howe, has his university fees paid by the local community, an act orchestrated by the schoolmaster, Patrick Jamison, the Domsie of the title:

> There was just a single ambition in those humble homes, to have one of
> its members at college, and if Domsie approved a lad, then his brothers
> and sisters would give their wages, and the family live on skim milk and
> oat cake, to let him have his chance.[19]

The sacrificial nature of the community's actions in ensuring that a special one amongst them goes on to university mirrors the Christian values of the Kailyard ('Ian Maclaren' was the pseudonym of the Reverend John Watson). When the lad o' pairts leaves the village, he carries the community with him as part of his moral value-system, thus representing the community to the outside world just as the Kailyard author fictionally represents the community. In death, George-as-hero is not only returned by his fictional maker to his spiritual maker, he is also returned to the community which is his moral maker. In the author-lad o' pairts the Kailyard community seeks its own impossible transcendence.

---

17   Francis Russell Hart, *The Scottish Novel: From Smollett to Spark* (Cambridge, MA: Harvard
       University Press, 1978), p. 402.
18   Andrew Nash, 'Introduction', Ian Maclaren, *Beside the Bonnie Brier Bush* (Glasgow:
       Kennedy & Boyd, 2009), pp. ix–xvi (p. ix).
19   Maclaren, *Beside the Bonnie Brier Bush*, p. 7.

Beside the Bonnie Brier Bush, along with other Kailyard works, 'offers a cele-bration of community values', according to Andrew Nash, as well as an 'idealis-tic view of a self-supporting community'.[20] The unified, organic nature of the Kailyard community not only suggests nostalgia for a lost sense of past community – Maclaren's *Beside the Bonnie Brier Bush*, for instance, while pub-lished in 1894, is set in the 1860s – but also glosses over many of the social divisions both within such small communities and in the larger urban centres of the late nineteenth century when much Kailyard fiction was written. While suggesting that Kailyard fictions are intended as 'morally improving [...] fairy tales', Gillian Shepherd states that '[i]n the Kailyard Eden the only serpents were the implicit threat of distant, urban squalor, poverty, riot and unrest, industrialisation and secularisation'.[21] Social class is undoubtedly the cuckoo in the Kailyard's nest. '*Class distinctions* are an important, if tacit, feature of kailyard', according to Campbell, while McCrone goes further, claiming that the 'political economy of the community inhabited by lads o' pairts is pre-capitalist' and '[t]he image of social identity which is held up for praise [in the Kailyard] is one of community, not class'.[22] McCrone's point – that 'commu-nity', as a mythic signifier of prelapsarian unity before the fall into the class discord of industrialisation, obviates class distinctions – is an important one, and worth quoting at length. In the Kailyard community,

> The commitment is to the parish, secular and religious, made up of sturdy and self-sustaining individuals. The social hierarchy of the parish is not questioned, and differences of economic and social power are taken for granted, rather than resented. Material rewards may even bring social and psychological disbenefits, if the social duties and obligations which wealth brings are not carried out. The unalloyed pursuit of profit offends the moral economy of the community (as the anti-Kailyard novels at the turn of this [the twentieth] century by George Douglas Brown, *The House with the Green Shutters* (1901), and by J. McDougall [sic] Hay, *Gillespie* (1914) set out to show. In this regard, they share the scepticism of Kailyard writ-ers like Ian MacLaren [sic] with his suspicion of 'mercantile pursuits').[23]

---

20   Nash, 'Introduction', *Beside the Bonnie Brier Bush*, pp. x, xi.

21   Gillian Shepherd, 'The Kailyard', in *The History of Scottish Literature, Vol. 3: Nineteenth Century*, ed. by Douglas Gifford (Aberdeen: Aberdeen University Press, 1989), pp. 309–18 (p. 312).

22   Campbell, *Kailyard*, p. 13. Italics in original. McCrone, *Understanding Scotland*, p. 99.

23   McCrone, *Understanding Scotland*, p. 99.

The House with the Green Shutters has, as McCrone suggests, been interpreted principally as Douglas Brown's attack on the Kailyard. This view has
been encouraged by the author himself: after the novel's publication he wrote
that he believed it to be 'more complimentary to Scotland [...] than the sentimental slop of Barrie, and Crockett, and Maclaren' and that it was 'antagonism
to their method' that compelled him to make the book so tragically dark.[24]
Young John Gourlay, forced to go to Edinburgh University against his will to
satisfy his father's competitiveness with his rival James Wilson, is a botched lad
o' pairts, and the 'nippy locality' of Barbie, which is characterised almost solely
by spiteful gossip and backbiting, is the antithesis of the absurdly sentimental
rendering of community found in the Kailyard.[25] However, the novel is much
more than simply a bomb thrown into the heart of the Kailyard community.
Carruthers, for instance, proposes along poststructual/postmodern lines that
The House with the Green Shutters 'might be read as a kind of game' that 'shifts
around in its mode [...thus] visiting upon the kailyard genre a shower of over-
wrought literary modes' which undermine the novel's reputation for literary
naturalism.[26] This has the merit of freeing the text from interpretative reliance
on the national traditional and the Kailyard, but somewhat misses the primary
point of what has been masked by the novel's Scottish overdetermination. We
have seen in McCrone's concept of the Scottish myth of egalitarianism that
class is shrouded through ideological recourse to 'community'. Equally, the priority of the Kailyard community in interpretations of *The House with the Green
Shutters* has disguised the extent to which the novel is actually a masterful critique of nineteenth-century commercial capitalism and its destructive effects
on individuals and communities. Cairns Craig argues that, in the shadow of
Calvinism, 'the potency of fear remains central to Scottish culture'; in particular, 'Douglas Brown's world of small-town Scotland is dominated by the word
"fear"'.[27] Fundamental to *The House with the Green Shutters* for Craig is the dialectic of fearful community (Barbie) and fearless individual who stands outside or against the community (Gourlay). He contends that even after Gourlay's
death, 'the house of Gourlay keeps its fearful dominance over the chorus of the
fearing and allows no exit from a dialectic in which the fearful and fearless

24   George Douglas Brown, letter of 24 October 1901, quoted in James Veitch, *George Douglas
      Brown* (London: Herbert Jenkins, 1952), p. 153.
25   George Douglas Brown, *The House with the Green Shutters* (Edinburgh: Polygon, 2005),
      p. 107.
26   Carruthers, *Scottish Literature*, p. 163.
27   Cairns Craig, *The Modern Scottish Novel: Narrative and the National Imagination*
      (Edinburgh: Edinburgh University Press, 1999), pp. 37, 48.

continually define and destroy each other'.[28] The fearfulness of the Scottish community has, for Craig, been inherited from the all-pervasive, God-fearing 'imaginative world that Calvinism projected'.[29] However, while this may have credence at an historical level, it is less convincing as interpretation of a novel that, as Craig himself acknowledges, is governed by a pre-Christian ethic presided over by the terrible fatedness central to Greek tragedy.[30] Rather than something to be feared, Christianity generally, and Presbyterianism in particular, are little more than a bad joke in the community of *The House with the Green Shutters*: the gossiping Deacon of the Presbyterian Church talks with a lisp that distorts the Word of God; the Cross no longer symbolises Christ's sacrifice, but is a place where, Judas-like, the town 'bodies' gather to backstab and betray their fellow townsfolk; the Free Kirk minister is denigrated;[31] and the Bible readings at the end of the novel, often seen as an indication of the Christian love and charity lacking in the Barbie community, are recited by Mrs Gourlay and her son in a 'high exaltation of madness' that parodies Kailyard deathbed scenes.[32] When a minister actually speaks – "'At the Day of Judgment, my frehnds," said Mr Struthers; "at the Day of Judgment every herring must hang by his own tail!"' – it is to express an individualistic ethos that the novel's narrator admits has as much to do with the 'keen spirit of competition' as it has with the fear of God.[33]

The governing dialectic of the Barbie community is not the Calvinist dialectic of fearfulness and fearlessness identified by Craig but the master–slave dialectic of capitalism. Gourlay may appear to be master of the community, Barbie's 'greatest man', but he is as much a slave to encroaching commercialisation and modernisation as are the town's meanest bodies.[34] Douglas Brown's novel is shot through with allusions to the growing capitalist impulse of the era, from the beginning of the railways to the use of English as opposed to Scots favoured by the likes of Wilson. The Scot is identified as 'largely endowed with the commercial imagination', enabling him to see 'a railway through the desert where no railway exists, and mills along the quiet stream', and it is Wilson, Gourlay's nemesis, who proves in this regard to have the larger vision.[35]

---

28   Craig, *The Modern Scottish Novel*, p. 51.
29   Craig, *The Modern Scottish Novel*, p. 37.
30   See Craig, *The Modern Scottish Novel*, p. 48.
31   Douglas Brown, *The House with the Green Shutters*, p. 70.
32   Douglas Brown, *The House with the Green Shutters*, p. 290.
33   Douglas Brown, *The House with the Green Shutters*, pp. 74, 75.
34   Douglas Brown, *The House with the Green Shutters*, p. 44.
35   Douglas Brown, *The House with the Green Shutters*, p. 114.

Although, the coming of the railway to Barbie is not merely Gourlay's downfall; as Zygmunt Bauman points out, 'a breach in the protective walls of community became a foregone conclusion with the appearance of mechanical means of transportation'.[36] Competitive commercialism and the desire for individual gain even infects personal relations, as one of the bodies tells how Gourlay came to marry his wife:

> 'I ken fine how he married her', said Johnny Coe. 'I was acquaint wi' her faither, auld Tenshillingland owre at Fechars – a grand farmer he was, wi' land o' his nain, and a gey pickle bawbees. It was the bawbees, and not the woman, that Gourlay went after! It was *her* money, as ye ken, that set him on his feet, and made him such a big man. He never cared a preen for *her*, and then when she proved a dirty trollop, he couldna endure her look! That's what makes him so sore upon her now. And yet I mind her a braw lass, too', said Johnny Coe the sentimentalist [...].[37]

Johnny Coe deploys an infamous levelling tactic and one of the more negative traits buttressing the Scottish egalitarian myth: 'I kent his (or her) faither', a jealous expression of contempt used to put down those who, especially from humble beginnings, have gone on to find success. Mrs Gourlay's father, 'auld Tenshillingland', is named after his farm, as was traditional; that it was also customary to name the farm after the worth of the land illustrates the deeply embedded nature of commercial values in the life of rural communities. The sentimentalism of Johnny Coe's reminiscences – 'She [Mrs Gourlay] had a cousin, Jenny Wabster, that dwelt in Tenshillingland than, and mony a summer nicht up the Fechars Road, when ye smelled the honey-suckle in the gloaming, I have heard the two o' them tee-heeing owre the lads thegither' – not only idealises the past and suggests how much happier Mrs Gourlay (and the community) was then, but in so doing evokes Kailyard prose by the likes of S.R. Crockett in *The Lilac Sunbonnet* (1894): 'No lassie in all the hill country went forth more heartwhole into the June morning than Winsome Charteris'.[38] The inscription of commercial value as shorthand for the farmer's true identity suggests, however, that such sentimental idealisation acted to mask much of the more hard-edged realities of nineteenth-century rural life, much

---

36   Zygmunt Bauman, *Community: Seeking Safety in an Insecure World* (Cambridge: Polity, 2012), p. 13.

37   Douglas Brown, *The House with the Green Shutters*, p. 78. Italics in original.

38   Douglas Brown, *The House with the Green Shutters*, p. 78. S.R. Crockett, *The Lilac Sunbonnet: A Love Story* (New York: D. Appleton and Company, 1894), p. 28.

as 'feeling' formed the literary countervail to the onset of industrialisation in the last decades of the eighteenth century. Likewise, the sentimental Kailyard, with the mythic community at its centre, is itself a product of the commercial imagination of the nineteenth-century Scot satirised in *The House with the Green Shutters*. Craig complains that '[w]hat makes Douglas Brown's novel so bleak as a projection of the national imagination is that there is no character within the community who is capable of representing, let alone sustaining, the author's values'.[39] In Barbie capitalist individualism promotes competitive spite. Yet the baker (the maker of bread, that staple and sustainer of life), whilst a minor character, a Burnsian like his author, trades the false sentiment of the Kailyard for sympathy and in so doing offers a humane model of what community should be, one that provides an antidote to the malevolence poisoning Barbie: 'folk should be kind to folk'.[40]

The Madness of Calvinist Community

The Kailyard community remained an important antagonistic spur to the movement for literary revival of the 1920–40s, itself influenced by the anti-Kailyard resonances of Douglas Brown's novel. Lewis Grassic Gibbon positions the small community of Kinraddie 'between a kailyard and a bonny brier bush in the lee of a house with green shutters' in *Sunset Song* (1932).[41] That it is the minister who makes these literary allusions to his baffled congregation is germane, for *Sunset Song* – notwithstanding the admiration shown in the novel for the Presbyterian Covenanters – is about the largely malign influence of religion, specifically Calvinism, upon the community of Kinraddie, which the Reverend Gibbon calls 'a rotten kailyard'.[42] John Guthrie, Chris's father, looks at her lustily like 'a caged beast', paces outside her bedroom during 'the harvest madness', and bids her sleep with him as they had done 'in Old Testament times'.[43] Chris's mother Jean kills herself rather than face yet another pregnancy forced upon her by Guthrie's religious beliefs, and her children Dod and Alec are taunted at school: *Daftie, daftie! Whose mother was a daftie?*[44] However, it is the village 'dafties' Andy and Tony who are the key to

---

39   Craig, *The Modern Scottish Novel*, p. 62.

40   Douglas Brown, *The House with the Green Shutters*, p. 216.

41   Lewis Grassic Gibbon, *Sunset Song* (Edinburgh: Canongate, 2008), p. 24.

42   Gibbon, *Sunset Song*, p. 84.

43   Gibbon, *Sunset Song*, pp. 60, 72, 108.

44   Gibbon, *Sunset Song*, p. 65. Italics in original.

understanding the madness which overtakes a community in the grip of Calvinist repression. Andy, who appears to be genuinely mentally disturbed, runs amok one day through Kinraddie molesting girls, whereas Tony, who is described as having 'once been a scholar and written books and learned and learned till his brain fair softened and right off his head he'd gone', is more insightful as to the nature of his own and the community's malady, calling the local minister 'only a half-witted cleric'.[45] Greeting Chae Strachan, one of the community's few genuinely good characters and 'a socialist creature' who believes in equality, Tony cries enigmatically: '*Ay, Chae, so the mills of God still grind?*', a proverbial saying with classical antecedents used by the American poet Henry Wadsworth Longfellow in 'Retribution'.[46] The retribution of 'a world gone mad' in war that tears Kinraddie apart and kills a generation of peasant farmers is suffered by a community ministered to by a hypocritical religion that renders learning futile (mere 'dirt') and love shameful.[47] Andy and Tony are holy fools bearing the names of saints: Scotland's patron saint Andrew becomes in Andy the perverted sex instinct of a country inhibited by Calvinist doctrine, while Tony as the mystic Saint Anthony represents the repressed spiritual intelligence of a community that has lost its way in the material temptations of a modernising world.

The critique of Calvinism in *Sunset Song* clears the way for new forms of religion and new ideas of community in the following two novels of the *Scots Quair* trilogy: the Reverend Colquohoun's humane but ineffectual Christian socialism in *Cloud Howe* (1933) and Ewan's anti-humanist revolutionary communism in *Grey Granite* (1934). Much has been made of the purportedly inclusive, communitarian use of 'you' throughout *A Scots Quair*, wherein the community speaks through individual characters and characters voice the community. Thomas Crawford claims that 'self-referring you [he is using Graham Trengove's phrase] serves to dramatise a character's thought; while generic you, equivalent to "everybody", strengthens the impression of universality'.[48] Cairns Craig has written of the 'You and I' central to the ethics of John Macmurray, whose philosophy releases the Self from the isolated ego to find existence in relation to the Other. As Craig explains, for Macmurray 'the Self is constituted in, through and by its relationships to others. [...] The Other

---

45   Gibbon, *Sunset Song*, pp. 15–16, 198.

46   Gibbon, *Sunset Song*, pp. 10, 204. Italics in original.

47   Gibbon, *Sunset Song*, p. 236.

48   Thomas Crawford, 'Introduction', *A Scots Quair*, pp. vii–xii (pp. xi–xii). See also Graham Trengove, 'Who is you? Grammar and Grassic Gibbon', *Scottish Literary Journal*, 2.2 (1975), 47–62.

is not an alien world antithetical to Self: Self is the Other in its relations'.[49] Crawford's argument that there is a communal aspect to Gibbon's use of 'you' tends to imply the 'You and I' of Macmurray: the Self in relation to others. But Gibbon's 'you' is not 'You *and* I' but rather 'You *as* I', you instead of I – a subtle yet crucial difference. 'You as I' constitutes an inability to speak in the first person, to act as a fully self-determining agent in the world. The communal element of Gibbon's 'you' is that 'You as I' comes from and is shared by the whole community's near pathological incapacity to assert its Self, a situation arising from the precedence of Standard English.[50] For instance, in *Sunset Song* Long Rob makes the point 'what a shame it was that folk should be shamed nowadays to speak Scotch', whereas Gordon counters that to advance materially people '*must use the English*'.[51] The movement from Scots to English, seen by Gordon as progress and by Long Rob as loss, indicates the demise of community at the hands of class-conscious individualism. Unable any longer to speak in the Scots language as an agent in the 'You and I' relation, the Self loses all self-identity as 'I' and retreats to the second-person 'you'. 'You as I' can be a way of not really speaking at all and can be negatively interpreted as stemming from self-alienation and the proletarianisation of the Scottish subject and community. 'You as I' illustrates not the triumph of mythic Scottish communalism but the Scottish community's subordination. 'You as I' is indicative of nation-as-class.

Class is central to Gibbon's opposition to Hugh MacDiarmid's modern Scottish Renaissance as a movement or community of writers with shared political and cultural aims, coalescing around the idea of an independent Scotland. Gibbon makes his hostility to the Scots Renaissance most clear in the *Scottish Scene* (1934) essay 'Glasgow': calling the movement for revival 'a homogenous literary cultus', he states that '[t]here is nothing in culture or art that is worth the life and elementary happiness of one of those thousands who rot in the Glasgow slums'.[52] Gibbon may wish not to belong to the Scots Renaissance, but his concern here with the Glasgow proletariat and urban life in the fictional

---

49   Craig, *The Modern Scottish Novel*, p. 90. See also Cairns Craig, 'Beyond Reason – Hume, Seth, Macmurray and Scotland's Postmodernity', in *Scotland in Theory: Reflections on Culture and Theory*, ed. by Eleanor Bell and Gavin Miller (Amsterdam and New York: Rodopi, 2004), pp. 249–83.

50   See Hanne Tange, 'Language, Class and Social Power in *A Scots Quair*', in *The International Companion to Lewis Grassic Gibbon*, ed. by Scott Lyall (Glasgow: Scottish Literature International, 2015), pp. 22–32.

51   Gibbon, *Sunset Song*, p. 156. Italics in original.

52   Lewis Grassic Gibbon, 'Glasgow', in Lewis Grassic Gibbon and Hugh MacDiarmid, *Scottish Scene, or The Intelligent Man's Guide to Albyn* (London and Melbourne: Hutchinson, n.d.),

Duncairn of *Grey Granite* shifts that movement's focus away from the small-town rural communities that were the background of many of its main protagonists, such as Gibbon and MacDiarmid, Nan Shepherd, Edwin Muir, Fionn MacColla, Neil Gunn, and Violet Jacob, and their work.

Willa Muir, born in Montrose of Shetland parentage, shared Gibbon's objections to the Scottish Renaissance as a unifying MacDiarmidian-nationalist movement. Her account of small-town Scottish community in *Imagined Corners* (1931) highlights the restrictive, claustrophobic nature of bourgeois family life for women. Set in the fictional town of Calderwick, and beginning in 1912, a year of feminist agitation and suffragette unrest prior to women fully winning the vote,[53] Alison Smith suggests that Muir's novel arose from her discontented sense that there was no place in Scottish society for 'women who feel *and* think'.[54] The Calderwick community portrayed in *Imagined Corners* is one of stifling social convention warping individuality and sex relations. Indeed, as the idealistic Elizabeth Shand begins to feel disillusioned in her marriage to Hector, the narrator comments: 'Wives, in Calderwood, were dull, domestic commodities, and husbands, it was understood, were unfaithful whenever they had the opportunity'.[55] Business success breeds manners and a correct middle-class way to behave; as Elise Mütze, recently returned to Calderwick from the continent, notes, Mabel, her brother John's wife, 'doesn't even know she's acting'.[56] Elise, formerly Lizzie Shand, for whom the God believed in by Calderwickians is 'merely an enforcer of taboos, and a male creature at that', escaped the restrictions of Calderwick's hypocritical Calvinist moral codes by leaving for Europe in her youth; on revisiting, she precipitates change in the community's relations, particularly in her true 'other half' Elizabeth, but also in herself, as she must learn to find peace with her younger self and her own relationship to the community.[57] In this sense, transformation comes to the community from outside – from Elise's freeing continental

pp. 114–25 (pp. 119, 124). See also Christopher Silver, 'Lewis Grassic Gibbon and Scottish Nationalism', in *The International Companion to Lewis Grassic Gibbon*, pp. 105–18.

53   See Leah Leneman, *A Guid Cause: The Women's Suffrage Movement in Scotland*, 2nd rev. edn (Edinburgh: Mercat Press, 1995).

54   Alison Smith, 'And Woman Created Woman: Carswell, Shepherd and Muir, and the Self-Made Woman', in *Gendering the Nation: Studies in Modern Scottish Literature*, ed. by Christopher Whyte (Edinburgh: Edinburgh University Press, 1995), pp. 25–48 (p. 44). Italics in original.

55   Willa Muir, *Imagined Corners*, in *Imagined Selves*, ed. by Kirsty Allen (Edinburgh: Canongate, 1996), p. 117.

56   Muir, *Imagined Corners*, p. 225.

57   Muir, *Imagined Corners*, p. 185.

influence – and from within, in that Elise is after all a native of Calderwick as well as someone who forces on others and herself an inner re-evaluation of life: as Elise realises, 'the one important thing in life [is] the integrity of the spirit'.[58] Yet cleaving to such personal spiritual integrity, the desire always 'to know the truth, the truth', is what sends Ned Murray mad.[59] Ned cannot be helped by his brother William, a Church of Scotland minister, who confesses to having 'been asleep' spiritually and is therefore no guide to the community's religious life.[60] Consulting a doctor as to Ned's prospects, William is told: 'our imperfect civilization may have been partly responsible for your brother's breakdown'.[61] However, the real blame lies closer to home. Like the 'dafties' of *Sunset Song*, Ned is a weathervane for Calderwick's own spiritual ills, in light of which his collapse into pessimism and paranoia, the feeling that the community is out to get him, is, as the doctor explains, entirely fitting:

> That persecution mania nearly always accompanies obscure breakdowns. It's one of the symptoms. Considering the long biological history of man, and the fact that herd animals nearly always reject their sick, it's not surprising if an unhappy human fears that he's to be rejected by his herd. [...] All communities persecute, and in that light persecution mania is reasonable enough.[62]

While it is tempting to assume that Scottish society became increasingly secular in the early decades of the twentieth century, and that therefore the fictional accounts by Gibbon and Muir overstate the influence of Presbyterianism, T.M. Devine claims that in fact during the 1920s and 1930s 'membership of the Church of Scotland was reasonably stable', with the real collapse in Kirk-going not occurring until the 1960s.[63] Many writers of the modern Scottish Renaissance were hostile to what they thought were Calvinism's harmful effects on the nation's spiritual and cultural health,[64] but *Imagined Corners* and *Sunset Song* cannily spotlight the madness wrought by Calvinism on Scottish communities.

---

58   Muir, *Imagined Corners*, p. 164.

59   Muir, *Imagined Corners*, p. 178.

60   Muir, *Imagined Corners*, p. 271.

61   Muir, *Imagined Corners*, p. 205.

62   Muir, *Imagined Corners*, p. 205.

63   T.M. Devine, *The Scottish Nation 1700–2000* (Harmondsworth: Penguin, 2000), p. 386.

64   See Scott Lyall, '"That Ancient Self": Scottish Modernism's Counter-Renaissance', *European Journal of English Studies*, 18.1 (2014), 73–85.

Although not usually associated with the Scottish Renaissance period, Muriel Spark's *The Prime of Miss Jean Brodie* (1961) is set mainly during the revival era in Thirties Edinburgh; indeed, Grassic Gibbon's characterisation of Edinburgh in this period as a 'disappointed spinster' chimes with the description of Jean Brodie as 'an Edinburgh spinster of the deepest dye', while Edwin Muir's view of the Scottish capital in his 1935 *Scottish Journey* as 'a city of extraordinary and sordid contrasts' is also captured by Spark.[65] Like the writers of the literary renaissance, Spark's novel links Calvinism and madness, or, at least, the pitiful self-delusion of Brodie who believes 'that God was on her side whatever her course'.[66] *The Prime of Miss Jean Brodie* is a parodic Kailyard novel, centred on education, with middle-class girls rather than lower-class lads o' pairts; it also tells of the tragedy of apparently self-sustaining, inward-looking community – *total* community[67] – as led by the teacher-dictator Jean Brodie. Calvinism is an enigma to the half-English Sandy Stranger, who as a schoolgirl in Edinburgh feels 'deprived' of a 'birthright' which 'pervaded the place in proportion as it was unacknowledged'.[68] Baffled she may be by the religion's essential nature and its expression in Edinburgh, but it is Sandy alone among the 'corporate Brodie set' who discerns the links between the teacher, the city and Calvinism. Brodie, who claims descent from the William Brodie whose 'double life' was dramatised by Robert Louis Stevenson and W.E. Henley, shuns the communion of the Roman Catholic Church and 'thinks she is the God of Calvin'.[69] Edinburgh's double life is demonstrated when Brodie takes her privileged Morningside and Bruntsfield girls on a trip through the Old Town; but for Brodie this is an historical tour in which she fails to see the community's poverty. In denouncing Brodie, Sandy is not only renouncing Calvinist Edinburgh, but also Brodie's aestheticisation of education and politics, which turns reality and imagination into sheer fantasy and Calvinism's elect/damned duality into fascism. Born as the Aesthetic Movement got under way in 1890 and dying just after World War Two, the route from aesthetics to fascism, mapped by Walter Benjamin in his 1936 essay 'The Work of Art in the Age of Mechanical Reproduction', is central to

---

65   Lewis Grassic Gibbon, 'Glasgow', in *Scottish Scene*, p. 114. Spark, *The Prime of Miss Jean Brodie*, p. 26. Edwin Muir, *Scottish Journey* (Edinburgh and London: Mainstream, 1999), p. 9.

66   Spark, *The Prime of Miss Jean Brodie*, p. 85.

67   The American sociologist Robert Nisbet uses this phrase to describe totalitarian regimes in his 1953 study *The Quest for Community: A Study in the Ethics of Order and Freedom* (Wilmington, Del: ISI Books, 2010), pp. 173–92.

68   Spark, *The Prime of Miss Jean Brodie*, p. 108.

69   Spark, *The Prime of Miss Jean Brodie*, pp. 40, 120, 85.

Brodie's life. While Benjamin warns against the 'negative theology' of 'pure' art, advocating instead a revolutionary art, Spark's novel cautions against truth being confused with fiction and lampoons art that merely reproduces versions of its maker in the same manner as Brodie imposes her reactionary politics on her pupils.[70] Sandy sees 'that the Brodie set was Miss Brodie's fascisti', just as Brodie's prime signifies not only the best (pre-menopausal) years of her life, which she sacrifices for her pupils, but the teacher as leader or dominant person, superior, cold and alone: Brodie, in contrast to Sandy's and Jenny's parents, has an indivisible prime rather than the relatedness of sexual intercourse, and questions the very meaning of 'social' when Eunice wants to absent herself from the set.[71] For all her idiosyncrasies, and her scorn for 'the team spirit', Brodie does not encourage individualism in her charges but the propagation of types within an enclosed, self-regarding community.[72] Significantly, it is the two non-elect girls of the set who die: Mary, who was not bright enough for Classics, is burnt to death in a hotel fire, and the 'outsider' Joyce Emily dies in Spain fighting for Franco on Brodie's encouragement.[73] While the Kailyard dominie exerts a positive influence over the community to liberate the lad o' pairts, Brodie's totalitarian instincts have an altogether more malign ending.

A Portrait of the Artist and the Community

Religion and education as repressive forces are also a considerable factor in Alasdair Gray's *Lanark*. The semi-autobiographical Duncan Thaw, who suffers asthma and eczema, is made ill by an environment discouraging of his artistic ambitions. Knoxian Presbyterianism has been blamed for a reputedly hostile attitude to creativity and the arts in Scotland, perhaps even any visible signifier of difference or 'specialness', and *Lanark* maintains the Scots Renaissance distrust of Calvinism. Knox glooms over Glasgow in the realist sections of the novel, where Thaw's mother has a view of Knox's statue from her ward in Glasgow's Royal Infirmary:

---

70   Walter Benjamin, 'The Work of Art in the Age of Mechanical Reproduction', in *The Norton Anthology of Theory and Criticism*, ed. by Vincent B. Leitch and others (New York and London: Norton, 2001), pp. 1166–1186 (p. 1172).

71   Spark, *The Prime of Miss Jean Brodie*, pp. 31, 16, 62.

72   Spark, *The Prime of Miss Jean Brodie*, p. 78.

73   Spark, *The Prime of Miss Jean Brodie*, p. 8.

Below them stood the old soot-eaten Gothic cathedral in a field of flat black gravestones. Beyond rose the hill of the Necropolis, its sides cut into by the porches of the elaborate mausoleums, the summit prickly with monuments and obelisks. The topmost monument was a pillar carrying a large stone figure of John Knox, hatted, bearded, gowned, and upholding in his right hand an open granite book. The trees between the tombs were leafless, for it was late autumn. Mrs Thaw smiled and whispered wanly, 'I saw a funeral go in there this morning'. 'No, it's not a very cheery outlook'.[74]

Knox is associated with sickness and death, not freedom and life, and in this dismal environment, Thaw, the budding artist, is frozen by repression. If Knox is petrified in stone, Thaw is petrified by an inheritance of Knoxian theology: anti-art and anti-sex. Yet as an artist he may hold the key to thawing his community through the use of the imagination.[75]

One of the novel's most quoted passages makes this point explicit. Thaw and his friend Kenneth McAlpin (who takes his name from the first King of Scots) climb a hill with a view of the city: '"Glasgow is a magnificent city," said McAlpin. "Why do we hardly ever notice that?" "Because nobody imagines living here," said Thaw'.[76] Thaw believes that Glasgow has been poorly served in artistic and literary representation and this has had a negative effect on the citizenry's sense of themselves and their habitat, for 'if a city hasn't been used by an artist not even the inhabitants live there imaginatively'.[77] Thaw may finally drown in his solipsistic self, but in theory he understands that the creation of art has communal implications. Art, in this view, imagines and re-imagines the community; without it the community remains dead to itself – a perspective that has been critically popular in Scotland during the last several decades, especially since the 1979 devolution referendum in particular, after which, only two years later, followed the publication of the enormously influential *Lanark*.

Thaw's story is similar to Mat Craig's in Archie Hind's *The Dear Green Place* (1966), cited in *Lanark*'s index of plagiarisms. Like Thaw, Hind's character is a budding artist. Craig is also thwarted by his Glasgow environment, yet wishes

---

74   Alasdair Gray, *Lanark: A Life in 4 Books* (London: Picador, 1991), p. 191.

75   See Cairns Craig, 'Going Down to Hell is Easy: *Lanark*, Realism and the Limits of the Imagination', in *The Arts of Alasdair Gray*, ed. by Robert Crawford and Thom Nairn (Edinburgh: Edinburgh University Press, 1991), pp. 90–107.

76   Gray, *Lanark*, p. 243.

77   Gray, *Lanark*, p. 243.

to write the great Glasgow novel, as Gray has done with *Lanark*. Significantly, Mat Craig works in a slaughter house, which ties into *Lanark*'s ideas of feeding and consumption, particularly in the fantasy sections of Gray's novel where humanity 'is the pie that bakes and eats itself' in a monstrous cannibalistic parable of the repressions and oppressions of capitalist individualism.[78] Both Thaw and Lanark have difficulties loving in this competitive system: Thaw, the artist, is asocial, whilst Lanark, the ordinary everyman is more social. This split is reminiscent of Stephen Dedalus and Leopold Bloom in James Joyce's *Ulysses* (1922). Stephen, like Thaw, is the asocial artist, Bloom the everyman hero: both have problems loving or expressing love; both are characters in their country's modern epic novel, as *Lanark* is Scotland's *Ulysses*. But the parallels go deeper, and while Gray mentions Joyce's *A Portrait of the Artist as a Young Man* (1916) in the index of plagiarisms, significantly he does not mention *Ulysses*. In *Ulysses* Stephen as an artist needs to find common ground with others and be more grounded and 'ordinary' if his art is ever to be realised; Bloom on the other hand, the adman everyman, is described as having 'a touch of the artist' about him.[79] As separate individuals these two figures never quite find balance in their own lives, but would do so by combining their respective virtues in one personality. This also applies to Thaw and Lanark. Thaw, like Stephen, has no romantic love or sex in his life; each is as sterile in this sense as his respective city and nation are perceived to be culturally. The post-Romantic 'artist' is mentally ill, a 'divided self' in R.D. Laing's phrase, because s/he is alienated and different from, not organically connected to, the community in a market society that monetises relations.[80] To re-imagine the community s/he needs to be more in touch with the community and have more of the common touch. Community, for the artist, can only be realised in a unity with the common. To adopt Gavin Miller's term, Thaw needs to find communion with others for his art to flourish; without that, he and his art can only remain repressed and be a comment on their society's repression.[81] Equally Lanark, who has some sort of social mission to understand the conditions of the Institute and Unthank and the machinations of Provan, needs to have more of the artist in his personality; he screams 'I'm not an artist!', refusing to recognise that side of himself, but his

---

78   Gray, *Lanark*, p. 62.

79   James Joyce, *Ulysses* (Harmondsworth: Penguin, 1992), p. 302.

80   'Ronald Laing's thoughts about the nature of madness appealed to many educated minds, including mine'. 'Of R.D. Laing', in Alasdair Gray, *Of Me and Others* (Glasgow: Cargo Publishing, 2014), pp. 205–07 (p. 205).

81   Gavin Miller, *Alasdair Gray: The Fiction of Communion* (Amsterdam and New York: Rodopi, 2005).

inflexibility, his very ordinariness, is the reason for Rima's departure and his own unhappiness.[82]

Community Contra Community

Lanark is a pathbreaking critique of Hobbesian Anglo-British capitalism. But the novel also maps the links between personhood and environment, character and community in a manner that is ambivalently influenced by Robert Owen's *A New View of Society* (1813–16). For Owen it is the social system that is responsible for the formation of good or bad character, not the individual, and the way to develop good people is through the creation of properly supportive communities: '*the happiness of self, clearly understood and uniformly practised [,…] can only be attained by conduct that must promote the happiness of the community*'.[83] An admirer of Jeremy Bentham, Owen's variety of utilitarianism illustrates that 'the very arguments of classical liberalism could and were readily turned against the capitalist society which they had helped to build'.[84] While the philanthropist reformer Owen put his theories to the test in founding the workers' community of New Lanark, there is neither a communitarian alternative to, nor personal escape from, the capitalist system in the dystopian *Lanark*. By the novel's publication in 1981, Thatcherite market deregulation and privatisation were well underway, the defeat of the miners' strike (1984–85) was on the horizon, and the very notion of community was being undermined ideologically through denial of 'society'.[85] Gray inhabited a community of writers – James Kelman, Agnes Owens, Tom Leonard, Jeff Torrington – whose vernacular style and focus on the Glasgow working class was declared in the 1980–90s as another defining renaissance in Scottish letters, but which drew criticism for its apparently narrow social and political focus.[86] Kelman would remain radically committed to writing from a working-class community, yet early novels such as *The Busconductor Hines* (1984) and *A Chancer* (1985) centre

---

82   Gray, *Lanark*, p. 389.

83   Robert Owen, *A New View of Society And Other Writings* (Harmondsworth: Penguin, 1991), p. 14. Italics in original.

84   Eric Hobsbawm, *The Age of Revolution, 1789–1848* (London: Abacus, 2014), p. 293.

85   Margaret Thatcher, 'Aids, education and the year 2000!' ['There is no such thing as society'], interview for *Woman's Own*, 31 October 1987, pp. 8–10 <http://www.margaretthatcher.org/speeches/displaydocument.asp?docid=106689> [accessed 5 September 2015].

86   See Douglas Dunn, 'Divergent Scottishness: William Boyd, Allan Massie, Ronald Frame', in *The Scottish Novel Since the Seventies: New Visions, Old Dreams*, ed. by Gavin Wallace and Randall Stevenson (Edinburgh: Edinburgh University Press, 1993), pp. 149–69.

on existential loners, while *A Disaffection* (1989) turns the noble Kailyard dominie into a cynical burnt-out teacher who can do little more for his pupils than warn them of the alienation to come upon leaving school.

Francis Fukuyama's *The End of History and the Last Man*, published in 1992, assumed the triumph of liberal capitalism over alternative economic and political systems, a mentality mirrored in the junky subculture of Irvine Welsh's *Trainspotting* (1993). Like Kelman's teacher Patrick Doyle, Welsh's novel also sees education as a dead-end for the working class, especially in an Edinburgh controlled by the Merchant school network. Instead, *Trainspotting*'s Leithers turn to popular culture, football and drugs. The callous ethics of capitalist individualism are endorsed by the novel's drug users: 'the real junky [...] doesnae gie a fuck aboot anybody else'; as the dealer Mother Superior says: 'Nae friends in this game. Just associates'.[87] This credo – 'Ah believe in the free market whin it comes tae drugs' – subscribes to no traditional political line, as the Sean Connery-obsessed Sick Boy explains:

> ...the socialists go on about your comrades, your class, your union, and society. Fuck all that shite. The Tories go on about your employer, your country, your family. Fuck that even mair. It's me, me, fucking ME, Simon David Williamson, NUMERO FUCKING UNO, versus the world, and it's a one-sided swedge. *It's really so fucking easy...* Fuck them all. *I admire your rampant individualism, Shimon.*[88]

Yet, the novel works both with and against its characters in order to define certain principles, being anti British Protestant imperialism, racism and sexism (although this last can seem difficult to discern in the welter of male violence and misogyny). Coming from or identifying with the traditionally Catholic, Irish-immigrant, Hibernian-supporting community centred round Easter Road and Leith, the main characters are already outside the city's hegemonic norm. As Renton's 'Choose life' mantra reveals, the junkies of *Trainspotting* also form a nihilistic community of individuals ranged against what they regard as the equally dysfunctional bourgeois values of family life, consumerism and 'getting on'. Theirs is a (non-)community opposed to the pretence that middle-class individualism was ever anything other than a community of self-interest. *Trainspotting*, a massively successful book and film, is both critique of and capitulation to the capitalism that eviscerates community.

---

87   Irvine Welsh, *Trainspotting* (London: Vintage, 2004), pp. 7, 6.
88   Welsh, *Trainspotting*, pp. 310, 30. Italics in original.

The End of Community?

As Kirstin Innes wrote in 2007, 'Scotland's literary landscape has never quite recovered from *Trainspotting*'.[89] Perhaps ironically, Welsh's Edinburgh novel has arguably most influenced the work of many of those contemporary writers Alan Bissett calls the 'New Weegies':[90] those based in and/or setting their work in Glasgow, such as Bissett's *Death of a Ladies' Man* (2009), Suhayl Saadi's Scots-Asian fusion *Psychoraag* (2004), and Zoë Strachan's *Negative Space* (2003), in which the narrator leaves Glasgow for Orkney to find healing after her brother's death, although Alan Warner's *Morvern Callar* (1995), filmed by Lynne Ramsay (2002), bucks the urban trend, positing an alternative rave community to the dystopic Kailyard of the Western Highland Port.[91] While Innes's statement implies the liberating power of *Trainspotting*, it can also be read more ambivalently. The apparent acceptance of 'end-of-history' postmodernism is troubling for the novel, a genre which has traditionally narrated communality. If community is under threat from *laissez-faire* individualism, neoliberalism, and cosmopolitan pop culture, then the end of community is best represented by a post-genre text such as Ewan Morrison's *Tales from the Mall* (2012). Like the mall, Morrison's book contains '[a]ll you'll ever need, under one roof': fiction; histories of the mall; real-life events.[92] *Tales from the Mall* mirrors capitalism in its range of content choice, its merging of styles and genres, and its lack of coherent narrative structure – a point made by Morrison:

> [O]ur era has no narrative; all that we require from a story – the struggle of the individual against all odds, towards a greater goal – is increasingly hard to envisage in an economy that undermines the lifelong project and in its place offers only quick fixes. It may be that consumerism and the struggle for daily survival in a deregulated job market of all-against-all

89   Kirstin Innes, 'Mark Renton's Bairns: Identity and Language in the Post-*Trainspotting* Novel', in *The Edinburgh Companion to Contemporary Scottish Literature*, ed. by Berthold Schoene (Edinburgh: Edinburgh University Press, 2007), pp. 301–09 (p. 301).

90   Alan Bissett, 'The "New Weegies": The Glasgow Novel in the Twenty-first Century', in *The Edinburgh Companion to Contemporary Scottish Literature*, pp. 59–67.

91   See Scott Lyall, 'The Kailyard's Ghost: Community in Modern Scottish Fiction', in *Roots and Fruits of Scottish Culture: Scottish Identities, History and Contemporary Literature*, ed. by Ian Brown and Jean Berton (Glasgow: Scottish Literature International, 2014), pp. 82–96 (pp. 92–93).

92   Ewan Morrison, *Tales from the Mall* (Glasgow: Cargo Publishing, 2012), p. 5.

has reduced our lives to short-term personal goals without a broader collective narrative.[93]

Like *Lanark*, the style of the book, with no logical beginning, structure or conclusion, can be described as postmodern, yet the contents can be seen as opposing some of the symptoms of postmodernity, such as mallification.

Morrison's guru in understanding postmodernity is Zygmunt Bauman, who defines the postmodern era as one of 'liquid modernity'. 'What makes modernity "liquid"', according to Bauman, 'is its self-propelling, self-intensifying, compulsive and obsessive "modernization", as a result of which, like liquid, none of the consecutive forms of social life is able to maintain its shape for long'.[94] This is very reminiscent of *The Communist Manifesto*'s idea that due to the revolutionary production relations of nineteenth-century capitalism 'all that is solid melts into air'.[95] However, while in the classic Marxian period of the nineteenth century, which Bauman calls 'heavy modernity', individuals were characteristically economic producers, 'postmodern society engages its members primarily in their capacity as consumers'.[96] If the distinguishing identity of the liquid modern era is that of the consumer, then the presiding characteristic of the liquid modern world is impermanence: impermanent relationships, employment, location, identities, and so on. Just as neoliberal capital is fluid and respects no borders, so the topos of postmodernity is a liquid impermanence.

Bauman argues that '[t]he function of culture is not to satisfy existing needs, but to create new ones'.[97] *Tales from the Mall* depicts the damaging results of the consumerist ethos for relationships and communities. Relationship breakdown is encouraged by capitalism creating never-ending consumer demand: 'now they've exhausted the family market, they're doubling their money with divorce', claims a character in 'Exits'.[98] Liquid modern relationships embody 'the mall within': transitoriness, lack of commitment, desire over need, and personal choice as a signifier of freedom.[99] Malls – the American name for shopping-centres is significant – are symptomatic of globalisation, which results in the loss of a *centre* in individual, local/regional and national

93   Morrison, *Tales from the Mall*, p. 9.
94   Zygmunt Bauman, *Culture in a Liquid Modern World*, trans. by Lydia Bauman (Cambridge: Polity, 2012), p. 11.
95   Karl Marx and Friedrich Engels, *The Communist Manifesto* (London: Vintage, 2010), p. 25.
96   Zygmunt Bauman, *Liquid Modernity* (Cambridge: Polity, 2012), p. 76.
97   Bauman, *Culture in a Liquid Modern World*, p. 17.
98   Morrison, *Tales from the Mall*, p. 204.
99   Morrison, *Tales from the Mall*, p. 207.

life, the consumerisation of personal and cultural space. As 'The Empty Space' indicates, malls literally have no centre (a disorientation tactic meaning there is nowhere to collect): 'the centre is a space, not a place'.[100] Metaphorically and literally, 'there is something empty at the heart of consumerism'.[101] David Harvey argues that malls 'instantiate rather than critique the idea that "there is no alternative"' to capitalism, with the ubiquity of the mall having done 'as much to signal the end of history as the collapse of the Berlin Wall ever did'.[102] The mall is a place that is a no place. Such decentring destroys communities and the very idea of community. The globalised world of 'Redacted', in which after '[e]ight hours on a plane [...] you haven't moved a mile', witnesses the death of a local town centre due to the opening of a mall that in contrast is 'busy, bustling, as if all the townsfolk have moved here'.[103]

Although *Tales from the Mall* instances acts of personal resistance against mallification, the ultimate act of opposition – the burning down of the mall in 'Borders' – is accidental, while the 'Twenty Top Tips for Brightening your Day in the Mall' details anarchist pranks rather than structured opposition. Morrison may be right to allege that '[t]he mallification of my country [Scotland] is an historic event, as important as the Jacobite Rebellion or the Highland Clearances', but his claim that '[t]he literature of my country is vehemently opposed to what it sees as a takeover of our national identity by multinational forces' implies some sort of corporate 'Scottish Literature' as well as the communal Scottish myth outlined by McCrone.[104] However, the activism of the Scottish independence referendum suggests a revitalisation of grassroots, community hall politics, and the redefinition of how we understand community and its relation and resistance to hegemonic politics.

One of the most significant and divisive aspects of the 2014 independence debate was the emergence of online communities as a means to campaign and propagandise for a Yes or No vote. 'Yes' in particular drew much support from culturalist communities such as National Collective and Bella Caledonia to challenge the dominant narratives of organisations such as the BBC and much of the Scottish and London print media, whose agenda was deemed to be Unionist by many Yes supporters.[105] 'New communications technologies have

---

100   Morrison, *Tales from the Mall*, p. 79.
101   Morrison, *Tales from the Mall*, p. 79.
102   David Harvey, *Spaces of Hope* (Edinburgh: Edinburgh University Press, 2002), p. 168.
103   Morrison, *Tales from the Mall*, pp. 60, 69.
104   Morrison, *Tales from the Mall*, pp. 8, 10.
105   See Iain Macwhirter, *Disunited Kingdom: How Westminster Won a Referendum but Lost Scotland* (Glasgow: Cargo Publishing, 2014), pp. 51–71, and *Democracy in the Dark: The Decline of the Scottish Press and How to Keep the Lights On* (Edinburgh: Saltire, 2014). For more on the referendum in relation to the British constitution, see Michael Gardiner,

catalyzed new styles for imagining and organizing communities of all sorts, including explicitly political communities', argues Patricia Hill Collins, for whom virtual communities can 'unsettle notions of a top-down public sphere, where elites control knowledge and public information'.[106] Whether such virtual communities, prone as they are to echolalia and self-promotion, adequately replace, or are merely revenants of, an old-school communitarian politics, or, indeed, actually suggest the triumph of hyperreal individualism, remain open questions. Benedict Anderson famously proposed that the 'basic morphology' of what would become the modern nation emerged in 'the convergence of capitalism and print technology'.[107] In a contemporary era that has seen traditional print media challenged by the rise of virtual communities, Anderson's equation, and what it means for nationhood and nationalism, needs to be reassessed. While Morrison's book would seem to suggest the end of community, the virtual communities established during the independence referendum show that the ends of community have emerged from the terrain of Scottish myth to become politically proactive communities in practice. These new imagined communities have contributed to a reshaping of the idea of community and the imagined community that is Scotland.

    Time and Action in the Scottish Independence Referendum (Basingstoke: Palgrave Macmillan, 2015).

106   Patricia Hill Collins, 'The New Politics of Community', *American Sociological Review*, 75.1 (2010), 7–30 (p. 17).

107   Benedict Anderson, *Imagined Communities: Reflections on the Origin and Spread of Nationalism* (London and New York: Verso, 2006), p. 46.

CHAPTER 1

The Lonely Island: Exile and Community in Recent Island Writing

Timothy C. Baker

Abstract

In much recent Scottish literature, writing about islands is often framed both as a form of cultural critique and a way to question ideas of community. Depictions of Scottish islands in mid-twentieth-century poetry and fiction often frame islands simultaneously as places of mythic renewal and necessary exile. More recent writers, including Christine De Luca, Angus Peter Campbell, Jen Hadfield, and J.O. Morgan, use this opposition to portray island communities as ever-shifting networks of individual relations.

Keywords

Islands – community – Iain Crichton Smith – exile – Shetland – J.O. Morgan – Christine De Luca – Charles Avery – Angus Peter Campbell – Gaelic – Jen Hadfield

In a recent discussion of the relation between writing and politics, Jacques Rancière makes the rather astonishing claim that the island 'is the metaphor for the book in general [...]. The space of the island and the volume of the book express each other and thus define a certain world, a certain way in which writing makes a world by unmaking another one'.[1] Islands, as many critics have noted, are places of shifting relationships, whether it is between ideas of centre and periphery, land and sea, or insider and outsider; they navigate the space between exile and belonging, between modes of expression and languages, and even between genres. Islands, in this formalist and aesthetic conception, present a way of rethinking the relationship between the individual and the community, and between differing views of history and cultural memory. As Fredric Jameson argues, islands present 'the ultimate rebuke of the centred

---

1 Jacques Rancière, *The Flesh of Words: The Politics of Writing*, trans. by Charlotte Mandell (Stanford: Stanford University Press, 2004), p. 100.

subject and the full deployment of the great maxim that "difference relates".[2] Like texts, islands must be considered as webs of relation: an island is both a world of its own and only visible in relation to other worlds. For Rancière, the world is seen not only through experience and imagination, but also through books, or texts, themselves. Texts and islands must be seen in relation to a continual process of making and unmaking.

In the same way, as Gillian Beer among others has noted, the island must be seen as the 'intimate, tactile, and complete relationship' or 'play' between earth and water.[3] The island, Beer argues, is both 'cultural' and 'pre-cultural', tied both to society and the individual, and both isolated and 'traceried by water, overflown by birds carrying seeds'.[4] The island is always known in relation to the external world: it can be known only as a place apart insofar as it is still defined by its connections to the mainland. Without going as far as Rancière's claim that the island is a metaphor for the text, both the island and the text can be seen to share key features, chief among them the notion that indeterminacy provides a position of critique. As Beer argues, islands are 'the space for exploration, self-inquiry, and satire of the writer's own culture'.[5] Peter Conrad similarly argues that the same experience that gives rise to an 'insular feeling, an aching symptom of isolation', can also provide 'a peculiar vantage point on the larger world'.[6] For each of these authors, the island is valued as providing a particular distanced perspective on mainland culture. Rather than looking at islands in relation to native inhabitants or cultures, or in terms of the history of particular islands, each of these critics focuses on the island as such. The island, thus abstracted, opens a space for consideration of the relationship between exile and community, as will be discussed below, as well as between place, culture, and text.

---

2   Fredric Jameson, *Archaeologies of the Future: The Desire Called Utopia and Other Science Fictions* (London and New York: Verso, 2005), p. 223.

3   Gillian Beer, 'The Island and the Aeroplane: The Case of Virginia Woolf', in *Nation and Narration*, ed. by Homi K. Bhabha (London and New York: Routledge, 1990), pp. 265–90 (p. 271).

4   Beer, 'The Island and the Aeroplane: The Case of Virginia Woolf', p. 271.

5   Gillian Beer, 'Discourses of the Island', in *Literature and Science as Modes of Exploration*, ed. by Fredrick Amrine (Dordrecht: Kluwer Academic Publishers, 1989), pp. 1–27 (p. 10).

6   Peter Conrad, *Islands: A Trip through Time and Space* (London: Thames and Hudson, 2009), p. 188. This perspective is exemplified by Jean-Jacques Rousseau, who finds on the Island of Saint-Pierre a secure 'resting-place' from which he can contemplate the 'constant flux' of the world. Jean-Jacques Rousseau, *Reveries of the Solitary Walker* [1782], trans. by Peter France (London: Penguin, 2004), p. 88.

The discourse surrounding islands is thus commonly focused on sets of binary oppositions. On the one hand, islands are often seen as prime examples of holistic or Durkheimian community; in J.G.A. Pocock's terms, they can be seen as 'relatively stable geographical communities, of whose pasts [...] history is supposed to consist'.[7] As necessarily finite geographical spaces in which a certain degree of interrelation is presupposed, the island is often figured as inherently unified, as can be seen in many utopian fictions from Thomas More onwards. At the same time, this separation from mainland cultures can lead to what Jacques Derrida calls a 'nostalgia as homesickness' that suggests a fundamental insularity and foregrounds the role of the solitary wanderer.[8] The island can thus be seen as both the ground of community and as a space in which the very idea of community can be questioned. Perhaps especially in Scotland, historians, sociologists, and anthropologists present Scottish islands in terms of unity, as is exemplified in the pioneering travel writing of Martin Martin, whose *A Description of the Western Islands of Scotland* (1703) presents each of the Western isles in relation to each other. Over the course of the twentieth century, however, Scottish authors have highlighted the relation between stability and insularity, as well as examining the potential divide between abstract conceptions of the island and the experience of a particular island. The tension between depictions of the island as a place of mythic renewal and as inherently unsustainable in mid-twentieth-century writers such as Iain Crichton Smith, George Mackay Brown, and Edwin Muir, among others, demonstrates the importance and variability of depictions of island life in Scottish writing.

Exile and Renewal in Scottish Island Writing

While many twentieth-century Scottish writers display an interest in the island's capacity for cultural critique noted by Beer and others, islands are more often seen as the locus of community: writing of the island becomes a way to address and critique ideas of community itself. Localised community represents how rural or island life differs from the life of the city. As the Lewis-raised poet and novelist Iain Crichton Smith writes in a late essay called 'Real People in a Real Place':

---

7 J.G.A. Pocock, *The Discovery of Islands: Essays in British History* (Cambridge: Cambridge University Press, 2005), p. 269.

8 Jacques Derrida, *The Beast and the Sovereign: Volume II*, ed. by Michel Lisse and others, trans. by Geoffrey Bennington (Chicago and London: University of Chicago Press, 2011), p. 95.

It is this sense of a community that one thinks of most when one compares the island with the city. It was because of the community that the fact of exile became so desolate and frightening. [...] The positive side [of the community] is the sense of warmth, settledness, that it gives, the feeling that one has a place, a name, that one will not be consigned to the chilly air of pure individuality. It is the sense that what one belongs to is a sustaining force [...although] it is nearly always conservative and hostile to change.[9]

Islands thus present a constant vision of community: the island community, by virtue of its separation, is stable. While careful not to present an overly idealised vision of island communities, Smith presents the island as a micro-cosmic and knowable society. A similar universality can be found throughout the works of Smith's Orkney-based contemporary George Mackay Brown. In a play called *The Well*, for instance, Brown depicts a small community's exis-tence across many centuries. The Keeper of the Well compares cyclical and progressive views of time. The former, rooted in the island, is eternal:

Time here, in the island, is a single day, repeated over and over. The same people, dawn to sunset. The same things: birth, love, death. The old die, the children come dancing into time. Water shines on the new-born and the dead.[10]

In this passage, and in many similar ones throughout his poetry, Brown intro-duces an almost mythic dimension to island life. The island exists outside of time, or rather, is constant in all times. For Brown the island can be seen as a place of individual and collective renewal: the island is where the individual meets the universal. For both Smith and Brown, islands become a place where abstract notions such as time and community are actualised and inhabited in a way they cannot be on the mainland.

This view of the island as both microcosm and place apart is often con-nected to an idea of the island as offering a vision of eternity. Derick Thomson, from Lewis, writes in 'Lewis in Summer': 'Probably there's no atmosphere in the world/that offers so little resistance to people/to look in at Eternity'.[11]

---

9   Iain Crichton Smith, *Towards the Human: Selected Essays* (Edinburgh: MacDonald, 1986), pp. 23–24 (p. 26).

10   George Mackay Brown, *Three Plays: The Loom of Light, The Well* and *The Voyage of Saint Brandon* (London: Chatto & Windus, 1984), p. 72.

11   Derick S. Thomson [Ruaraidh MacThomais], *Creachadh na Clarsaiach: Cruinneachadh de Bhardachd, 1940–1980/Plundering the Harp: Collected Poems, 1940–1980* (Edinburgh: MacDonald, 1982), p. 219.

Similarly, in 'Shores' the Raasay-born poet Sorley MacLean offers a depiction of several Hebridean islands, writing:

> And if we were together
> on Calgary shore in Mull,
> between Scotland and Tiree,
> between the world and eternity,
> I would stay there till doom
> Measuring sand, grain by grain.[12]

For both poets the island, considered both as an abstraction and as an experienced place, represents the border between the world as we know it and eternity. As in the work of the critics discussed above, in these texts the island is presented as a peripheral or liminal space, neither wholly of this world nor wholly out of it. Curiously, the particulars of a given island seem relatively unimportant for many of these poets. Brown equates each of the islands in Orkney, and MacLean, to an extent, covers much of the Hebrides. It is the idea of the island that is important in these texts: the island is poised not only between land and sea, but also between myth and modernity, and between varying notions of time. Looking at the island gives access to the world.

Especially within a Scottish literary tradition, however, there is a linked and opposed perspective in which the island stands for a unified culture that is either unsustainable or must be left behind. This can be seen in some of the works of both Brown and Smith, and especially in the writing of Edwin Muir. Muir and Smith, as well as many other writers, left the islands where they were raised and found it, in a sense, impossible to return. While not necessarily naïve, there is something of an Edenic or Arcadian perspective here: for Muir especially, Orkney represents not only his own personal past, but is a symbol for a larger human past of organic community where geographic and cultural identity are mutually founded. Orkney is figured as a mythic place apart; he writes in 'The Myth', for instance, 'My childhood all a myth/Enacted in a distant isle', a sentiment repeated in his autobiography, where he argues that '[t]he Orkney I was born into was a place where there was no great distinction between the ordinary and the fabulous; the lives of living men turned into legend'.[13] Leaving Orkney is Muir's own experience of the Fall; it is a necessarily innocent and premodern place that can only be figured in retrospect.

---

12   Sorley MacLean [Somhairle MacGill-Eain], *From Wood to Ridge/O Choille gu Bearradh* (Manchester and Edinburgh: Carcanet/Birlinn, 1999), pp. 141–43.

13   Edwin Muir, *The Voyage and Other Poems* (London: Faber and Faber, 1946), p. 31; *An Autobiography* (Minnesota: Graywolf Press, 1990), p. 14.

For Smith, likewise, the death of the island community can be seen both in the emigration of young people to the mainland and in the gradual eradication of Gaelic: once a people loses its native tongue, their identity both as individuals and members of a community becomes unstable. Writing in English about the Hebrides, and writing about the islands from the Scottish mainland, Smith suggests that whatever culture existed on the island can never be recovered or fully expressed. As he writes in an early poem called 'The Departing Island':

> It's the island that goes away, not we who leave it.
> Like an unbearable thought it sinks beyond
> assiduous reasoning light and wringing hands,
> or, as a flower roots deep into the ground,
> it works its darkness into the gay winds
> that blow about us in a later spirit.[14]

The island remains as a spirit or a thought, but can never be more than that: an island is not a place for self-inquiry and cultural evaluation, but a place that comes to exist only in the past or as a remnant of an unsustainable community. It is not a place from which to view eternity, but rather one of unreason and memory. For Smith, Brown, and Muir, the island can only be imagined from a certain perspective, whether cyclical, Edenic, or in terms of culture and language. Once the island changes, either through exile and diaspora or simply through encounters with a larger modernity, it can no longer be imagined. For each, arguably, the island is revealed simply as the locus of a past identity that can only be reconstituted through writing; an abstract or generalised approach to the island is necessitated by historical circumstance.

A third, related vision of islands, combining the ideas of exile and renewal, is exemplified in the work of John Buchan. At the end of *The Island of Sheep* (1936), Buchan's fifth and final Richard Hannay thriller, the action moves from England and Scotland to an almost deserted island in the Norlands, a fictionalised version of the Faroes. The island is depicted as 'a port outside the habitable world in some forgotten domain of peace'.[15] At the novel's close, however, the island is presented not simply as a refuge or utopia, but also as a place where violent international conflicts can be presented, and eventually solved, in microcosm; the novel repeats many ideas of an earlier volume of the same name that Buchan and his wife published under the names Cadmus and Harmonia. The characters who travel there represent a broad cross-section of

---

14   Iain Crichton Smith, *Collected Poems* (Manchester: Carcanet, 1992), p. 60.

15   John Buchan, *The Island of Sheep* (London: Hodder and Stoughton, 1936), p. 223.

European nationalities, while most of their personal and political allegiances have been formed by experiences in Africa and Asia. The island is at once a place of peace and action; indeed, as one character notes, the island's advantage is that it provides "'peace and leisure to do our will'".[16] It is precisely because the island is removed from the course of international events that it becomes a place where these events can be enacted. Buchan here foregrounds the way islands can be seen as case studies in both individual and collective history; as Fernand Braudel notes in his influential history of the Mediterranean, the role islands 'have played in the forefront of history far exceeds what might be expected from such poor territories. The events of history often lead to islands'.[17] *The Island of Sheep* presents just such a view of history: the island is a place of heightened political interest, if only by virtue of its assumed remove from the events of global politics. The island here, crucially, has no inherent qualities other than this remove. Although local customs and inhabitants are glimpsed, they are relatively unimportant. Instead, in Buchan's novel, the island is a place of temporary community.

Comparing these different versions of island community, it becomes clear that in twentieth-century Scottish writing islands are less stable than might be imagined. Even writers such as Mackay Brown, who in many of his texts insists on the stability of island community, ends several of his novels and stories – most notably *Greenvoe* (1972) and *Beside the Ocean of Time* (1994) – with scenes of apocalypse and renewal. These three tropes, where islands are figured variously in relation to eternity, exile, and temporary community, all continue to appear in more contemporary Scottish writing in a variety of genres. Examining a broad, though far from exhaustive, sampling of recent Scottish writing about islands demonstrates the extent to which the island continues to be used as a way to approach themes of exile and community.

Contemporary Island Writing

The tension between ideal or abstract visions of the island and those grounded in an experience of place is developed extensively in the work of the Shetland poets Christine De Luca and Jen Hadfield. In a recent poem called 'Nae Aesy Mizzer', De Luca imagines looking at a map of Shetland using a polar projection, where Shetland is placed in the centre of the map:

---

16   Buchan, *Island of Sheep*, p. 257.
17   Fernand Braudel, *The Mediterranean and the Mediterranean World in the Age of Philip II*, trans. by Sian Reynolds, 2 vols (London: Collins, 1972–73), I, p. 154.

Shetland isna banished tae a box
i da Moray Firt or left oot aa tagidder
– ta scale up da rest – but centre stage.
Peripheral has new meanin; an marginal.[18]

The polar projection provides a way of seeing Shetland as it is known to its inhabitants, making the peripheral central. Indeed, as Judith Schalansky writes, '[a]ny point on the infinite globe of the Earth can become a centre'.[19] In some ways this is reminiscent of Hugh MacDiarmid's conception of the universality he finds in Whalsay. Although MacDiarmid initially lamented his perceived exile in Shetland during much of the 1930s, he soon argued that 'I am no further from the "centre of things"/In the Shetlands here than in London, New York, or Tokio'.[20] De Luca's work is also reminiscent of Brown's older, or immemorial, perspective, with 'Nae satellites/ta fix a point', but rather a more simple 'element o winder'.[21] For De Luca, the experience of the island is fundamentally tied to individual self-conception: people come to know themselves in direct relation to the land they inhabit. As such, there will always be a tension between the way the island is central in the minds of its inhabitants and peripheral or marginal to mainland dwellers. As Donald E. Meek writes of his childhood in the Hebrides: 'I still cannot conceive of "edges" and "peripheries" in geographical terms [...]. If there was a "periphery" at all, it was the land mass of the Scottish mainland'.[22] For both writers the concept of the peripheral is based in lived experience, rather than abstraction. The relation between different conceptions of the island can, for De Luca, in part be addressed through language.

De Luca writes both in Shetland dialect and in English, implicitly arguing that the 'peripheral' language is as central to experience as the arguably more standard one. Her poetry is largely addressed towards her immediate community, and has predominantly been published locally: rather than explaining

---

18   Christine De Luca, *North End of Eden* (Edinburgh: Luath, 2010), p. 19.

19   Judith Schalansky, *Atlas of Remote Islands*, trans. by Christine Lo (London: Particular Books, 2010), p. 14.

20   Hugh MacDiarmid, *The Islands of Scotland: Hebrides, Orkneys, and Shetlands* (London: B.T. Batsford, 1939), pp. xv–xvi.

21   De Luca, *North End of Eden*, p. 19.

22   Donald E. Meek, '"It follows me, that black island...": Portraying and Positioning the Hebridean "Fringe" in Twentieth-Century Gaelic Literature', in *Centring on the Peripheries: Studies in Scandinavian, Scottish, Gaelic and Greenlandic Literature*, ed. by Bjarne Thorup Thomsen (Norwich: Norvik Press, 2007), pp. 153–63 (p. 153).

Shetland to an external audience, she represents it in its own language. In many of her recent poems she evokes a Muir-like conception of the island as a place apart. Even as she writes of ATMs and satellites, she also depicts Shetland in a rarefied manner, as in 'Faa fae Grace':

> We could vaige tae da fowr coarners
> o a treeless Eden, dis blissit gairden.
> Burns an lochs fed imagination,
> trowie-steyns led wis a mirry dance.[23]

Even in an account of the Fall, as this poem in many ways is, De Luca presents an Eden that is still in some ways accessible, through verse or through first-hand experience. Her Shetland is not wholly removed from the world, but it is still a refuge, a centre, and a place of becoming. Although this is an imagined Eden, it is significantly shaped by a collective voice: the shared stories and language create a particular experience of place.

Hadfield, on the other hand, is a poet from the mainland (Cheshire, in this case) who now resides in Shetland, and whose work is infused with Shetland words and phrases. Throughout her work the island is presented as a rejuvenating force that allows a simultaneous move both inwards and outwards. If De Luca writes from an avowedly insider's perspective, Hadfield writes as an outsider with insider knowledge. In many of her poems the island is seen as a place of linguistic as well as individual renewal; thinking of the island allows for a reconsideration of the structure and form of poetry. The movement between the worlds of text and experience can be seen in the title poem to *Nigh-No-Place*, which introduces a list of places without description, names without reference: 'Blowfly' and 'Salt Pie', 'North Light' and 'Hungry Hushes'. The sound of place becomes the place itself: 'Pity-Me-Wood' and 'Crackpot Moor' can only conjure the need to escape.[24] 'Nigh-No-Place' is also the name given to the volume's central section, in which the poems are directly concerned with Shetland; the title also foregrounds the page as a place in which texts move. The section includes list poems, prose poems both solid and divided, and untitled poems that cartwheel across the page. In form, language, and system of reference, none of these poems depicts a static place, but each instead highlights place as motion. The final lines of 'witless...' illustrate Hadfield's approach:

---

23   De Luca, *North End of Eden*, p. 66.
24   Jen Hadfield, *Nigh-No-Place* (Tarset: Bloodaxe, 2008), pp. 9–10.

grey-eyed, green-eyed, blue-eyed, pie-eyed,
my Macchu Picchu of the Kitchen Floor.
Now, will we visualise
the world? Cell by cell,
Saturn to Sedna, Hells to Valhalla
this and those universes,
aa'[25]

Here we are presented with the tension between the foreign ('Macchu Picchu') and domestic ('the Kitchen Floor'), the literal ('grey-eyed') and figurative ('pie-eyed'), the minute ('Cell by cell') and grandiose ('those universes'), English and Shetland. The lines physically swerve over the page; each new idea or image finds its own allotted place. Indeed, the poem arguably works as a physical depiction or illustration of the Shetland mainland itself, mixing the concrete and the metaphysical. The placement of the lines is not haphazard, but calls attention to the space surrounding them: the poem itself becomes an island, a world within a world.

A similar idea of the island as world can be found in Charles Avery's ongoing multi-media visual art project 'The Islanders'. Avery, now based in London but originally from Mull, combines drawing, sculpture, and text to explore the fictional world of 'The Island'. In its philosophical and surreal leanings, Avery's project offers a visual parallel to fantastical novels such as Alan Warner's *These Demented Lands* (1997) and Jess Richards's *Snake Ropes* (2012). The island, as Avery's maps show, is both the whole of the world and a tourist destination; like De Luca's polar projections, Avery's Island is defined as both centre and periphery. Avery's first major exhibition of the collected materials offers the diaries and observations of a visitor who comes, over the course of his stay, to consider himself a native. He writes:

Speaking from the point of view of an Islander, which I now regard myself to be, there are two states: the Island and Triangleland.

The term Triangleland refers to the character of the tourists, their apparent desire to label and classify everything and their complacency in their ability to do so. The first thing they will ask is, 'What is the name of the island?' This appears an absurd and irrelevant question, for it is akin to asking, 'What is the name of everything?' or, 'What is Tom's name?' Being the continent from which all the other islands in the

---

25   Hadfield, *Nigh-No-Place*, p. 30.

archipelago are isolated it is the archetype and as such does not require a name.[26]

At the same time, however, the visitor continues to make a taxonomy of the peculiar gods and beings on the Island, which is filled with strange gods and beings. In his various exhibitions, Avery introduces visitors to a fantastic world that only begins to make sense when it is taken apart and examined piecemeal, as the viewer focuses on a single drawing or sculpture. The viewer is made into a necessary outsider to this imagined island, and can never completely comprehend it, or understand its relation to the outer world: it is a marginal, peripheral land that both critiques and relies on flawed models of representation.

Avery's Island clearly illustrates some of the insider/outsider dynamics considered in relation to island life, if only because its surreal elements make it so clearly not of this world. The unease with such dynamics that Avery expresses in his interviews, as well as their necessity, can also be found in the Shetland writer Neil Butler's collection of interconnected stories *The Roost*. The collection focuses on several teenagers in Shetland, most of whom are reluctant to see their island as a functioning or stable community. In 'Shitmonster', the protagonist Ellie Tait invites herself to the birthday party of Rita Wheelwright, one of the very few characters in the text to speak in Shetland dialect. Rita argues that 'Du has to be proud o dy home, else what do you have?' and defines Shetland as 'da *folk*, and da *music*'; Ellie, on the other hand, finds only ganzies, puffins, '[a]lcoholism and parochial fools who can't see further than their own navels'.[27] Their debate ultimately centres on who has the more fantastical view of the island: Ellie, who sees it as stuck in an unviable past, or Rita, who sees that past as something to be preserved. On the whole, the text appears to side with Ellie, who reappears in the collection far more than Rita does. These visions of Shetland life are unified, however, in the way they both refer to other models. Rita's preferred Shetland is dedicated to recreating past traditions, rather than developing them, while Ellie simply seeks for Shetland to become more like mainland Britain or the United States. Neither character is especially at home in their given community; instead, both are looking to join a pre-existing community of which they are not yet part. Ellie reflects on this in another story where she speaks to her father and uncle:

---

26   Charles Avery, *The Islanders: An Introduction* (London: Parasol unit/Koenig Books, 2010), p. 103.

27   Neil Butler, *The Roost* (Edinburgh: Thirsty Books, 2011), p. 49. Italics in original.

They didn't *understand*. They'd stayed. Shetland was in them. They'd welcomed it, made it a part of them. She couldn't. She *refused*. She *was* going to escape, get to university, probably roll around on the ground there till she got the stink off her.[28]

As Ellie sees her relatives' situation, even for native inhabitants, Shetland identity or community is a choice. One is not a member of the community simply by birthright, but because one welcomes it.

In many respects Butler's presentation of island culture can be related to geographical approaches to island life. The South Uist writer Angus Peter Campbell argues in *Archie and the North Wind* that on an island there is 'no division between land and sea: such a choice was unimaginable'.[29] In Campbell's works the Hebrides are a place of constant variation. In *The Girl on the Ferryboat*, for instance, a character's immersion in Peruvian culture grants an experience of unified community that can be contrasted with Scottish islands, which are 'so open and exposed that nothing lasted'.[30] The variability of the landscape necessitates continually shifting relationships between the individual and the community. In each of these novels the protagonists are confronted with a vision of a traditional or holistic community to which they do not have access, whether because it is located in the past or only in the imagination. Their dilemma mimics that of Malcolm in Iain Crichton Smith's oft-anthologised 'An American Sky', who reflects on his return to his home island after years away that 'if one runs away one cannot be happy anywhere any more. If one left in the first place one could never go back. Or if one came back one also brought a virus, an infection of time and place'.[31] As the Lewis poet Anna Frater writes more recently in a poem called 'Bayble Island': 'I can't leave. There's no way back'.[32] Once the individual is separated – geographically or emotionally – from the island community, their original relationship with it cannot be recaptured. In Campbell's and Butler's texts, however, this division between community and exile, or between the desire to leave and the desire to remain, is less stable than it might appear: each feeds, and is seen in relation to, the other. Neither, crucially, is more authentic than the other: staying and leaving

---

28   Butler, *The Roost*, p. 140. Italics in original.

29   Angus Peter Campbell, *Archie and the North Wind* (Edinburgh: Luath, 2010), p. 16.

30   Angus Peter Campbell, *The Girl on the Ferryboat* (Edinburgh: Luath, 2013), p. 47.

31   Iain Crichton Smith, *The Red Door: The Complete English Stories 1949–76*, ed. by Kevin MacNeil (Edinburgh: Birlinn, 2001), p. 205.

32   *These Islands, We Sing: An Anthology of Scottish Islands Poetry*, ed. by Kevin MacNeil (Edinburgh: Polygon, 2011), p. 213.

are ultimately interconnected. Exile and belonging, framed in these various ways, are positioned as the central poles of island life.

A longer narrative of exile and return can be found in J.O. Morgan's book-length poem *Natural Mechanical*. A 'rendering of the true life stories of Iain Seoras Rockcliffe', according to the subtitle, the poem recounts a life on Skye in the middle of the twentieth century, a life, as Morgan takes pains to explain, that cannot come again. In this respect, Morgan follows the path set out by Muir and Smith: an organic island life is something intrinsically located in the past. For Morgan the life and community he wishes to depict is almost impossible to translate into a conventional, linear narrative. He begins *Natural Mechanical* with a lengthy 'Apologia': he notes that the scenes in the poem cannot appear in their original chronology; that though the language of the Inner Hebrides at the time of these scenes was Gaelic, the language used here is primarily English; that the poetic form of the narrative should be seen as secondary to its function as a biographical sketch; and that although all events are true, the poem 'has been approached by the author as a work of fiction'.[33] The content of the poem is not mediated by its structure so much as opposed to its structure. This is part of the poem's attempt to introduce the reader to a character who lives outside the confines of Standard English.

The poem begins by discussing the dyslexia of its hero, Rocky:

> At home it's the Gaelic that rolls from his tongue.
> Although he need not speak it very much.
> The language of streams, of rock, of wood –
> of nettles, as taught by their stings:
> that handled right can make a three-fold cord
> yet firm enough to catch a full-grown hare
> and hold it fast – is much more to his liking.
> The tongue of the classroom is English.
> *Read the words as you've been taught,*
> *or weren't you even listening.*
> As in a dream the letters stay as letters.
> They are glue. Have no perspective depth.
> Their shapes mean nothing other than their shapes.
> Have no relevance to sound, to throat. Un-word-like.[34]

---

33   J.O. Morgan, *Natural Mechanical* (London: CB Editions, 2009), [n.p.].
34   Morgan, *Natural Mechanical*, p. 2. Italics in original.

There are three languages discussed here: Gaelic, which Morgan insists cannot be translated or approximated, English, which is an impediment to communication, and the language of nature, which is the poem's primary concern. The notion that English and education act as a force of separation between children and an island environment is familiar from both Smith and Brown. Morgan further recognises, however, that the book's implied readership, including speakers of English and people who do not live on Skye, can only witness this experience through, as it were, the wrong medium. The reader can only approach Rocky's life through the written English that is a stumbling block to him, while the language of nettle ropes used to catch hares is what seems 'Un-word-like'. This potentially explains the simplified diction of *Natural Mechanical*: the language of the poem cannot be the language of the places and experiences it describes. While Hadfield looks to the island to find new words and forms for experience, and De Luca writes in a Shetland dialect that needs no explanation, but simply is the best tongue for the poems at hand, for Morgan the language of the island cannot be brought into the present, or into shared or cosmopolitan experience.[35] In a sense, Morgan's language is as innovative as Hadfield's, simply by drawing attention to all the things it cannot say and the experiences it cannot capture. Hadfield uses language to celebrate the island, while Morgan's language suggests that island experience can never be translated into the language of the mainland.

Towards the end of the poem, Rocky, while still a young child, makes a sudden decision to travel to France through a combination of stolen seats on trains and ferries, hitchhiking, and walking, making it as far as Lyon. He goes in part to experience the language, having previously been impressed by the French phrases of his schoolmates. Although his sojourn involves complete poverty and physical pain, as he goes barefoot through the streets of Paris and Lyon begging for his food, it allows him to understand better his place in the world. As he reaches the end of his journey, his connection with his home is reaffirmed:

> Just as a wounded animal seeks out
> the place where it is most at peace,
> so all that Rocky thinks of now
> is getting back to Skye.[36]

---

35   An alternative approach can be found in Robert Alan Jamieson's collection *Nort Atlantik Drift*, in which each poem in Shetland dialect is juxtaposed not only with an English gloss but also an archival photo so that the reader has three distinct avenues to approach a past community.

36   Morgan, *Natural Mechanical*, p. 55.

When he returns, and his feet are seen to by the doctor – amazed at the French bandages, as no one has believed his story – he is admonished never to 'do a thing like that again':

> And Rocky never does, although
> he cannot help but think upon
> the wider possibilities
> his opened world presents.[37]

For the remainder of the volume, Rocky's life is largely confined to a garage on Skye. Yet his trip to France as a child forms the poem's climax, and is one of the longest episodes presented in it. His trip away is important precisely because it allows him to be integrated into a community from which he has always felt estranged. Voluntary exile, in a sense, allows one to return. As with Butler's stories, in Morgan's poem island life is best seen as a choice, rather than a pre-existing state of being. One can only enter into island community once one has recognised what it is to live apart from that community.

This sense of disruption and return is arguably endemic to islands. As Gilles Deleuze argues, the island negates any assumed stability in the world. Islands, he argues, 'are either from before or for after humankind [...]. The island is both that towards which one drifts' and '*also the origin*, radical and absolute'.[38] The island both attracts and repulses: it both provides a place and idea of origins to which one always returns, often despite resistance. For Deleuze, however, this is not reductive, for the island is also the place of re-creation and re-beginning: the island is both origin and second origin, a place where everything can begin again. Although Deleuze is largely interested in an abstracted ideal, rather than any particular island, this movement can be seen in several of the stories of imagined Scottish islands in Campbell's *Invisible Islands*. The deserted island from which all life springs, as suggested by Deleuze, is given form on the island of Craolaigh, which has never had inhabitants. While Craolaigh has 'no story to tell', it is also the locus of all stories, as each visitor brings his or her own stories to the island: the visitors '[invent] an island whose earth was made of magic, whose sky was made of silk, whose people were the best dancers (as well as the best singers and boatmakers) in the whole wide

---

37   Morgan, *Natural Mechanical*, p. 57.
38   Gilles Deleuze, *Desert Islands and Other Texts, 1953–1974*, ed. by David Lapoujade, trans. by Michael Taormina (Los Angeles and New York: Semiotext(e), 2004), pp. 9–10. Italics in original.

world'.[39] The whole universe, Campbell writes, exists in this deserted island, insofar as every story finds a home there. Another island, Labhraigh, is notable for its speech system, which incorporates only the present indicative. With no past and future, everything happens 'now': 'nobody goes to the shop except now, nobody leaves the island except now, nobody dies except now, except that everyone knows, despite all the clamour, that the now they speak of is already past, or is yet to be'.[40] In Campbell's stories, as in Avery's exhibitions, the island is a place of infinite possibilities, including the redefinition of stories and language itself. At the same time, however, the island's challenge to conventional narratives of time and place is only partially disruptive: because the island is always figured in relation to the mainland (or the archipelago), it cannot operate at a complete remove. Instead, as in Deleuze's analysis, the island must be thought of as an origin that is also a second origin, a beginning that also refers back to the past.

This idea of a second origin similarly appears in a spate of recent novels imagining island communities from the outside. The use of islands as a place to gather disparate characters, so common in Scottish fiction of the first half of the century such as Buchan's, now seems largely relegated to genre texts by both Scottish and English authors, including mysteries such as Ann Cleeves's Shetland series (2006–present) and Peter May's Lewis Trilogy (2011–13), as well as contemporary Gothic novels including Alice Thompson's *Pharos* (2002) and *Burnt Island* (2013). The island is also used as a place where genres, as well as people, can be juxtaposed. In Louise Welsh's *Naming the Bones* and Sarah Moss's *Night Waking* academics from the mainland travel to deserted or quasi-deserted Hebridean islands in the hopes that they will be catalysts for self-discovery.[41] One character in *Naming the Bones* reveals that while she had thought of the island as 'an opportunity to create', it is finally symbolised by 'overcrowding, bad trips, drunkenness and sickness', as well as 'dark skies', 'relentless rain', and 'damp cottage[s]'.[42] The island is ultimately a place for Gothic adventure, a suitably otherworldly locale for witchcraft and murder. In *Night Waking*, Moss similarly alternates between academic comedy and Gothic imagery, but also uses the island to illustrate parallels between the past and present, as the story of modern academics is balanced with that of a nineteenth-century nurse. Living on and studying an island, the protagonist

---

39   Angus Peter Campbell, *Invisible Islands* (Glasgow: Otago, 2006), p. 13.

40   Campbell, *Invisible Islands*, p. 65.

41   A similar approach is taken in the English novelist Amy Sackville's *Orkney* (2013), where Orkney is depicted as an almost mythical place apart.

42   Louise Welsh, *Naming the Bones* (Edinburgh: Canongate, 2010), pp. 336–37.

discovers, 'offers a sharp illustration of the impossibility of untangling history and ideology'.[43]

Each of the texts mentioned above offers a way of seeing islands as a place of shifting relationships, whether it is between ideas of centre and periphery, between ideas of insider and outsider, between exile and belonging, and even between genres. In each, too, the question of islands is textually mediated; as in Campbell's stories, an island is known by how it is spoken of, and what sort of speech it demands. Similarly, many of these texts fluctuate between presenting the island as an ideal and as a place of particular lived experience. This tension is addressed in David Greig's play *Outlying Islands*, inspired by Robert Atkinson and John Ainslie's 1935 search for the Leach's Fork-Tailed Petrel as recorded in Atkinson's *Island Going*. Robert opens the play discussing 'the force that pulls us towards' outlying islands.[44] For the naturalists, every outlying island is the same: equally deserted, they are simply the unspoiled locations for scientific observation, and their beauty is enhanced by their distance from the mainland. Mr Kirk, however, the island's sole owner, argues that the island has been abandoned as divine punishment: the inhabitants' isolation led them to blasphemy, and Kirk hopes in turn to lease it to the government for anthrax testing. Kirk's niece Ellen, meanwhile, sees the island in terms of a timeless fairytale. Rather than moving towards a resolution between the scientific, religious, economic, and imaginative readings of the island, the play posits that the island can only be understood in terms of the relation between these ideas. Not only is each island different from any other, but each individual perspective on the island is equally different: no island can only be one thing.

This multiform approach to islands suggests a model of community predicated on individual difference, or what Jean-Luc Nancy calls singular plurality. Nancy argues that community can be thought of as a space in which individuals come together by recognising their difference: a sense of relation based not on similarity but difference and even rupture 'opens the sense of being' and allows the world to 'be conceived of as a creation of relations'.[45] Even more broadly, Roberto Esposito argues that '[c]ommunity refers to the singular and

---

43   Sarah Moss, *Night Waking* (London: Granta, 2011), p. 370. A longer exploration of this theme can be found in Robert Alan Jamieson's *Da Happie Laand* (2010), a Shetland novel that uses multiple timeframes and locations to trace the idea of islandness across generations, and novels of Scottish island diasporas by De Luca and Margaret Elphinstone.

44   David Greig, *Selected Plays 1999–2009* (London: Faber and Faber, 2010), p. 131.

45   Jean-Luc Nancy, *Adoration: The Deconstruction of Christianity II*, trans. by John McKeane (New York: Fordham University Press, 2013), p. 73.

plural characteristic of an existence free from every meaning that is presumed, imposed, or postponed'; community is the limit point that both separates and joins complete nihilism with immersion in the world.[46] For both thinkers community consists not only of individuals coming to know each other as individuals, but as the relation between poles of presence and absence. Community is not situated in a particular place, or predetermined according to a given group of people, but must be seen as a shifting set of relations.

This sense of community underlies the majority of texts discussed above, whether in terms of the momentary communities formed by outsiders in Welsh and Greig's texts or the discussion of exile and return in Butler and Morgan's works. In each, community, language, and even geography are not pre-established given facts, but must be constantly negotiated through acts of writing and speech. The island community is revealed as a choice made by the individual in relation to other individuals. As such, in many of these works the island becomes a symbol not for unity or organic communities, but for fragmented communities of individuals: the island community is something against which the individual defines him or herself. What makes these authors interesting in this regard is that few of them would be classed as experimental or postmodern writers.[47] Instead, by maintaining a focus on a particular island community, they reveal the extent to which an island can be thought of not as a stable locus, but as ever-shifting networks of individual relations. Exile and community are fundamentally linked in island writing simply because each is difficult to imagine without the other, and each contributes equally to the sense of the island.

---

46   Roberto Esposito, *Communitas: The Origin and Destiny of Community*, trans. by Timothy Campbell (Stanford: Stanford University Press, 2010), p. 149.

47   An exception might be made for the Devon-born, Skye-based poet Mark O. Goodwin, whose poem 'Skye' features the line: 'You've come over all postmodernist in Portree'. *These Islands, We Sing*, p. 182.

CHAPTER 2

Individual, Community and Conflict in Scottish Working-Class Fiction, 1920–1940

H. Gustav Klaus

Abstract

This chapter looks at a number of novels, many of them forgotten, which feature the growth and development of a working-class rebel against a background of poverty, hardship, industrial conflict and unemployment. These characters are embedded in their respective communities, but eventually move beyond them as the forces of history impinge on their lives.

Keywords

James Barke – Joe Corrie – Edward Gaitens – Lewis Grassic Gibbon – Edward Hunter – James C. Welsh – working-class writing – industrial fiction – labour history

'Most novels are in some sense knowable communities'.[1] No sooner had Raymond Williams stated the premise for his overview of the English novel than he went on to problematise it by stressing the importance of relationships, not only between the characters of a fiction, or the characters and a specific place, but also between the narrator and the range of social experience captured in the text. But since these relationships are assumed to be communicable, 'knowable communities' also comprises the author's relationship with his or her readers, including the kind of language used in and for the text. The instance of the reader, as well as that of the author, carries us beyond the text into the world of history and society.

In the real world, meanings of 'community' change over time and from one language and culture to another. Almost always positively connoted in English, in German some compound uses of it such as *Volksgemeinschaft* or even Max Weber's concept of the nation as a *Schicksalsgemeinschaft* have, since their

---

1 Raymond Williams, *The English Novel from Dickens to Lawrence* (London: Chatto and Windus, 1973), p. 14.

appropriation by Nazi ideology, become irremediably tainted. But the case for distinguishing between *Gemeinschaft* and *Gesellschaft* had already been made in the late-nineteenth century by Ferdinand Tönnies, the first standing for an organic social order characterised by natural social bonds, direct and recipro-cal relationships, mutual sympathy and interdependence; the latter represent-ing a mechanical formation (the state) in which isolated individuals are bound together in more formal and abstract relationships based on utilitarian prin-ciples. One can see how such a contrast connects with English cultural debates about a 'lost' organic social order, replaced by a mechanical entity, the one a warm, the other a cold place.

However, in a British context, community continues to interact with the nation and notions of a whole society. A recent monograph on George Mackay Brown, for example, has identified the following four predominant meanings of 'community': 'it signifies a local, geographically constituted region; a con-ception of shared national or political aims; a shared approach to ethics and morality; and, finally, the context for interpersonal relations and the emer-gence of the individual self'.[2] For the Scottish novels under consideration in this chapter, the first and the last of these meanings combined with the con-cept of the 'knowable community' will allow us to bear in mind a number of questions: How does the closely knit mining community in the novels of James C. Welsh, Edward Hunter, and Joe Corrie compare with the urban industrial scene in works by Lewis Grassic Gibbon, James Barke, and Edward Gaitens? What is the relationship between the gifted and idealistic male protagonist of these works and his local community? And how does that knowable place stand in relation to the larger unknown society and the unknowable dark forces of history?

Mining Novels

The modern Scottish working-class novel was born in 1920 when two miners who happened to be brothers-in-law each published a work of fiction. James C. Welsh's *The Underworld* was a bestseller in its day; the seventh edition of April 1923 registered an aggregated print-run of 81,500 copies.[3] By contrast, Edward Hunter's *The Road the Men Came Home* sank without a trace. A decade

---

2   Timothy C. Baker, *George Mackay Brown and the Philosophy of Community* (Edinburgh: Edinburgh University Press, 2009), p. 5.

3   Insert in the seventh edition of James C. Welsh, *The Underworld: The Story of Robert Sinclair, Miner* (London: Herbert Jenkins, 1923).

and a half earlier the two Lanarkshire miners had emigrated to New Zealand in search of better working and living conditions. Both eventually returned to Scotland, Welsh within fifteen months, Hunter after fourteen years. At home as well as abroad they had been active trade unionists. But the muse had also touched them. Before they ventured into fiction, they had already written songs, poems and sketches, which were, for example, published in the *Hamilton Advertiser* and the *Otago Witness*.[4]

At the centre of both novels there is an exceptionally gifted young man, a lad o' pairts, but one who subordinates his self and uses his talents for a common good: the cause of working-class emancipation. In each case the story is one of self-abnegation and self-sacrifice. Commitment comes at great personal cost: both works end with the central character's death, the one in an abortive rescue operation after a mining disaster, the other a victim of exhaustion and the miner's disease, phthisis. But there are also significant differences between the two works. As the subtitle of *The Underworld*, 'The Story of Robert Sinclair, Miner', suggests, Welsh's novel is in large part a proletarian *Bildungsroman*, starting with a childhood in a poverty-stricken miner's home, continuing with the boy's education, cut short by his decision – the first of many self-abnegating steps – to renounce secondary schooling in order to relieve the family purse, then following him into work, first at the pithead, then at the coalface, involving him in industrial disputes and portraying the stirring and frustration of young love.

The Road the Men Came Home manages without childhood scenes and a love triangle. Its broader take is evident not only from the title, but also from the all-embracing dedication 'To the Great Internationale of Men, Women, and Bairns. So to you millions of all lands, you myriad Dead, you of the Present, and you millions Yet To Be'.[5] The explicit mention of women and children puts Hunter in a league with some of his more radical utopian predecessors, such as the English Jacobin of Scottish descent, Thomas Spence, author of *The Rights of Infants* (1796), and the Chartist couple Goodwyn and Catherine Barmby, who developed a socialist feminist platform.[6]

---

4   Several of Welsh's poems were collected in his *Songs of a Miner* (London: Herbert Jenkins, 1917); see H. Gustav Klaus, 'James C. Welsh, Major Miner Novelist', *Scottish Literary Journal*, 13.2 (1986), pp. 67, 84 (note 7). Hunter followed in Welsh's footsteps by bringing out a handful of poems in the pamphlet-size *The Dream of Toil* (Glasgow, 1922) and a later more substantial collection, *When Sleeps the Tide: Pictures – Music – Songs and Poems* (Glasgow, 1943), both self-published. In New Zealand Hunter used the pen name Billy Banjo.

5   Edward Hunter, *The Road the Men Came Home* (London: National Labour Press, 1920).

6   See 'Early Socialist Utopias in England 1792–1848', in H. Gustav Klaus, *The Literature of Labour: Two Hundred Years of Working-Class Writing* (Brighton: Harvester, 1985).

The Road the Men Came Home begins on the eve of the protagonist's departure for New Zealand, where he is almost immediately thrown into the turmoil of industrial conflict, culminating in nothing less than a class war, during which Robin Laidlaw emerges as a leader. The story-line, insofar as there is one in this descriptive novel, closely follows the labour struggles in the years up to World War One. So strong is the documentary basis and political impulse behind the work that the unfolding drama (strikes, lockouts, divisions within the movement, victimisation, evictions, imprisonment, blacklisting, the bitterness of defeat) appears more controlled by the chronology of events than by the author's hand.

Both Robert Sinclair and Robin Laidlaw are embedded in their community and class, yet singular enough in their intelligence, courage, idealism and uprightness to stand out from the other colliers. They are working-class heroes, but neither of them is a lone wolf. Even when elected by their comrades into a leading position, as both Welsh and Hunter were in real life, they never once consider deserting their class. Laidlaw repeatedly fends off attempts by the coal magnates' chief to buy him off: 'I'll die before I leave my ain folk'.[7] Welsh condemns the move out of the working class through the figure of Mysie, Robert's sweetheart, who is seduced by the dream of rising into the cushioned and cultured world of the bourgeoisie – and who will bitterly regret her mistake, dying, in an echo of Dickens's Stephen Blackpool, with the words: 'It was a' a mistak".[8] For Robert (and for Welsh), community means the family, the street, the neighbours, the school, the village, the workplace, and, by extension, union activity and eventually class action. The closely-knit mining community of Lowwood even includes an old-type caring coal master and his son, neither of whom is the villain of the piece. One thing, however, does not enter the picture: the kirk (as opposed to the language of religion) – something which is also true of *The Road the Men Came Home*. The explanation is given in a remarkable chapter of that novel, in which the old folks back in Scotland comment on the news from New Zealand. They are proud of Laidlaw's devotion to the cause, comparing him with the likes of Bob Smillie, Keir Hardie and Ramsay MacDonald, and mentioning Welsh in one breath:

> Robin – him and Jamie Welsh, a pair o' rumstougerous callants. [...] Wha wad hae thocht he'd ding the maisters an' land in jile? Man I'm pleased, gie pleased, to hear o' that this nicht. [...] [A]lthough thae hae left the kirk, the Grace o' God 's i' their he'rts.[9]

---

7 Hunter, *The Road the Men Came Home*, p. 39.
8 Welsh, *The Underworld*, p. 237.
9 Hunter, *The Road the Men Came Home*, pp. 108–09.

We are not told when Robin was politicised. He is twenty-three when *The Road the Men Came Home* opens and knows a good deal about the abject conditions in which his ancestors in the Scottish coalfields were kept until the early-nineteenth century, 'serfdom' being not an inappropriate term for their legal and social status. The experience of recent British unionism, such as the push to federate the separate regions, is also in his baggage when he arrives in his new environment. But the different generic possibilities of *The Underworld* allow Welsh to trace his hero's political awakening, while still a boy, to his having attended visits by Robert Smillie and Keir Hardie to the mining village. In other words, the outside world introduces socialism and class politics, which have a wider dimension, to the community. Again, Robin's first agitation in the Shepherd Creek Mining Camp is over the miserable fifteen minutes 'crib-time', which he compares with the habitual Scottish half-hour 'piece-time'.

Thus the visitor or migrant can impart knowledge and experience not previously available in the self-enclosed community. The itinerant agitator is an important figure both in real history and in fiction at least since the days of Chartism. Interestingly, Welsh conflates the two levels by refusing to disguise Smillie and Hardie, as will practically all the writers discussed in this chapter. But, then, there is flux not only into but also out of the community; for example, migration from economic necessity, as with Robin. Or take Robert, who, as a delegate of his union, regularly goes to Hamilton, and attends conferences in Edinburgh and London (where, in contrast to the above-mentioned working-class leaders, the cabinet members are not identified by name, though Lloyd George is recognisable). Yet Robert remains ill at ease in the wider world and always returns to his native village, and it is there that he will give his life in the attempt to rescue the trapped miners. Neither his trajectory nor that of Robin, who moves around the New Zealand coalfields, passes beyond the confines of the working class. The only socially mobile figure is Mysie, who, bitten by remorse and lacking the face-to-face contact and warmth of the community, is withering away in Edinburgh where she is to be educated in the manners of the middle class. Her fate suggests that a cross-class romantic encounter can only bring disaster for a working girl, even if it is her own ill-judged choice that produced it, and not the result of seduction or rape and abandonment. 'It was a' a mistak" at once personalises and through the grammatical tense singularises her error of judgment; it does not point to a continuing and general social problem as does Dickens's Stephen Blackpool's ''Tis aw a muddle' in *Hard Times*.

The camps in *The Road the Men Came Home* bear little resemblance to the mining villages of Scotland or elsewhere in Britain. These settlements have something rough and ready about them, with the miners shifting about a good deal. Robin also drifts, but his peripatetic life is due to his work for the union or, later, his having been blacklisted. During his wanderings he meets up with a Maori, 'the last of the tribe', whose story reveals the dark side of the incursion of the outside world into a community: "'White man, he come one day – he bring Bibles. Pakeha, he see te land. Te land Maori. Now te Maori got te Bibles. Pakeha got te land'".[10] Although only a vignette, it is a powerful tale of dispossession and expulsion, effective precisely because the narrator abstains from commenting on it. Hunter's partisanship for the indigenous population is remarkable when compared to his more famous near-contemporary and fellow-socialist writer from Australia, Henry Lawson, whose stories are not free from racist assumptions about the Aborigines and imported Chinese labour, in part because, along with important sections of the labour movement, he felt that cheap labour undercut the pay for the white working class. It is likely that Hunter came across some of these stories published in major Australian magazines, but also in collections. Though different in content, a chapter in *The Road the Men Came Home* carries a title very similar to one of Lawson's great stories, 'The Union Buries Its Dead'.[11]

The third mining novel under consideration, Joe Corrie's *Black Earth*, published in book form in 1939, but previously serialised in *Forward* from June to September 1928, is a very different kind of work. It focuses on an ordinary working-class family, appropriately called the Smiths, rather than a gifted young man. What talent one of their sons has goes into playing football rather than rebelliousness, and that talent is used for entirely personal, even egoistic ends. But the perspective often shifts from the Smiths to the gaffer (later manager) of the mine, or, in a moment of strife, to the Red Three, the Communists who run the union, and even beyond the community, in a devastating character sketch, to the national union secretary and member of parliament, 'a wet blanket, a damper of enthusiasm, a constitutional complaint'.[12] While the novel's large cast allows for some differentiation, including sober and drunken miners, decent women and gossips, strikers and blacklegs, the overall picture of the community is one of a deadening environment. The stark naturalism announces itself from the start:

> The boys of Brandon were doomed the day they were born, doomed to do battle with the coal [...] doomed to be caged in the dirty little town, marry and settle down there to rear still more children to step on the cage. [...] Once a miner, always a miner, and those who come after us too.[13]

---

10   Hunter, *The Road the Men Came Home*, p. 120.

11   Henry Lawson, 'The Union Buries Its Dead', in *While the Billy Boils* (Sydney: Angus and Robertson, 1907).

12   Joe Corrie, *Black Earth* (London: Routledge, 1939), p. 93.

13   Corrie, *Black Earth*, pp. 8, 11.

The Smiths had vowed to let their gifted son study rather than send him down the mine, but a mining accident robs them of their breadwinner; the story repeats itself with the daughter. Maggie, the mother, desperately tries to hold the disintegrating family together, but with a bed-ridden husband who has since his accident become an irascible bully and betting addict, she feels 'now in a cage where there could be no escape'.[14] Those who have escaped, or are trying to, are without exception negatively portrayed as careerists or opportunists: not only Jimmy, the footballer, or the national union secretary and MP, but also the gaffer who, pushed on by his ambitious middle-class wife, has risen to the position of manager and eventually the company's mines supervisor. 'Did that make him happier?' a character asks.[15] Locked as he is in a loveless and childless marriage, we know the answer. Even the two boys from the village who managed to go on to university are failures, one becoming a snob, the other dying – in neither case is the sacrifice of the family rewarded. When it comes to social mobility, Corrie takes the same line as Welsh in *The Underworld*.

An interesting facet, and one that bears a resemblance with contemporary working-class writing from Wales,[16] is the solitude and solace that a character seeks away from the community, in nature. Edward Gaitens in *Dance of the Apprentices* (1948) comments on this feature. His main character

> had read in novels of men who went out to commune with Nature when faced with a critical turn in their lives. For long hours they walked by field or river seeking in solitude for guidance and strength. Sometimes such men carried with them a book, their favourite essayist or poet.[17]

In the Welsh works this withdrawal characteristically leads them to a mountain top, from which they at once scan the countryside and try to clarify their thoughts; in the Scottish works the protagonists often seek refuge and consolation in the moor. Like their Welsh counterparts, they temporarily flee from the cramped, squalid and oppressive conditions of their village or slum, but often they also need to calm down after some desperate act and take courage again. Thus we have Maggie Smith in *Black Earth* shuddering at the thought that in

---

14   Corrie, *Black Earth*, p. 243. Ian Haywood rightly emphasises the sympathy with which Maggie is drawn, one of the few figures in the novel to enjoy that status; see his *Working-Class Fiction from Chartism to Trainspotting* (Plymouth: Northcote House, 1997), p. 72.

15   Corrie, *Black Earth*, p. 280.

16   Examples include works by Lewis Jones, *Cwmardy* (1937), Alun Lewis, 'The Mountain over Aberdare' (1942), Gwyn Thomas, *All Things Betray Thee* (1949), and Raymond Williams, *Border Country* (1960).

17   Edward Gaitens, *Dance of the Apprentices* (Edinburgh: Canongate, 1990), p. 127.

utter desperation she had raised a poker at her husband when she had discovered that he had squandered all the money, which in an exemplary act of solidarity had been raised by the colliers on the family's behalf. Or Robert Sinclair of Welsh's *The Underworld*, similarly worked up after his first rebellious act at school: 'The spell of the moor took possession of him, and his wounded soul was soon wrapped in the soft folds of its silence. The balm of its peace comforted him, and brought ease and calmed the rebellion in his blood'.[18] The bitter irony is that Robert is killed by the very moss rising in the shaft from which he tries to rescue the trapped miners, and which has already imprisoned them.

City Novels

In his essay 'Politicians' from *Scottish Scene* Hugh MacDiarmid refers to 'Jimmy Welsh' and Joe Corrie as 'negligible scribblers', and is only slightly more generous to 'my friend Bob Hislop' [*sic*], the English miner writer.[19] In the works of all those novelists, from Welsh to Harold Heslop, the protagonists are born into the working class and consider themselves as part of a community.[20] None of this applies to the principal characters in *Grey Granite* (1934), the novel of MacDiarmid's co-author from *Scottish Scene*, Lewis Grassic Gibbon. On arriving in the fictional industrial town of Duncairn, both Chris, the heroine of the trilogy *A Scots Quair*, of which the novel forms the last part, and her son, Ewan, are outsiders. Chris, the widow of a minister, takes up a partnership in a boarding-house; Ewan, having decided not to continue his further education after the death of his stepfather, enters a steel plant. The one is regarded as 'gentry', the other as a 'toff', a book-reader looked at with suspicion by the other 'keelies' in the factory. In part their distance from the working class has to do with the overall conception of *A Scots Quair*, which symbolically traces Scotland's movement from a peasant nation to an urban and industrial society, so that at the start of each part of the trilogy Chris appears as an incomer to a community.[21] But the urban industrial novelist is also faced

---

18   Welsh, *The Underworld*, p. 40.

19   Lewis Grassic Gibbon and Hugh MacDiarmid, *Scottish Scene, or The Intelligent Man's Guide to Albyn* (London: Hutchinson, 1935), p. 253.

20   For Heslop, see 'Harold Heslop: Miner Novelist', in Klaus, *The Literature of Labour*. Edward Hunter reviewed Heslop's novel *The Gate of a Strange Field* (1929) under the title 'The Underworld' in the *Labour Leader* of 26 April 1929.

21   See *Scottish Literature in English and Scots*, ed. by Douglas Gifford and others (Edinburgh: Edinburgh University Press, 2002), pp. 593–94.

with a more general problem in that the immeasurably larger, more frag-mented and anonymous a society is, the greater the difficulty of adequately representing all shades and layers of a community within it, or deciding on which of these to focus.

We first glimpse a section of the working class through Chris's eyes. She has taken a tram into town for some shopping and is suddenly confronted with the unemployed, and as in the days when she supported the miners during the General Strike (in *Cloud Howe*, the second volume of the trilogy), she cannot help feeling sympathetic to them: 'aye plenty of them, yawning and wearied, with their flat-soled boots and their half-shaved faces', they might 'chirp a bit filth to a passing quean', but 'you didn't much mind, were you wearied yourself and half-fed, you thought, with nothing to do, you'd do worse than chirp'.[22] But when accosted one evening by a lumpenproletarian in a dark alley, she is natu-rally afraid, her sympathy later turning to anger when she realises that a slug-gard has wheedled money from her. In the altercation she becomes uncertain of her own social status. To the beggar's remark, *'enjoy your money while you have it. There's a time coming when your class won't have it long'*, she proudly retorts: *'My class? It was digging its living in sweat while yours lay down with a whine in the dirt'.*[23]

Ewan's story is by and large one of a gradual and hesitant integration into the working class, which entails an abandonment of his staunchly indepen-dent, almost insular stance. Only after having been provoked into a brawl and having proved his masculinity in the process is he accepted by his fellow apprentices, though he himself remains cool and detached as before, aggres-sively asserting his individuality and self-centredness: 'I'm myself'.[24] It takes some political arguing by his girlfriend-to-be Ellen and his accidentally being drawn, from a sense of justice, into a pitched battle between unemployed marchers and the police to finally side with a community, that of the jobless. Hand-to-hand fighting appears as an initiation rite into Ewan's manhood and socialism, and by implication into the working-class community. Even so he continues to be nagged by doubt about his attitude to them: 'They DON'T con-cern you. BREAK with it all'.[25] Yet the dividing line between the unemployed and the keelies is porous precisely because the apprentices risk being sacked at the end of their term. Anyone can lose his job, whether for the sake of greater profit or as a result of victimisation, as Ewan and other Reds find out.

---

22   Lewis Grassic Gibbon, *Grey Granite* (London: Pan, 1973), p. 19.
23   Gibbon, *Grey Granite*, p. 32. Italics in original.
24   Gibbon, *Grey Granite*, pp. 26, 48.
25   Gibbon, *Grey Granite*, p. 76. Emphasis in original.

The many violent scenes in the novel, present in a good deal of socialist fiction of the 1930s, serve not only to highlight the indignation of the poor and the bitterness of the class struggle, but also motivate the steeling of Ewan's character, underlined by the ever harder minerals (Epidote, Sphene, Apatite and Zircon) that head the four sections of the book. When Ewan is arrested on suspicion of having flung pepper into the faces of bludgeoning police and having had a hand in the drowning of a strike-breaker, he is beaten up in his cell, not into confession or submission, but into a tough and indestructible disposition: that of a Communist. With this development he enters into yet another community, the Internationale, as it were, of the 'tortured and tormented'. Gibbon specifically mentions the victims of Nazi terror, the 'torment-pits' of Polish Ukraine, the fate of the Nanking Communists and the castration of blacks in US prisons, and then in a grand historical sweep connects these examples with the slave revolt under Spartacus and more generally the common folks' 'enslavement and oppression of six thousand years'.[26] Neither Ewan nor Gibbon, though they are by no means one and the same, harbours any illusion about the ruling class's readiness to resort, in the last instance, to terror to uphold its power, nor, come to that, about the Communist Party's ruthlessness regarding the means to overthrow them; it was 'the fight of class against class, till they dragged down the masters and ground them to pulp', reflects Ewan after his release from prison.[27] Setting the local struggle in an international and historical context reveals a Marxist consciousness. It is thus only logical that the novel ends with Ewan leading a hunger march to London, from the periphery to the heart of capitalism and to the larger concerns of world history, whereas Chris returns to her roots on the land.

Gibbon broadens his vision of an urban working-class community in the grip of the Depression by employing a narrator who can have one or several voices.[28] An early example is the view of a tenement where an unnamed husband and wife and their daughter ponder over their hopeless and meaningless lives in a claustrophobic and squalid environment, in stark contrast to the genteel guesthouse where Chris and Ewan live.

> And a man would get up in a Paldy tenement and go along the passage to the WC, blasted thing crowded, served a score of folk, not decent, by

26   Gibbon, *Grey Granite*, p. 149.
27   Gibbon, *Grey Granite*, p. 158.
28   See William K. Malcolm, *A Blasphemer & Reformer: A Study of James Leslie Mitchell/Lewis Grassic Gibbon* (Aberdeen: Aberdeen University Press, 1984), p. 154.

God what a country to live in. On the Broo since the War and five kids to keep, eating off your head – och, why did you live? [...]

And the wife would turn as she heard him come back, lie wakeful and think on the morn's morning – what to give the weans, what to give the man, fed he must be ere he took the streets to look for that weary job he'd not find [...]. Hardly believe it was him you had wed, that had been a gey bit spark in his time, hearty and bonny, liked you well; and had hit you last night, the bloody brute coming drunk from the pub – a woman couldn't go and hide in booze, forget all the soss and pleither, oh no, she'd to go on till she dropped [...].

And the quean would turn by the side of her sisters, see the faint glow of the dawn, smell the reek of the Paldy heat – would she never get out of it, get a job, get away, have clothes, some fun? If they couldn't afford to bring up their weans decent why did father and mother have them?[29]

There is heartfelt compassion in this cameo, but not an iota of sentimentalism. Nor are the agents of change, the Communists, idealised, as the branch treasurer's absconding with the Party funds or Ewan's callous treatment of Ellen, who is under threat of being sacked as a teacher due to her political beliefs, demonstrate.

If *Grey Granite* is, among other things, a document of the disastrous 'class against class' policy pursued by the Communist International between 1928 and 1934, which helped to split the labour movement and thereby facilitated the rise to power of the Nazis, James Barke's *Major Operation* (1936) is a representation of the new Popular Front policy implemented in 1934–35, as a consequence of the failure of the previous line. The Popular Front aimed not only to unite the various working-class organisations but also to build alliances with the progressive and liberal sections of the middle class, all with a view to stem the rising tide of Fascism. In alternating chapters Barke's novel contrasts the lives of a group of bored and conceited bourgeois people around the coal merchant George Anderson with the family, relatives and comrades of the shipyard worker Jock MacKelvie, whose paths coincidentally cross in a hospital ward. 'Two Worlds' apart (thus the subtitle of Section 1 of the novel), both are nonetheless in due time hit by the Depression, which in Barke's scheme opens the way to a 'Unity of Opposites' (the subtitle of Section 3) – a union eventually achieved not between equals, but effectively by winning a weakened Anderson over to the working-class cause, which is either a flaw in the plot construction or unintentionally betrays the bad faith of the Communists.

---

29   Gibbon, *Grey Granite*, p. 21.

Gibbon's portraiture of the forces opposed to the working class, from the minister of the kirk to the Tory press to the bailie, borders on caricature, enlivened only by sardonic humour, but Barke's middle class, with the exception of Anderson, a decent man, is a set of stereotypes, starting with the notion that in this milieu it is everyone for themselves. Once Anderson is bankrupt and in hospital with a duodenal ulcer, he is deserted by friends, business colleagues and wife alike. He receives not a single visitor, letter or phone call, whereas with MacKelvie 'there had been complaints about the number of people who came to see' him.[30]

Big Jock, a product of the Partick slums, is one of those titanic proletarians populating the socialist fiction of the 1930s. An inexhaustible source of energy, he leads the toughest gang in the shipyard, the red-leaders, at the beginning of the narrative (c.1927) and, unperturbed by years on the dole, organises the all-Scottish hunger march seven years later. A steely militant like Ewan or, more to the point, the Communist Jim Trease in *Grey Granite*, he serves time in prison. At the same time, he is also a working-class intellectual, citing Kant, Hegel, James Jeans and Eddington in his lengthy discussions with Anderson, winning the argument and converting him to socialism. But the author never dramatises MacKelvie's family life, tenement, close or street, as Gibbon had done in the vignette quoted above and Edward Gaitens was to do in more elaborate ways in *Dance of the Apprentices*. Instead we get mainly naturalistic descriptions of slum life:

> The subway entrance breathed out its stale decayed air. Immediately beyond, where they turned into Walker Street, a warm, odoriferous waft of slumdom met them. It was not a smell that could be escaped. There were identifiable odours of cats' urine: decayed rubbish: infectious diseases: unwashed underclothing, intermingled with smells suggesting dry rot: insanitary lavatories, overtaxed sewage pipes and the excrement of a billion bed-bugs.[31]

No doubt in an attempt to counter the gang warfare image of Glasgow as delivered by Long and McArthur's *No Mean City* (1935), Barke keeps the 'razor slashers, wife beaters, incestmongers, adulterers, drunkards, blackmailers, [and] gangsters' offstage, but in so doing he goes to the other extreme.[32] His workingmen are practically without blemish, and the most morally upright of them all

---

30 James Barke, *Major Operation* (London: Collins, 1936), p. 311.
31 Barke, *Major Operation*, p. 72.
32 Barke, *Major Operation*, p. 41.

is MacKelvie himself, a man without weaknesses, with a cast-iron conviction, at one with whatever particular segment of the working class he finds himself in, whether his shipyard mates, the slum-dwellers, the unemployed or the patients. MacKelvie is an indomitable fighter compared by Anderson to the likes of the Communist leaders Thälmann and Dimitrov and, in one of several echoes from *Grey Granite*, with the Scottish Covenanters and the victims in the 'torture dens' of Nazi Germany. Yet despite the heroic stature there is something static and bloodless about this figure. It is not even clear how MacKelvie evolved from a red-leader, disappointed about the outcome of the General Strike, with no serious interest left in politics, to a Red leader.

In view of the fact that Barke criticised Gibbon's handling of his working-class characters it is curious that he should end up with such pitfalls.[33] Jack Mitchell has a point when, with Barke in mind, he argues that some writers '*romanticised* the workers and then embraced their own romantic creation'.

> Their attitude had more of moral idealism than historical materialism. The proletariat is seen not so much as a historically developing class but rather as an absolute and therefore de-historicised *moral category* whose superiority over the bourgeoisie lies in its moral excellence.[34]

This idealisation extends to the females. Compared to the spoiled and conceited figure of Anderson's wife, 'a social parasite [whose] only aim in life had been to achieve mating with another social parasite: a gentleman', MacKelvie's wife, Anderson's secretary and several sisters in the ward are model women, all tirelessly devoted to their work, endowed with an open-minded and healthy sexuality and remarkably self-assured in their conduct with men.[35] Anderson is the far more interesting, tragic figure, a man who loses everything: his business, his social standing, his wife and daughter, his physical health, his sexual potency, the faith in his middle-class values, the ability to earn a livelihood, his self-respect and finally his life – not by putting an end to it as he had contemplated doing, but as a victim of police brutality during a hunger march, so that in the concluding graveside oration MacKelvie can praise him as 'one of the best types produced by the bourgeoisie', who had displayed exemplary loyalty and courage 'at the most dangerous and difficult moment of our mighty

---

33   James Barke, 'Lewis Grassic Gibbon', *Left Review*, 2.5 (1936), 220–25.
34   Jack Mitchell, 'The Struggle for the Working-Class Novel in Scotland 1900–1939', *Zeitschrift für Anglistik und Amerikanistik*, 21.4 (1973), p. 410. Italics in original.
35   Barke, *Major Operation*, p. 216.

demonstration'.[36] Having dropped out of his own class, Anderson had, despite lodging with the MacKelvies after his discharge from hospital, never fully integrated into the working-class community but remained stranded in a no man's land between the classes.

As a figure allowed to have his doubts, worries and anguish, Anderson offered himself to the experimental style Barke occasionally resorts to, imitated from James Joyce, with due credit given ('good lad Joyce'), but paddling his 'own canoe in the stream of consciousness'.[37] Here we have Anderson, still looking at the world through his middle-class blinkers, though already sensing the impact of the economic crisis, held up by a demonstration of the 'Second City's waste human labour':

> Hadn't seen anything about that in the papers. Unemployed becoming a menace. Silly of them demonstrating during business hours. Dislocating traffic. Silly at any time, come to that. Break into a riot, loot shops. Give police lot of bother. Addition to rates. High enough already. Too high. Hadn't they got the dole? Want jam on it. [...]
>
> Damned shame to bring women and children. Better at home cooking their husbands' dinner. Nothing to cook maybe. Still they could wash and mend clothes. No right to have children in any case. Bringing children into squalid poverty. Always the way: poor breed like rats. Reason for being poor. Cheapest of all pleasures – cheapest initial cost. Yours to-day: nothing to pay. Compound interest in the long run. Not very long either – nine months. [...]
>
> South Partick Unemployed Workers' Flute Band. [...] What about *The Red Flag* – dismal thing: no good to march to. What was it Bernard Shaw called it...funeral march of a fried eel? Witty old buffer Shaw – socialist at that. No flies on him though. Knows what side of his bread is buttered.[38]

As a budding writer Barke had been briefly in touch with Bernard Shaw.[39] Now, with four novels in quick succession to his credit, he found himself approached

---

36   Barke, *Major Operation*, pp. 491, 493.

37   Barke, *Major Operation*, pp. 124, 123.

38   Barke, *Major Operation*, pp. 128–29.

39   Barke had sent Shaw a copy of his first novel *The World His Pillow* (London: Collins, 1933) and received a photo of the author with an autograph in response. The autobiographical Duncan in the novel thinks: 'Innumerable young men had been attacked with the Shaw fever' (p. 247). See H. Gustav Klaus, 'James Barke: A Great-Hearted Writer, a Hater of Oppression, a True Scot', in *A Weapon in the Struggle: The Cultural History of the Communist Party in Britain*, ed. by Andy Croft (London: Pluto Press, 1998).

by an aspiring writer, Edward Gaitens, actually his senior by eight years, seeking advice in early 1938 about the publication of a manuscript entitled *Dance of the Apprentices*. In one letter Gaitens added a list of the publishers who by that time had already rejected the book, all operating from London, where Gaitens lived at the time: 'Down here they jib at the dialogue and unfamiliar atmosphere'.[40] It was left to the small Glasgow firm of McLellan to remedy the situation. In 1942 several chapters were extracted from the novel and appeared as part of a collection of short stories, *Growing Up*. The publication of the novel six years later confused readers, and continues to mislead critics because of the reappearance of much of the material from the earlier book.[41] However, Barke's detailed criticisms of the manuscript in a letter of 3 February 1938 leave no doubt that the novel came first and was practically in the finished form in which it was published ten years later. In all likelihood the breaking up of the material for the purposes of a short story collection was an expedient, possibly suggested by another reader.

Book 1 of *Dance of the Apprentices* is set in the Gorbals district of Glasgow before World War One and in part confirms the notoriety of the place. We witness scenes of insanitary conditions, debauchery and domestic violence that Barke had spared us. But Gaitens sticks firmly to his chosen social spectrum, the Macdonnel family and their neighbours from the tenement and close. Sensationalism has no place in his work. Characters constantly repair to the corner pub once they have secured the necessary change, but we are rarely inside one. Nor does gang warfare and street violence play a role. Even the illegal prize fight involving a gifted pugilist from the tenement is shown only in terms of its outcome. The tableau of *misérabilisme* is relieved not only by moments of raucous humour, reminiscent of scenes in a Sean O'Casey play, but, more importantly, by glimpses of the slumbering potential in the family and beyond. Three of the seven Macdonnels are book-readers. Eddy, a plasterer's apprentice in the shipyard, and his two friends, the other apprentices of the title, are filled with higher aspirations. Self-taught, except for attending a study circle, they quote from and discuss Emerson, Marx, Nietzsche, Shaw, and Jack London, and write essays on Milton, Free Will and Determinism, and Individualism. Nor is this an exclusively male prerogative. On a visit to his friend Neil, Eddy is intimidated by the fact that in this household the six sisters 'were all studious, all prize-winners at school and disconcertingly

---

40   The correspondence is in the James Barke papers held by The Mitchell Library, Glasgow.

41   James Campbell, 'Introduction', Edward Gaitens, *Dance of the Apprentices* (Edinburgh: Canongate, 1990), p. vi. See also Moira Burgess and Hamish Whyte's entry in the *Oxford Dictionary of National Biography*, vol. 25, pp. 285–86.

intelligent', two of them sitting reading, two younger ones occupied with copy-books and school-primers.[42] The very opening of the novel sets the tone, as we find the eighteen-year-old Eddy reading Robert Herrick's poem 'To Daffodils' in *The Golden Treasury*. The trio's longing for beauty, knowledge and truth is serious, if not free from conceit and self-importance. Sincere socialists all three of them, they represent different shades of the creed, from constitutionalism to revolutionary socialism to anarchism. They attend mass meetings of Tom Mann and go to John Maclean's Sunday class. All three, having the courage of their convictions, end up as conscientious objectors.

Book II traces the fortunes of the trio and three of Eddy's brothers, apprentices by extension, after the war up to the mid-1930s – the likely date of composition of the novel. But there are two exceptions to the chronology: one concerns news of the death in action of Eddy's elder brother, which breaks into a hilarious lottery for housewives organised in the Macdonnel kitchen, making the arrival of the letter all the more dramatic; the other is Eddy's case, where the author shies away from facing his alter ego's path and concentrates instead on his harrowing experiences as a conscientious objector in Wormwood Scrubs prison. Both episodes are set in 1918, framing the narrative in Book II – an infraction of the chronological sequence that had exasperated Barke. But the point Gaitens wants to make is abundantly clear, if not necessarily convincing. These apprentices in social idealism have all been failures in one sense or another. Jim, the older brother, giving in to the taunts directed at a stay-at-home, volunteered against his better instinct and paid the price; John settles in an unhappy petty-bourgeois marriage; Francie, the other radical thinker in the family, goes mad. Of Eddy's friends, Donald, suffering from depression, attempts suicide for the second time, having previously 'dropped all serious reading', 'his former certainties, his cocksure atheism and materialism [...] now empty fallacies'; Neil, author of the eulogy on Individualism, blacklisted among Glasgow's book-keeping firms following his time in prison as a conscientious objector, is tricked into a dead-end marriage; Eddy goes through the hell of solitary confinement, after having vainly tried to incite his fellow-prisoners to open rebellion.[43] So disillusioned is he and so gloomy his outlook at the end that he even questions the validity of his and the other conscientious objectors' sacrifice: 'All the arguments in the multitudes of books, the historic, organised attacks upon Capitalism had not prevented this war. Sentimental appeals to the spirit of world-brotherhood were futile'.[44]

---

42   Gaitens, *Dance of the Apprentices*, p. 89.

43   Gaitens, *Dance of the Apprentices*, pp. 197, 196.

44   Gaitens, *Dance of the Apprentices*, p. 252.

Gaitens's own traumatising experiences as an 'Absolutist', refusing to labour in a Government Work Centre, have left their mark on the second half of *Dance of the Apprentices*. But the bitterness and rancour, resulting from the infamous treatment of war resisters, not only during their time in Work Centres or prisons, but continuing well into the postwar years, is not allowed to sour the slice of life of the Gorbals community, which remains the triumph of the novel. It is a world of pawn and betting tickets, of borrowing and scrounging, of quarrels and family fights complete with screams and blows, of 'bad language' and self-pitying sentimentality, but also of generosity when money is there, as when the sailor-son returns from a voyage, of warmth and humour, of familial and social cohesion. Amid the overcrowded tenement blocks with their universal squalor, stark poverty, pitiful waste and human weakness, Gaitens detects and brings to life a rich variety of characters, figures that may appear only once or twice such as the boxer, or Blind Mary, 'the wonder of the Gorbals', who 'drank hard and regularly and stood it better than the toughest men'.[45] At times the author seems to despair, as when the Macdonnel father or mother take the pledge and their resolve does not survive a week or even day. But, contrary to the doubts cast over the apprentices' high-flown social and political idealism, cynicism towards his creations never gains the author's upper hand.

'Community is frequently viewed as a central theme in Scottish literature', notes Timothy C. Baker.[46] In the light of the comparative perspective applied at the beginning of this chapter such a preoccupation appears indeed as something distinctly Scottish (and, perhaps, also Welsh). Community in the sense of *Gemeinschaft* is, if not unthinkable, extremely unlikely to be used as an angle from which to approach the study of contemporary German literature. As observed before, the concept owes its fascination in part to its oscillation, or tension, between the poles of *Gemeinschaft* ('community') and *Gesellschaft* ('society'). But the ongoing debate about the Scottish nation's uncertain political status has undoubtedly added to its continued relevance. Where there is no state to shape the destiny of a nation, other factors such as religion, education, language, law, culture and, indeed, community, can act as bonds that unify and give identity to a society.

A community is always grounded in a historical moment and a particular place. This is as true of real-life communities as of fictional ones, but in the latter case it is the writer's moment in history and place in society that matters. *Grey Granite* apart, the novels discussed here come from hands that were, around World War One, labouring in mines and shipyards. These experiences

---

45   Gaitens, *Dance of the Apprentices*, p. 33.
46   Baker, *George Mackay Brown and the Philosophy of Community*, p. 5.

have gone into the works; Williams's 'knowable community' is in large measure that of a particular segment of the working class. The mining novels, for example, show the connections between the location of an industry, the special work experience (including the loss of work through conflict or accident), and a particular place, the mining village, founded after the sinking of a mine and constituted as much by the natural and built environment as by the people inhabiting it. To that extent the communities in these novels conform to the first of Baker's four meanings of the term, being set in a 'local, geographically constituted region'. At the same time, their heavy working-class imprint delimits them socially. Only in Welsh's *The Underworld* does the community include the other side, the mine-owner. What we see of those of higher social class in the other novels excludes them from the community. This is even more evident in the city novels, where the slum community is, as Barke had it, a 'world' apart, cordoned off from, say, the West End.

These working-class communities also provide 'the context for interpersonal relations and the emergence of the individual self', Baker's fourth definition. Family, community, and books nurture the individual. The community is a *Heimat*, but one whose shaping pressures (family obligations, work, conforming to social expectations) can become constraints that may stifle or harm the self and its mission. As these novels demonstrate, just as the outside world intrudes into the community through boom and slump, national labour struggles and international conflicts such as war, so the protagonist as social idealist must needs transgress the local community's boundaries and move into the society at large; for his affiliation is to the 'Cause', which, though in the interest of his community, must be fought for in the wider world. The references to the 'Great Internationale of Men, Women, and Bairns' in Hunter, and to revolutionary leaders and struggles in Gibbon, Barke and Gaitens acknowledge this resolution, whatever the consequences of the rebel's action.

CHAPTER 3

Speaking for Oneself and Others: Real and Imagined Communities in Gaelic Poetry from the Nineteenth Century to the Present

Emma Dymock

Abstract

A sense of community pervades much of Scottish Gaelic literature through the centuries in both the classical bardic tradition of panegyric as a mode of praise for both clan and individual hero, and the vernacular tradition of song, which celebrates the everyday life of the community and often includes a community-based dimension to its composition. This chapter examines how that legacy of Gaelic community in poetry survives and continues into the later nineteenth century to the present day and will argue that far from keeping Gaelic poetry in stasis, it has actually been one of the most significant vehicles of innovation, stimulating Gaelic poets in confronting and understanding their self-imposed role as spokespersons for both real and imagined communities. Historical themes such as the Highland Clearances, the Land Agitation and Land Reforms, emigration and the World Wars will be studied in relation to perceptions of community, as well as the effect of literary and socio-political circumstances, including the rural–urban experience, the influence of Gaelic learners on the literature, and the concept of 'native' authenticity.

Keywords

Gaelic poetry – Highland Clearances – Land Agitation – World War One – World War Two – urban Gaels – crofting community

If the clan was the main marker of group identity for the Gaels, from the time of the Lordship of the Isles (arguably from the 1330s to 1493) to the Jacobite Risings (the period 1688–1746), then it was community, particularly the crofting community, which reinforced and, in some cases, replaced, clan society in the nineteenth century onwards. Taking into account traumatic events such as the Battle of Culloden in 1746 and its aftermath – the breakdown in the traditional relationship between chief and clan as chiefs became increasingly more akin to landowners – and the Highland Clearances, John MacInnes concludes that 'the poets of the nineteenth century inherited a broken world'.[1] Poetry is the genre of literature with the oldest pedigree in the Gaelic world; the poets of this literary tradition were the spokespersons for their society, with the official bards of the clans charting the history and genealogy of their people. Despite circumstances in the eighteenth century severely undermining this order, the role of the poet was still respected by the people. Poetry had previously been integral to clan life and it continued to pervade all aspects of Gaelic community; if the formation and cultivation of 'community' was a way for the Gaels to make sense of their changing world, then poetry was one of the means which united this community. The ceilidh-house was the centre of the community, a way for individuals to share stories, songs, cultural traditions and current news. Poetry was often practised in a community setting; the waulking song is a good example of the way in which a community can not only shape its literature, but uphold and preserve it by its habitual usage.[2]

Alexander Carmichael's publication in 1900 of the first two volumes of his *Carmina Gadelica*, with its prayers, hymns, charms, blessings, poems and songs gathered in communities of the Highlands and Islands from 1860, firmly established the notion that Gaelic culture was a treasure to be preserved, even if its own communities were sometimes affording it less respect than it deserved.[3] Significantly, the genesis of the *Carmina Gadelica* was more connected to the political aspect of community life than may be imagined and can be traced back to 'Grazing and Agrestic Customs of the Outer Hebrides', the second appendix Alexander Carmichael contributed to the *Report* of the Napier Commission in 1884,[4] in which Carmichael attempts to represent the crofters as part of an ancient and noble culture, lending them an air of respectability in the process. The information that Carmichael had collected for this study

---

1   John MacInnes, 'Gaelic Poetry in the Nineteenth Century', in *Dùthchas Nan Gàidheal: Selected Essays of John MacInnes*, ed. by Michael Newton (Edinburgh: Birlinn, 2006), pp. 357–79 (p. 357).

2   A folksong with a verse and chorus, usually sung in Gaelic by a group of women, while waulking (cleansing) cloth. The song helped the women to maintain rhythm as the newly woven tweed was beaten against the table.

3   See, for example, Alexander Carmichael's introduction to *Carmina Gadelica*, vol. 1 (1900), pp. xxxv–xxxvi, in which a woman from Lewis explains how her community has turned its back on its oral tradition and customs in favour of Evangelical Protestantism.

4   The Napier Commission was the Royal Commission and public inquiry into the condition of crofters and cottars in the Highlands and Islands. The Commission was a response to the events of the Land Agitation or Land War, when crofters finally rebelled against excessively high rents, lack of security of tenure and rights of access to land.

convinced him to pursue the subject in more detail.[5] More politically motivated still had been much of the poetry of the Skye poet, Mary MacPherson
(Màiri Mhòr nan Òran) (1821–98), who had supported the actions of the
crofters during the Land War.

Any sense of cohesion and celebration of Gaelic community life that survived
after the wound inflicted by the Highland Clearances turned out to be short lived –
Ronald Black described the 'Parnassian spring' of the *Carmina Gadelica* as 'an
idyll smashed by the realism of the First World War'.[6] With a whole generation of
Gaelic speakers being acutely depleted in World War One, there were severe
repercussions on community life and the transmission of the Gaelic language to
the next generation of speakers. As the twentieth century progressed, Gaelic
poets continued to find ways to express their feelings regarding community, even
if that community was becoming more imagined than physically existent for a
number of writers. The (self)-perceived role of the poet was still a reality, even
when poetry became more reliant on written forms and publication, appearing to
usurp the poetry that was orally transmitted and shared by local communities.

It is this role of the poet, both self and publicly bestowed, coupled with the
concept of community in its myriad forms which will form the basis of this
chapter. If Gaelic scholars are ever to develop a literary theory which will be
both suitable and innovative enough to adapt to the specific and unique characteristics of Gaelic literature and facilitate in the understanding of their
meanings, the idea of community with all its nuances will have to be considered as an integral part of this theory. This chapter will provide a reading of
some of the ways that Gaelic poetry from the late-nineteenth century to the
present has embraced and rejected community, dealt with the loss and fracture of community and continued to create, reassemble and reimagine community. This will be a thematic study because poets from different periods
have had similar experiences in their envisioning of community, irrespective
of social, educational and cultural contexts.

Concepts of Homeland and Issues of Social Change

While it would be tempting to make the assumption that all nineteenth-
century poetry in Gaelic was awash with nostalgia and sentimentalism for a

---

5 Alexander Carmichael, 'Grazing and Agrestic Customs of the Outer Hebrides', *Report of Her
   Majesty's Commissioners of Inquiry into the Conditions of the Crofters and Cottars in the
   Highlands and Islands of Scotland* (Edinburgh, 1884), pp. 451–82.
6 *An Tuil: Anthology of Twentieth-Century Scottish Gaelic Verse*, ed. by Ronald Black (Edinburgh:
   Polygon, 1999), p. xxi.

lost 'golden age' of Gaelic culture, poets such as Mary MacPherson, William Livingston (1808–70) and Neil MacLeod (1843–1913) were not necessarily responding to social change in their communities in exactly the same way. It is really Neil MacLeod who best fits the description of nostalgic poet in his dedication of his native Skye in 'An Gleann san robh mi Òg' ('The Glen where I was Young'), in which he appears resigned to the loss of a 'golden age' of Gaeldom and recalls past days in particularly sentimental style:

> Ann an dùbhlachd gharbh a' gheamhraidh
> Cha b' e àm bu ghainn' ar spòrs;
> Greis air sùgradh, greis air dannsa,
> Greis air canntaireachd is ceòl;

> (In the wildest depths of winter,/there would be no limit to our fun;/times at jesting, times at dancing,/times at pipe music and tunes).[7]

Donald Meek has pointed out that 'such reflection neutralises the ability to condemn purposefully or react constructively'.[8] As a contrast to this attitude, in MacPherson's 'Nuair bha mi òg' ('When I was young'), stanzas which at first appear nostalgic for forgotten community events – 'A' falbh sa gheamhradh gu luaidh is bainnsean' ('going off in winter to waulks and weddings') – also hint at hopes for a future community – ''S nam faicinn sluagh agus taighean suas annt',/Gum fàsainn suaimhneach mar bha mi òg' ('if I could see them peopled, and houses built there,/I would become joyful, as I was when young').[9] Livingston's 'Fios chun a' Bhàird' ('A Message for the Poet') successfully shows the figure of the poet to be at the centre of the protest against the social and cultural change which came about when the chiefs took on the role of landowner (with more emphasis on economic advance at the expense of their tenants) and, by describing his native Islay as being transformed into a beautiful yet vacant landscape, he laments the community which made its mark on that landscape through its agricultural work.

> Tha taighean seilbh na dh'fhàg sinn
> Feadh an fhuinn nan càrnan fuar;
> Dh'fhalbh 's cha till na Gàidheil;

---

7   *Caran an t-Saoghal: Anthology of Nineteenth-Century Scottish Gaelic Verse*, ed. by Donald Meek (Edinburgh: Birlinn, 2003), pp. 56–57. Gaelic translations as in original publications.

8   *Caran an t-Saoghal*, p. 33.

9   *Caran an t-Saoghal*, pp. 20–23.

Stad an t-àiteach, cur is buain;
[…]
'Mar a fhuair 's a chunnaic mise,
Leig am fios seo chun a' Bhàird'.

(The houses once owned by those departed/lie throughout the land in frigid heaps;/the Gaels have gone, never to return;/ploughing, sowing and reaping have ceased;/[…]/'Just as I found and as I saw,/let this message reach the Poet'.)[10]

Donald Meek writes that the verb *caochail* ('change, die') has been employed by these poets as a means of describing the change in the complexion of these communities: 'The characteristics of *caochladh* included the arrival of sheep, the loss of the native population, the disappearance of traditional customs, and an accompanying coldness as the community decayed or collapsed, sometimes dramatically'.[11] While twentieth-century Gaelic poets addressed these same issues of change and death, they did so in more symbolic terms and, perhaps due to the benefit of the passage of time, the characteristics of *caochladh* were not irreversible, despite the desperateness of the situation. Derick Thomson's (1921–2012) 'An Tobar' ('The Well') is a good example of a meditation on the fate of his native community in the Isle of Lewis: an old woman asks a young boy to fetch her water from a nearly forgotten spring, with the old woman and the well representing a community near the end of its life. Significantly, to take Meek's allusion to 'a change in the complexion of a community' a stage further, the old woman's complexion is colourless, and it is hoped that the water will bring colour to her cheeks. By extension, the well, with all its connotations as a source of sustenance and renewal for a community, must be nurtured if it is not to become dried up. Thomson's message is perhaps bleak, but it is not necessarily a dead end for the culture or for community life. He writes, 'Dh' fhaodadh nach eil anns an tobar/ ach nì a chunnaic mi 'm bruadar' ('It may be that the well/is something I saw in a dream').[12] Thomson views his community as being in a sleeping-state, brought on after the depression of the nineteenth century. In this case, the poet's role is therefore to awaken the community to its responsibility of retaining and re-energising its culture and language in the face of past injustice and hardship.

---

10 *Caran an t-Saoghal*, pp. 42–49.
11 *Caran an t-Saoghal*, p. 33.
12 Derick Thomson, *Creachadh na Clàrsaich/Plundering the Harp: Cruinneachadh de Bhardachd/Collected Poems 1940–1980* (Edinburgh: MacDonald Publishers, 1982), pp. 48–49.

The Effect of War on Perceptions of Community

World War One made a huge impact on the Gaelic communities, leaving in its wake a sense of desolation and a loss of innocence, and Gaelic poets were not slow to catalogue their responses. While conflict has always garnered reactions in Gaelic literature, World War One, with the horrors of trench warfare, was a very different experience. Dòmhnall Ruadh Chorùna (1887–1967), the North Uist-born poet who is regarded as the Gaelic Voice of the Trenches, is perhaps best-known for his poem 'An Eala Bhàn', which is a love poem or *cianalas* for his homeland and for his lover back in Uist. Undoubtedly, this sort of poem or song would be understood and appreciated by the people who shared that homeland with him. Many of the poet's songs and poems could be viewed as a means of describing his war experiences to those back home in his community, for instance, 'Air an Somme' ('On the Somme') and 'Òran a' Phuinnsein' ('Song of the Poison'), but it is also significant that Dòmhnall Ruadh Chorùna shows an aware-ness of a very different 'community' during a time of war, with his regiment, many of whom were Gaelic speakers, fulfilling the same purpose as his home community. In 'Tha mi duilich, cianail, duilich' ('I am sorry, anguished, sorry') his fellow soldiers are described as 'brothers' and their battlefield traditions mirror the traditions of the ceilidh-house: 'Le'm bu mhiann a bhith 'nam chòmhradh/ Cur mun cuairt nan òran Gàidhlig' ('Who loved to converse with me/And take turns at Gaelic songs').[13] However, the sense of community felt by Gaelic poets during World War One had subtly altered by World War Two, going beyond the themes of traditional solidarity within their own societies. While Sorley MacLean (1911–96) was still very much aware of his sense of Gaelic and clan identity – 'tha mi de dh'fhir mhòr a' Bhràighe' ('I am of the big men of Braes') – his socialist and communist influences ensured that the community he most valued was the international community of the common people.[14] Likewise, George Campbell Hay (1915–84) goes to great lengths to show the damage inflicted on other com-munities across the world during wartime. In 'Bisearta' ('Bizerta') the North African people are unknown to him, but the destruction of streets and houses echoes the suffering of the families and communities inside:

C'ainm a-nochd a th' orra,
Na sràidean bochda anns an sgeith gach uinneag

---

13   *Songs of Gaelic Scotland*, ed. by Anne Lorne Gillies (Edinburgh: Birlinn, 2005), pp. 134–39.

14   Sorley MacLean, 'Dol an Iar' ('Going Westwards'), in *Caoir Gheal Leumraich/White Leaping Flame. Sorley MacLean: Collected Poems*, ed. by Christopher Whyte and Emma Dymock (Edinburgh: Polygon, 2011), pp. 198–201.

A lasraichean 's a deatach,
A sradagan is sgreadail a luchd thuinidh

(What is their name tonight,/The poor streets where every window
spews/Its flame and smoke,/Its sparks and screaming of its inmates)[15]

Here there is a sympathy and sense of shared experience with other cultures,
which is often present in Hay's poetry and is nowhere better expressed than in
his long and unfinished poem 'Mochtar is Dùghall', which synthesises Arab
and Gaelic culture in the descriptions of two people, showing how individuals
can carry the cultural heritage of a whole people within themselves. In this
context, Ronald Black has rightly described 'the untimely death of an individual in war' as 'a cultural act'.[16] Hay's war poetry advances the descriptions of
the horrors experienced by the Gaelic poets of World War One by internation-
alising the loss of culture and community that war brings in its wake, and
ensures that the theme of community in twentieth-century Gaelic poetry is
not centred solely on local issues.

Fractured Community: Loss and Resilience

Sorley MacLean's 'Hallaig' stands alone in a literary landscape of poems
inspired by the Highland Clearances; there has certainly never been anything
like it written in Gaelic about the effects of the Clearances before or since
MacLean's poem was first published. 'Hallaig' began its published life as a
poem centred on Gaelic identity, even if now its reputation has grown far
beyond this community to other cultures and individuals who feel a kinship
and emotional connection to the themes in the poem. Hallaig is a township
north of Beinn na Lice on Raasay, MacLean's birthplace. It was cleared after
1846 by George Rainy, who had purchased the island in November 1843. Rainy
is a name synonymous with the betrayal of the people in MacLean's poetry.
'Hallaig' is not the only poem of MacLean's which mentions Rainy, whose
greatest duplicity from MacLean's standpoint was that, as the son of a minister
from a notable Highland family, he ensured that the blame for these (in some
cases) forced clearances was placed firmly at the feet of one who must be, to
some extent, identified as Gaelic. MacLean was always aware of the scars left

---

15 *Collected Poems and Songs of George Campbell Hay*, ed. by Michel Byrne (Edinburgh:
    Edinburgh University Press, 2003), pp. 176–77.
16 *An Tuil*, p. xxxviii.

on the landscape after the Clearances and subsequent emigration took place. MacLean's time as a teacher on Mull (the traditional lands of Clan MacLean) was the genesis for another of his poems, 'An Cuilithionn', which also deals with themes of injustice within local communities, before moving outwards to encompass the history of people across the world against the evils of capitalism. While 'An Cuilithionn' centres on the symbol of the mountain, the emblem of 'Hallaig' is the tree, specifically the birch tree, which is a regenerative symbol, being the first tree to repopulate a landscape after natural or unnatural destructive influences have cleared woodland. The birch tree and other trees mentioned in the poem have a firm base in reality for the poet.

> Up to the Second World War, there were in Raasay many of the native birches, hazels, rowans, elders and planted conifers of many kinds, and also a relatively large area of deciduous trees, beeches, chestnuts, elms, ash, oaks, thujas, aspens – even eucalyptus, planted by a wealthy English family of landlords from 1875 onwards. With the War they were nearly all cut down, and replaced by quick-growing conifers. I soon became very fond of the 'old woods' of Raasay.[17]

In 'Hallaig' these trees become representative of the people who no longer populate the township, who have disappeared and whose only traces are the ruined homes that they once inhabited.

> Ann an Sgreapadal mo chinnidh,
> far robh Tarmad 's Eachann Mòr,
> tha 'n nigheanan 's am mic 'nan coille
> a' gabhail suas ri taobh an lòin.
>
> (In Screapadal of my people/where Norman and Big Hector were,/their daughters and their sons are a wood/going up beside the stream.)[18]

There is a strong sense of possession and self-identification with these absent people in the use of 'mo chinnidh' ('my people'), while the naming of specific individuals also serves to strengthen the poet's assertion of kinship.

'Hallaig' is a modern poem on several counts; it could only have been written in the mid-twentieth century, with the experiences of the Clearances being

---

17   Sorley MacLean, *O Choille gu Bearradh/From Wood to Ridge: Collected Poems* (Edinburgh: Carcanet/Birlinn, 1999), p. xv.

18   *Caoir Gheal Leumraich*, pp. 230–35.

sufficiently removed to allow a poet such as MacLean to assess its damage from a distance. However, 'Hallaig' is also a modern poem of the Clearances on account of its style and use of imagery. MacLean describes the trees as animate, giving the impression that the movement of the wood as it 'repopulates' the area is mirroring the movement and habits of the people:

O Allt na Feàrnaibh gus an fhaoilinn
tha soilleir an dìomhaireachd nam beann
chan eil ach coitheanal nan nighean
a' cumail na coiseachd gun cheann.

A' tilleadh a Hallaig anns an fheasgar,
anns a' chamhanaich bhalbh bheò,
a' lìonadh nan leathadan casa,
an gàireachdaich 'nam chluais 'na ceò

(From the Burn of Fearns to the raised beach/that is clear in the mystery of the hills,/there is only the congregation of girls/keeping up the endless walk,/coming back to Hallaig in the evening,/in the dumb living twilight,/filling the steep slopes, their laughter a mist in my ears)[19]

The landscape has been imprinted by the people's very footsteps; they have left such a residue that their presence is still tangible. But here lies the philosophical quandary at the poem's heart: this is an individual's reaction to the absence of community, and the re-emergence and sustainability of this community is reliant on the sheer strength of mind and imagination of one person. MacLean underlines this issue clearly when, in the closing stanzas of the poem, he describes the vehement bullet which will come from the gun of love:

's buailear am fiadh a tha 'na thuaineal
a' snòtach nan làraichean feòir;
thig reothadh air a shùil sa choille:
chan fhaighear lorg air fhuil rim bheò.

(and will strike the deer that goes dizzily,/sniffing at the grass-grown ruined homes;/his eye will freeze in the wood,/his blood will not be traced while I live.)[20]

---

19   *Caoir Gheal Leumraich*, pp. 230–35.
20   *Caoir Gheal Leumraich*, pp. 230–35.

This final stanza raises the question of whether a community, with its memories and traditions, can survive simply by being preserved by one individual, albeit one who is rooted in that tradition. With 'Hallaig', MacLean takes the traditional role of the Gaelic poet as spokesperson for the people to a Modernist conclusion. He manages to speak for an absent majority and reanimate the past in the present while nevertheless leaving the future hanging in the balance.

Urban Responses to Community in Gaelic Poetry

As the twentieth century progressed, it became increasingly difficult to confidently locate Gaelic community solely in its traditional heartlands of the Highlands and Islands. Changing economic situations have understandably contributed to the migration of Gaelic speakers from rural areas to urban centres in Scotland. The demographic of Gaelic speakers has also contributed to an altered picture of Gaelic community, with growing numbers of fluent learners in cities such as Edinburgh and Glasgow, who are embracing the language, choosing to educate their children in Gaelic medium schools, and identifying themselves as 'Urban Gaels'. This has meant that while certain Gaelic speakers with familial Highland links often have a personal understanding of the markers of traditional community that were practised by their grandparents, other Gaels have no connection to these markers and are creating their own meaningful sense of community. Gaelic literature clearly has a part to play here; the Gaelic experience of urban environments and how Gaelic community has responded and adapted can be traced through the literature.

Some of the earlier examples of twentieth-century poetry are quite conventional and based in an environment in which the oral tradition is dominant. The South Uist poet Donald John MacDonald (1919–86) composed a lament, 'Taigh a' Bhàird' ('The Poet's House'), to the home of a bard, John Campbell. It is an interesting poem in that it uses the conventions of a traditional lament but, by mourning the loss of creativity since Campbell's death, MacDonald lends the house anthropomorphic status. The now cold and silent house is a symbol of the greater loss of ceilidh culture, which MacDonald was witnessing in his community and beyond.

> Nach iomadh seanchas is òran
>   A dh'èist an òige bhon aois
> Taobh a' ghealbhain dhe d' chòmhlaidh
>   'S an teine mònadh 'na chraos;

Gillean gasta 'nad chèilidh
  A thataidh lèirsinn do ghaoil,
'S b'e lasair theine ceann fhòidean
  Bu tric a threòraich na laoich.

(So many stories and songs/Did youth listen to from age/On the hearth-side of your door/With the peat-fire ablaze;/Fine lads at your ceilidh/ Whom your love's sight caressed,/It was mostly peat fire flame/That brought them home to rest.)[21]

This poem is also an interesting modern example of how the concept of nature can be extended to human-made structures in the landscape. According to Michael Newton,

> some poets describe the dynamics of their local environment in similar terms to how they describe the functioning of their human community. Indigenous cultures realise that there is no easy division between the human actors, animal inhabitants, and the natural landscape. [...] The health of the human community and nature are intimately connected.[22]

In reflection of this, the poet's house in MacDonald's poem has become so steeped in the life of the people that it has itself taken on human traits.

Donald MacIntyre's (1889–1964) poem 'Bùth Dhòmhnaill 'IcLeòid' ('Donald MacLeod's Pub'), in contrast to MacDonald's state of mind, provides the other side of the story – a transplanted ceilidh-house in an urban environment, where the immigrant Gaels have regrouped and continue their communal traditions.

Ann am bùth Dhòmhnaill 'IcLeòid bidh gach seòrs' innte cruinn
Thig o thaobh Abhainn Chluaidh 's cuid tha nuas ás na glinn;
Bidh a' chàbraid cho cruaidh ann an cluasan do chinn
'S ged bhiodh bard ris gach gualainn dhiot 's fuaim ac' air seinn
  Ann am bùth Dhòmhnaill 'IcLeòid.

(In Donald MacLeod's pub folk of all sorts foregather/That come from the bank of the Clyde and down from the glens;/The babble's as loud in the

---

21 *An Tuil*, pp. 424–27.
22 Michael Newton, *Warriors of the Word: The World of the Scottish Highlanders* (Edinburgh: Birlinn, 2009), pp. 294–95.

ears of your head/As if you'd a poet at each shoulder singing his head off/
In Donald MacLeod's pub.)[23]

The pub in question was near Paisley Road Toll in Glasgow and celebrates the
sort of establishment which became a focal point for uprooted Gaels in the
city. However, the celebratory earlier stanzas of the poem take a depressing
turn, much like a drinker becoming morose at the end of a riotous drinking
session. The poet complains about the price of drink, and the decline of
Highland communities is also mourned:

> Thràigh iad fuaran nam buadh, dh'fhàg iad sluagh ann an càs,
> Tha na ceàrnachan tuath 's iad air thuar a bhith fàs;
> Tha na fàrdraichean fuar a bha uaireigin blàth,
> 'S chan eil àbhachd aig cluais mur eil fuaim a' mhuir-làin
>   Far am b' àbhaisteach ceòl.

> (They dried up the magic well, they left folk in a strait,/The northern dis-
> tricts are almost deserted;/The dwellings are cold that were formerly
> warm/And no ear has good cheer but the incoming tide/Where once
> there was music.)[24]

This change of pace reduces the social and cultural value of Donald MacLeod's
pub, thereby placing it in the position of 'poor relation' to the Highland ceilidh-
house. Iain Crichton Smith (1928–98) has also lamented the dilution of Highland
community traditions in the cities. In his article 'Real People in a Real Place' he
explores the changing nature of the ceilidh:

> The songs sung at modern ceilidhs have nothing to do with those sung
> at traditional ceilidhs. The new ceilidh has become a concert, with 'stars'
> in kilts twinkling from platforms in great halls in Glasgow or Edinburgh.
> The songs have now become nostalgic exercises, a method of freezing
> time, of stopping the real traffic of Sauchiehall Street, a magic evocation
> of a lost island in the middle of the city. The traditional ceilidh which
> was held in the village ceilidh house was a celebration of the happen-
> ings of the village, it was alive, it was a diary and a repeated record. The
> ceilidh as it is now practised is a treacherous weakening of the present,

23   *An Tuil*, pp. 180–85.
24   *An Tuil*, pp. 180–85.

a memorial, a tombstone on what has once been, pipes playing in a graveyard.[25]

There is clearly concern for the way in which Gaels are in danger of allowing their traditions to become devoid of their former meaning (and, by extension, permitting them to be parodied by those who have no interest in or intimate connection to the community from which they originated). A number of Gaelic poets have explored urban issues and group identity by employing Modernist depictions of urban space, leaning towards Surrealism and a sense of unreality and dislocated visions. It is perhaps no coincidence that the poets who have successfully navigated these themes in the mid-twentieth century are those with an academic background, such as Derick Thomson and Iain Crichton Smith, who have created in their poetry a sense of self-imposed exile in relation to their native communities. In the case of Thomson, who studied as an undergraduate at the University of Aberdeen, and later in life settled in Glasgow, becoming Professor of Celtic at Glasgow University in 1963, the impression given in much of his work is that his exile from his native Lewis is psychological as well as physical. The dislocation felt in a city, which is so far removed from his native community, is palpable in "'Bùrn is Moine 's Coirc'" ("'Water and peats and oats'"):

'Bùrn is mòine 's coirc' –
facal am beul strainnseir
ann an dùmhlachd a' bhaile,
ann am baile nan strainnsear.
Boile!

('Water and peats and oats' –/a word in a stranger's mouth,/in the throng of the town,/in the town of strangers./Madness.)[26]

The idea that certain words, lines of songs or fleeting images can conjure up a sense of homeland in an environment outside that community is explored

25   Iain Crichton Smith, 'Real People in a Real Place', in *Towards the Human: Selected Essays* (Edinburgh: MacDonald Publishers, 1986), pp. 37–38. Moray Watson has recently explored in detail Smith's sense of duality and the issues of Gaelic in bilingual communities in his plenary lecture at Rannsachadh na Gàidhlig 2014 (University of Edinburgh, 25 June 2014), entitled 'The Gaelic Writer, Iain Crichton Smith...', which has provided crucial discussion of an under-researched area in Gaelic scholarship.

26   *Creachadh na Clàrsaich*, pp. 130–31.

further in Crichton Smith's poem 'Innsidh mi dhut mar a thachair' ('I'll tell you how it happened'). Like Thomson a native of Lewis, Smith raises the notion that his life in the city is a pale reflection of the colourful, rich life that was familiar to him in his native community and culture, which he has left behind:

> Ach tha e àraidh
> a bhith fuireach ann am baile
> 's a' coiseachd troimh shràidean
> cho buidhe 's cho falamh
> 's a' coimhead òrain dhathte

> (But it's odd/to be living in a city/and walking through streets/so yellow and so empty/and seeing coloured songs)[27]

As well as harbouring an often misplaced feeling of having betrayed their native sense of place and community, these Gaelic poets, who left their communities and were exposed as students to non-Gaelic intellectual influences, appear to have developed a duality in their work, being simultaneously 'insiders' and 'outsiders'. This is almost certainly why Gaelic poetry has become more 'literary' in content and conception, with a move away from the markers of orally transmitted song and poetry, with its tendency towards storytelling, local events and gossip, and the naming of specific individuals known in the district, towards more formal and written poetry. Ronald Black has highlighted this change in poetic styles and outlook, pointing out that such a revolution in Gaelic literature could not be achieved 'without letting of blood' and likening the quarter of the century between the founding of *Gairm* in 1952 and the late 1970s as a time in which something akin to a 'holy war was fought between tradition and innovation for the soul of Gaelic poetry'.[28] Black has also categorised the separate camps of tradition and innovation in Gaelic poetry and it is evident that issues of community play a significant role in how this separation occurred. The 'innovative' poet seldom lived at home, according to Black, and there was a separation from traditional community life, while they were highly literate in Gaelic with excellent skills in English. This is in sharp contrast to the 'traditional' poet who was often non-literate (but never illiterate) in Gaelic, with sometimes poor English.[29] Poets such as Derick Thomson, Sorley MacLean, George Campbell Hay, Donald MacAulay, and Iain Crichton Smith

---

27   *An Tuil*, pp. 524–27.
28   *An Tuil*, p. xliv.
29   *An Tuil*, p. xlvi.

never lost their awareness of tradition, but there is also willingness towards implementing innovation in their work. MacLean has written at some length of his pre- and post-university influences, giving the impression that exposure to new forms of literature had a considerable impact:

> I think that the first great 'artistic' impact on me was my father's mother singing some of the very greatest of Gaelic songs, and all in her own traditional versions. [...] I had read no modern English poetry before I came to Edinburgh University at the age of 17 [...;] the lyrics of Hugh MacDiarmid might very well have destroyed any chances I ever had of writing poetry had my reading of them not been immediately followed by my reading of *The Drunk Man* [*sic*], *Cencrastus*, and *Scots Unbound*. [...] In them I saw a timeless and 'modern' sensibility and an almost implicit 'high seriousness' and an unselfconscious perfection of rhythm that could not be an exemplar because it was so rare.[30]

It is significant that MacLean's 'traditional' education was oral, and steeped in family and community, while his journey into non-Gaelic modern literature was more of a personal discovery, albeit one in which other university friends journeyed alongside him.

MacLean's work is often described in terms of merging tradition with innovation, but perhaps it is also necessary to take this reading of his work a stage further and appreciate it in broader terms relating to the community and the individual. Certainly, not all of MacLean's work was readily accepted by his own community. He was aware of the disapproving gaze of the community and, while it did not hinder the creative process of his poetry, it did create issues during the publication process. In a letter to Douglas Young of 30 July 1942, MacLean expressed worry regarding some of his poetry:

> As for my stuff, I am rather disturbed by [MacLean's brother] John's attitude to the publication of my godless stuff. It means of course that for various reasons John is terribly afraid of its effect on my mother and father, who are Seceders of a kind. My mother, I know, will be especially worried by a new manifestation of my godlessness at this time. Of course it is all my responsibility not yours. I sometimes think that all my stuff is

---

30   Sorley MacLean, 'My Relationship with the Muse', in *Ris a' Bhruthaich: The Criticism and Prose Writings of Sorley MacLean*, ed. by William Gillies (Stornoway: Acair, 1985), pp. 6–14 (pp. 7, 10–11).

not worth any added worry to anybody but now that it is ready, the responsibility is mine.[31]

These comments illustrate some negative effects of community, particularly community with a strong religious influence. Meg Bateman has described the rejection of established religion in the 1940s as 'almost [...] an orthodoxy amongst Gaelic *literati*'.[32] It may be the case that the satisfaction in the rejection of religion had more to do with the denunciation of rigid patterns and viewpoints of the respected elders within the community than philosophical issues of belief. Donald MacAulay's 'Rabhd Eudochais' ('Cry of Despair') could be viewed in this light:

Dè nì ceòl no cainnt sgeilmear
no craobh a' fàs craobhach dealbhach
no blàth caomh a' chinnidh daonna
[...]
dhan an fheadhainn a roghnaich
boidhr' agus doille –
's a tha 'n aghaidh ris a' bhailbhe?

(What's the use of music or polished diction/or trees that grow branching and shapely/or the gentle blossom of humanity/[...]/to those who have chosen/deafness and blindness –/and are facing dumbness?)[33]

The Postmodern Community

This dichotomy between tradition and innovation has continued in more recent Gaelic poetry. It could be argued that the high Modernism of the mid-twentieth-century poets, who were tackling large issues, has given way to a more postmodern style of approaching issues of community, and the conclusions that one can draw from these poems are more ambivalent for this reason. This postmodernism has reached its zenith in a very recent poetry collection, *Aibisidh* (*ABC*), by Angus Peter Campbell (1954–), who was born and still lives on the Isle of Skye. The whole collection has been described as an examination

---

31   Letters from Sorley MacLean to Douglas Young, Acc 6419 Box 38b, National Library of Scotland.

32   *An Tuil*, p. xlvii.

33   *An Tuil*, pp. 540–41.

of the 'fragmentation of language and identity in our modern global age', and 'the ways in which the dissolution of certainties challenges us to discover new connections – between individuals, communities, and cultures'.[34] In the title poem of the collection, Campbell plays with the idea of translation; the poem is made up of lines of songs but, while the Gaelic side of the page has poems and songs from the Gaelic tradition, the English side includes modern pop songs and musicals. 'Aibisidh' does not provide a translation for the songs and poems associated with Campbell's Gaelic community. Instead, Campbell shows that he exists in two places, with at least two cultures vying for his attention. By leaving these two cultures untranslated he is giving them equal weight, although it is perhaps telling that there are more lines of English due to there being more letters within the English alphabet than within the Gaelic one, raising questions of the limitations of the minority language of Gaelic against the more powerful world language of English. For Campbell in *Aibisidh*, his Gaelic community is as much an imagined community as it is a real one, kept alive by the possibilities of language:

> Thig an tè
> a chruthaicheas
> an ath eapaig
> Ghàidhlig
>
> o bhonn na mara.
> [...]
> Thig i le a h-òran fhèin,
> a' sèideadh bholgain-ciùil
>
> (The creator/of the next/Gaelic epic/will rise/from the bottom of the sea./[...]/She will arrive with her own song,/blowing a bubble of music)[35]

Gaelic learners have also had an effect on Gaelic literature. Learners of Gaelic who choose to write poems in Gaelic do so for multiple reasons, one of which may be the decision to become part of a Gaelic literary community. Sometimes the literary and physical Gaelic communities are interconnected. For instance, there is a very clear awareness of the politics of community in the poetry of Meg Bateman (1959–), who was born in Edinburgh, studied Gaelic at Aberdeen University and now lives on Skye. Her biographical section in Black's *An Tuil*, to

---

34 Angus Peter Campbell, *Aibisidh* (Edinburgh: Polygon, 2011). From the book's cover.
35 Campbell, *Aibisidh*, pp. 106–07.

which she clearly had an input, states that during her early life in Edinburgh 'her only misgivings took the form of a yearning for a community that was not class-based, for a way of life that was less technological, and for a mode of expression that came more easily than piano-playing'.[36] Her work does show that she has embraced Gaelic traditions and has a real respect for these traditions and the communities from which they originated. In 'Do Alasdair MacIlleMhìcheil' ('To Alexander Carmichael') she longs for the traditions practised by the communities from which Carmichael collected his folklore for his *Carmina Gadelica*. Bateman's wish in the poem appears to be that she can live more mindfully. Thus, the television, rather than the hearth fire, is now 'smoored' at the end of the night.[37] Bateman is commenting on the danger of losing the human interaction of community, and she is aware that, in the postmodern present, consumerism has overtaken the reciprocity that was at the centre of Gaelic community. But there is also a knowing self-consciousness in this awareness. In 'Ealaghol: Dà Shealladh' ('Elgol: Two Views') she does not fail to see either the humour or the irony of this situation. While looking at an old postcard of the houses and landscape of Elgol in Skye with an old man who has lived there all his life, she sees a time before there was a divide between the sacred and the secular, and work and play, 'mus d' rinneadh goireas de bheanntan', whereas the old man's reaction is quite different.

> 'Eil sin cur cianalas ort, a Lachaidh?'
> dh'fhaighnich mi, is e na thost ga sgrùdadh.
> 'Hoi, òinseach, chan eil idir!
> 's e cuimhne gun aithne a bh'agam oirrese',
> is stiùir e ri bò bha faisg oirnn san deilbh,
> 'Siud an Leadaidh Bhuidhe, an dàrna laogh aig an Leadaidh Bhig –
> dh'aithnichinn, fhios agad, bò sam bith
> a bhuineadh dhan àite sa rim bheò'.

> ('Does it make you sad, Lachie?' I asked/as he scrutinised it in silence./'Sad? Bah! Not at all!/I just couldn't place her for a moment',/and he pointed to a cow in the foreground./'That's Yellow Lady, Red Lady's second calf –/I'd know any cow, you see,/that belonged to me in my lifetime'.)[38]

---

36   *An Tuil*, p. 815.

37   *Modern Scottish Women Poets*, ed. by Michel Byrne and Dorothy McMillan (Edinburgh: Canongate, 2003), p. 217.

38   Meg Bateman, *Soirbheas/Fair Wind* (Edinburgh: Polygon, 2007), pp. 10–11.

Lachie's place in the community and on the landscape is undisputed in his own mind, but it is the seemingly small details that add weight to his sense of identity; in this instance animals are as important to him as the human population.

Not every Gaelic poet even deems it necessary to be rooted in the more traditional or fixed idea of Gaelic community. With 'Bho Leabhar-Latha Maria Malibran' ('From the Diary of Maria Malibran'), Christopher Whyte (1952–) has composed a long poem on a distinctly non-Gaelic subject matter. Whyte has described his poem on the Spanish opera singer Malibran as being about the 'preservation of self'.[39] The final italicised section is of a different nature to the rest of the poem, and appears to be the poet's address to a Gaelic readership and his own struggle with identity and authenticity, in relation to a real and/or imagined Gaelic community. The poem is a challenge to those who might expect that Gaelic poetry will simply deal with apparently Gaelic themes.

> Dè 'm fàth dhomh bhith 'nam bhreugaire? Carson
> nach aidichinn e? A luchd-leughaidh chaoimh,
> chan iad sin na cuspairean as fheàrr leibh.
> Nam b' e bhith còrdadh ribh a bha nam rùn,
> bu chòir dhomh sgrìobhadh air cùis eadar-dhealaicht'.

> (Why should I lie to you? Why shouldn't I/state the truth openly? Kind readers, shall you/look in my book for topics that you value?/If keeping you happy were my design,/a very different sermon would be mine.)[40]

Whyte is not prepared to categorise himself in order to fit in with preconceived ideas and ideals of Gaelic poetry. The issues raised in the poem may be deliberately set up in opposition to the type of view expressed by Bill Innes:

> [T]he authentic voice of modern Gaelic poetry [...] has evolved naturally out of the tradition[,] using simple images to convey deep emotion. [...] By contrast, I read some contemporary Gaelic poetry that does nothing for me as a Gael. The thought process is European [...]. In appealing to

---

39   Christopher Whyte, *Bho Leabhar-Latha Maria Malibran/From the Diary of Maria Malibran*, Gaelic poems with English versions by Michel Byrne, Sally Evans, W.N. Herbert, Ian MacDonald, Niall O'Gallagher and the author (Stornoway: Acair, 2009), p. 145.

40   Whyte, *Maria Malibran*, pp. 86–91.

the intellect rather than the heart, the work often fails to move. Worst of all, it fails to communicate with the ordinary Gael.[41]

Such an essentialist standpoint is in danger of not only ostracising Gaelic poets who are out of step with conservative notions of what is authentically 'Gaelic', but also fails to note that Gaelic poetry in traditional community settings has often tackled themes of a global nature. Whyte in 'Bho Leabhar-Latha Maria Malibran' is calling for a new community, one which he is unsure may even exist at the time of writing:

Deudan a th' annta, air neo dèideagan,
aig a' cheann thall tòisichidh iad a' fàs,
cnàmhan is crè is craiceann aig gach fear dhiubh,
's an leabhar ùr fa chomhair nan sùl ùr ac',

(though these are words, not teeth or pebbles – words,/when they are ready they will start to grow,/springing in flesh and bone from top to toe,/ and their new eyes will study what I've done)[42]

Whyte also appears to be heavily critical of the Gaels who lament their lost language but who do little to pass it on to their children, thereby assisting in the loss of the community's language and tradition – 'a dhiùltamaid a bhruid-hinn ris a' chloinn' ('the rich language our children can't join in').[43] There is little doubt that, in this poem at least, Whyte is painfully aware that he is an outsider. Nevertheless he uses Gaelic as his language of choice in his poetry and lays claim to this language identity, irrespective of whether or not he feels part of a greater community. This is unprecedented in Gaelic poetry in the twentieth century. The very act of stepping outside of a community which holds little or no meaning for an individual while simultaneously furthering the literature of that language community is both a triumph of individual will-power and the best answer to one's detractors.

The Gaelic poetry of the late-nineteenth century, and the subsequent poetry that has emerged in the twentieth and twenty-first centuries, has the capacity to celebrate community life but has more often than not been preoccupied with coming to terms with the loss of community values and traditions. While

---

41   Bill Innes, 'Poetry of the Oral Tradition: How Relevant is it to Gaelic in the 21st Century?', *Transactions of the Gaelic Society of Inverness*, 62 (2004), 79–109 (pp. 107–08).

42   Whyte, *Maria Malibran*, pp. 86–91.

43   Whyte, *Maria Malibran*, pp. 86–91.

the nineteenth-century poets do not entirely escape the trap of yearning for a lost 'golden age', poets have since risen to the challenge of envisioning the possibilities of community inherent in their changing world. In the twentieth century, both native speakers and learners of Gaelic have played a part in this process, showing that community can flourish in both rural and urban contexts. Community is adaptive and, while not always a purely positive force for these Gaelic poets, who have perceived 'community' as casting a censorious gaze on their work, the influence of community pervades the work of even the most self-contained and individual of poets. Rather than keeping Gaelic poetry in stasis, the theme of community has actually been one of the most significant vehicles of innovation, stimulating Gaelic poets in confronting and understanding their self-imposed role as spokespersons for both real and imagined communities and ensuring that the voices of others will always be a presence in their ears.

CHAPTER 4

Hugh MacDiarmid's Impossible Community

Scott Lyall

Abstract

This chapter suggests two main related points. The overarching contention is that
Hugh MacDiarmid was a poetic, political, polemical, and metaphysical impossibilist
(rather than merely the extremist of caricature). More particularly, in an attempt to
escape the impossible community of the Kailyard – provincial, retrogressive, Christian,
Scotland-as-Brigadoon – MacDiarmid fashioned an equally impossible if conflicting
community, profoundly singular yet ultimately spiritual, that nonetheless contained
residual Kailyard archetypes. The argument is traced through examination of
MacDiarmid's attitude to the Kailyard; work relating to the small communities in
which he lived and wrote, and to cities; and the question of his anti-Englishness.

Keywords

Hugh MacDiarmid – community – impossibilism – communism – Scottish Renaissance –
Scottish nationalism – Kailyard – Jean-Luc Nancy

'He would walk into my mind as if it were a town and he a torchlight proces-
sion of one'.[1] Norman MacCaig's graveside encomium on Hugh MacDiarmid is
a fitting memorial to the brilliance of his friend. It is also an apposite, if troublingly revealing, description of MacDiarmid's relationship to community as
both an idea and a lived reality in his work and life. MacDiarmid recognised
and indeed cultivated his own extreme singularity, likening his role in Scotland
to that of the 'cat-fish that vitalizes the other torpid denizens of the aquarium'.[2]
The multiplicity of Christopher Murray Grieve's pseudonyms – including
A.K. Laidlaw, A.L., Arthur Leslie, Gillechriosd Moraidh Mac a' Gheidhir, Isobel
Guthrie, James Maclaren, Mountboy, Pteleon, and Stentor, utilised chiefly for

---

1 Norman MacCaig, quoted in Alan Bold, *MacDiarmid: Christopher Murray Grieve: A Critical
   Biography* (London: John Murray, 1988), p. 434.
2 Hugh MacDiarmid, *Lucky Poet: A Self-Study in Literature and Political Ideas, Being the
   Autobiography of Hugh MacDiarmid* (*Christopher Murray Grieve*), ed. by Alan Riach
   (Manchester: Carcanet, 1994), p. xxv.

© KONINKLIJKE BRILL NV, LEIDEN, 2016 | DOI 10.1163/9789004317451_006

journalism and reviews – of which 'Hugh MacDiarmid' was the most famous, illustrates the poet's sense that if he was to sing alone, he would need to swell the chorus with his own community of voices.[3] In his persona as MacDiarmid, Grieve intended to be 'an impossible person'.[4] 'That pride of being tested. Of solitude' that Seamus Heaney writes of a poem to MacDiarmid is a mission statement implying a kind of self-imposed spiritual task.[5]

MacDiarmid was a poet in revolt against accepted standards, as were those whom he regarded as being among his main poetic influences: Pound, Rilke, Rimbaud, and Mayakovsky.[6] For instance, in his autobiography, *Lucky Poet*, he claimed to 'share to the full [...] Rimbaud's detestation of the whole of *bourgeois* culture'.[7] Such pronouncements can be aligned with the irrational-ist philosophy of *A Drunk Man Looks at the Thistle* and its narrator's desire to 'aye be whaur/Extremes meet'.[8] But where does the impulse to *épater le bour-geois*, to alienate his politico-aesthetic practice and beliefs from the under-standing of 'the vast majority o' men' and women,[9] leave MacDiarmid's work in relation to the idea of community, very broadly defined as a complex of shared values? This is an important question to ask of a writer who is gener-ally acknowledged to be modern Scotland's greatest poet, who thought of himself in the 1930s as 'by far the most powerful non-Conservative personal force in Scotland today',[10] and who claimed, in a poem published after his death but probably written in the early 1940s, to be responsible for the upsurge in political and cultural movements and bodies with a community of interest in envisioning Scotland as a self-determining nation:

> I have succeeded. See behind me now
> The multiplicity of organisations all concerned

---

3   I will throughout this chapter refer to the poet, journalist, political activist and man as Hugh MacDiarmid.

4   Letter to Neil M. Gunn, 22 June 1933, in *The Letters of Hugh MacDiarmid*, ed. by Alan Bold (London: Hamish Hamilton, 1984), p. 252. See also David Goldie, 'Hugh MacDiarmid: The Impossible Persona', in *The Edinburgh Companion to Hugh MacDiarmid*, ed. by Scott Lyall and Margery Palmer McCulloch (Edinburgh: Edinburgh University Press, 2011), pp. 123–35.

5   Seamus Heaney, 'An Invocation', *London Review of Books*, 14.15 (August 1992), p. 16.

6   See letter to Edith Trelease Aney, 7 February 1952, in Hugh MacDiarmid, *New Selected Letters*, ed. by Dorian Grieve, O.D. Edwards and Alan Riach (Manchester: Carcanet, 2001), p. 291.

7   MacDiarmid, *Lucky Poet*, p. 411. Italics in original.

8   Hugh MacDiarmid, *Complete Poems, Volume I*, ed. by Michael Grieve and W.R. Aitken (Manchester: Carcanet, 1993), p. 87.

9   MacDiarmid, *Complete Poems I*, p. 87.

10   Letter to Neil M. Gunn, 25 November 1933, in *The Letters of Hugh MacDiarmid*, p. 254.

With one part or another of that great task
I long ago – almost alone – most imperfectly – discerned
As the all-inclusive object of high Scottish endeavour
The same yesterday and today, and forever.
Fianna Alba and the Saltire Society,
The Scottish Socialist Party and Clann nan Gaidheal,
And a host of others all active today
Where twenty years ago there was not one to see.[11]

'MacDiarmid's revolt was in the name of a future Scotland which could only be grasped partially and intuitively', according to Bob Purdie, 'which is why his political thinking was fundamentally utopian'.[12] This begs several questions, not altogether answerable, such as: What does the 'future Scotland' of the present-day make of MacDiarmid, particularly during the Scottish Independence Referendum of 2014? Is MacDiarmid's 'future Scotland' ever truly graspable? And what does posting to the future in this utopian manner do to the present and the past? Gregory Claeys argues that '[u]topianism may be seen, in part, as an attempt to recapture a lost sense of community', as well as having its roots in a religious instinct to rediscover a prelapsarian, uncorrupted wholeness or pursue the bliss of the afterlife.[13] Indeed, seen in this light, community for Jean-Luc Nancy is a longing for the divine – that is, the impossible – with the increasing secularity of modernity as the driver of political projects such as communism that wish to return to *total* community: 'the thought of community or the desire for it might well be nothing other than a belated invention that tried to respond to the harsh reality of modern experience: namely, that divinity was withdrawing infinitely from immanence'.[14] Community, for Nancy, communion with an immanent deity that can no longer be reached, *is* loss.[15] This has profound implications for MacDiarmid's impossibilism, by which is

---

11   Hugh MacDiarmid, 'I Have Succeeded' [untitled], in *The Revolutionary Art of the Future: Rediscovered Poems of Hugh MacDiarmid*, ed. by John Manson, Dorian Grieve and Alan Riach (Manchester: Carcanet, 2003), p. 56.

12   Bob Purdie, *Hugh MacDiarmid: Black, Green, Red and Tartan* (Cardiff: Welsh Academic Press, 2012), p. 124.

13   Gregory Claeys, *Searching for Utopia: The History of an Idea* (London: Thames & Hudson, 2011), p. 129.

14   Jean-Luc Nancy, *The Inoperative Community*, trans. by Peter Connor et al. (Minneapolis and London: University of Minnesota Press, 2008), p. 10.

15   For more on Nancy's recoil from utopian thinking, see Jean-Luc Nancy, 'In Place of Utopia', in *Existential Utopia: New Perspectives on Utopian Thought*, ed. by Patricia Viera and Michael Marder (New York and London: Continuum, 2012), pp. 3–14.

meant his uncompromising stretching of the parameters of the conceivable, and its relation to community as a political idea, to which we shall return. The lost community is also fundamental - in a sense, too, that is ultimately metaphysical – to the Kailyard.

Kailyard

As the Introduction to this volume makes clear, the Kailyard is essential to understanding community in modern Scottish literature. It is also one of the key factors in MacDiarmid's revolt against what he regarded as the provincialisation of not merely Scottish literature, but Scotland as a cultural and political entity. Kailyard for MacDiarmid delimits Scottish experience in profoundly existential terms, cutting off the Scots from a fuller perception of their own identity, as well as their national past, present and future. Community as represented by the Kailyard is not only for MacDiarmid damagingly nostalgic and sentimental for a lost or non-existent Scotland, it is indicative of Scottish inferiorisation within a Britain controlled by metropolitan elites. The Kailyard extends beyond the Kailyard School of writing of Barrie, Maclaren and Crockett, to include the Burns Cult and Scottish comedians such as Harry Lauder. Kailyard becomes for MacDiarmid an attitude of mind, one entirely at odds with his view of the Scots as fearless eccentrics. Kailyard is the cultural substratum of the canny Scot, the respectable, penny-pinching and dour Presbyterian that MacDiarmid believed to be a national stereotype arising from 'the horrible psychological revolution' inaugurated by the Reformation and solidified by the Union of Crowns and Parliaments.[16] Kailyard, for MacDiarmid, makes a laughingstock of the Scots, and is synonymous with the 'Scottish cringe'.

Andrew Nash argues that, '[m]ore than any other writer, MacDiarmid was responsible for placing Kailyard at the centre of discussions over Scottish literature in the twentieth century'.[17] MacDiarmid's opposition to the Kailyard came initially from his negative assessment of post-Burnsian poetry in Scotland, in particular that of the Vernacular Circle of the London Robert Burns Club set up in 1920; according to Nash, he 'was the first writer to use the

---

16   Hugh MacDiarmid, *Scottish Eccentrics*, ed. by Alan Riach (Manchester: Carcanet, 1993), p. 298.

17   Andrew Nash, *Kailyard and Scottish Literature* (Amsterdam and New York: Rodopi, 2007), p. 207.

term consistently to refer to a poetic tradition'.[18] MacDiarmid's drunk man
laments that 'owre the kailyaird-wa' Dunbar they've flung' and that Kailyard
poetry is fit only for 'ploomen's lugs [ears]',[19] a point underlined in *Albyn, or
Scotland and the Future* (1927):

> The rediscovery of Dunbar can solve the difficulty for every would-be
> Scots writer who stands divided between his reluctance to go over bag
> and baggage to English literature and his inability to rise above the
> Kailyard level through the medium of Kailyaird Scots.[20]

MacDiarmid considered the Kailyard to constitute 'a false tradition in Scottish
literature', and his influence in defining what 'Kailyard' means in ideological
terms has, argues Nash, affected not only how we view the Kailyard itself, but
how we perceive Scottish literature and culture more generally.[21] MacDiarmid
set up the Kailyard to be the irreconcilable opposite of everything he stood for:
if the Kailyard was a tawdry example of Scottish popular culture, he would be
a Modernist elitist; while the Kailyard, as far as he was concerned, had nullified
the Victorian period in Scottish literature, the Scottish Literary Renaissance
would provide challenging high art; because it was a ruralist and reactionary
expression of Scottish provincialism, the Kailyard needed to be replaced by an
avant-garde, internationalist movement that connected Scottish cultural life to
progressive developments in Europe. Most significantly, though, MacDiarmid's
prognosis that 'Kailyairdism' is a 'disease' which is harmful to the cultural body
politic has influenced subsequent analyses such as that by George Blake, Tom
Nairn, and Craig Beveridge and Ronald Turnbull in their views, variously
expressed, that there are aspects of Scottish culture which are sick and in need
of an intellectually prescribed cure.[22]

   To identify a literary movement as being harmful to the health of a national
culture and then to isolate it from the national tradition is arguably to create the

---

18   Nash, *Kailyard and Scottish Literature*, p. 209.
19   MacDiarmid, 'A Drunk Man Looks at the Thistle', *Complete Poems I*, p. 106.
20   Hugh MacDiarmid, *Albyn: Shorter Books and Monographs*, ed. by Alan Riach (Manchester:
     Carcanet, 1996), p. 17.
21   Nash, *Kailyard and Scottish Literature*, p. 216.
22   C.M. Grieve, 'Newer Scottish Fiction (1): Norman Douglas; F.W. Bain', in Hugh MacDiarmid,
     Contemporary Scottish Studies, ed. by Alan Riach (Manchester: Carcanet, 1995), p. 342.
     George Blake, *Barrie and the Kailyard School* (London: Arthur Barker, 1951); Tom Nairn,
     The Break-Up of Britain: Crisis and Neo-Nationalism (London: NLB, 1977); Craig Beveridge
     and Ronald Turnbull, *The Eclipse of Scottish Culture: Inferiorism and the Intellectuals*
     (Edinburgh: Polygon, 1989).

very problem you seek to solve; as Ian Campbell argues, '[t]o reject the kailyard is to reject much that is central to any attempt to define "Scottishness"'.[23] MacDiarmid, eager to instigate a Scottish cultural revival, was, however, insistent that 'renaissances do not grow in kailyards'.[24] Yet the modern Scottish Renaissance in which he played such a central role may have been guilty of creating its own Kailyard-like vision of Scotland. Almost all of its main protagonists were from small Scottish communities, and many, including MacDiarmid, disliked Scotland's urban centres, a theme to which I shall return. Moreover, in much Scottish Renaissance writing, as in the Kailyard, there is a sense in which spiritual recovery, the revelation of a metaphysical Scotland, arises in a rural setting that stands for the essential nation; this is true of Edwin Muir's Orcadian Eden, Lewis Grassic Gibbon's Land, Neil M. Gunn's Highlands, and Nan Shepherd's northeast. The Kinraddie of Gibbon's *Sunset Song* was 'fathered between a kailyard and a bonnie brier bush in the lee of a house with green shutters', references to Ian Maclaren's immensely popular stories *Beside the Bonnie Brier Bush*, and George Douglas Brown's dark rejoinder to the Kailyard, *The House with the Green Shutters*.[25] Gibbon is making the point, according to Nash, 'that any fictional representation of a Scottish village had the fiction of Maclaren and Brown – and the structures of Kailyard and Anti-Kailyard – as its anxiety of influence'.[26] For all the internationalist aspirations of the modern Scottish Renaissance as propagandised for by MacDiarmid, this dialectic of Kailyard and anti-Kailyard remains fundamental to the movement for revival, as well as to MacDiarmid's work more specifically and how he conceives of community. The Kailyard, appearing in the shadow of Scotland's industrialisation, sought to resurrect a lost past, one underlain by a soft Christianity and an impossibilism captured most fantastically in Vincente Minnelli's *Brigadoon* (1954), by most accounts filmed in Hollywood because the producer, Arthur Freed, could not find the real Scotland on location.[27] The impossible community of MacDiarmid is principally prospective rather than being retrospective in the manner of the Kailyard, yet it remains impossible in seeking a communion with a reality that can never be realised.

---

23   Ian Campbell, *Kailyard: A New Assessment* (Edinburgh: The Ramsay Head Press, 1981), p. 16.

24   C.M. Grieve, 'Leaves from a London Scottish Diary', 12 May 1923, in Hugh MacDiarmid, *The Raucle Tongue: Hitherto Uncollected Prose, Volume I: 1911–1926*, ed. by Angus Calder, Glen Murray and Alan Riach (Manchester: Carcanet, 1996), p. 46.

25   Lewis Grassic Gibbon, *A Scots Quair* (Edinburgh: Canongate, 1995), p. 24.

26   Nash, *Kailyard and Scottish Literature*, p. 215.

27   See Forsyth Hardy, *Scotland in Film* (Edinburgh: Edinburgh University Press, 1990), p. 1.

The Place of Community

MacDiarmid's conception of community was fostered by his small-town upbringing in Langholm in the Scottish Borders. He remembered his boyhood in Langholm as 'the champagne days' of his life, claiming that Langholm and the surrounding area 'has always haunted my imagination and has probably constituted itself as the ground-plan of my mind'.[28] Not only did Langholm feed MacDiarmid's creativity, making it 'possible that I would in due course become a great national poet of Scotland', his upbringing there also allowed him to understand 'the spirit of Scotland and the Scottish folk'.[29] MacDiarmid relished the rural beauty of Langholm, calling it 'the bonniest place I know', yet the communist poet still aligned himself 'wholly on the side of the industrial workers and not the rural people' of the town, despite, as we shall see, often castigating the *urban* industrial proletariat.[30] In 'Out of the World and into Langholm', published in 1946, MacDiarmid argues that small towns such as Langholm, where 'we all know each other, and as a rule we know all about each other and past generations', are 'preferable to the anonymity of great cities'.[31] This sense of community is particularly beneficial as a way to militate against international conflict, such as the recently-ended World War Two. For MacDiarmid, to be 'properly rooted' in one's 'natural environment' is 'one of the best guarantees against the [...] destructive tendencies' of modernity.[32] MacDiarmid, internationalist, communist and Modernist, makes a statement redolent of the Kailyard when he says that '[a] remarkable fact about small places is the index of how far we have gone astray in the modern world'.[33] Just as the Kailyard was focused on the small rural town, for MacDiarmid, Langholm, and small Scottish communities like it, *is* Scotland. Langholm helped inspire what he called the 'racy Scots' of some of his best poetry,[34] such as this from 'Scots Unbound':

> No' the Esk that rins like a ribbon there
> But gi'es and tak's wi' the cluds in the air

---

28   Hugh MacDiarmid, 'Growing Up in Langholm' (1970), in Hugh MacDiarmid, *Selected Prose*, ed. by Alan Riach (Manchester: Carcanet, 1992), pp. 271, 272.

29   MacDiarmid, *Selected Prose*, p. 271.

30   MacDiarmid, *Selected Prose*, pp. 268, 270.

31   Hugh MacDiarmid, *The Raucle Tongue: Hitherto Uncollected Prose, Volume III: 1937–1978*, ed. by Angus Calder, Glen Murray and Alan Riach (Manchester: Carcanet, 1998), p. 102.

32   MacDiarmid, *The Raucle Tongue III*, p. 103.

33   MacDiarmid, *The Raucle Tongue III*, p. 102.

34   MacDiarmid, *Lucky Poet*, p. 16.

And outwith its stent boonds lies at the root
O' the plants and trees for miles roondaboot,
And gethers its tributaries, yet pulse-beats back
Up through them and a' that mak's it helps mak'
Sae I wad that Scotland's shape 'ud appear
As clear through a' its sub-shapes here
As whiles through my separate works I see
    Their underlyin' unity.[35]

MacDiarmid here sees that Scotland is diverse, multiform, but he views this as troublesome and hopes that in and through his poetry the nation will find cultural and political wholeness.

MacDiarmid lived in small towns for most of his life, and it was in the small communities of Montrose on Scotland's northeast coast during the 1920s and Whalsay in Shetland in the 1930s that he did his best work. Montrose, in particular, was a place of intense creativity for MacDiarmid: he wrote the Scots lyric poems collected in *Sangschaw* (1925) and *Penny Wheep* (1926), and the epic *A Drunk Man Looks at the Thistle* (1926); he instigated the Scottish Renaissance Movement; and he was immensely active within the community as a journalist, councillor, Justice of the Peace and provincial public intellectual. Yet Montrose is also represented by MacDiarmid as a suffocating and philistine community of Kailyard values in which the poet's artistic aspirations and metaphysical enquiries find little sustenance. In *A Drunk Man*, the use of Scots embeds the drunk man within the community, while the sheer ordinariness of his environment provides a comical juxtaposition to the extravagance of his philosophical wanderings. Tensions emerge though, as when the sacrificial poet-Christ finds his fellow townspeople to be spiritually void:

And in the toon that I belang tae
– What tho'ts Montrose or Nazareth? –
Helplessly the folk continue
To lead their livin' death!...[36]

Yet in returning him to his wife Jean at the end of the poem, MacDiarmid ensures that the drunk man's peregrinations remain within the bounds of the imagination, with little to trouble the community's normalcy. In the 'Frae Anither Window in Thrums' section of *To Circumjack Cencrastus* (1930), which

---

35   MacDiarmid, *Complete Poems I*, p. 343.
36   MacDiarmid, *Complete Poems I*, p. 88.

alludes to both a painting by the Scottish Modernist artist William McCance and J.M. Barrie's book of 1889, life and art clash much more fundamentally, and the roots of this conflict can be ascribed, at least from the poet's perspective, to the narrowness of the community in which he lives.[37] Montrose becomes Thrums, the archetypal Kailyard community, and the poet, while writing copy for the local newspaper, searches for his absent Muse, Athikte, the young female dancer of Paul Valéry's 'L'âme et la danse'. The unknown poet of 'Frae Anither Window in Thrums' attempts to resist the easy Kailyard lure of Neil Munro and Annie S. Swan by citing international giants such as Dostoevsky and Proust, yet the Kailyard ultimately triumphs, stealing over him like sleep, and he realises that his own preoccupations are not shared by the community or its rich and famous entertainers: 'The problems o' the Scottish soul', he complains, 'Are nocht to Harry Lauder'.[38] MacDiarmid believed Barrie's work to be 'destitute of spiritual purpose'; in the Kailyard community of 'Frae Anither Window in Thrums', the poet has reached a similar impasse.[39]

The Impossible Community

On moving to Whalsay in 1933, MacDiarmid left behind the vigorous communitarianism of his Montrose period. Yet it was while he was living in Shetland that he formalised his commitment to a communitarian politics by joining the Communist Party of Great Britain (CPGB), while at the same time pursuing the impossibilism of revolutionary politics premised, in his case, upon spiritual self-realisation.

As Mark Ryan Smith points out, MacDiarmid was 'extraordinarily productive' in Shetland, writing 'all the poems from page 385 to 1035' in the *Complete Poems*.[40] This poetic prodigiousness is in inverse ratio to his engagement with the local community. MacDiarmid mixed socially with the likes of the local doctor, to whom he dedicated *The Islands of Scotland* (1939), and Whalsay's laird; although he held ill-attended communist meetings on the island, to the locals he was 'gentry'.[41] MacDiarmid 'remained an outsider' in

---

37   See Margery Palmer McCulloch and Kirsten Matthews, 'Transcending the Thistle in *A Drunk Man* and *Cencrastus*', in *The Edinburgh Companion to Hugh MacDiarmid*, pp. 58–67.

38   MacDiarmid, *Complete Poems 1*, p. 248.

39   Grieve, 'Sir J.M. Barrie', in MacDiarmid, *Contemporary Scottish Studies*, p. 15.

40   Mark Ryan Smith, *The Literature of Shetland* (Lerwick: The Shetland Times Ltd, 2014), p. 114.

41   See Scott Lyall, *Hugh MacDiarmid's Poetry and Politics of Place: Imagining a Scottish Republic* (Edinburgh: Edinburgh University Press, 2006), pp. 117–18.

Shetland.[42] Indeed, the persona of the exiled Celtic bard was one he cultivated increasingly in the 1930s, and it is central to his autobiography *Lucky Poet* (1943), written mostly in Shetland.[43] MacDiarmid described Shetland as 'Scotland's greatest exclave, the neglected of the neglected, a sphere of lapsed traditions and unapprehended possibilities'.[44] Shetland is 'bare and desolate and destitute of all the rich variety to be found elsewhere', but this is something he relished as anticipating 'the end of the old world; and the beginning of the new'.[45] MacDiarmid does not explain what he means here by 'the old world' and 'the new', but in Shetland he attempted to carve out a new existential reality for himself which included turning to communism. Purdie points out that MacDiarmid joined the CPGB 'after reconnecting with his working class origins through an imaginative return to the Langholm of his youth' in *The Muckle Toon* poems, although he did show an earlier interest in Lenin while in Montrose.[46] Despite formalising his communism by joining the CPGB in 1934, MacDiarmid's 'Marxism looks distinctly odd', as Purdie explains:

> He never expressed a belief in class struggle as the driving force of human development nor that individuals are the products of their social and economic circumstances. He rarely quoted from the Marxist classics, and when he did so it was usually at second hand. He did not depict industrial workers as the most important progressive force in society, nor did he laud the struggles of working class communities.[47]

MacDiarmid's communism shows little concern for the exploited and oppressed, the wretched of the Earth Alphonso Lingis terms 'the community of those who have nothing in common'.[48] Nor is MacDiarmid especially

---

42   Smith, *The Literature of Shetland*, p. 119.

43   See Stephen P. Smith, 'Hugh MacDiarmid's *Lucky Poet*: Autobiography and the Art of Attack', in *Hugh MacDiarmid: Man and Poet*, ed. by Nancy K. Gish (Edinburgh: Edinburgh University Press, 1992), pp. 275–94.

44   Hugh MacDiarmid, 'Life in the Shetland Isles' (1934), in MacDiarmid, *Selected Prose*, p. 98.

45   Hugh MacDiarmid, 'The Shetland Islands' (1933–34), in Hugh MacDiarmid, *The Raucle Tongue: Hitherto Uncollected Prose, Volume II: 1927–1936*, ed. by Angus Calder, Glen Murray and Alan Riach (Manchester: Carcanet, 1997), pp. 511, 512.

46   Purdie, *Hugh MacDiarmid*, p. 71. For more on *The Muckle Toon*, see W.N. Herbert, *To Circumjack MacDiarmid: The Poetry and Prose of Hugh MacDiarmid* (Oxford: Clarendon Press, 1992), pp. 98–119; for MacDiarmid's Leninism in Montrose, see Lyall, *Hugh MacDiarmid's Poetry and Politics of Place*, p. 83.

47   Purdie, *Hugh MacDiarmid*, p. 77.

48   Alphonso Lingis, *The Community of Those Who Have Nothing in Common* (Bloomington and Indianapolis: Indiana University Press, 1994).

interested in the working people of Shetland. Smith correctly points to *Stony Limits* (1934), MacDiarmid's first collection of poems after coming to live in Shetland, as containing 'a deep and fundamental engagement' with the Shetland landscape, especially in an important poem such as 'On a Raised Beach'.[49] But in and through his engagement with this landscape, MacDiarmid creates of Shetland a no-place, a *terra incognita* through which to rediscover himself; he feels little connection with Shetlanders, a point illustrated in 'Shetland Lyrics', where, while he celebrates the world of sea, fish and birds, his appreciation of natural beauty is alien to the 'primitive minds' of the fishermen ('Deep-Sea Fishing'), and his real 'delight' is in 'naethingness' ('De Profundis').[50]

With 'On a Raised Beach' MacDiarmid breaches the confines of lived community to create a place of the mind that is at once inspired by the Shetland landscape, the passage of geological time, and his own existential needs. As Christ went into the desert – a comparison we are invited to make by the poet's tone of biblical prophet ('We must be humble') and his being 'enamoured of the desert at last' – so MacDiarmid finds his spiritual salvation in 'this stone world now'.[51] This is a poem about faith, but the faith the poet finds is an acceptance of the Earth, through the stones; an acceptance that there is no transcendental reality; a metaphysical acceptance of the reality of the *real*. 'On a Raised Beach' is a poem of 'difficult knowledge', a phrase from 'The Kind of Poetry I Want'.[52] How do we apprehend the stoniness of the stone? How do we understand the stone and the world scientifically, as composed of atoms and energy? These are difficult questions for poetry to answer, and the unfamiliar, technical and scientific terms at the beginning and end of the poem are in part MacDiarmid's bid to transmit this difficulty. It is also a poem of difficult knowledge in that it seeks to understand the world from a materialist perspective, but in a way that still allows us to remain open to wonder. Poetry alone is not sufficient to comprehend the world in materialist terms, yet neither, one might argue, is geology or any other science. A materialist theology, a re-sacralisation of the non-transcendental realm, and the dialectic of two apparently divergent worlds, spirit and science, is what MacDiarmid is reaching for in 'On a Raised Beach'. While the 'Sea of Faith' is 'withdrawing' in Matthew Arnold's 'Dover Beach', published in 1867, the same year as Arnold's *On the Study of Celtic Literature*, so a new wave of scientific discovery underlies

---

49   Smith, *The Literature of Shetland*, p. 119.

50   MacDiarmid, *Complete Poems I*, pp. 438, 440.

51   MacDiarmid, *Complete Poems I*, pp. 425, 431, 426.

52   Hugh MacDiarmid, *Complete Poems, Volume II*, ed. by Michael Grieve and W.R. Aitken (Manchester: Carcanet, 1994), p. 1013.

Modernism.[53] A new ecology of cultural materialism evolves in 'On a Raised Beach', and this combines with MacDiarmid joining the Communist Party.

Communism is, or at least was before Stalinism and the fall of the Berlin Wall, 'a utopian hypothesis', according to Judith Balso.[54] In this regard, communism not only has historical political importance, but, as Nancy argues, it is also of foundational philosophical significance:

> Communism, as Sartre said, is 'the unsurpassable horizon of our time', and it is so in many senses – political, ideological, and strategic. But not least important among these senses is the following consideration, quite foreign to Sartre's intentions: the word 'communism' stands as an emblem of the desire to discover or rediscover a place of community at once beyond social divisions and beyond subordination to technopolitical dominion, and thereby beyond such wasting away of liberty, of speech, or of simple happiness as comes about whenever these become subjugated to the exclusive order of privatization; and finally, more simply and even more decisively, a place from which to surmount the unraveling that occurs with the death of each one of us – that death that, when no longer anything more than the death of the individual, carries an unbearable burden and collapses into insignificance.[55]

Communism is community in the face of our shared finitude, death being that which at last we all have in common. This, then, is less a communion in traditional spiritual terms, a final communion with God, and more what Nancy calls 'a community of being', by which he means that 'being is *in* common, without ever being common'.[56] Communism, for Nancy, 'does not belong to the political' but rather 'comes before the political' because it 'means the common condition of all singularities of subjects, that is, of all the exceptions, all the uncommon points whose network makes a world'; in these terms,

---

53   Matthew Arnold, 'Dover Beach', in *Selected Poems*, ed. by Timothy Peltason (London: Penguin, 1994), pp. 102–03.

54   Judith Balso, 'To Present Oneself to the Present. The Communist Hypothesis: A Possible Hypothesis for Philosophy, an Impossible Name for Politics?', in *The Idea of Communism*, ed. by Costas Douzinas and Slavoj Žižek (London and New York: Verso, 2010), pp. 15–32 (p. 15).

55   Nancy, *The Inoperative Community*, p. 1.

56   Jean-Luc Nancy, 'Of Being-in-Common', in *Community at Loose Ends*, ed. by the Miami Theory Collective (Minneapolis and Oxford: University of Minnesota Press, 1991), pp. 1–12 (pp. 1, 8). Italics in original.

communism 'is not politics, it is metaphysics or, if you prefer, ontology'.[57] To link Nancy's thought to MacDiarmid's poetics may seem surprising: whereas Nancy has sought to rescue the idea of communism from the disaster of Soviet totalitarianism, MacDiarmid was a Party member in the 1930s when 'On a Raised Beach' was written, subsequently became a Stalinist, and rejoined the CPGB following the Soviet crushing of the 1956 Hungarian Uprising. Yet the Nancian understanding of communism as idealised existential community is vital to the poet of 'On a Raised Beach', even, or particularly, in his apartness from lived community. 'Death is a physical horror to me no more [...]. It is reality that is at stake', claims MacDiarmid's poet.[58] Spiritually *in extremis*, beyond even the claims of suicide, the poet sees reality truly for the first time with visionary eyes ('The beginning and the end of the world'), in existential terms ('My own self'), and in communion with the commons of the world ('as before I never saw/The empty hand of my brother man').[59] The poem ends with the reflection that, for all our natural fear of personal extinction, life is harder than death, and what is hardest of all is 'to get a life worth having'.[60] While 'Great work cannot be combined with surrender to the crowd', it is at the same time 'the impossible and imperative job' of the 'Intelligentsia' to reach 'the mob'.[61] Yet the Nietzschean loneliness of the poet, the ascetic 'Self-purification and anti-humanity' he adjures himself to find, both belies and reveals the poem's politics. For Nancy, in a post-secular world, 'death is itself the true community of mortal being; their impossible communion'; as such, community 'takes upon itself the impossibility of its own immanence, the impossibility of a communitarian being as subject'.[62] 'On a Raised Beach' is a communist poem proclaiming the impossibility of community.

Cities

On leaving Shetland in 1942, MacDiarmid was conscripted to do munitions work in Glasgow. MacDiarmid did not like cities, something he shared in

---

57   Jean-Luc Nancy, 'Communism, the Word', in *The Idea of Communism*, pp. 145–53 (pp. 149, 150).
58   MacDiarmid, *Complete Poems I*, p. 428.
59   MacDiarmid, *Complete Poems I*, p. 432.
60   MacDiarmid, *Complete Poems I*, p. 433.
61   MacDiarmid, *Complete Poems I*, pp. 429, 432.
62   Jean-Luc Nancy, quoted in Maurice Blanchot, *The Unavowable Community*, trans. by Pierre Joris (Barrytown: Station Hill, 1988), p. 11.

common with the Kailyard: as Ian Campbell confirms, the Kailyard is mainly 'a *rural* form, a literature which prefers the small town or farming countryside to the burgeoning cities which were increasingly the everyday reality of Scotland in the later nineteenth century' of the Kailyard's heyday.[63] MacDiarmid's model of community was based on the rural town of Langholm, which during his childhood (from 1892 until around 1908, when he went to Edinburgh) could be described as a 'little community', defined by Robert Redfield as characterised by 'distinctiveness, smallness, homogeneity, and all-providing self-sufficiency'.[64] Anthony P. Cohen points out that for Redfield the traditional values and stability of the 'little community', or folk community, provide 'the classical repository of community', whereas the movement to city life brings about 'the loss of community'.[65] The degeneration discerned by Redfield in the shift from rural community to urban *anomie* chimes with MacDiarmid's depiction of the city as a modern wasteland. In *Lucky Poet*, he complains of cities that he had 'never been able to find one that was not full of reminders of the fact that Cain, the murderer, was also the first city-builder'.[66] He was particularly hard on Glasgow and Edinburgh, although in *Scottish Scene* (1934), which MacDiarmid co-authored with Lewis Grassic Gibbon, all four of the main Scottish cities are portrayed in a negative light. MacDiarmid writes on Dundee and Edinburgh in *Scottish Scene*, while Gibbon covers Aberdeen and Glasgow. Dundee is dismissed as 'a great industrial cul-de-sac', a city culturally saturated with 'kailyard products' due to the monopoly of D.C. Thomson, publishers of *The Scots Magazine*, *The People's Friend*, *The Courier* and *The Evening Telegraph*, publications that 'stand in a category quite by themselves as one of the most incredible freaks in the history of Scottish journalism', and all of which MacDiarmid viewed as 'old Kailyaird guff which has no correspondence to Scottish realities'.[67] Dundee is divided between a radical working population and a conservative press and factory-owning class of Jute Barons. The city has been damaged, though not destroyed, by *laissez-faire* capitalism, but it is, MacDiarmid believes, 'the principal stronghold of Communism in Scotland'.[68]

---

63   Campbell, *Kailyard*, p. 12. Italics in original.

64   Robert Redfield, *The Little Community*, in *The Little Community* and *Peasant Society and Culture* (Chicago and London: Phoenix Books, 1963), p. 4.

65   Anthony P. Cohen, *The Symbolic Construction of Community* (Abingdon: Routledge, 2015), p. 27.

66   MacDiarmid, *Lucky Poet*, p. 105.

67   Hugh MacDiarmid, in Lewis Grassic Gibbon and Hugh MacDiarmid, *Scottish Scene, or The Intelligent Man's Guide to Albyn* (London: Hutchinson, n.d.), pp. 160, 161, 160, 52.

68   MacDiarmid, *Scottish Scene*, p. 159.

Dundee may be the home of the MacDiarmid's *bête noire*, the Kailyard, but it is also 'the centre of a struggling colony of Scottish artists – men like Stewart Carmichael, Walter Grieve, David Foggie and others'.[69] Edinburgh, in contrast, 'lives on manifestations of the creative spirit made elsewhere'.[70] When listing Edinburgh's cultural achievements, MacDiarmid can think only of Chopin's time in the Scottish capital, and that Thomas Common, translator and author of a book on Nietzsche, lived there. There is no mention of the great philosophical accomplishments of the Scottish Enlightenment, although Hume does gain a passing reference. Edinburgh may be beautiful, but it is intrinsically empty: 'The husk is everything; there is no kernel'.[71] MacDiarmid renders Edinburgh a cultural 'blank' in much the same manner as Edwin Muir in *Scott and Scotland* (1936), published two years after *Scottish Scene*.[72] While MacDiarmid mentions Walter Scott, he makes nothing of his significance to Edinburgh, and he complains that no Scottish novelist has done for Edinburgh what Joyce's *Ulysses* did for Dublin. He makes a similar observation about the relationship of Edinburgh to poetry:

> If Edinburgh has not given the creative spirit due place, the creative spirit has not been deluded as to Edinburgh's false position. It is a significant fact that with all the romance attached to it it has never been the subject of any good, let alone great, poem. It could not have failed to inspire the poets if there had not all along been something wrong with its pretensions – some essential falsity the instincts of their genius could never be deluded by.[73]

MacDiarmid is suggesting that the city itself is to blame for the apparent absence of great poetry on Edinburgh. Muir comes to a similar conclusion on the city as part of his assessment of why Scott is not in the first rank of writers. Edinburgh for MacDiarmid, as for Muir, is *lacking*; the absence at the heart of Edinburgh's creative dearth is, argues MacDiarmid, political power: it is 'a capital that is not one; a magnificent provision for an unfulfilled function'.[74] For all

69   MacDiarmid, *Scottish Scene*, p. 162.

70   MacDiarmid, *Scottish Scene*, p. 71.

71   MacDiarmid, *Scottish Scene*, p. 72.

72   Edwin Muir, *Scott and Scotland: The Predicament of the Scottish Writer* (Edinburgh: Polygon, 1982), p. 2.

73   MacDiarmid, *Scottish Scene*, p. 78.

74   MacDiarmid, *Scottish Scene*, pp. 80–81.

that, MacDiarmid, then living in Shetland, believed there is nowhere else for an artist to live in Scotland but Edinburgh.

MacDiarmid's poems on Edinburgh do not give the lie to his judgement that the city has failed to inspire great poetry. 'Edinburgh' from *Lucky Poet* confirms MacDiarmid's view that the city does not exhibit creative capacity, repressed as it is by 'a monstrous acquiescence' to the bourgeois values of an acquisitive society; the poem is a call to find 'the primal power' that is necessary to repossess ourselves of 'the mighty impetus of creative force', but MacDiarmid's windy rhetoric falls short of the task.[75] The military tattoo is attacked in 'Edinburgh's Tattoo Culture', while 'Edinburgh', an early poem of 1921, describes Edinburgh's setting and panorama as arising from 'a mad god's dream', whereas 'Dundee is dust', 'Aberdeen a shell', and 'Glasgow is null'.[76]

MacDiarmid's Glasgow poems seek ostensibly to attack the capitalist system, but often end up denigrating the people who suffer most at its hands. 'Glasgow, 1960' is a satire on the lack of intellectual hunger in this famously football-loving city, while 'Glasgow' (in *Lucky Poet*) describes Glaswegians as 'hoodlums', 'callous Scots', and – with magnificent malevolence – 'Half glow-worms and half newts'.[77] 'Glasgow', from the 1962 *Collected Poems*, claims:

> The houses are Glasgow, not the people – these
> Are simply the food the houses live and grow on
> Endlessly, drawing from their vulgarity
> And pettiness and darkness of spirit [...].
> Everything is dead except stupidity here.[78]

Glasgow for MacDiarmid is a capitalist and cultureless hell, as Brecht's 'Contemplating Hell' imagines London and Los Angeles to be. Yet where Brecht's poems largely show understanding and humanity to the workers' plight, MacDiarmid displays a Modernist disdain, nowhere more so than in his Glasgow poems. Other writers of the modern Scottish Renaissance, such as Edwin Muir and Fionn MacColla, envisaged Glasgow as hell, while the fictional city of Duncairn is seen as a threatening, disintegrative force in Lewis Grassic Gibbon's *Grey Granite*, dedicated to MacDiarmid. Even George Douglas Brown's *The House with the Green Shutters*, an anti-Kailyard novel that kick-started the

---

75   MacDiarmid, *Complete Poems I*, pp. 644, 645, 646.

76   MacDiarmid, *Complete Poems II*, p. 1204.

77   MacDiarmid, *Complete Poems I*, pp. 647, 648.

78   MacDiarmid, *Complete Poems II*, p. 1049.

revival's anti-parochialism, sees young John Gourlay return home to Barbie in disgrace from Edinburgh. For MacDiarmid, '[t]here is little relationship between Thrums and Clydebank'.[79] We might expect a communist to dismiss a rural folk community such as Barrie's Thrums as being at a previous stage of revolutionary development to industrial Clydebank. Yet there is a tension here in that MacDiarmid's idea of community is patterned on the 'little community' of Langholm, while his city poems consolidate a Kailyard-like view of urban centres as distant and alienating places of contamination.

Immigration and the 'English Problem'

In the Kailyard, according to Campbell, 'change is something which happens' in the cities, 'far-off Dundee or "Edinburry"'.[80] That the Kailyard is an almost changeless rural community is emphasised by its Christian, implicitly Presbyterian values, in stark contrast to the 'distant atheist cities' of the industrial Lowland conurbation with its influx of immigrants looking for work.[81] According to Gerard Delanty:

> As cities become more and more diverse and unstable due to changes in the nature of capitalism and industrialization, a sense of place and attachment, which is generally related to ethnicity, can be possible only in small localities or neighbourhoods.[82]

The Kailyard provided certainty amidst the violent change suffered by much of the Scottish population during the Industrial Revolution. Indeed, in trying to account for the Kailyard's immense popularity, George Blake focuses on the unparalleled changes wrought by industrialisation, and the internal dislocation and immigration that followed. The Industrial Revolution, he argues, 'knocked the old Scotland sideways [...] and turned the Clyde Valley almost overnight into a Black Country'.[83] The immigration of Irish, Lithuanians and others into the cities in this period, and the accompanying tensions, is not represented in Kailyard fiction. While the cities were a flux of shifting and diverse populations, the Kailyard remained an almost static community.

---

79   C.M. Grieve, 'Leaves from a London Scottish Diary', 19 May 1923, in MacDiarmid, *The Raucle Tongue I*, p. 48.

80   Campbell, *Kailyard*, p. 12.

81   Campbell, *Kailyard*, p. 15.

82   Gerard Delanty, *Community*, 2nd edn (Abingdon: Routledge, 2010), p. 40.

83   Blake, *Barrie and the Kailyard School*, p. 8.

MacDiarmid's exasperation with the industrial proletariat in his city poems is largely contrasted by his positive views on immigration. He particularly welcomed Irish immigration to Scotland, and opposed the sectarian fearmongering of the Church of Scotland over the increasing number of Irish Catholics coming to the country in the 1920s. However, MacDiarmid's positive views on the Irish come mainly from his sense that Irish Catholic immigrants would help to offset the Anglicisation of Scotland, especially during a time when many Scots were emigrating. He argues in 1927 that 'the vital thing is not the influx of Irish and other aliens; but the exodus of Scots' due to insufficient wages and opportunities.[84] Sectarianism is the 'religious and social' consequence of 'political and economic' issues and the solution is the 're-orientation of Scottish affairs on such a basis that Scottish industries and interests would not be systematically sacrificed to English' priorities.[85] MacDiarmid points out that there are a native Catholic people and a Catholic cultural tradition in Scotland, and that anti-Irishness merely allows the Protestant Churches to play the sectarian card, thus blinding Scots to the more serious issue of Anglicisation. The solution to all of this is Scottish nationalism. However, MacDiarmid opposed fellow nationalists, such as the poet Lewis Spence and the Duke of Montrose, who were anti-immigrant ethnic nationalists:

> His Grace [the Duke of Montrose] contends that Scottish people can look after their own interests without the help of Irish, Poles, English, and other aliens. The answer is – then why haven't they done so? Even His Grace's efforts over many years have failed to stir them up, and Scottish interests have been sacrificed all along the line. In any case, these aliens are citizens of Scotland and their interests are bound up with its condition. Does His Grace propose to disenfranchise them – or, like Mr Spence, to evict them? Why can't he face the practical political situation, recognize them for the important, permanent, and increasing factors they are in our electorate, and be ready to welcome any signs they show of identifying themselves with Scottish interests and becoming true citizens of our country?[86]

This progressive endorsement of civic nationalism is arguably somewhat undone, coming as it does in an article announcing the emergence of Clan

---

84   Special Correspondent, 'The "Irish Invasion" of Scotland', in MacDiarmid, *The Raucle Tongue II*, p. 87.

85   MacDiarmid, *The Raucle Tongue II*, pp. 87, 88.

86   Hugh MacDiarmid, 'Clan Albainn' (1930), in MacDiarmid, *Selected Prose*, p. 56.

Albainn, an extremist Scottish nationalist group that proposed to adopt 'militant action' to secure independence.[87]

While the English are included in MacDiarmid's rejoinder to the ethnic nationalism of Spence and the Duke of Montrose, he did worry that increasing numbers of English people coming north would spell the de-nationalisation of Scotland. 'Taking other foreign elements into account', he writes in 1923, 'it is appalling to find that there is one non-Scot in every nine of Edinburgh's population and one in eight in Glasgow's'.[88] Here he is responding mainly to what he perceives as the demographic unbalance created by English immigration to Scotland. This is important for MacDiarmid because, as a Scottish nationalist, he believes English influence within the United Kingdom to be disproportionately large and therefore likely to militate against Scottish political and cultural self-determination. Neal Ascherson, alluding to the poet's attitude to the English, believes that 'MacDiarmid was, for much of his life at any rate, a racist'.[89] For Ascherson, MacDiarmid 'wasted time trying to prove Scotland's superiority over England, when he should have been emphasising what historians know with increasing clarity: that England is the exception of Europe' and that the 'English problem', what Tom Nairn calls the 'English Enigma'[90] – England's early industrialisation and embedded landed gentry stymieing a revolutionary moment –, is one 'Scotland shares with France, Ireland, Norway, Poland and so forth'.[91] MacDiarmid's problem with the English, tantamount to racism, blinded him to the structural inequalities emerging from English exceptionalism, described by Ascherson as the 'English problem'.

However, contra to Ascherson's view, MacDiarmid was exceedingly aware of the 'English problem' in the terms later mapped out by Ascherson and Nairn, as shown in an essay such as 'English Ascendancy in British Literature'. Here he argues that '[c]onfinement to the English central stream is like refusing to hear all but one side of a complicated case', and he promotes the study of all of the British cultures in a manner that would undermine English cultural dominance within the British Isles.[92] This is in opposition to the ideas of T.S. Eliot, who in 1931 published 'English Ascendancy in British Literature' in *The*

---

87   MacDiarmid, *Selected Prose*, p. 55.

88   Unsigned, 'English Invasion of Scotland', in MacDiarmid, *The Raucle Tongue I*, p. 115.

89   Neal Ascherson, 'MacDiarmid and Politics', in *The Age of MacDiarmid: Essays on Hugh MacDiarmid and his influence on contemporary Scotland*, ed. by P.H. Scott and A.C. Davis (Edinburgh: Mainstream, 1980), pp. 224–37 (p. 233).

90   See Nairn, *The Break-Up of Britain*, pp. 291–305.

91   Ascherson, *The Age of MacDiarmid*, p. 232.

92   MacDiarmid, *Selected Prose*, p. 68.

Criterion. Eliot regarded Ireland, Wales and Scotland as mere regional satellites to a national English culture, having questioned whether there was or had ever been a Scottish Literature.[93] For Eliot, the best in Scottish, Irish and Welsh culture is consumed by English culture so making the latter stronger, but he also believes that the local cultures benefit through connection to the metropolitan culture: 'For Ireland, Scotland and Wales to cut themselves off completely from England would be to cut themselves off from Europe and the world'.[94] Eliot's analysis rests on a conservative and centrist view of British culture, which imagines that cultures, at least the great ones, are organic, natural, unbroken traditions assimilating the finest that the non-metropolitan nations have to offer and condemning the remnants as provincial. In this sense, MacDiarmid's work, and his seemingly intolerant attitude towards English culture and its penetration into Scotland, can be seen as questioning what he regarded as the false universals of an imperious English Literature. The ideas of national community in MacDiarmid's work are not simply those imagined by the Scottish poet, but those that he was reacting against.

Scotland 2014

MacDiarmid's impossibilism and the perception of his anti-Englishness are undoubtedly the main reasons his work and ideas played little positive part in the debates leading up to the 2014 Scottish independence referendum. The Scottish composer and Unionist James MacMillan alluded to what he saw as MacDiarmid's support for fascism when claiming that the poet's 'art and his wild, radical, "progressive" idealism can be difficult to disentangle'.[95] From a feminist perspective, the playwright and transwoman Jo Clifford gave her reply to Alexander Moffat's painting *Poets' Pub*, the very masculine community of poets to which MacDiarmid is central, with her 'Unnamed Woman in "Poets' Pub"'.[96] Work by Angela Bartie, Eleanor Bell and Linda Gunn on the changing nature of Scotland in the 1960s sees MacDiarmid as a figure to be challenged.[97]

---

93   T.S. Eliot, 'Was There a Scottish Literature?', *Athenaeum*, 1 August 1919, 680–81.

94   T.S. Eliot, *Notes Towards the Definition of Culture* (London: Faber and Faber, 1948), p. 55.

95   James MacMillan, 'Scottish independence essay: arts and the referendum', *The Scotsman*, 30 April 2014 <www.scotsman.com/what-s-on/theatre-comedy-dance/scottish-independence-essay-arts-and-the-referendum-1-3393306> [accessed 10 July 2015].

96   <www.thespace.org/artwork/view/dearscotlandpoetspub#.U7ajb_ldWzQ>.

97   Angela Bartie, *The Edinburgh Festivals: Culture and Society in Post-war Britain* (Edinburgh: Edinburgh University Press, 2013). *The Scottish Sixties: Reading, Rebellion, Revolution?*, ed. by Eleanor Bell and Linda Gunn (Amsterdam and New York: Rodopi, 2013).

Ironically perhaps, it was the writer and broadcaster Andrew Marr, perceived by many as a supporter of the British Establishment, who sought to defend MacDiarmid and promote his work as being centrally influential to contemporary Scottish culture and the burgeoning support for a new political vision of Scotland.[98] MacDiarmid wanted to be a 'disgrace to the community', and his legacy remains challenging and confrontational, shattering the provincial limits of the Kailyard, while revealing new regions in the realm of the impossible.[99]

---

98   *Andrew Marr's Great Scots: The Writers Who Shaped a Nation*, BBC2, first broadcast 30 August 2014.

99   MacDiarmid, *Lucky Poet*, p. 426.

CHAPTER 5

Becoming *Anon*: Hamish Henderson, Community and the 'Folk Process'

Corey Gibson

Abstract

Hamish Henderson (1919–2002) was a celebrated songwriter, war poet, political activist, folklorist, and perhaps the most visible campaigner on behalf of the modern folk revival in Scotland. Henderson developed a theory of the 'folk process' by which contemporary singers, poets, and even audiences and readers, are absorbed into a vast anonymous community of 'tradition-bearers'. This proposal presents obvious problems for conventional notions of community based on national, local, historical, political or ideological paradigms, as it transcends the boundaries that we rely on to distinguish a given 'community' and extends, even beyond death, to encompass all of human history. This chapter will describe the formulation of this notion of the 'folk process' through the 'discovery' of the folk culture of the travelling people, and through Henderson's use of *Anon* as an idealised descriptor for the sphere from which the 'folk process' springs.

Keywords

Hamish Henderson – community – travelling people – *Anon* – tradition – folk culture – balladry – identity – politics

In 1955 Hamish Henderson embarked on his great 'tinker project'. This was to be a research programme that would deploy the full gamut of the University of Edinburgh's School of Scottish Studies' resources in an in-depth and wide-ranging survey of 'the entire traveller set-up in Scotland from a historical, anthropological and folk-cultural point of view'.[1] The 'discovery' behind this ambitious proposal appears frequently in Henderson's essays and articles. Its prominence increases over time, especially when later in his career Henderson sought to reconcile his work as a folk revivalist with that as a folklore scholar.

---

1   Hamish Henderson, *Alias MacAlias* (Edinburgh: Polygon, 2004), p. 168.

The revival was, at least in part, a project in cultivating class consciousness through a nationally framed and seemingly autochthonous cultural tradition. Though Henderson rejected Hugh MacDiarmid's faith in the intellectual vanguard, investing instead in the 'commonweal' and its inherent revolutionary potential, he did share the poet's notion that their ideals could be effectively engendered in art.[2] In contrast, the collection and analysis of folklore was, especially after the advent of the portable tape-recorder, an exercise in academic humility. Henderson wrestled with the vanity of the folklorist's work: charting a process defined by its boundlessness, and therefore by its capacity to transcend any ideological claims on its fundamental nature. Against this backdrop the 'discovery' of the travellers' lore came to represent a new extension of the field in folklore studies. After the balladry of the Borders and the northeast, and the folklore of the *Gàidhealtachd*, this was the 'third great zone of Scottish folk culture'.[3] The first two 'zones' can each be loosely associated with their respective developments in antiquarianism, song collection, and folk scholarship, through the Romantic period and the so-called Celtic Twilight. The popular and academic contexts for the discovery of this third 'zone' were, without the advantage of hindsight, more difficult for Henderson to articulate.

The folk culture of the travellers would not only provide scholars with untapped 'tradition bearers' and unrecorded song and tale variants; it would, according to Henderson, usher in a new era in the discipline. The relative dearth of folktales collected from the field in English and Scots was, for example, redressed in this 'discovery'. The status of established ballads and folk tale types was reaffirmed as they were found alive and well in the travellers' communities. And the geographical and historical coverage of traditional folk scholarship seemed suddenly to open up, reaching further and deeper than it had previously. The revivalist was encouraged by the vitality of this 'living tradition', but troubled by the circumstances that seemed to have fostered it because they were so distant from those in the urban centres where the revival was being staged. The folklorist was bolstered by the wealth of material uncovered, but unsettled by the deferral that comes with such a 'discovery': that the more of the folk process is glimpsed, the more this confirms that the whole is, indeed, unknowable.

---

2   See Henderson and MacDiarmid's various 'flytings' in the pages of *The Scotsman* (1959–60, 1964 and 1968) for a sense of the shared and contested grounds in their respective cultural politics. A selection of these exchanges is compiled in *The Armstrong Nose* (Edinburgh: Polygon, 1996), pp. 70–100, 117–41, 162–70.

3   Hamish Henderson, 'The Man with the Big Box', in *The Summer Walkers*, ed. by Timothy Neat (Edinburgh: Canongate, 2002), pp. 65–86 (p. 65).

These informants, or 'tradition-bearers', were distinguished by their mobility and their 'unpropertied lifestyle'.[4] They returned annually to the same camps, the same seasonal work, gathering and redistributing songs and tales along the way. The travellers belonged to no one locale, but were distinguished by their movement between settled communities. In Henderson's view therefore, their culture came to represent an 'unframed mirror within which Scotland can view and be herself – backwards and forwards in time'.[5] The travellers' cultural heritage as 'discovered' could function as a synecdoche for the vast, anonymous folk process at work in Scotland. It gave Henderson a way of channelling the local and the universal through a national framework, despite the dispassionate and decontextualised vision promised by an 'unframed' mirror. This chapter will examine Henderson's 'discovery' of the folk culture of the travelling community and the implications it had for his understanding of the place of folklore in modernity. It will then turn to Henderson's veneration for the anonym and his notion 'Alias MacAlias', used to conceptualise the interconnections and interstices between Scotland's folk and literary traditions. Finally, the chapter will consider some of the ways in which Henderson's long and often fraught relationship with these ideas might help inform our analyses of the ways in which the national literary tradition was imagined in the twentieth century.[6]

Travelling People and the Folk Process

From his first official experience of fieldwork – 1951, armed with a portable tape recorder, and investigating alongside Alan Lomax (1915–2002), the renowned American folklorist – and through his appointment to the School of Scottish Studies in 1952, Henderson often encountered 'Scotland's indigenous nomads'. Their contributions impressed upon him the profundity of a culture that was the 'most substantially ancient', but also the most 'vital', of Scotland's various 'towering folk traditions'.[7] The travellers, for instance, exhibited a living connection with the great ballad tradition, one that did not appear to have relied on scholarly interventions or publications for its transmission.

---

4   Henderson, as cited by Neat, *The Summer Walkers*, p. 195.
5   Henderson, as cited by Neat, *The Summer Walkers*, p. 195.
6   For an in-depth examination of Henderson's work, see Corey Gibson, *The Voice of the People: Hamish Henderson and Scottish Cultural Politics* (Edinburgh: Edinburgh University Press, 2015).
7   Henderson, 'The Man with the Big Box', p. 65.

Perhaps Henderson's 'greatest discovery', certainly his most celebrated, was that in 1953 of the singer Jeannie Robertson (1908–75). He later remarked that he could walk from Robertson's house, where Child ballads and recent compositions were sung side-by-side, to the Library at King's College, University of Aberdeen, where the ballad scholar Gavin Greig's manuscripts were preserved. In 'a short journey in space and time' he would find himself among researchers working on the mistaken assumption that these papers were 'relics' of a now-vanished culture.[8] Henderson travelled between these sites, drawing both from the living (the song as sung) and the latent (the song in the archive). Due in no small part to Henderson's own work, it has long been understood that the ballads, not to mention folk tales and other traditional song forms, predate their first documented appearances, often by some considerable distance.[9]

The nomadic community to which Robertson belonged had, until recent generations, been substantially non-literate. Despite the fact that increasing numbers of travellers were settling in the immediate post-war years, Henderson found a cultural inheritance that appeared to have circumvented, or at least diminished, the influence of those hallmarks of the modern world that were frequently blamed for the suppression, or dispersal, of folk culture elsewhere: print, the educational establishment, mass culture, urbanisation, and industrialisation. In the explanatory notes, appendices, and introductory essays of many folklorists, and later, in the clubs and ceilidhs frequented by purists in the burgeoning folk music scene, the socio-historical contexts that separate us from the communities out of which these older ballads and songs first sprung were something to be regretted, elided, or even denied completely. Though collectors and antiquarians traditionally framed their task in terms of preservation, the extinction that threatened their artefacts was always imminent, but never realised.[10] Among the modern revivalists in particular, folk music was not to be regarded as a measure of historical or cultural distance, but of consanguinity, of something shared and inherited precisely because of its continually reaffirmed relevance. In this sense, history stands to either corrupt or displace the common folk inheritance. This, in turn, gives a great deal of cultural authority to a

---

8   Henderson, *Alias MacAlias*, p. 38.
9   See Hamish Henderson, 'The Ballad and Popular Tradition to 1660', in *The History of Scottish Literature, Volume 1: Origins to 1660*, ed. by R.D.S. Jack, 4 vols (Aberdeen: Aberdeen University Press, 1988), pp. 263–83. Henderson, *Alias MacAlias*, pp. 78–94.
10   Henderson was perturbed, for example, at the moribund status of folk culture implied by the title posthumously given to a selection from Gavin Greig and the Rev. James Duncan's folk song collection, *Last Leaves of Traditional Ballads and Ballad Airs* (1925), in *Alias MacAlias*, pp. 20, 38, 132.

group who appear to function as custodians for a once common, now largely lost, folklore. The travellers invite speculative histories, and therefore, alternate presents. In keeping with the more patronising practices and assumptions of the Romantic folklorist, the travelling people were, therefore, liable to be cast as 'contemporary ancestors' for the nation, even in the twentieth century.[11] Where some modern literary figures, such as Edwin Muir and Fionn MacColla, reflected on the national cultural inheritance that had been denied by the Reformation,[12] Henderson focused not on transformational events or conjectural histories but on the fragments of folk culture that seemed to have survived *despite* history, and the prevailing cultural, political, and social conditions of modernity. This led him to develop a distinctive rhetoric on this subject: he frequently referred to the 'underground', 'chthonic' character of folk culture, and to its perennially embattled, subaltern status.[13]

In describing the qualities of folk song, Henderson had a great number of epithets and metaphors. One of these – 'living on the lips of the people' – he used to invoke the durability and immediacy of folk culture.[14] In the travellers, he found a people whose folk culture seemed to live almost entirely on the lips. He would later regard this 'discovery' as a defining phase in his career, one so critical to the young folklorist's ideas, and especially his notion of the 'folk process', that it seemed to him to be fate that brought them together.[15] Here was a living archive that not only showed what had thrived through oral transmission and what had remained relevant to the lives of the travelling people, but also described the lineage of these songs and tales. In the performance of a travelling person from an established nomadic clan like the Stewarts, Whytes, or MacPhees, Henderson could project onto that song or tale an informed line

---

11   Neat uses this phrase in *The Summer Walkers*. It is most commonly associated with William Goodell Frost's infamous article on the mountain communities of Eastern Kentucky, which were said to have preserved the folk cultures of the colonists and people of the frontier, 'Our Contemporary Ancestors in the Southern Mountains', *Atlantic Monthly*, 83 (March 1899), 311–19.

12   See Edwin Muir, *Scott and Scotland: The Predicament of the Scottish Writer* (Edinburgh: Polygon, 1982) and Fionn MacColla, *At the Sign of the Clenched Fist* (Edinburgh: M. MacDonald, 1967).

13   See 'Enemies of Folk-song' (1955), 'The Underground of Song' (1963), and 'Zeus as Curly Snake: The Chthonian Image' (1995) for a sense of how this terminology was used in the early days of the revival compared to its later, more conceptual deployment, in *Alias MacAlias*, pp. 45–50, 31–36, 427–35.

14   Henderson, *Alias MacAlias*, p. 45.

15   Timothy Neat, *Poetry Becomes People (1952–2002)* Vol. 2, *Hamish Henderson: A Biography* (Edinburgh: Polygon, 2009), p. 23.

of descent, secure in the knowledge that its living context had not been so wholly transformed in the years between its conception and the present, as it had with those proffered by his other, settled informants. In the discovery of a more concentrated and resilient body of living folk-song, Henderson rediscovered what Greig had found in the northeast around the turn of the century: 'folk-song admits of no delimitation either in a geographical or a secular way, reaching forth ultimately to the ends of the earth through countless affinities, and back to primeval times through an unbroken chain of derivation'.[16]

In his fieldwork Henderson found that the travellers were also quite conscious of those qualities that made their culture, and the place of folklore in particular, distinctive. One young 'tinker' differentiated his people from the 'Irish tramp': 'That sort of lad just lives from day to day, but we (tinkers) live entirely in the past'.[17] This worldview might find a causal explanation in the lifestyle and lore repeated and revisited with every intergenerational transition: migratory patterns, sites for and types of itinerant labour – pearl fishing and berry picking – rituals, etiquette, superstitions, songs and tales. Generation, however, cuts both ways. It can be conceived as cohort: a broad, horizontal relationship with the living that stretches to a mass of anonymous peers; or as descent: a narrow, vertical relationship extending to the long dead and the not yet born.[18] The travellers, at least in Henderson's account, have the latter conception at the heart of their community identity, perhaps to the expense of the former. In this way, the singular song performance stands as a symbol of the accumulated generations that have precipitated it. On hearing Robertson's recording of 'Lord Donald, my son' (version B of Child no. 12 'Lord Randal') Willa Muir recognised this dynamic:

> I was at once caught up into a timeless world – a world, at least, where time bore no relation to the clock, giving a curiously reassuring sense of endless duration [...]. The singer's voice is quite impersonal; she is merely the vehicle through which flows a remarkable sense of duration, almost of inevitable ceremony and ritual.[19]

Henderson repeated the American folklorist Marguerite Olney's comments on Robertson's style: 'no trained singer could possibly imitate it. It has to be inherited'.[20]

---

16   Gavin Greig, *Folksong of the North-East* (1963), as cited in *Alias MacAlias*, p. 93.

17   Henderson, *Alias MacAlias*, p. 229. Parenthesis in original.

18   This distinction is examined in depth in David I. Kertzer, 'Generation as a Sociological Problem', *Annual Review of Sociology*, 9 (1983), 125–49.

19   Willa Muir, *Living with Ballads* (London: Hogarth, 1965), pp. 44–46.

20   Henderson, *Alias MacAlias*, p. 21.

The travellers became symbolic of this inheritance. Nevertheless, Henderson did acknowledge that the travellers did not live in a vacuum. Before he set out on the 'tinker project', his encounters with the travellers were not always immersive studies limited to a coherent or self-identifying community; they were often more transient, and very mixed affairs, such as the picking season in the berry fields of Blair.

Here, the travelling people made up only part of the pool of informants. The other major constituency was the urban working-class families pleased to have a holiday in the countryside that would pay for itself:

> But the pickers who give the berry fields their distinctive atmosphere, who set the tone, and do most to make the whole area a vast pounding maelstrom of folk music and song are the 'travellers'. [...] They, in chief, are the carriers, dispensers, performers and glorifiers of one of the most voluminous oral cultures in Europe, and the all-star cast of the world's most successful unofficial folk festival.[21]

Henderson co-opts this 'festival', implying its complicity in the project of popular folk revivalism despite the fact that it appears to preclude any effort at a cultural-political agenda. Deploying another of his favourite images, this time to describe the act of collecting, Henderson wrote of recording in the berry fields as like holding a 'tin-can under the Niagara Falls; in a single session you can hear everything from ancient Ossianic hero-tales, whose content reflects the life of primitive tribesmen, to the caustic pop-song parodies thought up by Clydeside teenagers the same afternoon'.[22] In this scene, the ancient but vital folk culture of the travellers is set alongside the folk idiom of the city children and their lampoons of contemporary music hall and radio hits. The fixed parameters of a concerted study on the travelling people's particular folk culture might have appealed to Henderson – the connection between the living and the ancient was, after all, the aspect he celebrated most fervently. However, it was the comparison with the world of settled populations, and especially with the more diluted and transient folk culture they seemed to sustain, that made them interesting in the first place.

The travellers are, wrote Henderson, 'a small minority group, but they are generous, frequently noble and aristocratic people tied together by kinship, lifestyle, and historical circumstance'.[23] This triple bond inspires and sustains

---

21   Henderson, *Alias MacAlias*, p. 101.
22   Henderson, *Alias MacAlias*, p. 102.
23   Henderson, 'The Man with the Big Box', p. 66.

the myriad ways in which travellers measure their distance from settled communities, and from the established authorities that govern the behaviour of those populations. For instance, Henderson notes that the travellers' language, cant, was often deployed as a kind of 'cover tongue', 'to be used when the speaker wants to disguise his meaning' from 'flatties' ('non-tinkers').[24] This measuring of distance from the structures that bind wider society is also a major structural feature in Betsy Whyte's popular memoirs, *The Yellow on the Broom* (1979) and *Red Rowans and Wild Honey* (1990).[25] The title of the former refers to the seasonal prompt for the family to 'escape' from the 'dark wee hole' of the house they wintered in, and go out 'into the open air again'.[26] The title of the latter refers to the joys and sorrows of life; the metaphor similarly lifted from the roadside. Nobility, gentry, policemen, 'cruelty men',[27] farmers, schoolmasters, doctors and gamekeepers all recur; and the Welfare State and the Second World War also make their incursions. Henderson was careful to emphasise the 'persecution complex' suffered by this community, and in typical style, he turned to lore to substantiate his claims.[28] While 'flatties' have long traded on the image of the 'tinker' as 'child-stealer', Henderson discovered an equally well-established, and more potent fear among the travellers – that of the 'burkers' and 'noddies', murderers or body-snatchers and medical students respectively, who were said to lie in wait and take travellers separated from their group to supply the medical schools with cadavers. The travellers threaten the settled community's sense of itself, and serve as bogeymen for the children; the doctors are symbolic of the institutionalised world from which the travellers are separated. If they are to come into contact, this behemoth will literally consume the traveller. In this example, Henderson's rendering of the 'unframed mirror' through which Scotland might see itself is borne out.[29] The folk beliefs of this community emerge not in direct response to their opposites, but in a more nuanced reflection of these reciprocal constructions of the 'other'.

It is this reflective quality that later prompted poststructuralist thinkers to adopt 'nomadism' as a notion that challenges the logic of the nation, the state,

---

24   Henderson, *Alias MacAlias*, pp. 229, 238.
25   Like Jeannie Robertson, Betsy Whyte had a long-standing relationship with the School of Scottish Studies and with Henderson in particular. See the School's archives: <http://www.tobarandualchais.co.uk>.
26   Epigraph, Betsy Whyte, *The Yellow on the Broom* (Edinburgh: Chambers, 1979).
27   Term used in particular to refer to inspectors for the National Society for the Prevention of Cruelty to Children, but often for any representative of local authorities, or the State.
28   Henderson, *Alias MacAlias*, p. 230.
29   Neat, *The Summer Walkers*, p. 195.

and the historical narratives that describe them.[30] However, if the travelling people exist outside of and as a counterpoint to these structures, Henderson would have to proceed carefully in his efforts to extrapolate wider truths about the 'folk process' from their example, unless he was willing to concede that folk culture functions as myth, opposed to, and outside of, history. As a counterpoint for national self-reflection the travellers' culture lets Scotland 'view and be herself – backwards and forwards in time' in the sense that it exists entirely in a sphere that predates and precludes the national past.[31] It does not furnish those outside of that community with a vision of their future; it gives them a glimpse of something that will be unchanged by it. In *Out Of History* Cairns Craig reminds us that in Walter Scott's novels, history is enacted alongside the counter-history it inevitably invokes.[32] We might see Henderson, and the difficulties incurred by the folklorist more generally, as outliers in Craig's analysis. Confronting the living past of the travellers' worldview means acknowledging the failures and obstinacy of the dominant models of historical understanding during the preceding two hundred years. To turn to the travellers and to 'nomadism' is one way (though perhaps not the one intended) of taking Craig's closing directive to heart: 'listen for the voices from the dark, listen to the mingling of the voices in and out of history'.[33]

As Willa Muir recognised in Robertson's performance, the travellers' song culture conjures a 'timeless world' and inspires a sense of 'endless duration'. It does not speak of 'progress' or of the 'slow march' of history. In his introduction to Duncan and Linda Williamson's collection of stories of the Scottish travelling people, Henderson struck upon some word play that, perhaps inadvertently, embodies this disjuncture. Describing the pervasiveness of the 'Happy Man's Shirt' tale type and specifically its relationship with Hans Christian Andersen's 'The Shoes of Happiness', where we are taught that happiness is not derived from material belongings nor even from basic provisions like shoes or clothes, he concludes: 'Luck and happiness are everywhere, it seems, *sans chemise*, if not *sans culotte*'.[34] The moral remains constant, only the details differ. The travellers' culture is one that heads out shirtless 'into the open air', free from context. Historicism collapses because even in their high drama the songs

---

30   See Pierre Clastres, *Society against the State* (1974), Gilles Deleuze and Félix Guattari, *A Thousand Plateaus* (1980), and Rosi Braidotti, *Nomadic Subjects* (1994).

31   Neat, *The Summer Walkers*, p. 195.

32   Cairns Craig, *Out of History: Narrative Paradigms in Scottish and British Culture* (Edinburgh: Polygon, 1996), pp. 70–72.

33   Craig, *Out of History*, p. 225.

34   Henderson, *Alias MacAlias*, p. 222.

and tales embody 'endless duration', a constant equilibrium. They are not embroiled in the revolutionary forces (*sans-culottes*) of history. In an early article promoting the folk revival, Henderson reflected on the power of balladry to rewrite past events, claiming victories for the clans, for example, that were in fact spectacular defeats: 'If history, as Ernst Toller said, is the propaganda of the victors, balladry is very often the propaganda of the defeated'.[35] Henderson sought out an indomitable 'folk process' resistant to all the forces that might threaten it, from the Reformation through the Industrial Revolution, and the dawn of mass culture. Among the travelling people he found a long-established proof for this theory, yet the success of this ancient but vital folk culture seemed to rely on the very fact that it had not been reconciled with modernity. Its resistance to these historical forces was not radical, but passive and adventitious.

Throughout the 1950s and 1960s Henderson's fieldwork, his archival work, and his assiduous studies tracing the potential descent of song and tale fragments, convinced him of the endless adaptability of the folk process. The travellers equipped him with a dense complex of observable connections to the oldest documented evidence of this process. But elsewhere, Henderson found traces of a nimbler, more thoroughly transformative aspect, one that seemed to absorb or respond to new socio-historical contexts altogether more successfully. The folk revival, for example, saw new generations of singers from the urban centres very consciously take up the mantle. Combining his findings as a folklorist, and his conviction as a revivalist, Henderson began to see that this folk process moved at various speeds. Political songs written to popular melodies with a great degree of assumed knowledge on current affairs would wax and wane far more quickly than a Child ballad. There were always precedents and antecedents that went unnoticed. In fact, the process was predominantly unobservable, and the travellers represented an anomaly in this regard. They sustained a visible folk culture that appeared to have thrived due to its isolation. In describing this quality, Henderson often reached for Federico García Lorca. The Andalusian poet venerated gypsy folk culture, in particular, the *cante jondo* or 'deep song', where depth denotes not only profundity or emotional poignancy, but longevity and resilience. 'Deep song' is that which has remained constant while history happens all around. Those strains of the great 'folk process' that are not propelled solely by oral transmission – the chapbooks, ballad scholar's manuscripts, field recordings, LPs, radio broadcasts – are less dissolvable. They provide us with markers against which we might intimate the greater process, which is vast, unknowable, and *oral*.

---

35   Henderson, *Alias MacAlias*, p. 29.

The travellers helped Henderson to mediate between these two extremes – between the documentary and the ethereal, the deep songs and the shallow.

Becoming *Anon*

If the travellers' culture was cast as a living model of the folk process, this did not necessarily help Henderson in formulating his cultural political agenda. Here was proof of the possibility of a simultaneously ancient and vital folk culture. However, it was not instigated, it was simply inherited. It could not provide a viable blueprint for the 'genuine people's culture' he hoped to elicit in modern Scottish society.[36] The greater part of Henderson's written work, from his translations of the Italian Marxist Antonio Gramsci to his autobiographical sketches, can be seen in light of this aim, the foundation of which was put succinctly in the 1952 Edinburgh People's Festival Programme: '[to restore] Scottish folksong to the ordinary people in Scotland, not merely as a bobbysoxer vogue, but deeply and integrally'.[37] Like Gramsci in his prison notebooks, and MacDiarmid in his public flytings, the travellers articulated a challenge that would be constant throughout Henderson's long career: explaining the political relevance of folk culture in the present, and for the future. His discoveries as a folk scholar aided his response to this challenge, giving him grounds for the notion of an adaptable and indomitable folk process constantly at work 'underground'. This is not to say that Henderson regarded folklore as perennially counter-cultural. It was not so contrived. The folk process is involuntary and inimitable, and, most importantly, it is communal.

In order to account for the vast folk process without jeopardising the cultural and political integrity of the modern folk revivalist's project, Henderson needed to find ways of talking about it that would neither spin off into pure abstraction, nor focus too narrowly on the individual song or song performance. On the one hand he risked disconnecting the process from those who sustained it, and on the other he was vulnerable to that greatest sin of the modern Scottish writer: parochialism. This dilemma prompted Henderson to turn to the anonym, where folk culture and literary history often coincide. Timothy Neat reports that one of Henderson's favourite phrases was: 'when you become *Anon*, you've arrived'.[38] This describes not only his creative endeavour – he was thrilled when his songs were thought to be 'traditional' – but also describes

---

36   Henderson, 'Freedom Becomes People', *Chapman*, 42 (1985), 1–7 (p. 1).

37   Henderson, *Alias MacAlias*, p. xxiv.

38   Neat, *Poetry Becomes People*, p. 317. Italics in original.

what Neat refers to as his use of 'invisibility' as a 'cultural weapon', and his implementation of a 'silent "underground methodology"'.[39] To win accession to *Anon* is, in this account, to deploy a purposeful cultural-political strategy. The relative dearth of published creative works in Henderson's corpus is often explained in these terms.[40] Indeed, it has become a measure of his commitment to the cultivation of a so-called 'genuine people's culture' that he would happily forsake his potential as an 'art-poet' – the promise of the *Elegies for the Dead in Cyrenaica* (1948) and the recognition of the Somerset Maugham Award (1949) – in favour of a self-effacing dissolution in the anonymous mass of 'tradition-bearers'.

In an important essay on the history of Scots in folk song and literature, titled 'At the Foot o' yon Excellin' Brae' (1983), and ranging from the popular ballads to the poets of the mid-twentieth century, Henderson reflected:

> If prose and poetry in a self-conscious literary Scots came increasingly [by the 1940s] to seem documentations of a sad case of arrested development, the anonymous ballad-makers continued on their way, knowing little and caring less of the niceties of hyperborean lingo and prosody. They were, in any case, operating in a zone which ignored national and political boundaries.[41]

Anon promises freedom from artifice and conceit. The anonymous song-makers are unmoved by the pursuit of innovation or originality in form or subject, unfettered by philology or linguistics, and unconcerned with the cultural claims of the nation. Henderson compared the anonym and the poetaster in terms of intent: the poet who 'operated with a hopeful eye to print' was set beside those who 'spontaneously and for preference entrusted their wares to the discerning minds and deft mobile tongues of the traditional singers'. He celebrated the historical 'predilection for making direct oral contact with a receptive community', and insisted on its continuance in the twentieth century, particularly through the performances, publications, and workshops that were crucial to the programme of the popular revival.[42] The designation, *Anon*, especially when used by a folklorist, invokes the Romantic ballad collection,

---

39   Neat, *Poetry Becomes People*, p. 317.

40   See Joy Hendry, 'The Scottish Accent of the Mind', in *Borne on the Carrying Stream: The Legacy of Hamish Henderson*, ed. by Eberhard Bort (Ochtertyre: Grace Note, 2010), pp. 195–203, and Neat, 'The Unknown Soldier', *Scotland on Sunday*, 11 November 2007, [n.p.].

41   Henderson, *Alias MacAlias*, p. 53.

42   Henderson, *Alias MacAlias*, pp. 72–73.

but Henderson's use has an interesting inflection: it is not simply a signed marker for what is not known – the name of the author – but rather becomes a common pseudonym for all of the unnamed. To aspire to *Anon* is to hope to borrow the authority of the accumulated works that share this status. As short-hand for the collective and cumulative it overlaps with the 'folk process', and as such, its usefulness as a 'weapon', a methodology, or a strategy, is limited. It is disengaged from any agenda that these terms might imply in the moment of its becoming. *Anon*, like the 'folk process', will not be directed or overseen.

The word 'anonymous' first came into the English language in the sixteenth century, 'as if it took print to make the absence of an author's name an important fact'.[43] In the early-nineteenth century unattributed literary works were as numerous as those with named authors. By the beginning of the twentieth century this use of the term, as concerned with authorship, was most commonly associated with the discussion of ancient literary works, or else traditional song and folk poetry. Anne Ferry describes the literary history and origins of the word 'anonymity' (and its parent adjective) in an effort to explain how it became 'so packed with presuppositions and preoccupations that we can often sense the structure of feelings associated with it to be present even in contexts where the word is not explicitly used'.[44] This means going beyond the root – 'without name' – and pushing into twentieth-century lexical meanings long separated from the issue of authorship, and comprising the impersonal and the indistinguishable, especially in the modern city. This is anonymity as a cultural phenomenon. Neither of these approaches is, however, sufficient with regard to Henderson's use of *Anon*. It does not describe an absence, nor does it necessarily conjure anxieties about mass culture and modernity. Instead, it is aligned like the travellers' folk culture, with a vast cohort of creative agents and 'tradition-bearers' wielding a collective and cumulative influence.

In his 1925 pamphlet on anonymity, E.M. Forster comes closer to a compatible concept. Gesturing towards but not arriving at Barthes's 'Death of the Author' (1967), Forster asserts that 'all literature tends toward a condition of anonymity [...;] it wants not to be signed [...]. It is alive – not in a vague complementary sense – but alive tenaciously, and it is always covering up the tracks that connect it with the laboratory'.[45] In this formulation, then, the question of

---

43   John Mullan, *Anonymity: A Secret History of English Literature* (London: Faber and Faber, 2007), p. 296.

44   Anne Ferry, 'Anonymity: The Literary History of a Word', *New Literary History*, 33 (2002), 193–214 (p. 194).

45   E.M. Forster, *Anonymity: An Enquiry* (London: Hogarth, 1925), p. 14.

a named author is immaterial; anonymity is contingent to literature. These are the truths Henderson found, though more explicitly so, in the 'folk process'. Its vitality comes from those aspects of itself that are most difficult to isolate: its origins and its reach. Indeed, Henderson insisted that the divergence of song and poetry was 'a passing phenomenon', that for the greater part of their existence this distinction was not needed, and that they would return again to this state.[46] To reach for *Anon* was to reach for this pre-history, and this promised future. As with the travelling people, the anonym was a way of conceiving of the 'timeless world' that has never diminished though it has been neglected. However, to insist that the greater part of modernity has been an anomaly in this respect is not an easily defensible position. Henderson tried to show that, in fact, this truth was consummated even in the present, and could be traced throughout the Scottish literary tradition, not just among those who wrote, sung, or lived, in Craig's terms, entirely 'out of history'.

The most striking feature of Scottish literature was, for Henderson, the 'constant fruitful cross-fertilisation' between 'high-art' and the 'native demotic tradition'.[47]

> [O]ne has the impression that many ballads which now exist in numerous variants must have stemmed from original versions composed by craftsmen-balladeers who took the inherited skills of their art very seriously indeed. By the same token, art-poets have often operated like folk-poets, appropriating opening lines or even whole stanzas from earlier or contemporary authors or from popular tradition – and using them as a basis for their own productions.[48]

Given the proximity of Henderson's notions of *Anon* and of the 'folk process', we can see that not only does literature 'tend toward' anonymity, as Forster would have it, but that the anonym is also present in the work of the named author. The 'folk process' will always infiltrate the literary, but this relationship, at least in Henderson's understanding, sits closer to the surface in the Scottish tradition. The major influence in the development of Henderson's conception of *Anon*, the 'communal bin' foraged in by art-poets and folk-poets alike, was not Robert Burns but Hugh MacDiarmid.[49] Though the great doyen of the Scottish Literary Renaissance is renowned

---

46   Henderson, *Alias MacAlias*, p. 451.

47   Henderson, *Alias MacAlias*, p. 4.

48   Henderson, *Alias MacAlias*, p. 427.

49   Henderson, *Alias MacAlias*, p. 430.

for lifting entire passages from other writers, through extensive quotation and audacious plagiarism alike, Henderson placed this practice in a broader context and came to see MacDiarmid as a paragon for the whole sweep of the Scottish literary tradition.

The Golden Treasury of Scottish Poetry (1940), edited by MacDiarmid, is an anthology replete with ballads and other anonymous works. They are scattered throughout, appearing alongside medieval makars, Romantic poets, translations from Gaelic and Latin, and contemporary figures alike. With typical flair, MacDiarmid writes in his introduction: 'It is certainly no exaggeration to say that it is with Scottish literature as it is with an iceberg – only a small fraction of it is visible above the obliterating flood'.[50] In Henderson's terms, the flood obliterates authorship first; it is the vast, perdurable drift of folk culture from which the literary emerges. MacDiarmid goes on to cite at some length W.J. Entwistle's tome *European Balladry* (1939), which remains one of the most ambitious and accessible surveys on this subject:

> Entwistle writes of the ballads and folk-songs that 'have clung to life, sometimes during four to seven centuries, and that without any aid from courtly society, nor from the schools [...] nor from official literature, contemptuous of such wild snatches'. Since Scottish poetry has not developed away from these great staples of poetry to anything like the same extent, it is at once a reassurance [...] and a warning with regard to English poetry to read [...] that the amazing survival and appeal 'in widest commonalty spread' of these kinds of poetry is 'a glory not often achieved by the great artistic poets, and, when achieved, it is through some partial endowment of the generous ballad simplicity'.[51]

Despite the dismissive, and sometimes fierce, attitude MacDiarmid later expressed with regard to the modern folk revival, his conception of the Scottish literary tradition rested on the claims that balladry and folk-song allowed him to make.[52] This was typical of those who identified with the prospect of a national literary renaissance. In his 1948 pamphlet *The Scottish Renaissance*, the anthologist Maurice Lindsay insisted that contemporary successes in 'closing the gap' between poetry and the public were due to the national literary

---

50   *The Golden Treasury of Scottish Poetry*, ed. by Hugh MacDiarmid (London: Macmillan, 1941), p. xiv.

51   MacDiarmid, *The Golden Treasury of Scottish Poetry*, p. xviii.

52   In particular, see MacDiarmid's contributions to the so-called 'Folk-song Flyting' of 1964, in *The Armstrong Nose*, pp. 117–41.

tradition and its fundamentally 'popular (i.e. of the people)' character, as opposed to the 'rarefied, aesthetic varieties' of the English canon.[53]

Henderson also drew from MacDiarmid's poetry to reaffirm his notion of the pervasive influence of *Anon* in the Scottish literary tradition. He speculated that the poet might have been thinking of a singer like Jeannie Robertson when he wrote in 'First Hymn to Lenin':

> Descendant o' the unkent Bards wha made
> Sangs peerless through a' post-anonymous days,
> I glimpse again in you that mighty poo'er
> Than fashes wi' the laurels and the bays
> But kens that it is shared by ilka man
>   Since time began.[54]

Again, the perseverance of anonymous song in the age of the named author is a constant reminder of that 'mighty poo'er' that is not concerned with plaudits but with timelessness and universality. Henderson was not alone in ascribing something of the force of anonymous song to MacDiarmid's work. In his contribution to a collection of poems dedicated to the poet on his seventy-fifth birthday, Norman MacCaig wrote:

> Kick him – that's nothing. Kick his ideas, then
> The poor rise up, the dead slide from their stones.
> Then he's himself and he's Anonymous.
> It's not his hand that strikes, but everyone's.[55]

Henderson revelled in the absence of a 'hard and fast line between the "popular" arts and the "elite" arts of individual excellence' in Scotland.[56] In articulating the receptiveness of Scottish literature to all that is denoted by *Anon*, Henderson took up the notion of 'Alias MacAlias'. He adapted the phrase from Moray Maclaren's *New Statesman* article 'MacAliases' (1960), which described the pervasiveness of 'Scottish anonymists and pseudonymists' as compared with other national literatures.

---

53   Maurice Lindsay, *The Scottish Renaissance* (Edinburgh: Serif, 1948), pp. 5–6.

54   MacDiarmid, 'First Hymn to Lenin', as cited by Henderson, *Alias MacAlias*, p. 430.

55   Norman MacCaig, 'Hugh MacDiarmid (1)', in *Poems Addressed to Hugh MacDiarmid and Presented to him on his Seventy-Fifth Birthday*, ed. by Duncan Glen (Preston: Akros, 1967), p. 31.

56   Henderson, *Alias MacAlias*, p. 430.

Modelled on MacDiarmid, Henderson's notion of the 'Alias MacAlias' stands for that confluence of original arrangement and the vast complex of direct sources and indirect influences that go into the conception of a literary work. It stands, therefore, as the nexus between the named author and *Anon*. To demonstrate his thinking, Henderson pointed to well-known instances in MacDiarmid's corpus: Glyn Jones's prose versified in 'Perfect'; Compton Mackenzie's role in 'The Little White Rose of Scotland'; and Erich Heller's article on Karl Kraus for the *Times Literary Supplement*, which became a portion of *In Memoriam James Joyce*.[57] Perhaps the most satisfying for Henderson's purposes is the example of 'Jenny Nettles', an anonymous eighteenth-century folk song that supplied the first and third lines of one of MacDiarmid's most celebrated early lyrics, 'Empty Vessel'. While MacDiarmid's debt to John Jamieson's *Etymological Dictionary of the Scottish Language* (1808) is well understood, Henderson suggests we look deeper and consider that the words he found there had come from the folk poetry he claimed to despise. In this instance, the original folk source had likely reached the poet through David Herd's *Ancient and Modern Scottish Songs* (1776).[58] 'Plagiarists of genius', writes Henderson, 'are the justified sinners of literature'.[59]

Within Henderson's corpus there are a series of essays tracing folk songs and tales through their many incarnations. By isolating plot structures, tropes, motifs, or lexical features, any given variant can be analysed in the context of its other known relations, probable lines of descent can be sketched, and the significance of any one phrase can be considered in light of its recurrence among the fragments with which the scholar plots the 'folk process'. For Henderson the Scottish literary tradition, and MacDiarmid's work in particular, invites the same kind of analysis. Indeed, the influence of folk song is explicit in much of the Scots poetry most often associated with the interwar Scottish Literary Renaissance. This becomes especially apparent in the work of those writers who perhaps shared many of MacDiarmid's characteristics, particularly with regard to style and the example of the early lyrics, but who were not so in thrall to the editorial agenda, its fierce promotion and its haughty defence. Violet Jacob, Marion Angus, and William Soutar, for example, make

---

57   On Glynn Jones and 'Perfect', see *Alias MacAlias*, p. 438; on Compton Mackenzie and 'The Little White Rose of Scotland', see Alan Bold, *MacDiarmid: Christopher Murray Grieve: A Critical Biography* (London: John Murray, 1998), pp. 429–30; on Erich Heller and *In Memoriam James Joyce*, see Henderson, *The Armstrong Nose* (Edinburgh: Polygon, 1996), pp. 174–81, 189–93.

58   Henderson, *Alias MacAlias*, p. 443.

59   Henderson, *Alias MacAlias*, p. 439.

extensive use of the ballad stanza, and various other motifs and tropes typical of Scottish folksong. However, Henderson came to apply this interpretative framework more broadly. Any literary historical study was incomplete without sensitivity to the 'folk process'. In one sense, to imagine a literary tradition is to subsume the '"elite" arts of individual excellence' into a continuum that foregrounds a causal or developmental narrative. Given the boundlessness of the 'folk process', Henderson was predisposed to complicate this trajectory and provide a looser, more permeable account of the national literary tradition. In seeking out those instances where *Anon* pokes through, where a vital and ancient folk culture like the travellers' can be glimpsed, Henderson not only suggested that the literary critic prioritise the relationship between literary and folk production, he proposed that the practices of the 'folk process' be emulated by writers in the interests of inciting a 'genuine people's culture'. The contradiction at the heart of Henderson's cultural politics is revealed in this combination of the active and passive. He encourages us to submit to the anonymous process that abides just beneath the surface of our literary cultures, whilst purposefully setting out to instigate a conscious engagement with, or emulation of, this process. Agency belongs, therefore, both to us and to the folk culture with which we are negotiating. Neither seems able to exert dominance over the other.

The 'tinker project' of 1955 was intended to do more than satisfy Henderson's academic interests. If he could understand the travelling people from a 'historical, anthropological and folk-cultural point of view', perhaps he could better understand the ways in which a 'genuine people's culture' is sustained. These lessons would seem invaluable for the 'principal strategist' of the modern folk revival. Due to its relative isolation, and its reliance on a sense of the past and its presence, the travellers' folk culture animated songs and tales that were, by the middle years of the twentieth century, thought to have been the reserve of folklore scholars. Through the revival Henderson hoped to re-establish the popularity of these works in communities that had not 'inherited' them; that had, through the incursions of socio-historical change, apparently been denied this cultural continuity. However, it was clear that the conditions that made this continuity possible (or, at least, a belief in the possibility of such continuity) could not be fabricated. The 'endless duration' evoked by Jeannie Robertson's performances, the distinguishing feature of the psychology of the 'tinker' – 'living entirely in the past' – and the 'ancient' and 'vital' qualities of the folk culture, all contributed to Henderson's conception of the 'unframed mirror' through which Scotland might see itself and move freely among contested histories and possible and impossible communities. Henderson's experience of the travellers represented what Edwin Muir called a 'time-accident' when describing his move from the Orkney of his childhood, reminiscent of the eighteenth century, to the Glasgow of his young adulthood in the twentieth century.[60] It was a pre-industrial and even pre-national past against which modernity and history could be measured. As such, it demonstrated a political passivity that troubled Henderson. To harness popular folk culture as a force for political and social change, as Henderson ventured, was to contradict the observable constants of the 'folk process' – those made visible by the travellers.

Beyond literary authorship, anonymity inhabits a similarly contradictory space: it is politically passive in the sense that it guarantees some freedoms and inherently undermines others. A free election requires the secret ballot to protect us from external intimidation and corruption, for example. But while it may be deployed to protect the collective will, it can also be used to distort it – accountability is inversely proportional to anonymity in this regard. An equivalent tension is at work in the literary sphere. To accede to Henderson's vaulted *Anon* is to break the connection between author and text, or at least, to submerge it in a collective will that can barely be traced, let alone scrutinised with any authority. As Forster asserted, literature always seeks to conceal its provenance. Becoming *Anon* and submitting to the 'folk process' is simply the consummation of this tendency. Henderson knew that at many stages of the process 'individual minds [...] set their seal on new variants', but this kind of composition was distinguished by its immersion in 'musical and linguistic traditions', and by the 'time-honoured prescriptive idiom' that gave it shape, rather than by the individual efforts of the 'craftsman-poet'.[61] The task of the folklorist is to uncover the transmissions and byways of this boundless, anonymising process, despite the fact that its political and cultural significance (and its longevity) is derived from its resistance to such efforts.

If, as Henderson asserts, the Scottish literary tradition is distinguished by its 'constant fruitful cross-fertilisation' with the folk tradition, then it is exposed to the same tensions and contradictions that arise from his analyses of the travellers' culture and the power of *Anon*. Adopting Shelley's dictum, Liam McIlvanney has described modern Scottish novelists as 'unacknowledged legislators'.[62] In a similar vein, an aphorism attributed to Andrew Fletcher of

---

60   Edwin Muir, *The Story and the Fable: An Autobiography* (London: George Harrap, 1940), p. 263.

61   Henderson, *Alias MacAlias*, p. 73.

62   Liam McIlvanney, 'The Politics of Narrative in the Post-War Scottish Novel', in *On Modern British Fiction*, ed. by Zachary Leader (Oxford: Oxford University Press, 2002), p. 181–208 (p. 186).

Saltoun (1655–1716), which features on the Canongate Wall of the Scottish Parliament Building, reads: '(I knew a very wise man who believed that) if a man were permitted to make all the ballads, he need not care who should make the laws of a nation'.[63] Needless to say, Henderson was sympathetic to this message. These two statements – one from the period of the Union of the Parliaments, the other from the twenty-first century, though borrowed from the Romantic era – endow writers and balladeers with great political import. In the first the novelist is given an invisible role at least metaphorically equivalent to that of the lawmaker; in the second, the songwriters completely supplant the lawmakers. However, the 'unacknowledged' and the qualifying 'if' reveal a great deal. Shelley's original claim in *A Defence of Poetry* states:

> Poets are [...] the mirrors of the gigantic shadows which futurity casts upon the present, the words which express what they understand not, the trumpets which sing to battle and feel not what they inspire; the influence which is moved not, but moves. Poets are the unacknowledged legislators of the World.[64]

Like the travellers' folk culture, the poet is a mirror. That is not to say that the poets, or the travellers for that matter, are prophets. They are unconscious conduits for these bigger processes. While the writer, or the folk revivalist, might try to conceive of a greater ideal in its totality, in all of its possible iterations, and promote this in their work, they cannot escape this limitation: they are the 'influence which is moved not, but moves'. In Fletcher's statement, the 'if' is a concession to the fact that it is an impossible proposition to 'make all the ballads'. The 'folk process' on which the ballads rely is immune to the directives of any individuated agenda. Its political significance and its passivity are the ramifications of this fact. Both of these quotations are based on the impossibility of being conscious of this 'legislative' role in the act of creation. They are precise statements on the unattainable perspective that looks out with transhistorical omniscience and sees the sum of inherited cultural influences. The power Shelley and Fletcher invoke is the power that can only be realised by submission to the collective and communal force that Henderson describes in the 'folk process'.

---

63   As cited by Henderson, '"It Was in You That It A' Began": Some Thoughts on the Folk Conference', in *The People's Past: Scottish Folk, Scottish History*, ed. by Edward J. Cowan (Edinburgh: Polygon, 1980), pp. 4–15 (p. 6).

64   Percy Bysshe Shelley, *The Major Works*, ed. by Zachary Leader and Michael O'Neill (Oxford: Oxford University Press, 2003), pp. 674–701.

A fresh examination of the ways in which Henderson 'discovered' and sought to understand the 'folk process' might afford new insights into the origins and development of the central pillar of Scottish literary exceptionalism: its *democratic* tendency.[65] In the 1950s and 1960s, looking out on Scotland's literary and cultural tradition from the increasingly reified foundation of the 'folk process', Henderson was able to infer community from the songs that are sustained by it. Where many of the writers examined in the present volume perhaps deferred to the past, to the communities of their childhood, or else to the marked absence of community in their present, Henderson needed only to find a song, or even a tattered fragment. From there, a single line of descent could be confidently asserted (though its particular route might not be discerned), and, given the vastness and variety of the oral tradition, many more could be tentatively supposed.

Henderson thought both deductively and inductively about folk-song. He had predictions and assumptions about its process that he looked to prove through his scholarship and collecting, but conversely, he inferred a great deal from the mass of fragments and variants he compiled. A song's survival in the 'living tradition' is a small outpost of resistance to the overwhelming force of history and its tendency to absorb without trace the lives of those who go uncelebrated in its literature. Henderson sought to overcome the isolation of the artist in twentieth-century Scotland by committing himself to a community so immense that it excluded no one. In doing so he invalidated community based on any other principle: the locale, the faith group, the political party, the workers of a given industry, the family, and the nation are all transcended. Henderson described the impossibility of this expansive form of community even while arguing for it.

---

65   The resilience and pervasiveness of this conception among critics, especially in the period since devolution and through more recent debates about constitutional resettlement, has attracted some scrutiny in recent years; see Alex Thomson, '"You can't get there from here": Devolution and Scottish Literary History', *International Journal of Scottish Literature*, 3 (2007); and Scott Hames, 'On Vernacular Scottishness and its Limits: Devolution and the Spectacle of "Voice"', *Studies in Scottish Literature*, 39.1 (2013), 203–24.

CHAPTER 6

The Alternative Communities of Alexander Trocchi

Gill Tasker

Abstract

This chapter analyses Alexander Trocchi's centrality to the formation of three alternative communities throughout the 1950s and 1960s. Charting Trocchi's role in the formation of the magazine *Merlin* through to the Situationist International in Paris, then
project sigma in London, it is argued that these countercultural communities were
rooted in Trocchi's longstanding interest in existential philosophy. The chapter deter-
mines that Trocchi promoted a model of radical subjectivity as a strategic means to
react against the stifling conservatism of the moral status quo, while also offering an
alternative to the paralysing political dichotomy of the Cold War.

Keywords

Alexander Trocchi – Jean-Paul Sartre – existentialism – subjectivity – sigma –
Situationist International – *Merlin* – counterculture – *littérature engagée* – Cold War –
1950s – 1960s – alternative communities

Alexander Trocchi's avant-garde *oeuvre*, his cosmopolitan lifestyle and experimental aestheticism, are typically associated with French existentialism, the
Beat Generation, and the 1960s London counterculture. While living in Paris
in the 1950s, Glasgow-born Trocchi sought to emulate Jean-Paul Sartre's model
of *littérature engagée* as a means to achieve self-determination and personal autonomy; while Sartre's engagement suggests direct political association, Trocchi used its emphasis on the existentially subjective self to instead
promote his stance against the dichotomous politics of the Cold War.[1] The
sigma project, with its roots in the Situationist International of the 1950s,
enabled Trocchi to envisage cultural revolution through subjectivity in the
1960s, and subjectivity was central to Trocchi's vision of a cultural reawaken-
ing as a means to reject the Cold War opposition between capitalism and

---

1 For Sartre's politics, see Alan Sinfield, *Literature, Politics and Culture in Postwar Britain*
(London: Continuum, 2004), p. 99.

communism.[2] Through his position as editor of publications such as the magazine *Merlin* and the sigma portfolio, Trocchi came into contact with many other like-minded individuals whose shared belief in radical subjectivity led to the formation of alternative communities.

Trocchi was greatly influenced by Parisian postwar existentialism, particularly Sartre, who established the primacy of subjectivity through individually determined choice and action. Each individual is alone in the world and solely responsible for their being and making because '[m]an is nothing else but what he makes of himself. Such is the first principle of existentialism. It is also what is called subjectivity'.[3] Trocchi read English Literature and Philosophy at Glasgow University and after graduating he received a travelling scholarship in 1950.[4] After an initial visit to Paris, he relocated there permanently.

> I went to France, not London, from Scotland. I found the English attitude towards existentialism – French existentialism in particular – unsympathetic after the war. They had a very patronising attitude towards existentialism and Literature Engagé [*sic*]. They thought of the term engagé in the old 30s sense of 'commitment', whereas *engagement* could have the sense of refusing to be identified with either capitalism or communism. You could, in fact, be Engagé as an outsider.[5]

This highlights Trocchi's interest in existentialism and the idea of engagement, but significantly he views himself as an outsider because he rejects the dominant political ideologies of the Cold War. The central concepts of postwar existentialism – the importance of the individual, subjectivity and choice, authenticity and freedom – were a strategy through which Trocchi could refuse the total politics of the Cold War era. This belief in autonomy through subjective consciousness is in marked contrast to state reliance – whether that be in the capitalist West or what was then the communist Soviet bloc – on mass conformity and mass culture. Trocchi acknowledges this situation in 1962,

---

2   See Timothy Brown and Lorena Anton, 'Introduction', in *Between the Avant-garde and the Everyday: Subversive Politics in Europe from 1957 to the Present*, ed. by Timothy Brown and Lorena Anton (New York: Berghahn, 2011), pp. 1–10 (p. 1).

3   Jean-Paul Sartre, *Existentialism and Human Emotions* (New York: Citadel, 1994), p. 15.

4   Andrew Murray Scott, *Alexander Trocchi: The Making of the Monster* (Edinburgh: Polygon, 1991), p. 25.

5   Murray Scott, *Alexander Trocchi*, p. 33. Italics in original.

describing the era as 'what is often thought of as the age of the mass'.[6] Mark Donnelly describes the postwar years in the West as being propelled by 'an emphasis on the needs of consumption (in other words spending)'.[7] Equally, as George W. Breslauer points out, the 'mass-oriented basis of early Soviet political culture' also meant that postwar communism sought to mobilise the masses as a means to ensure authoritarian bureaucracy.[8] In contrast to these state-led and impersonal political ideologies, Todd Gitlin believes that existentialism's premise, which focused on the individual, heralded a new way of thinking in the Cold War era, whereby 'authority would always have to prove itself, minute by minute'.[9] In this way, existentialism presented the opportunity for a critique of totalitarian politics, something that Trocchi saw as a means to achieve a more authentic, autonomous, and individualised existence.

Richard Seaver acknowledges the influence that existentialism had on Trocchi as a young writer living in Paris:

> There was a great ferment after World War II. You had Sartre and Camus who were in rebellion against the French establishment, both politically different but trying to forge something new, both in literature and in politics, and I think Alex saw himself as the equivalent in the English language. When I first met him there were no drugs in his life. His radical stands were concentrated on literature.[10]

An example of this radicalism was the Paris-based journal *Merlin*, founded by Trocchi and which he edited from 1952 to 1955. Existing in friendly rivalry with the *Paris Review*, the first issue of *Merlin* was published on 15 May 1952.[11] The journal's mission statement declared that 'MERLIN will hit at all clots of rigid categories in criticism and life, and all that is unintelligently partisan'.[12] Seaver, a colleague of Trocchi's at *Merlin*, claims that 'Paris may have been our mistress,

---

6   Alexander Trocchi, 'The Invisible Insurrection of a Million Minds', in *Invisible Insurrection of a Million Minds: A Trocchi Reader*, ed. by Andrew Murray Scott (Edinburgh: Polygon, 1991), pp. 177–91 (p. 165).

7   Mark Donnelly, *Sixties Britain: Culture, Society and Politics* (London: Routledge, 2013), p. 2.

8   George W. Breslauer, in *The Soviet Polity in the Modern Era*, ed. by Erik P. Hoffmann and Robbin Frederick Laird (New York: Aldine de Gruyter, 1984), p. 23.

9   Todd Gitlin, *The Sixties: Years of Hope, Days of Rage* (London: Bantam, 1993), p. 30.

10   Richard Seaver, in *A Life In Pieces: Reflections on Alexander Trocchi*, ed. by Allan Campbell and Tim Niel (Edinburgh: Rebel Inc., 1997), pp. 58–62 (p. 60).

11   John Calder, *Garden of Eros: The Story of the Paris Expatriates and the Post-War Literary Scene* (Richmond: Alma, 2014), p. 64.

12   Alexander Trocchi, *Merlin Collection*, 2.1 (1952), p. 57.

but the political realities of the time were our master'.[13] For Seaver, the magazine 'bore the weight of the early Cold War world on its meagre shoulders', and he points out that the political contexts of the time in Paris are essential to understanding *Merlin*'s ethos and its stand as an alternative community:

> We were not just different from our Paris-based elders who had filled the cafés in Montparnasse in the twenties, we were the extreme opposite: pure literature in the sense that a Joyce or a Gertrude Stein understood it, experimentation as an end in itself, seemed impossible.[14]

Seaver argues that *Merlin* rejected the absolute aestheticism of the 'art for art's sake' attitude and instead sought to embody a new socio-political consciousness alongside a fundamentally existential approach:

> There was no way we could remain neutral, for neutrality was the death of the soul. In a debate between Camus and Sartre that rent the European literary establishment in those days, we clearly sided with the political scrapper over the detached philosopher, the *engagé* over the *non-engagé*.[15]

Alluding to the debate surrounding *littérature engagée*, which had led to the public and long-lasting fallout between Sartre and Camus, Seaver says that *Merlin* supported Sartre. Although Sartre's philosophy is rooted in individuality through its emphasis on subjectivity, whereby 'I am responsible for everything', it does however encompass wider humanist terrain, what Maurice Cranston calls 'the notion of community'.[16] Sartre writes that where 'man is responsible for himself, we do not mean that he is responsible for his own individuality, but that he is responsible for all men', meaning that in addition to being responsible for himself, man (the gendered human) is responsible for all humans because 'in choosing myself, I choose man'.[17] Alistair Braidwood also acknowledges the concept of community in his claim that 'Sartre's existentialism is primarily concerned with the potential of the apparently

---

13   Richard Seaver, 'Introduction', Alexander Trocchi, *Cain's Book* (London: Calder, 1992), pp. xi–xx (p. xxi).
14   Seaver, 'Introduction', *Cain's Book,* p. xiii.
15   Seaver, 'Introduction', *Cain's Book*, p. xiii.
16   Jean-Paul Sartre, *Existentialism and Human Emotions*, p. 57. Maurice Cranston, *Sartre* (Edinburgh: Oliver and Boyd, 1970), p. 80.
17   Sartre, *Existentialism and Human Emotions*, pp. 16, 18.

alienated subjective individual to influence and affect wider society'.[18] In tandem with the existential connection of all of humankind, Sartre also argued that existentialism is 'a doctrine of action', and although this idea of action primarily relates to individuals because they must actively choose their own existence, it also had wider social implications.

The notion of communal subjectivity is particularly pertinent to the context of postwar Paris in which Sartre and Trocchi were living and writing, and in which *Merlin* was established. Writing of the role of the engaged writer, Sartre states: 'he knows that words, as Brice-Parain says, are "loaded pistols". If he speaks, he fires'.[19] Trocchi responds to this model by wielding words as weapons in the provocatively titled 'Words and War' editorial, which develops into a lengthy diatribe in which he posits subjective theories to be 'an extremely subtle and effective type of moral armament' against the culture of impersonal, totalitarian politics.[20] Trocchi's unwavering belief in the authenticity of existential subjectivity is clear, and he believes that this approach of inwardness must be implemented in order to influence

> certain aesthetic theories [which] have become widely accredited, and which, in their attempt to impose arbitrary structure on history and on cultural processes, past, present, and future, represent an imminent threat, parallel and confederate with the same kind of thinking in politics, to our civilisation.[21]

Echoing Sartre's engagement, Trocchi believes that the writer has the potential to highlight and even change 'cultural processes' by influencing society.

Like 'Words and War', Trocchi uses another *Merlin* editorial as an opportunity to strike out against what he calls 'fixed categories' and to assert subjectivity as a weapon against the political absolutism of the Cold War:

> It is symptomatic of the Orwellian situation which exists in the world today that politicians on both sides of the iron curtain cry indignantly for 'justice'; both sides claim to be 'right' and think that they are describing a fact when they call the other 'wrong', the east in the name of Marx or

---

18   Alistair Braidwood, 'Iain Banks, James Kelman and the Art of Engagement: An Application of Jean-Paul Sartre's Theories of Literature and Existentialism to Two Modern Scottish Novelists', (unpublished doctoral thesis, University of Glasgow, 2011), p. i.

19   Jean-Paul Sartre, *'What Is Literature?' And Other Essays* (Cambridge: Harvard, 1998), p. 38.

20   Alexander Trocchi, 'Words and War', *Merlin*, 3.2 (1954), 141–43 and 209–27 (p. 209).

21   Trocchi, 'Words and War', p. 209.

'historical necessity', the west even more ambiguously in the name of 'humanity' or 'God' or 'democracy'. It is the uncritical acceptance of such categories as these (Jew, Nigger, American, Bolshevik – and others) that allows men, always liable to act in accordance with stock responses, to be herded into armies keyed up to destroy 'the enemy'.

Here man is at the mercy of words. And it is precisely here that the writer has a vital social function to perform. If he is not alive to the snares of language he is a more dangerous fool than his audience. [...]

In what way can a literary magazine most effectively combat that tendency in the human being to form rigid and uncompromising attitudes? For if it does not combat that tendency it merely panders to those forces which will explode the world for a third time. Obviously, as was suggested in *MERLIN* Number Two, it must proceed by hitting at fixed categories, by persuading men to analyse their own attitudes, to suspend their responses, to think critically, and then, in the historical context, *to act*.[22]

While Trocchi acknowledges that *Merlin* is 'a literary magazine', he dismisses a purely 'literary' function by instead portraying it as an independent and radical publication that aims to influence its readers into thinking and acting. In this way, Trocchi argues that writers are inherently 'engaged' because they have a 'vital social function to perform', and this affirms Sartre's social vision that 'the writer is, *par excellence*, a mediator and his engagement is mediation'.[23] Moreover, Trocchi suggests that 'man is at the mercy of words', which again warns of language's dangerous or corrupting potential when used loosely or for merely propagandistic ends. Trocchi aims to destablise 'rigid and uncompromising attitudes' by calling readers to 'analyse their own attitudes' in opposition to the fixed nature of apparently absolute categories: he suggests that subjectivity must be used strategically to bring about action to secure existential freedom and truth for individuals in the face of political ideologies. Crucially, he urges readers 'to think critically' and to use their subjectivity 'to *act*' to form radically alternative communities against the conformity of the Cold War political order. Indeed, Trocchi is aligned with Sartre's belief that 'literature should not be a sedative but an irritant, a catalyst provoking men to change the world in which they live and in doing so change themselves'; in *Merlin*, this meant also opposing the nuclear agenda of the United States and the Soviet Union.[24]

---

22   Alexander Trocchi, 'Editorial', *Merlin Collection*, 3.1 (1952–53), p. 117. Italics in original.
23   Sartre, *'What Is Literature?'*, p. 77.
24   David Caute, 'Introduction', in Sartre, *'What is Literature?'*, pp. vii–xxi (p. xi).

Tom McGrath, a fellow Scot and friend of Trocchi's during the 1960s through his role as editor of the *International Times*, claims that 'Trocchi had no patience for Marxism or any other political approaches, which he regarded as outmoded. Instead his revolution began in inner space, within human consciousness itself'.[25] In a 1955 letter to his family in Scotland from Paris, Trocchi addresses this idea of revolution coming through the subjective self as an alternative to putting his belief in the masses:

> I reject the entire system [...;] the answer is *revolution*. Not in the objective, idealistic sense, but there in the heart of every man [...] a new attitude [...;] the Revolution has already taken place in me. I am outside your world and am no longer governed by your laws.[26]

In his particular vision of subjectivity as a means to create change, Trocchi again describes himself as an outsider: he is 'outside *your* world' of conventional laws and politics. The letter is significant because, writing contemporaneously in *Merlin*, Trocchi also acknowledges, and promotes, the revolutionary potential of this new stance: 'We know that it is attitudes which are important. It is attitudes that are effective'.[27] Gitlin has termed such radical apolitical sensibility as 'the impulse to go it alone', which sought 'a heady truth in this image of self-creation' and that later became typically associated with the 1960s, despite being rooted in and stemming from a reaction to the political ideologies of the 1950s.[28]

> With left-wing politics in a state of collapse [in the 1950s], most of these oppositional spaces were cultural – ways of living, thinking, and fighting oneself free of the affluent consensus. Most were indifferent or hostile to politics, which they saw as yet another squandering of energy. But even the antipolitical enclaves opened a space for later and larger oppositions, both the New Left and the counterculture, oppositions compounded – however contradictorily – of politics and culture.[29]

It is clear that for Trocchi, writing his *Merlin* editorials in the 1950s and echoing these ideas in letters back to Scotland, the personal became a means of

---

25   Tom McGrath, 'Remembering Alex Trocchi', *Edinburgh Review*, 70 (1985), 36–47, (p. 37).

26   Trocchi, in Murray Scott, *Alexander Trocchi*, p. 64. Italics in original.

27   Trocchi, 'Editorial', *Merlin Collection*, 3.1, p. 117.

28   Gitlin, *The Sixties*, p. 27.

29   Gitlin, *The Sixties*, p. 28.

resisting the dominant Cold War political ideologies. In this way he can be regarded as anticipating the apolitical ethos of the counterculture in the 1960s through his belief that the way out of the status quo was through moving inwards into the subjective self.

Trocchi's time in Paris also brought him into contact with a collective of radical thinkers who used their subjectivity strategically in their aim to achieve personal authenticity and political freedom by forming an alternative community. The group was the Lettrist International, which Trocchi described as a 'closed society, a clandestine group, which was to be my whole world' and which forced him to sever contact with friends and associates.[30] Existing from the mid-1940s, Lettrism was founded by Isodore Isou in Paris, and stemmed ideologically from Dada and Surrealism. Like the Situationist International, Lettrism sought to integrate all art forms into its radical cultural-political theory, and Situationist impresario Guy Debord joined in 1951. Debord then covertly started the Lettrist International in 1952, with Trocchi joining in October 1955. Trocchi's Lettrist International affiliation led him to attend the 'Italian First World Congress of Free Artists' in 1956, after which he and eight others, including Debord, founded the Situationist International (SI) in 1957. The extent of Trocchi's involvement with the SI is somewhat difficult to determine because at the time of the Situationist International's formation Trocchi had moved from Paris to the United States. Although Trocchi was absent in the flesh as a member of the SI, when he was arrested for allegedly sexually assaulting and dealing narcotics to a minor in 1960, *Internationale Situationniste #5* published 'Resolution of the Fourth Conference of the Situationist International Concerning the Imprisonment of Alexander Trocchi' to support him and oppose his arrest. Having fled from America due to the impending drugs charges, the SI community continued to support Trocchi well into his relocation to London, until Debord 'resigned' him from the SI's Central Council via a letter in 1964. It is however vital to acknowledge the Situationist International in order to trace the trajectory of Trocchi's use of subjectivity as a strategy to achieve existential and artistic freedom.[31]

---

30   Murray Scott, *Alexander Trocchi*, p. 64. Gavin Bowd, *'The Outsiders': Alexander Trocchi and Kenneth White, An Essay* (London: Akros, 1998), p. 8.

31   For more on Trocchi and the SI see Michael Gardiner, 'Alexander Trocchi and Situationism', in *Aesthetics and Radical Politics*, ed. by Gavin Grindon (Cambridge: Cambridge Scholars Publishing, 2008), pp. 63–82; 'Alexander Trocchi's Invisible Insurrection', in Samuel Martin Cooper, '"A Lot to Answer For": The English Legacy of the Situationist International' (unpublished doctoral thesis, University of Sussex, 2012); and 'Trocchi and Project Sigma', in Bowd, *'The Outsiders'.*

The 1960s saw Trocchi channel his previously established ideas regarding both individual and collective subjectivity and existential autonomy into a new venture, the sigma portfolio. Trocchi initially introduced sigma in 1960 in an article entitled 'project sigma: Cultural Engineering', which was printed in a special edition of the Situationist International's journal *Manifesto Situationiste*. Sigma's idea of revolution in inner space was undoubtedly indebted to the SI's philosophy and is explicitly evident in Trocchi's writing and principles in sigma, despite the fact that Debord resigned Trocchi from the Situationist International in 1964 because he felt that sigma was moving in too different a direction from the SI.[32] Bowd echoes this point, while also acknowledging that sigma's apolitical stance jarred with the SI's Marxism:

> If sigma did not attribute a messianic role to the proletariat, it nevertheless had close affinities with the Situationists: the desire for a collective organisation overthrowing separations between culture and everyday life; the refusal of existing hierarchies; the importance of town-planning and the organisation of space.[33]

Sigma's official headed paper boldly proclaims 'SIGMA GENERAL INFORMATION SERVICE EXISTENTIAL CONSULTANTS LONDON PARIS NEW YORK'. Although somewhat ambiguous, sigma was fundamentally a transnational network of associates – Trocchi termed these associates 'sigmaticians' and described sigma as an 'international index' – and the project was mainly administered and promoted through publication of pamphlets under the title 'the sigma portfolio'. Pamphlets were a popular mode of publication at the time due to being relatively inexpensive to produce. Proclaimed as 'an entirely new mode of publishing', Trocchi explains why this method was chosen: 'the writer reaches his public immediately, outflanking the traditional trap of publishing-house policy, and by means of which the reader gets it, so to speak, "hot" from the writer's pen, from the photographers lens, etc.'.[34] Trocchi, as founder and leader, wrote many of sigma's pieces and his contributions best convey its radical ethos. According to Andrew Murray Scott, 'sigma was Alex

---

32   Debord's letter resigning Trocchi reveals Debord's concern that 'the SI might find itself discomforted if certain aspects or collaborators on this project were compared to the SI's other declarations'. Guy Debord, letter to Alexander Trocchi, 12 October 1964 <http://www.notbored.org/debord-12October1964.html> [accessed 13 May 2012].

33   Bowd, *'The Outsiders'*, p. 9.

34   Alexander Trocchi, 'Subscription Form', *Sigma Portfolio*, 12 (1964), [n.p.].

and Alex was sigma', and between 1964 and 1967 a total of thirty-nine issues of the 'sigma portfolio' were produced;[35] contributors were to include William Burroughs, R.D. Laing, Colin Wilson, Kenneth White, Joan Littlewood, Robert Creeley, and Michael McClure. Trocchi explains the rationale for choosing the name 'sigma': 'Commonly used in mathematical practice to designate all, the sum, the whole, it seemed to fit very well with our notion that all men must be eventually included'.[36] Sigma launched in 1962 with publication of the seminal 'Invisible Insurrection of a Million Minds', followed by 'sigma: A Tactical Blueprint', which sought to 'inspire and sustain self-consciousness in all men' by catalysing an 'international association of men who are concerned individually and in concert to articulate an effective strategy and tactics for this cultural revolution'; Trocchi was keen to clarify that sigma's revolution 'must be in the broad sense cultural', with culture signifying both society and creativity.[37]

That Trocchi's ambitious proposals emphasise the revolutionary potential of the individual may seem at odds with sigma as a collective network. However, this is conceptually similar to Sartre's vision of engagement, whereby individual self-consciousness evolves to become subjectivity that is shared among like-minded individuals as a means to subvert capitalism. Rather than constructing praxis that focused on the lives of the elite, like the Situationist International, sigma sought instead to critique and change everyday life. Indeed, the 'everyday' was a concept central to writing in the Parisian postwar context: SI member Raoul Vaneigem's *The Revolution of Everyday Life* (1967) and Michel de Certeau's *The Practice of Everyday Life* (1980) both demonstrate how a focus on the everyday was vital to critiquing the established order. In an attempt to break down political and socio-economic divisions in their focus on everyday life, sigma called for the 'man in the streets' to be involved, because 'all men must eventually be included' in sigma's proposed alternative community.[38]

Sigma centred on the principle of subjectivity as a strategy of defiance against state-led political decree. In its ambitious vision of a '*coup de monde*', Trocchi used the sigma portfolio to propose his idea of a worldwide cultural revolution through the power of individual subversion:

35   Murray Scott, *Alexander Trocchi*, p. 128.

36   Alexander Trocchi, 'Sigma: A Tactical Blueprint', in *Invisible Insurrection of a Million Minds*, pp. 192–203 (p. 193).

37   Alexander Trocchi and Phillip Green, 'project sigma: Cultural Engineering', in *A Life In Pieces*, pp. 189–93 (p. 189).

38   Trocchi, 'The Invisible Insurrection of a Million Minds', in *Invisible Insurrection of a Million Minds*, p. 181. Trocchi, 'sigma: A Tactical Blueprint', in *Invisible Insurrection of a Million Minds*, p. 193.

The so-called 'seat-of-power' must shift. We must stop externalising it so absolutely. The power is in us, and we can use it together if we use our heads. We must do everything to attack the 'enemy' at his base within ourselves. We must take nothing for granted. Certainly not what men call the 'state' [...]. The word 'state' was well-chosen. It is an existential absurdity.[39]

Trocchi suggests that subversion is necessary for people to reclaim power from political systems, and it is clear that he believes subversion can only be achieved through subjectivity: he correlates power with individual inwardness, arguing that 'the power is in us if we use our heads' and the attack comes from 'within ourselves'. The 'technique of subversion' outlined here is a means to achieve existential freedom in opposition to the 'the "enemy"': impersonal, and absurd, political systems. In 'project sigma: Cultural Engineering', Trocchi and co-writer Philip Green make it clear that sigma exists outside this conventional milieu:

[W]e propose immediate action on an international scale, a self-governing (non-)organisation of producers of the new culture beyond, and independent of, all political organisations and trade and professional syndicates which presently exist; for there is not one of those which does not have the fogs and vapours of ataxia in its own basement.[40]

Trocchi emphasises that sigma is international, self-fulfilling, and ideologically autonomous. Writing in an explicitly existential style in the aptly titled 'The Invisible Insurrection of a Million Minds', Trocchi rallies writers and thinkers to awaken and assert their individual subjectivity as a strategy to oppose the paralysing quality of politically-dictated existence:

The individual has a profound sense of his own impotence as he realises the immensity of the forces involved. We, the creative ones everywhere, must discard this paralytic posture and seize control over the human process by assuming control of ourselves. We must reject the conventional fiction of 'unchanging human nature'. There is in fact no such permanence anywhere. There is only *becoming*.[41]

---

39   Trocchi, 'The Invisible Insurrection of a Million Minds', in *Invisible Insurrection of a Million Minds*, p. 181. Alexander Trocchi, 'Potlach', *Sigma Portfolio*, 4 (1964), p. 4.

40   Trocchi and Green, 'project sigma', in *A Life In Pieces*, p. 192.

41   Trocchi, 'The Invisible Insurrection of a Million Minds', in *Invisible Insurrection of a Million Minds*, p. 178. Italics in original.

Just as Sartre believed that 'becoming' through 'subjectivity must be the starting point' for an authentic and free existence, in sigma Trocchi similarly outlines his vision of subjectivity as a strategy to overturn the 'impotence' of the individual caused by the Cold War duopoly of fear.[42] Trocchi also alludes to the existential premise that in a world without God nothing is permanent or predetermined, there is 'only becoming' through subjective self-determination.

By encouraging individuals to re-engage with and ignite their own subjectivity and creativity, sigma, like the SI, also suggested that art and leisure enabled humans to transcend banal consumerist conformity and experience an authentic and more meaningful existence. While Trocchi rejected capitalist structures, he was also against communism's ideology of mass-oriented labour: both systems encouraged conformity through state-led, rather than self-led, control. Trocchi puts forward these ideas in sigma in order to overturn the monotony and lethargy of what he terms the 'poor working man':

> So much for hard work. Which is fit for machines only. And always was, except in the mouths of hypocrites who found it profitable to make a virtue of others' underprivilege. Work does not ennoble and beer did. Experience en-nobles. Living fully. Applying oneself to life. And that is art and craft and consciously becoming, not work [...]. This attitude, these thoughts, are at the bottom of the contemporary interest in the 'happening', an existential situation in which the protagonists adopt a meta-catagorical posture and play at discovering themselves, together, at leisure, freedom unrestrained by external constraints.[43]

Trocchi's dismissal of work and his playful preference for 'applying oneself to life' is a reaction against the dehumanising industrial construct of the human-machine. Rather than being brain-dulled through the impersonal mode of relentless capitalist production, Trocchi instead saw art as a route to 'consciously becoming', or in other words, as presenting the opportunity for subjectivity through the heightening of individual consciousness to enlighten and expand human existence. Emphasising the subjective nature of creativity, Trocchi defines 'art' in sigma as 'the products of all the expressive media of civilisation', whereby art is *the* agent for overcoming capitalist alienation, not

---

42   Sartre, *Existentialism and Human Emotions*, p. 13.
43   Alexander Trocchi, 'Sigma: General Informations' "Third Impression"', *Sigma Portfolio*, 5 (1964), p. 3.

an agent.[44] The absolute centrality of art to Trocchi in sigma marks a departure from the earlier ideology and praxis of Debord and the SI, which, according to Merlin Coverley, attempted to tackle the 'more broadly philosophical themes of time, society, and history'.[45] Although aestheticism played a significant part in Debord's overall praxis, sigma arguably elevated art to become almost the entirety of their vision of subjectivity as strategy. This shift is acknowledged by Coverley, who claims that 'Debord [...] became [so] increasingly preoccupied with Marxist revisionism that he had little time for the unfettered Romanticism that Trocchi had so fondly recalled'.[46]

Trocchi's 'The Invisible Insurrection of a Million Minds', which is influenced by Situational International ideas such as Debord's 'Never Work',[47] outlines his radical vision of an alternative community based on leisure, or what he calls 'play', rather than work:

> A great deal of what is pompously called 'juvenile delinquency' is the inarticulate response of youth incapable of coming to terms with leisure. The violence associated with it is a direct consequence of the alienation of man from himself brought about by the Industrial Revolution. Man has forgotten how to play.[48]

Sigma, like the Situationist International before it, believed there was no teleology to work, and that through capitalism individuals had become alienated from each other and from themselves by being subsumed into the economically driven consumerist masses. The concept of *homo ludens* (generally translated as 'playing man' and a reference to the title of the Dutch historian Johan Huizinga's 1938 text), is recurrent throughout Trocchi's *oeuvre*. For instance, the protagonists in the novels *Young Adam* (1954) and *Cain's Book* (1960) actively reject the working mentality and instead advocate a lifestyle of play. Although Joe Necchi in *Cain's Book* is employed as a scow captain on the waterways around Manhattan, he rarely engages in any labour and he is portrayed as almost always lying around: 'lying on the bunk'; 'I had been lying in the bunk for over an hour'; 'I found myself lying on my

---

44   Trocchi, 'The Invisible Insurrection of a Million Minds', in *Invisible Insurrection of a Million Minds*, p. 188.

45   Merlin Coverley, *Psychogeography* (London: Pocket Essentials, 2010), p. 102.

46   Coverley, *Psychogeography*, p. 101.

47   Guy Debord, *Panegyric* (London and New York: Verso, 2009), p. 84.

48   Trocchi, 'The Invisible Insurrection of a Million Minds', in *Invisible Insurrection of a Million Minds*, p. 180.

bed'; 'we lay down on the bed'; 'I spent most of my time lying on the roof of my shack'.[49] The scow is not a place of productivity but a place of idleness and experiment; it is where Necchi smokes, indulges in illicit sex, philosophises, and gets high on heroin. In *Young Adam*, Joe is employed as a barge-hand but he is similarly lazy – he and the skipper Leslie are described as frequently feeling 'a bit uncomfortable there on deck and doing nothing because Ella never seemed to stop working'.[50] The barge is also where Joe instigates an illicit affair with Ella, Leslie's wife, and as such the barge is rendered as both a site of play and of labour.

In the sigma portfolio Trocchi furthers his stance against capitalist conformity by critiquing the role of literature. Sartre's model of engaged literature, in which literature must perform a progressive social function, may be in Trocchi's mind as he warns of the danger of all writing being essentially 'an economic act with reference to economic limits', and argues that if literature is written within the confines of capitalist society it is by default 'an economic act'.[51] Trocchi claims that this renders literature a 'business', something which sigma appeared to oppose despite the fact that Trocchi charged a subscription fee for the sigma portfolio and was always appealing to readers for monetary donations.[52] Albert Camus claimed that 'the society based on production is only productive, not creative', and although Trocchi singles out literature as the artistic medium for his attack, the point he makes is generally applicable to all creativity: for freedom to be achieved through revolution, *all* art must escape being part of commerce-driven production and consumption.[53] Trocchi suggests a community of subjectivities as a means to realise this, arguing that 'the conventional spectator-creator dichotomy must be broken down' and that 'the traditional "audience" must participate'.[54] Trocchi's ideas regarding art in sigma anticipate those later expressed by Guy Debord in *The Society of the Spectacle* (1967), which proposed that rather than being passive and alienated spectators caught up in impersonal economic mechanisms, individuals must be active and subjective participants in order to break free from and overcome the isolation inherent in the capitalist system. To instigate collective subjective action against such existential lethargy and social convention, sigma adopted the

---

49   Alexander Trocchi, *Cain's Book* (London: Calder, 1992), pp. 10, 65, 123, 132, 183.
50   Alexander Trocchi, *Young Adam* (Richmond: Oneworld Classics, 2008), p. 27.
51   Trocchi, 'sigma: A Tactical Blueprint', in *Invisible Insurrection of a Million Minds*, p. 194.
52   Trocchi, 'sigma: A Tactical Blueprint', in *Invisible Insurrection of a Million Minds*, p. 194.
53   Albert Camus, *The Rebel* (London: Penguin, 2000), p. 237.
54   Trocchi, 'sigma: A Tactical Blueprint', in *Invisible Insurrection of a Million Minds*, p. 194.

Situationist International's concept of the 'situation'.[55] According to Debord, the situation was the main plank of the SI's *modus operandi*: 'Our central idea is that of the construction of situations, that is to say the concrete construction of momentary ambiences of life and their transformation into a superior passional quality'.[56] The situation was rooted in individual subjectivity and was an act of subversion against the capitalist commodification of life and art; because the situation was not a tangible product it would thus transcend capitalism. As the name suggests, and as Debord acknowledges, the situation was a fleeting moment: 'Our situations will be ephemeral, without a future. Passageways', because '[e]ternity is the grossest idea a person can conceive of in connection with his acts'.[57]

In his own attempt to form a new society, or what he called a 'true Situationist culture', Trocchi proposed the formation of the 'spontaneous university' or 'sigma-centres'.[58] The spontaneous university would act as an 'experimental laboratory' and be a counterpoint to a traditional university education, which Trocchi dismissed since 'universities have become factories for the production of degreed technicians'.[59] The fundamental ethos behind the spontaneous university was an attempt to make permanent the ephemeral situation conceived by the SI. The proposed place of alternative learning would be modelled on the avant-garde Black Mountain College in North Carolina, founded in 1933, which Trocchi described as being 'a situation constructed to inspire the free play of creativity in the individual and the group'.[60] Short on neither ambition nor self-belief, Trocchi hoped that the spontaneous university would form 'the nucleus of an experimental town'.[61] In Trocchi's vision in sigma of subverting

---

55   For more on the situation in relation to sigma and the SI see Howard Slater, 'Towards Situation', *Variant* <http://www.variant.org.uk/14texts/Variant_Forum.html> [accessed 6 April 2012].

56   Guy Debord, 'Report on the Construction of Situations and on the International Situationist Tendency's Conditions of Organisation and Action', *Bureau of Public Secrets* (1957) <http://www.bopsecrets.org/SI/report.htm> [accessed 5 June 2013].

57   Debord, 'Report on the Construction of Situations and on the International Situationist Tendency's Conditions of Organisation and Action'.

58   Trocchi, 'The Invisible Insurrection of a Million Minds', in *Invisible Insurrection of a Million Minds*, p. 186. Trocchi, 'sigma: A Tactical Blueprint', in *Invisible Insurrection of a Million Minds*, p. 193.

59   Trocchi, 'sigma: A Tactical Blueprint', in *Invisible Insurrection of a Million Minds*, p. 197.

60   Trocchi, 'The Invisible Insurrection of a Million Minds', in *Invisible Insurrection of a Million Minds*, p. 188.

61   Trocchi, 'The Invisible Insurrection of a Million Minds', in *Invisible Insurrection of a Million Minds*, p. 189.

economic production by creating a community that was fundamentally unproductive in commercial terms, he imagined that the transnational sigma associates would come together to participate in their experimental township and participate in what he termed a 'cultural "jam session"',[62] allowing sigma's 'cosmonauts' or 'astronauts' to 'either congregate or be in contact'.[63] In his concept of a subversive society centred around sigma it is apparent that Trocchi sought not only to connect people psychologically through inner space but also physically through shared outer space, thus creating a spatially and spiritually distinct alternative community.

Trocchi, a heroin addict, also used sigma to promote his pro-drug perspective. His drug-induced vision of shared subjectivity is ostensibly synonymous with Timothy Leary's quintessentially 1960s countercultural coinage 'turn on, tune in, drop out'. Today this cultivated escapism from society in pursuit of pleasure can seem somewhat dated: as Thomas De Quincey in *Confessions of an English Opium-Eater* (1821), William Burroughs in *Junky* (1953) and others show, the road of excess often leads only to the palace of the self and no further. However, for Trocchi intoxication would become fundamental, perhaps vital, to the formation of alternative communities. Writing just after the demise of sigma in 1968, the Paris-based artist Jean-Jacques Lebel equates the happening or the situation with the use of narcotics, which positions Trocchi's proposed sigma methods within a wider context of countercultural collectivity:

> The only reality in art is furnished by the hallucinatory experience, around which crystallize (ephemeral) rites, and around which our mystical thoughts express themselves. The communication of this experience is essential to the life of the mind, yet it is clear that it has been interrupted. Every possible means must be used to re-establish it. The era of hallucinogenic drugs ushers in a new state of mind, breaks with industrial preoccupations, in order to develop itself to the revolution of being. Cubism, dadaism, surrealism, expressionism, or abstract impressionism, or even 'kinetic' or 'op' paintings have (timidly) tried to approximate certain aspects of hallucinatory experience. Now, it is no longer a matter of representing it, but of living it, and making it possible for others to live it.[64]

---

62   Trocchi, 'The Invisible Insurrection of a Million Minds', in *Invisible Insurrection of a Million Minds*, p. 186.

63   Trocchi, 'sigma: A Tactical Blueprint', in *Invisible Insurrection of a Million Minds*, p. 194.

64   Jean-Jacques Lebel, 'On the Necessity of Violation', *The Drama Review*, 13 (1968), 89–105 (p. 94).

Lebel's ideas can be read as a defence of sigma's principle of the spontaneous university as a place for drugged-up and dropped out inner-space cosmonauts to congregate and live the hallucinogenic experience together and individually – those, like Trocchi, who considered themselves to be pioneering explorers of the inward realm of the existential subjective self. Lebel positions drug taking in direct opposition to industry and capital and argues that drugs are implicit in 'the revolution of being' by emphasising 'mythical thoughts' and 'a new state of mind' based on exploring the individual's inner subjective consciousness in a shared environment. This subjectivity-enhancing narcotic practice can be viewed as analogous to Lebel's radical stance: drug-taking in the 1960s was often a strategic attempt to subvert dominant social systems through heightening the individual's subjective experience and emphasising what Lebel describes as the 'revolution of being'.

The centrality of narcotics to sigma's model of alternative community is best exemplified by Trocchi's decision to organise a meeting at Brazier's Park in Oxfordshire between sigma associates and a collective of transnational radical psychiatrists, centered around R.D. Laing, called 'The Philadelphia Foundation'.[65] Jeff Nuttall, who helped Trocchi to organise the weekend, highlights how nonconformist behaviour was high on the agenda:

> The [London-based] group I represented was turned into the examination of their own minds, partly driven there by the fear and hatred of anything outside their own minds, with an angry contempt for the most ordinary conventions and all regulations, with no intention of wanting to pay their way for a place where they could go a little madder than they already were.[66]

The initial idea – that attendees would come together for an intensive weekend-long exchange of ideas on (amongst other topics) the role of narcotics in existential psychiatry – fundamentally failed, as Nuttall's testimony confirms: 'We had lunch. [...] The picnic got wilder and drunker. Wine got into people like the sun got into butter. The picnic table became an image of the whole meeting.

---

65   Murray Scott, *Alexander Trocchi*, p. 140. The sigma portfolio had an interest in radical psychiatry and their readership represented this. Issue 17 (1964) comprised a 'list of people interested', which includes nine psychologists or psychiatrists including R.D. Laing.

66   Jeff Nuttall, *Bomb Culture* (London: Paladin, 1968), pp. 213–14. Tom McGrath also details his experience of Brazier's Park in 'Remembering Alex Trocchi' in *Edinburgh Review*, 70 (1985), 40–43.

Discordant, messy, runny, sticky, and finally abandoned'.[67] Rather than being a meeting of minds, the narcotics-fuelled weekend was steeped in chaos. Trocchi, at the centre of it all as organiser, struggled to hold it together in-between over-dosing on heroin, while the invited guests – who according to Nuttall '*dreaded meeting each other*' – frequently squabbled.[68] There is no doubt that Brazier's Park failed to be the somewhat utopian vision of shared subjectivity based on harmony and a deep sense of community that Trocchi envisaged as a 'cultural jam session'. Instead, it reveals the difficulties of coming together as a united alternative community that the attendees experienced and suggests that per-haps sigma's ideas, now seen as emblematic of the 1960s, were more cohesive and convincing on paper than in practice.

It must also be recognised that the collective sensibility at the heart of Trocchi's 'engaged' vision markedly contrasts with his fiction, in which charac-ters are often absolutely alone and isolated due to their predominantly inward and solipsistic existence. While Trocchi sought worldwide revolution in his polemical writing, by the time he turned to write 'The Long Book', his last work of fiction contracted by John Calder and that he failed to finish, he instead cre-ates a character that conversely does not – and more tellingly cannot – engage with the world at all. Indeed, a chronological trajectory of increasing alien-ation can be traced from Joe in *Young Adam* to Necchi in *Cain's Book* to the bizarre character of 'The Existential' in 'The Long Book', who has no arms and legs and lives in a coffin-like box.[69] Trocchi's 'dirty books', such as *Thongs* (1955), *Helen and Desire* (1953), *School for Sin* (1954) and *Sappho of Lesbos* (1960), many published by Maurice Girodias's infamous Olympia Press, simi-larly depict various protagonists' journeys as they leave their home communi-ties to travel abroad alone. Although Trocchi's fictional *leitmotif* of isolation, and the (often explicit) rejection of community that accompanies this stance, is ostensibly at odds with calls for collective revolution in sigma and *Merlin*, James Campbell describes Trocchi as 'a philosopher, one who invites you to consider the contradictions inherent in the statement that reads: "[t]his state-ment is not true"'.[70] This concept of philosophical paradox is absolutely central to Trocchi's complex *oeuvre* which, spanning fiction and non-fiction, seems to

---

67   Nuttall, *Bomb Culture*, p. 216.

68   Nuttall, *Bomb Culture*, p. 215. Italics in original.

69   For in-depth analysis of this trajectory see Chapter 2 of my doctoral thesis, '"Cosmonaut of Inner Space": An Existential Enquiry into the Writing of Alexander Trocchi' (unpub-lished doctoral thesis, University of Strathclyde, 2015).

70   James Campbell, *Syncopations: Beats, New Yorkers, and Writers in the Dark* (Berkeley: University of California, 2008), p. 201.

both affirm and reject the concept of community, and prevents any neat or simple conclusion being reached.

Writing for *Merlin* and forming the Situationist International in 1950s Paris, then establishing the sigma project in London in the 1960s, it is however clear that Trocchi's long-lasting position of subjectivity can be considered as part of a wider, and indeed transnational, radical sensibility of engagement. While not explored in this chapter, the framework of subjectivity established here can also be extended to include parallels with elements of the American Beat Generation and the French *nouveau roman*, two groups with which Trocchi is also affiliated, whose bold experimentalism also sought to disrupt the socio-cultural norm through developing a pioneering and distinctive literary aestheticism based on authenticity.[71] Subjectivity through existential inwardness became a strategy for Trocchi to reject totalitarian systems and enabled him to remain outside such political control, whilst bringing him together with those who also sought to reject the political hegemonies of the postwar era. These connections were primarily made possible through journals, as indicated by the existence of both *Merlin* in the 1950s and the sigma portfolio in the '60s. The way in to the subjective self became the way out of the stifling conformism of postwar politics and society for Trocchi and many others, united by the shared radical sensibility of their alternative communities.

---

71   For more on subjectivity, the Beat Generation, and the *nouveau roman*, see Tasker, '"Cosmonaut of Inner Space": An Existential Enquiry into the Writing of Alexander Trocchi', Chapter 1.

CHAPTER 7

Scottish Drama: The Expanded Community

Trish Reid

Abstract

This chapter traces the ways in which the idea of community has been imagined and embodied on the Scottish stage since the mid-twentieth century. While working class, urban and typically masculinist conceptions of community dominated for much of the period – largely under the influence of Glasgow Unity Theatre, 7:84 Scotland, and a more general Clydesidism – in recent decades definitions of community on the Scottish stage have proliferated and expanded in ways that are productive and welcome. In particular, the generation of female playwrights who came to prominence in the 1980s extended the vocabulary of Scottish theatre in relation to both thematic focus and setting. The reinvention of political Europe in the aftermath of the fall of the Berlin Wall further informed Scottish playwriting in the 1990s as did the growing appetite for autonomy in Scottish politics and culture, and the inevitable cultural bounce that accompanied devolution. While populist political traditions persist in Scottish theatre, and contemporary stagings of communal or shared values are marked by these traditions, nevertheless such stagings are considerably more inclusive than they have been in the past.

Keywords

Theatre – 7:84 Scotland – Glasgow Unity – National Theatre of Scotland – community

As a public and social art form, theatre has long been understood as a platform for the exploration of communal identities and shared values. Communities are apparent in theatre both in the many and varied ways that they are imagined and embodied on stage, and also in the working practices of theatre companies. My aim in this chapter is to consider the ways in which modern Scottish theatre has intersected with shifting social and political attitudes, and how these intersections have affected our understanding of the term 'community' as it relates to a distinctively Scottish theatrical tradition. Broadly speaking, I aim to trace the processes by which the workers' theatre movement in the mid-twentieth century became emblematic of a distinctively Scottish theatre culture and also to note the ways in which this paradigm has been complicated and extended in the last twenty years or so. As well as focusing on the content of particular plays and the working practices of specific companies I also want to pay attention to how Scottish theatre makers have sought to imagine and engage their audience. This focus will, I hope, contribute to a deeper understanding of how Scottish theatre operates, and has operated, in the public sphere and how it understands its role in relation to that sphere. This chapter does not pretend to be a comprehensive survey; instead, it focuses on a number of key moments when, by consensus, the vocabulary of Scottish theatre has been expanded and consequently its focus broadened.

My use of the phrase 'public sphere' clearly recalls Jürgen Habermas, who defined it as 'a realm of our social life, in which something approaching public opinion can be formed'.[1] Habermas's discursive understanding of the public sphere is important for my understanding of how theatre functions because it implies both a jurisdiction where discussion of public interests can take place and also an area of social life generated through such discussion. Scottish civic society and by extension Scottish theatre relies on discourse and, most specifically, on the existence of a public capable of forming common understanding though conversations of one kind or another. Given the scope and rate of cultural and constitutional change in Scotland in the last fifteen years, it is perhaps unsurprising that many contemporary Scottish theatre practitioners assume the existence of a public sphere and consciously produce work that engages discursively in it. The 2012 *Review of the Theatre Sector* commissioned by Creative Scotland noted this trend:

> [T]here is no lack of things for theatre to talk about. Whatever happens in the independence referendum, people in Scotland are facing the biggest political and constitutional decision of their lives and already we can see evidence of theatre makers working through the issues of statehood and nation building beyond the simplicity of the 'yes/no' arguments.[2]

As a theatre scholar, I am invested in the idea that theatre has an important role to play in working through issues of identity, community and nationhood. However, it is not my intention in what follows to exaggerate its importance in this regard, but simply to note, as Nadine Holdsworth has reminded us, that

---

1   Jürgen Habermas, 'The Public Sphere: An Encyclopedia Article', *New German Critique*, 3 (1974), 49–55 (p. 49).

2   Christine Hamilton Consulting, 'Review of the Theatre Sector in Scotland for Creative Scotland', 2012, p. 6 <http://www.creativescotland.com/resources/our-publications/sector-reviews/theatre-sector-review> [accessed 30 June 2015].

theatre can be 'one of the ways that members of a nation contribute to public discourse, a national conversation, which opens up the possibility for reflection and debate'.[3] This was clearly a view shared by the newly elected devolved Scottish Executive, when in 2000 it agreed in principal to the idea of funding a national theatre company. The subsequent establishment of the National Theatre of Scotland (NTS), which began producing work in early 2006, was the most significant development in twenty-first century Scottish theatre.

The NTS's genesis is of interest here because it reinforced a sense of the Scottish theatre sector as a community of artists. In 2001, in the aftermath of the opening of the Scottish Parliament in 1999, a working group set up by the Scottish Arts Council (SAC) to explore available options had recommended the new national theatre company be building-less and essentially nomadic. Importantly, in arriving at this conclusion, the SAC working group had been strongly influenced by a 2000 report by the Federation for Scottish Theatre (FST) under the chairmanship of Hamish Glen, in which the FST outlined the model for a building-less company later developed by the SAC working group. In this way the operating structure of the NTS emerged from the Scottish theatre community itself, in what can only be described as a moment of consensus. The NTS thus conceived would, and indeed does, act as a 'creative producer [...] working with and through the existing Scottish theatre community to achieve its objectives'.[4] The NTS is a strikingly modern institution, a national theatre company characterised by mobility, flexibility and adaptability that has made work with local collaborators across Scotland, from Dumfries to Shetland, from Stornoway to Dunfermline. However, although widely praised for its innovative co-producing structure and the range and quality of new and experimental work it has brought to audiences across Scotland, the NTS has attracted criticism in relation to its perceived lack of interest in major Scottish plays of the past. As Joanne Zerdy has noted, the 'national organization has frequently traded in extant dramatic literature for contemporary adaptations, site-specific events, or collaboratively devised and digitally disseminated work'.[5] It is not my intention to discuss this criticism – some of which has been unpleasant and ethnically oriented – here, except to note, as I have argued elsewhere, that the emphasis on small scale, new and experimental work in

---

3   Nadine Holdsworth, 'Introduction', in *Theatre and National Identity: Re-imagining Conceptions of Nation*, ed. by Nadine Holdsworth (New York: Routledge, 2014), p. 2.

4   Scottish Arts Council, *Scottish National Theatre: Final Report of the Independent Working Group*, 2001 <http://www.sac.org.uk/nonhtdocs/single-page-pdf> [accessed 30 June 2015].

5   Joanne Zerdy, 'Fashioning a Scottish Operative: *Black Watch* and Banal Theatrical Nationalism on Tour in the US', *Theatre Research International*, 38.3 (2013), 181–95 (pp. 188–89).

the NTS's programme need 'not be read as evidence of indifference to a unified national tradition in Scottish playwriting'.

> It should instead be considered a welcome manifestation of locally grounded and resistant performance practices working in the interests of a small nation and its diverse communities in opposition to expectations of both the cultural elite and larger centralising forces.[6]

In the event, although it has been far from the mainstay of its output, the NTS has not completely avoided reviving older Scottish plays. Questions of how and why particular plays have been selected for restaging are therefore worth exploring because as a state-sanctioned and state-funded institution the NTS is inevitably implicated in the process of canon building. Unsurprisingly this process involves the privileging of certain quite specific versions of Scottish community and the exclusion of others.

On 17 August 2014 a shortened version of the NTS production of Joe Corrie's *In Time O' Strife* (1926) was staged in the debating chamber during the Scottish Parliament's annual Festival of Politics. The event was advertised as marking the thirtieth anniversary of the miners' strike. *In Time O' Strife* is an early example of grassroots Scottish working-class drama. Its author, the poet and playwright Joe Corrie, was a member of the Fife mining community from which the play's subject matter is drawn. Written during a lock-out to raise money for strikers' soup kitchens, *In Time O' Strife* is an emotionally charged domestic drama characterised by vigorous realism and the use of earthy colloquial Scots. It tells the tale of the middle-aged miner, Jock Smith, his family and neighbours, and of young Jenny Smith's fiancé, Wull Baxter, an ambitious young man who becomes a strike-breaker, much to Jenny's despair. Adapted, designed and directed by Graham McLaren, with additional poems and songs, the NTS revival played successfully in October 2013 at the Pathhead Hall in Kirkcaldy, where *The Scotsman* critic Joyce McMillan praised it as 'memorably angry, vivid and theatrical'.[7] In the autumn of 2014, a UK tour followed the performance at the Scottish Parliament.

Although *In Time O' Strife* is a regularly cited example of indigenous working-class drama, it has not been regularly staged in Scotland since its original semi-professional production in the late 1920s. Prior to 2013, the play had attained

---

6   Trish Reid, 'Staging Scotland: National Theatre of Scotland and Shifting Conceptions of Scottish Identity', in *The Media in Europe's Small Nations*, ed. by Huw David Jones (Newcastle: Cambridge Scholars Press, 2014), pp. 105–20 (p. 109).

7   Joyce McMillan, 'Theatre Review: *In Time O' Strife*', *The Scotsman*, 7 October, 2013, p. 17.

only one major professional revival, by 7:84 Scotland in 1982 as part of its Clydebuilt season. However, it had also been given a rehearsed reading as part of the NTS's 2011 Staging the Nation project, a series of events designed specifically to address questions relating to Scotland's theatre history and its legacy. As part of this project, a number of leading Scottish playwrights were asked to select plays that had been formative in their development as artists and that they would particularly like to see re-staged. Peter Arnott, who had seen the 7:84 Scotland revival of *In Time O' Strife* in Glasgow in 1982, chose Corrie's play, crediting it with opening up 'the possibility that theatre rooted in a place and a moment could speak across time and tell something like the truth'.[8] Doubtless the rehearsed reading provided a useful stepping-stone towards McLaren's full-scale revival in 2013, but it had the added benefit of asserting continuity between the NTS and 7:84 Scotland, a company that under the directorship of John McGrath in the 1970s and '80s had achieved legendary status in the field of politically-engaged theatre. Although lacking McGrath's explicitly Marxist agenda, the NTS has nonetheless privileged his conception of a popular theatre that engages its audience by refiguring the theatrical event as a celebration. McLaren's adaptation of *In Time O' Strife* with additional poems from elsewhere in Corrie's *oeuvre*, music and songs by Michael John McCarthy and a three piece band, and intensely choreographed dance sequences by Imogen Knight, recalled the populist approach favoured by 7:84, as did the choice of a community hall in Kirkcaldy as venue.

In Time O' Strife was written at a time when the professionalisation of Scottish theatre was in its early stages. Consequently, as Donald Smith has argued, Corrie 'opened a new social and artistic route into professional theatre, of which he himself could not take full advantage'.[9] Scottish theatre in the 1920s and '30s was not 'yet ready to accommodate and support drama by a political artist of Corrie's origins and stature, leaving him isolated'.[10] Nonetheless, in foregrounding the perspective of victimised workers and in asserting communal bonds between stage and audience via a shared vocabulary of language and lived experience, *In Time O' Strife* carried strong 'implications for a specifically Scottish socialism' in the theatre, and can be readily understood as part of

---

8   Peter Arnott, 'Joe Corrie: *In Time O' Strife* and Me', *Staging the Nation: A Conversation about Theatre*, 2011 <http://stagingthenation.com/peter-arnott-joe-corrie-in-time-o'-strife-and-me/> [accessed 30 June 2015].

9   Donald Smith, 'The Mid-Century Dramatists', in *The Edinburgh Companion to Scottish Drama*, ed. by Ian Brown (Edinburgh: Edinburgh University Press, 2011), pp. 118–29 (p. 119).

10 Smith, 'The Mid-Century Dramatists', in *The Edinburgh Companion to Scottish Drama*, p. 119.

a tradition that found fuller expression in the work of Glasgow Unity Theatre in the 1940s and 7:84 Scotland in the 1970s and '80s.[11] By reviving the play, the NTS asserted both its understanding of, and its place in, this history, not least, as I have noted, because the only other professional revival of Corrie's play had been the 7:84 Scotland one that had so affected Arnott. This lineage was also emphasised in 2011 when the NTS revived the most critically acclaimed of Glasgow Unity's Scottish plays, Ena Lamont Stewart's *Men Should Weep* (1947), which had also been revived by 7:84 Scotland as part of its 1982 Clydebuilt season.

Any discussion of community in modern Scottish drama should acknowledge the influence of Glasgow Unity, not only because its principles and its working practices shaped the praxis of later Scottish companies, but also because, as Adrienne Scullion has shown, 'its writers redefined the repertoire of twentieth-century Scottish drama; and its critical and academic recovery helped shape a critical orthodoxy within Scottish theatre studies that prefers a history of working-class and broadly naturalistic drama and theatre'.[12] Between 1940 and 1951, latterly under the directorship of Robert Mitchell, Glasgow Unity became the most successful and influential theatre company in Scotland. Rejecting the London-centric diet of middle-class theatre that had monopolised Scottish stages in the mid-century, and working in a largely social realist tradition, Unity strove to create a populist theatre that would reflect the lived experience of working-class Scots, especially Glaswegians. To this end, the company was extremely clear in setting out its aims and objectives. In a programme note for its 1943 production of Clifford Odets's *Golden Boy*, for instance, it defined itself as

> a group of Glasgow workers, interested in theatre, who intend to put on Real Plays for the entertainment and education of our fellow workers. Our main purpose is to build a People's Theatre in Glasgow. All of our activities are centred to this aim, for we believe that Glasgow has great need for a Real Theatre, where life can be presented and interpreted without prejudice or without being biased by the controlling interests which have so far strangled the professional theatre.[13]

11   Randall Stevenson, 'Drama, Language and Revival', in *The Edinburgh Companion to Scottish Drama*, pp. 73–84 (p. 78).

12   Adrienne Scullion, 'Glasgow Unity Theatre: The Necessary Contradictions of Scottish Political Theatre', *Twentieth Century British History*, 13.3 (2002), 215–52 (pp. 215–16).

13   John Hill, 'Towards a Scottish People's Theatre: The Rise and Fall of Glasgow Unity', *Theatre Quarterly*, 7.27 (1977), 61–70 (p. 63).

Alongside introducing working-class audiences to international classics, Unity's main achievement was in creating a repertoire of new Scottish plays that combined the traditions of European realist political theatre with the robust humour associated with popular forms such as pantomime and Music Hall that had long been adored by Scottish audiences, especially in Glasgow. Unity was also important as an example of community-based working practice because it was formed by the amalgamation of a number of politically-engaged theatre groups, including the Glasgow Corporation Transport Players, the Glasgow Workers' Theatre Group, and the Jewish Institute Players. Unity also ran an 'Outside Group', which toured sketches and short reviews to hospitals, factory canteens and trade union meetings. The company can therefore be credited with developing a model, admittedly on a small scale, that shaped the practices not only of 7:84 but of the NTS, whose emphasis has been less on large scale main stage productions for adult audiences than on small scale, education, outreach and community projects.

Unity's most commercially successful show was Robert McLeish's *The Gorbals Story* (1946), which ran for more than six hundred performances and was seen by one hundred thousand people in its first six months. Based on the dramatist's own experience, and set in a crowded lodging house in the Gorbals area of the city, McLeish's play utilised Glasgow's rich demotic speech patterns to full comic effect while at the same time offering a powerful attack on the causes of the contemporary housing crisis. The play features a wide array of characters, including Hector, a baker from the Highlands, Jean and Wullie Mutrie, an older couple now reduced to living in a single room despite having once had a house of their own, Peggie, a young women without regular employment, Peter Reilly, an Irish labourer and his family, and Ahmed, an Indian peddler who is visiting the lodging house. The play dealt with a topical issue in exploring the chronic post-war housing shortage, but its wider themes, as Paul Maloney has noted, include 'the social injustice of economic condition; post war disillusionment [...] the effects of racism and sectarianism pervading Scottish society; and grinding poverty's destructive and undignified effects'.[14]

Like *The Gorbals Story*, Ena Lamont Stewart's *Men Should Weep* utilises the vernacular, local reference and humour in centring on the effects of poverty on working-class Glaswegian communities. Set in a tenement during the Depression, Lamont Stewart's play was unusual for its time in focusing on female experience. Its central character, Maggie Morrison, a long-suffering wife and mother, is weighed down by the daily grind of making ends meet. Her

---

14 Paul Maloney, 'Twentieth-Century Popular Theatre', in *The Edinburgh Companion to Scottish Drama*, pp. 60–72 (p. 64).

husband John is affectionate but jobless. Her troubles proliferate. She has responsibility for her ailing mother-in-law, and her youngest son Bertie is hospitalised with tuberculosis. Her eldest, Alex, returns to the overcrowded tenement with his quarrelsome wife, and her headstrong daughter Jenny leaves home to set up house with a married man. In its original version, *Men Should Weep* had a particularly bleak ending in which Maggie died in childbirth, John fell off the wagon, Alex murdered his unfaithful wife, Jenny returned destitute to the family home, and Bertie died of tuberculosis.

As Holdsworth has pointed out – and this insight might also be extended to *In Time O' Strife* – this level of misery in the play's resolution amounts to 'a risky dramatic tactic: teetering close to melodrama'.[15] Clearly both plays needed to make very real and visceral connections with their audiences to remain viable. In both cases the realism of the language, the accurate rendering of authentic demotic Scots, was key, as was the use of humour to offset the worst aspects of poverty. 'Here is Glasgow humour, quick, raw, homely, at its best, and it is "put over" with punch and vigour by a company of outstanding ability', observed *The Scotsman* theatre critic of Lamont Stewart's play.[16] Unusually for the period, *Men Should Weep* also offered a subtle but extremely effective critique of patriarchy, especially the gendered division of labour. Although jobless, John Morrison makes no effort to alleviate the domestic labour that so overburdens his wife and, one might even argue, eventually kills her. Instead, he clings belligerently to his culturally determined role as the head of the household. Elsewhere in the play, men emasculated by the vagaries of industrial capitalism – admittedly through no fault of their own – take refuge in drink or assert control over their lives via domestic violence, while women, including Jenny, and Maggie's sister, Lily, take action. Consequently, despite its tragic ending, *Men Should Weep* staged a working-class community of women that was resourceful, resilient and capable of sharing meagre resources. This aspect of the content must have made uncomfortable viewing for a significant section of the original audience. Indeed, Robert Mitchell later attributed the play's limited success to this focus:

[I]t was such an indictment of men's responsibilities in the home, that... well they liked it at the start...they laughed at the funny bits...but it was

---

15   Nadine Holdsworth, 'Case Study: Ena Lamont Stewart's *Men Should Weep*, 1947', in *The Cambridge History of British Theatre: Volume 3 from 1895*, ed. by Baz Kershaw (Cambridge: Cambridge University Press, 2004), pp. 228–41 (p. 229).

16   Anonymous, 'Men Should Weep', *The Scotsman*, 31 January 1947, p. 6.

so near [to] home in Glasgow…it was hitting the man in Glasgow…well somehow they didn't go[:] 'well you must see that'.[17]

Although mounting financial problems meant that Glasgow Unity ceased to exist in 1951 it remained an important touchstone because of its commitment to non-bourgeois audiences, to new writing that was authentic, populist and indigenous, and to work that was urban and working class.

Although different in style and intention, the work of Glasgow Unity remained an important inspiration for 7:84 Scotland in the 1970s and '80s not least because it evidenced the existence of a workers' theatre tradition in Scotland on which the later 7:84 could draw. McGrath's *The Cheviot, the Stag and the Black, Black Oil* (first performed in 1973) remains the most widely acclaimed example of Scottish political theatre of the period, but McGrath's work alongside the archivist and researcher Linda Mackenney in uncovering left-wing playwrights, plays, and companies of the 1920s, 1930s, and 1940s was equally important in establishing a paradigm for a truly 'Scottish' theatre. This work reached its high point in 7:84's hugely influential Clydebuilt season in 1982. In addition to the revival of Corrie's *In Time O' Strife*, which had such a formative impact on Peter Arnott, the season included George Munro's *Gold in his Boots* (1947), Ewan MacColl's *Johnny Noble* (1946), and, perhaps most significantly, Giles Havergal's production of a revised version of Lamont Stewart's masterpiece; it was this production that definitively secured *Men Should Weep*'s reputation. Perhaps mindful of the gains made by second-wave feminism, Lamont Stewart revised the text for the 1982 revival, allowing Maggie to survive and achieve some small measure of control over her situation.

Lamont Stewart was Unity's only female playwright and for much of her career she remained an isolated figure. Gender bias was not peculiar to the stage during this period, of course, but Scottish culture and by extension Scottish theatre continued to be particularly saturated in masculine imagery. Well into the 1970s, as Ian Brown and John Ramage have noted, while Scottish theatre remained politically engaged it continued to be 'dominated by a reaffirmation of traditional Scottish values – the values of a male dominated traditional working class culture'.[18] This trend is exemplified in works such as Bill Bryden's *Willie Rough* (1972), Tom McGrath and Jimmy Boyle's *The Hard Man* (1977), and John Byrne's *The Slab Boys* (1978), all of which drew their energy

17   Robert Mitchell, 'Interview with Robert Mitchell', *Scottish Theatre Archive*, 1967, University of Glasgow, Tape 60.

18   Ian Brown and John Ramage, 'Referendum to Referendum and Beyond: Political Vitality and Scottish Theatre', *The Irish Review*, 18 (2001), 46–57 (p. 48).

from the creative use of working-class Scots while retaining a focus on masculine concerns. Thankfully, the early 1980s, when the positive effects of second-wave feminism finally began to become apparent, witnessed the beginning of a sustained focus on women's lives on Scottish stages. Building on the achievements of Lamont Stewart, Scotland's female dramatists began to make significant inroads, troubling in the process preconceived notions of how Scottish communities could and should be represented on stage.

Like other feminist playwrights of their generation, Scottish women dramatists questioned the efficacy of realism as a mode for representing female experience, often drawing on mythic and folkloric elements to critique historically determined representations of woman. Sue Glover's *The Seal Wife* (1980), for example, utilised the legend of the selkies to explore the domestic restrictions placed on women in a coastal village in southern Fife. According to tradition, a selkie would transform into human form then marry and bear children, only to return to the sea at some later date. In *The Seal Wife*, Glover's protagonist Rona is dissatisfied with her culturally assigned role as wife and mother and eventually abandons her family. Glover thus transforms the legend from a narrative of seduction and deceit to one of resistance and release, in the process critiquing the cultural pressures that bear upon Scottish women and assign them unproblematically to domestic roles. Similarly, Rona Munro's *The Maiden Stone* (1995) takes as its setting the rural northeast in the early part of the nineteenth century, and draws on and inverts local myths of chastity in order to expose the fear and hatred of female sexuality that is symptomatic of patriarchal ideology. More recently, in *The Last Witch* (2009), Munro reimagines the life of Janet Horne, who in 1727 became the last women to be burned as a witch in Scotland. Munro's play figures Janet as a strong, willful and eccentric fantasist and the superstitious and claustrophobic community that turns on her, not as resilient, couthy and resourceful, but as profoundly misogynistic. The devil 'appears in many guises' in *The Last Witch*, noted *The Guardian*'s Lyn Gardner wryly, 'but all of them are male'.[19]

In the event, the decade that witnessed the 7:84 revival of *Men Should Weep* saw the emergence of a number of significant Scottish women playwrights including Liz Lochhead, Marcella Evaristi, Ann Marie Di Mambro, Sharman Macdonald, Rona Munro, Anne Downie and Aileen Ritchie. As well as challenging the domination of masculinist content on the Scottish stage, these women also took the lead in extending the range of possible settings in theatre, moving beyond the tenement and workplace interiors of industrial working-class Scotland. The narrative of Sharman Macdonald's *When I Was a Girl*

---

19   Lyn Gardner, 'Theatre Review: *The Last Witch*', *The Guardian*, 25 August 2009, p. 8.

I used to Scream and Shout (1984) for example, unfolds largely on an east-coast beach as does Glover's *The Seal Wife*. Glover's award-winning *Bondagers* (1991) recounts a year in the life of a group of nineteenth-century female farm labourers in the Scottish Borders, while her *Shetland Saga* (2000) is set in Lerwick. Themes of displacement, marginalisation and isolation recur in Scottish women's drama, as does a tendency to explore these issues in personal terms and in specific localities. Such dramas complicate and problematise the working class 'resilience in adversity' version of community privileged by the realist dramas of the mid-twentieth century. Arguably, the play that refigured the tenement drama most comprehensively, however, was Chris Hannan's *Elizabeth Gordon Quinn* (1985).

Although her narrative unfolds against the backdrop of the 1915 Glasgow rent strikes, with her defiant cry, 'I am not the working class: I am Elizabeth Gordon Quinn. I am an individual', the eponymous anti-heroine of Hannan's tenement drama bears little or no resemblance to Maggie Morrison.[20] Hannan's play is less an attempt at an accurate portrayal of tenement life in early twentieth-century Glasgow, than an exploration of the newly emerging cult of the individual in Margaret Thatcher's Britain. Despising collective action in all its forms, Elizabeth refuses to join the 1915 Rent Strike. Disdaining menial work, she prefers to live in conditions that are squalid even in comparison with her neighbours. She is, in fact, something of a monster. In a fit of patriotic fervour she goads her son into giving up his job as a Post Office clerk and enlisting, only to end up with a deserter on her hands. She also drives her long-suffering husband away. On the other hand, although Elizabeth's attitudes are as delusional as they are destructive, Hannan's achievement is that he invests her with a kind of terrible grandeur. She is a magnificent and tragic embodiment of false consciousness, expending all her energies in keeping up a performance that fools precisely no one. Her final lines, offered by way of explanation, are also the closing lines of the play and exemplify her bizarrely indomitable spirit: 'I refused to learn how to be poor. That's my whole story. And I still refuse!'[21]

The relevance of Hannan's theme to the political culture of the 1980s is obvious. An important development in public discourse in that decade was the tendency to refer to people as consumers and to attribute authority to individuals on these grounds. Moreover, and quite deliberately, to attribute authority to consumers in this way is to undermine or deny that traditional forms of authority are operative, especially those associated with collectivism and

---

20   Chris Hannan, *Elizabeth Gordon Quinn*, in *Scot-Free: New Scottish Plays*, ed. by Alasdair
      Cameron (London: Nick Hern Books, 1990), pp. 105–46 (p. 122).
21   Hannan, *Elizabeth Gordon Quinn*, p. 146.

working-class life. In the aftermath of the No vote in the devolution referendum in 1979 and the re-election of a Conservative government in 1983, the working-class communities that had been the powerful focus of Glasgow Unity's work seemed to be not only in crisis but in terminal decline. Consequently the dramaturgy of politically-engaged theatre shifted. Tony Roper's *The Steamie* (1987), set in a 1950s washhouse on Hogmanay, was an undoubted hit for Wildcat later in the decade but its tone was largely nostalgic and sentimental, celebrating 'a vanishing way of life and sense of community' rather than examining the lives of contemporary working-class Glaswegians with the aim of engendering social or political change.[22]

For Scottish playwrights in the 1990s the reinvention of political Europe in the aftermath of the fall of the Berlin Wall in 1989 fed into an ongoing examination of political and cultural Scotland and offered a very different worldview than those that had held sway in Scotland in earlier decades. This shift in focus and perspective is particularly if by no means exclusively apparent in the work of David Greig, whose output in the 1990s as an independent playwright, and as part of Suspect Culture, the performance company he co-founded, established him as a leading playwright of his generation. A prominent feature of Greig's work in the '90s was its focus on the effects of globalisation on existing notions of identity, community and belonging. A significant quantity of his earlier works explored these questions in settings outside Scotland, from 'perspectives that are not constrained by particular regional boundaries'.[23] A number of important plays of the 1980s, including Peter Arnott's *White Rose* (1985) and John Clifford's *Losing Venice* (1985), had also utilised settings outside Scotland, but this trend was to become more pronounced in the 1990s, offering a further challenge to the orthodoxy of playwrights focusing on working-class Scottish communities or on figures and incidents from Scottish history. *Europe* (1994), the earliest play by Greig to appear in print, provides a good example of this new direction in Scottish playwriting.

Europe is set in autumn in a small decaying provincial town near an unnamed border somewhere in the heart of Europe. The arrival of two foreigners, Sava and his daughter Katia, seeking shelter and safety, provokes a range of responses from the locals, from sympathy and sexual attraction, to suspicion and hatred. Most of the action unfolds in the town's dilapidated railway station, which is staffed by Fret the stationmaster and his daughter Adele, a porter.

---

22   Maloney, 'Twentieth-Century Popular Theatre', in *The Edinburgh Companion to Scottish Drama*, p. 72.

23   Anja Müller and Clare Wallace, in *Cosmopotia: Transnational Identities in David Greig's Theatre*, ed. by Anja Müller and Clare Wallace (Prague: Univerzita Karlova, 2011), p. 2.

It is in this station, at which trains no longer stop, that Sava and Katia, refugees from war, set up camp. In *Europe* the disused station operates as a very rich and powerful metaphor through which Greig explores tensions between mobility and stasis and the existence of vastly unequal cultures of movement in late-twentieth-century Europe. His characters exist in situations of transition, instability and uncertainty. For example, the ground on which Fret has built his sense of identity and community continually shifts, and he appears cut off from the outside world and from history. In the second half of the play, the town is no longer near a border because the border has moved.

In his introduction to David Greig's *Plays: One*, Dan Rebellato notes that the kind of 'severance from history' we encounter in *Europe* is 'particularly important to Scotland where national identity is often linked with the defence of cultural memory'.[24] This observation explains the popularity history plays on Scottish stages, a trend explored elsewhere by David Archibald and Ian Brown among others.[25] Much of the work of Scotland's female playwrights since the 1980s, although sometimes drawing on history, problematises the idea of a stable and coherent Scottish body politic by focusing on marginalised figures, on outsiders and the periphery. A sustained concern with the politics of inclusion and exclusion and on the idea of community as suffocating and oppressive as well as liberating and inclusive has also been evident across the generation of Scottish dramatists who emerged in the 1990s. David Harrower, for instance, exhibited a persistent ambivalence about the possibility of shared values in his early work. His acclaimed debut, *Knives in Hens* (Traverse, 1995), is a compelling and subtle exploration of how patriarchal power relations are enforced through language. Indeed, the play's central character – 'young woman' – is so oppressed by patriarchal discourse that she does not even have a name. Set in an ill-defined preindustrial past and in no identifiable country, *Knives in Hens* is an intensely lyrical and atmospheric play that tells how the young woman eventually escapes the clutches of her oppressive husband by joining forces with her lover to murder him. The many failures in communication that characterise its bleak poetry create a sense of characters isolated and irrevocably trapped in their own subjective realities.

24   Dan Rebellato, 'Introduction', in David Greig, *Plays: One* (London: Methuen, 2002), pp. ix–xxiii (p. xiii).

25   David Archibald, 'History in Contemporary Scottish Theatre', in *The Edinburgh Companion to Scottish Drama*, pp. 85–94. Ian Brown, 'Plugged into History', in *Scottish Theatre Since the Seventies*, ed. by Randall Stevenson and Gavin Wallace (Edinburgh: Edinburgh University Press, 1996), pp. 84–99.

Alongside Greig and Harrower, Anthony Neilson has also emerged as a distinctive voice. Originally coming to attention in the 1990s as part of what Aleks Sierz labelled the 'in-yer-face' school, Neilson's work in the new millennium has been consistently formally experimental.[26] Especially in works such as *The Wonderful World of Dissocia* (2004), *Realism* (2006), *Relocated* (2008) and *Narrative* (2013), Neilson has privileged felt experience over culturally imposed notions of 'normality' and community, by staging – in a cocktail of flash back, fantasy, nightmare and naturalism – the insides of characters' heads. Neilson's focus on marginalised and often traumatised individual subjects, combined with an almost complete absence of reference to contemporary Scottish political debates in his work, means that, among other things, his plays provide an eloquent counterbalance to reductive or essentialist conceptions of Scottish identity. Although very different in form and emphasis, his work, like that of Harrower and Greig, and indeed many of the female playwrights discussed earlier in this chapter, has extended the vocabulary of Scottish theatre in ways that are both welcome and productive. This is not to imply that contemporary Scottish theatre has entirely abandoned its existing iconography in the new millennium. On the contrary, by far the most successful Scottish production of the twenty-first century has been Gregory Burke's *Black Watch* (2006), a play that is uncompromisingly populist, masculinist and working class in its focus.

Burke has consistently produced work that privileges masculine perspectives, particularly the vantage points of disaffected working-class men struggling to find their place in a post-industrial Scotland. In his debut, *Gagarin Way* (2001), a play which, like *Black Watch*, features an all-male cast, self-educated factory worker Eddie and his accomplice Gary, a disillusioned political activist, kidnap Frank, a visiting factory manager, in what proves to be a futile and violent act of resistance against the vagaries of global capitalism. *Gagarin Way* is a dark heist comedy about four men who are, very specifically, the sons and grandsons of Fife miners. They exist in a world of outsourcing and are buffeted by the forces of international capitalism, but they are more or less painfully aware of their community's radical past: the nearby mining village of Lumphinnans was once dubbed Little Moscow because of its communist affiliations. *Gagarin Way* had an immediate impact, transferring from Edinburgh's Traverse to the National Theatre in London, but its success was overshadowed by that of *Black Watch*. Although it began life as a site-specific Fringe production, *Black Watch*, in an NTS production by John Tiffany, has by now achieved celebrated status, winning numerous awards, including four Oliviers and a New York Drama Circle award, and touring extensively internationally and

---

26   Aleks Sierz, *In-Yer-Face Theatre: British Drama Today* (London: Methuen, 2001).

in the UK. *Black Watch* has in effect become 'emblematic, both of renewed confidence among Scottish theatre makers and a distinctively Scottish approach to the medium'.[27] Burke reinvigorates and reanimates the iconography of the Scottish soldier, in the process painting a picture of an exclusively masculine community established through centuries of shared experience. 'We're a fucking tribe ourselves', its central character informs the audience in one of the play's many moments of direct address.[28] Focused firmly on the shared experience of a group of working-class men, and featuring music by Davey Anderson and movement direction by Stephen Hogget, *Black Watch* utilises a wide range of performance modes and registers, in the process drawing on the legacy of both Glasgow Unity and 7:84 Scotland. While it certainly does not embrace McGrath's explicitly Marxist agenda, it does draw freely on his conception of a popular theatre that engages its audience by conceiving of the theatrical event as a celebration and as an expression of community. This emphasis on celebration and community can be seen elsewhere in the output of the NTS. David Greig's *The Strange Undoing of Prudencia Hart* (2011), for instance, drew with some degree of wit and assurance on the conventions of the medieval folk ballad and was designed to be performed by a small group of actor-musicians in pubs, howfs and function rooms, not in traditional theatre spaces. Similarly, Kieran Hurley's *Rantin* (2013), a collection of songs and monologues about contemporary Scotland co-devised with Gav Prentice, Julia Taudevin and Drew Wright, was a 'gorgeous piece of ceilidh theatre', according to *The Herald*'s Mary Brennan, delivered with an 'unforced rollicking charm'.[29]

I have been arguing that the recent NTS revivals of *Men Should Weep* and *In Time O' Strife* illustrate a continued investment in the efficacy of the populist political tradition that created them. Cora Bissett and David Greig's musical *Glasgow Girls* (2012) evidences the re-emergence of a more direct form of political engagement in Scottish theatre, one that calls to mind the practices of Glasgow Unity and 7:84 Scotland. Indeed, this connection was quite obvious. *The Herald*'s Mark Brown observed that not, 'perhaps, since 1973 – when John McGrath and his 7:84 theatre company staged their legendary play *The Cheviot, The Stag and The Black, Black Oil* – has Scottish musical theatre packed a political punch as hard as *Glasgow Girls*'.[30] *Glasgow Girls* is certainly strikingly optimistic in tone in comparison with *Elizabeth Gordon Quinn*, *Europe* or *Gagarin*

27   Trish Reid, *Theatre and Scotland* (Basingstoke: Palgrave Macmillan, 2013), pp. 15–16.
28   Gregory Burke, *The National Theatre of Scotland's Black Watch* (London: Faber and Faber, 2007), p. 31.
29   Mary Brennan, '*Rantin*', Cottiers Theatre, Glasgow', *The Herald*, 19 April 2013, p. 12.
30   Mark Brown, 'True Test of Girl Power', *The Herald*, 4 November 2012, p. 17.

Way, and in this sense it recalls Glasgow Unity's fundamental belief in the power of theatre to effect change. Unity's intention, as its membership form made explicit, was 'to present plays which, by truthfully interpreting life as experienced by the majority of the people, can move the people to work for the betterment of society'.[31]

Glasgow Girls tells the true story of seven Glaswegian schoolgirls and their teacher, who in 2005 conducted an award-winning campaign against dawn raids on asylum seekers in their local community. It is set largely in Drumchapel, a peripheral Glasgow housing estate built in the 1960s as an exercise in slum clearance. The girls' campaign exemplifies the child's appetite for justice, and indeed this might seem sentimental were it not for the cruelty and brutality that surrounds them. Their collective action is triggered by the arrest of Agnesa, a member of their friendship group with whom they have shared a classroom for five years. One of the remarkable, and one might think unfashionable, things about the show is that it repeatedly exposes itself to sincerity and directly challenges cynicism in its moments – mostly musical – of breath-stopping exuberance. The structure is not fiercely dialectical, like McGrath's *The Cheviot, the Stag and the Black, Black Oil*, nor is it intended to pull produc-tively against the limitations of realism; instead, it privileges emotional space. Many significant events take place in between scenes (the arrest of Agnesa and her family, the deportation of a mother and son, for instance), so that rather than concretise these highly charged moments in a particular representation, Bissett and Greig open up spaces in the dramaturgy for the intense emotional responses of the young protagonists to inhabit, allowing such emotions to situ-ate themselves beyond the precise world of the play in the auditorium.

Such a reading is of course unashamedly optimistic and aligns itself neatly not only with John McGrath's thesis in *A Good Night Out* (1981), but also with Jill Dolan's more recent arguments in *Utopia in Performance* in which she insists on

> the potential of different kinds of performance to inspire moments in which audiences feel themselves allied with each other, and with a broader more capacious idea of a public, in which social discourse articu-lates the possible, rather than the insurmountable obstacles to human potential.[32]

---

31   Glasgow Unity Membership Forms (194?), *Scottish Theatre Archive*, University of Glasgow, Ar Box 1/7.

32   Jill Dolan, *Utopia in Performance: Finding Hope at the Theater* (Michigan: The University of Michigan Press, 2005), p. 2.

The success of *Glasgow Girls* evidences the return, admittedly in a new incarnation, of the kind of politicised populism that characterised Scottish theatre in the 1940s and again in the 1970s. The theatre sector in which this work has flourished has become considerably more complex and nuanced however, not least because of the valuable contributions made by female playwrights and those working under the influence of postmodern trends in contemporary performance across Europe. Operating from the twin sites of gender and national culture, these writers have enriched the vocabulary of Scottish theatre immeasurably, in the process evidencing a cultural determination, shared by key institutions and individuals, to develop a sustainable theatre culture in Scotland in which the careers of theatre practitioners can develop beyond the first flush of success. This determination found its most concrete expression in the establishment of the National Theatre of Scotland, an institution that by retaining an emphasis on small-scale collaborative projects, and by being geographically inclusive, has explored the many and various communities that make up contemporary Scotland in the locations where these communities live and work.

CHAPTER 8

Alienation and Community in Contemporary Scottish Fiction: The Case of Janice Galloway's *The Trick is to Keep Breathing*

Alex Thomson

Abstract

The refusal of innovative Scottish fiction published in the 1980s and 1990s to appeal to community as a solution to social alienation has led to it being accused of nihilism. This chapter explores this stylistic ambivalence through a case study of Janice Galloway's *The Trick is to Keep Breathing*.

Keywords

Alienation – contemporary Scottish fiction – community – critique – Janice Galloway – *The Trick is to Keep Breathing* – William McIlvanney – *The Kiln*

While commentators have agreed that the 1980s and 1990s saw the development of distinctive new styles of fiction in Scotland, the nature and consequences of those developments remain disputed. For James English, the 'strong emergence' of Scottish fiction in the period, 'formally and linguistically as well as thematically [distinguished] from the accepted norms of the English novel', is part of a larger differentiation of British fiction 'into a whole range of commercially and symbolically important subcategories'.[1] Responses by Scottish critics confirm this symbolic importance: the addition of significant new novels to continuing strengths in drama and poetry has been seen as crucial to the literary revival of the period. This reflects the novel's status as the preeminent modern literary form, as well as the greater portability of fiction to international audiences. Writing in 1993, Gavin Wallace argued that:

> The period since 1970 is likely to be seen with hindsight as a phase in
> which the Scottish novel flourished with a maturity and consistency

---

1 James F. English, 'Introduction', in *A Concise Companion to Contemporary British Fiction*, ed. by James F. English (Oxford: Blackwell, 2006), pp. 1–15 (p. 4).

reminiscent of the heyday of Galt, Scott and Hogg in the nineteenth century or Gibbon, Gunn, McColla [*sic*], Linklater and Mitchison in the twentieth, producing reputations of an analogous stature and influence which have extended well beyond the native.[2]

Yet studies of this period repeatedly identify an apparent contradiction: the formal innovation and artistic success of the Scottish novel is often paired with a strongly negative assessment of contemporary Scottish society. For Douglas Gifford, it is 'the paradox of what looks like a revival of Scottish writing, but the theme of which is pessimism about the very events the revival describes'; a revival 'whose subject matter is the dearth of real culture and aesthetic freedom in modern Scotland'.[3] Cairns Craig contrasts 'the bleak and depressing worlds inhabited by [...] typical characters of post-devolutionary Scotland' with their representation 'in novelistic styles that are radically innovative and energetically ambitious'.[4]

For some commentators, the negativity and alienation of the new Scottish fiction is simply a reflection of social reality. Echoing James Kelman's comment that 'all you've got to do is follow some people around and look at their existence for 24 hours and it will be horror. It will just be horror', Gavin Wallace suggests that:

> A substantial majority of the most significant novels, in fact, published since the 1970s comprise a catalogue of Kelman's 'horror' in its range of constituent complaints: the spiritual and material deprivations of unemployment and decaying communities; failures to find – or accept – self-fulfilment in education, work, emotional relationships; inarticulacy and alienation escaped through alcoholism; destructive mental instability; the paralysing hyper-awareness of class and cultural differentiation; crippling incapacities to give love, or to receive it.[5]

---

2 Gavin Wallace, 'Introduction', in *The Scottish Novel Since the Seventies*, ed. by Gavin Wallace and Randall Stevenson (Edinburgh: Edinburgh University Press, 1993), pp. 1–7 (p. 2).

3 Douglas Gifford, cited in Scott Hames, 'The New Scottish Renaissance?', in *The Oxford History of the Novel in English, vol. VII: British and Irish Fiction Since 1940*, ed. by Peter Boxall and Bryan Cheyette (Oxford: Oxford University Press, 2016), pp. 494–511 (p. 495).

4 Cairns Craig, 'Devolving the Scottish Novel', in *A Concise Companion to Contemporary British Fiction*, pp. 121–40 (p. 127).

5 Kirsty McNeil, 'Interview with James Kelman', *Chapman*, 59, (1989) 1–9 (p. 9). Gavin Wallace, 'Voices in Empty Houses: The Novel of Damaged Identity', in *The Scottish Novel Since the Seventies*, pp. 217–31 (p. 217).

Wallace's comments reflect a sense of national crisis, in which the impoverish-
ment of some specific Scottish communities, although rooted in much longer-
term economic transformations, acquired a new symbolic centrality in articulating
the impact of the political and social changes of the 1980s. In William McIlvanney's
The Kiln (1996), the novelist Tom Docherty makes a representative confession of
his inability to understand Thatcherite Britain:

> He couldn't believe how quickly a largely decent society had been condi-
> tioned to prey on itself. [...] One woman, with all the vision of a soldier
> ant, had managed to screw up the UK. Dehumanisation by statute. There
> is no such thing as society. A self-fulfilling idiocy.[6]

In both these examples, the loss of community – meaning something like the
sense of common belonging that guarantees mutual co-operation – is a prior
historical and social fact. Literature can either merely reflect this loss, or by
giving it expression can help to combat it. This latter ambition is made explicit
in *The Kiln*, in which the novelist (in this case, both McIlvanney and Docherty)
re-affirms the roots of his art through its connection to the ability of the people
around them to truly inhabit a social world through imagination – to 'find
a sense of community in some shabby council houses and a few bleak streets';
or 'an awareness of the horizons [Docherty's] mother can still see, no matter
how enclosed her circumstances'.[7]

However, for other critics, the literature of alienation is not a reflection of
failed community but rather a challenge to the communitarian political horizons implicit in the quotations from Wallace and McIlvanney. In her study of
the period, Eleanor Bell argues that 'writers have often been interested in [...]
questioning limits and borders of Scottishness, which literary and cultural critics have often been hesitant to address'.[8] Similarly, Scott Hames sees the fiction
of the 1980s and 1990s as defined precisely by its rejection of what Francis Hart
had argued in 1978 was the traditional 'moral primacy of community' in the
Scottish novel: 'the "new renaissance" novels broach collective identity primarily to address more fundamental and intractable ethical dilemmas centred on
the individual'.[9] This chapter will build on the work of critics such as Bell and
Hames by arguing that the stylistic and critical distinction of the new Scottish

---

6   William McIlvanney, *The Kiln* (London: Sceptre, 1996), p. 257.
7   McIlvanney, *The Kiln*, pp. 212, 241.
8   Eleanor Bell, *Questioning Scotland: Literature, Nationalism, Postmodernism* (Basingstoke:
    Palgrave Macmillan, 2004), p. 98.
9   Hames, 'The New Scottish Renaissance?', p. 508.

fiction of alienation rests not simply on its ethical orientation towards individual rather than community, or its rejection of the Romantic model in which literature is conceived as the imaginative recreation of community, but on its specific forms of equivocation on this issue. This allows us to give shape to the essential political difference between the confidence displayed by McIlvanney's protagonist in his attribution of blame, and the specific *ambivalence* characteristic of the new style.

Rahel Jaeggi suggests that since the birth of the concept in European Romanticism, there have been two divergent currents of thinking about alienation in philosophy and social theory. Broadly speaking, one perspective is existentialist, and the other Marxist. For the latter, 'alienation is understood as alienation *from* the social world, whereas in the former case the condition of being immersed in a public world is itself regarded as the source of alienation, understood as the subject's loss of authenticity'.[10] One approach concludes in social critique and the subordination of individual to community: only the freedom of the social whole will resolve the problem of individual unfreedom. The other seems to point to the rejection of social goals, including the aspiration for a critically renewed society, as an intrusion on the self. What strikes critics as the 'paradox' of the fiction of alienation is its refusal to clearly decide between these two positions. This refusal is striking in the context of local and international resurgence of identity politics in the 1980s and 1990s – what Arjun Appadurai describes as the global production of locality.[11] As Gillian Rose argued at the time, the 'currency of "community" avoids any immediate implication of state, nation, sovereignty, representation – of power and its legitimation – yet it insinuates and ingratiates the idea of the perfectly enhanced individual and collective life'.[12] The renewal of identity thinking places literature under new pressure to contribute to the production of community. This runs the risk not only of relinquishing literature's aspiration to critical distance from social life but also of contributing to the abnegation of the analysis of political and social process.

This stylistic ambivalence helps explain the reluctance of some writers and critics to give due credit to the new fiction of alienation. While some nationalist critics, including Gifford and Craig, resolve the tension by presenting the

---

10   Rahel Jaeggi, *Alienation*, trans. by Frederick Neuhouser and Alan E. Smith (New York: Columbia University Press, 2014), p. 9. Italics in original.

11   Arjun Appadurai, 'The Production of Locality', in *Modernity At Large: Cultural Dimensions of Globalization* (Minneapolis: University of Minnesota Press, 1996), pp. 178–99.

12   Gillian Rose, *The Broken Middle: Out of Our Ancient Society* (Oxford: Blackwell, 1992), p. 297.

new fiction as the aesthetic overcoming of social and political failure, other commentators have been concerned that the gloomy worldview of these novels has helped sustain a representational malaise which has led to Scotland becoming imprisoned in its own negative stereotypes. A recent cultural pamphlet urges Scots to move beyond 'miserabilism' in literature and film: the self-fulfilling and repetitive perpetuation of archetypes of a damaged culture.[13] This complaint has a long pedigree. Writing in 1996, for example, Kenneth C. Steven saw the new wave of Scottish writing as the repetitive expression of an empty 'malaise [...] without a cause; just a kind of bitter tiredness that will not go away'. Steven argues that this is not the renewal, but the destruction of traditional literary values: writing was now being judged on its commercial potential, or its ability to shock, rather than for the aspiration to any kind of transcendence. Most worrying for Steven, the new styles are not so much the renewal of Scottish tradition but its abolition: for much contemporary Scottish writing 'there is nothing beneath it. It seems to exist in a vacuum, to pay no attention to what has gone before, even in the earlier part of this century'.[14] If literature is taken as the guarantor of national community, the literature of alienation becomes not only a symptom of nihilism but an accelerant of cultural devastation.

The persistence of this debate suggests its significance. Underlying it are differences over the relationship between fiction and society, perhaps particularly starkly drawn as a result of what Hames has described as the 'remarkably strong claims for the political efficacy of the contemporary literary novel' made in Scotland in the period.[15] Moreover, the very social processes that seem to have driven the revival of Scottish fiction have been understood in terms of the shattering of tradition. For Christopher Harvie, Scotland's renascent nationalism coincided with 'market and information revolutions which shattered structures and hierarchies, leaving a hyper-individuation exhausted by its technology, and overwhelmed by its data: deconstructed texts, rejected canons, literature or culture fixed in local constellations'.[16] Harvie catches the ambiguity arising from the celebration of innovation and the experience of

---

13   Eleanor Yule and David Manderson, *The Glass Half Full: Moving Beyond Scottish Miserabilism* (Edinburgh: Luath, 2014).

14   Kenneth C. Steven, 'The Nihilism of the New', *The Herald*, 1 June, 1996, p. 23.

15   Hames, 'The New Scottish Renaissance?', p. 494.

16   Christopher Harvie, *Scotland and Nationalism: Scottish Society and Politics from 1707 to the Present*, 4th edn (London: Routledge, 2004), p. 212; cited in Scott Hames, 'On Vernacular Scottishness and Its Limits: Devolution and the Spectacle of "Voice"', *Studies in Scottish Literature*, 13 (2013), 203–24 (p. 213).

the exhaustion of older models: it gives rise to a stylistic freedom apparently unregulated by tradition or precedent, in which forms of connection have to be reimagined. Finally, we might also speculate that the same ambiguity will play out in the novel's exploration of the relationship between individual and society. For as John Brenkman has argued, the transformation of the novel in the twentieth century is best seen not as the forgetting of its traditional concerns, but their renewal:

> The imperatives of realism – to illuminate individual life histories in the flow of collective histories, to represent how time and impersonal forces move through individual experience and intimate relationships, to assess the boundaries of moral action – are manifest across these writers diverse projects and varied styles. The realist imperative is ingrained in the very innovations that get labelled 'modernist' or 'postmodernist'.

Brenkman suggests that in confronting the modern subject with the experience of modernisation, the novel as a form has in fact run ahead of the philosophers in dealing with reality. As a result, it proves hard to locate within critical schemata that seek to derive a critical value from the opposition between the sphere of the aesthetic and that of market capitalism, or to identify a solution to alienation in the experience of art: 'the art of the novel is not some pure countermovement to nihilism'.[17] The concept of tradition is predicated on an understanding of community – of the consciousness of shared cultural characteristics which relate the members of a social group in more than merely pragmatic ways. When tradition is under stress, the precarious tie between aesthetics and community may fracture in ways which expose the fragility of the claims of either as resistance to modernisation processes.

The Case of *The Trick is to Keep Breathing*

The Trick is to Keep Breathing (1989) provides an excellent case study of the tensions between alienation and community in contemporary Scottish fiction. Quickly recognised as a major achievement, the novel is both informed by and a response to the formal developments of the Scottish novel in the 1980s. Indeed the novel's protagonist includes both Kelman and Gray in a list of

---

17   John Brenkman, 'Innovation: Notes on Nihilism and the Aesthetics of the Novel', in *The Novel, Volume 2: Forms and Themes*, ed. by Franco Moretti (Princeton: Princeton University Press, 2006), pp. 808–38 (pp. 810, 829).

her reading materials, while the book as a whole adopts the typographical device of indicating section breaks by a series of three characters – 'ooo' – from Kelman's *The Busconductor Hines* (1984) and *A Chancer* (1985). The novel's first-person perspective and its use of typographical breakdown to indicate points of intense psychological or textual disturbance echo Gray's *1982 Janine* (1984). Its complex exploration of narrative perspective is more evidently indebted to Kelman, although thematic concerns with guilt and responsibility connect it to both predecessors, and to what had by the end of the decade emerged as a hallmark of the new Scottish fiction. Where the book seems to break new ground is in mixing these stylistic traits with more overtly feminist thematic concerns, already given powerful articulation in Scottish poetry by Liz Lochhead, such as consumer culture, the domestic sphere, mental health and female friendship.[18] Galloway is not simply working within a national context. Like Kelman, she is influenced by post-war European experimental fiction, particularly in French. Moreover, there are few precedents in Scottish tradition for the disavowed lyricism in her work that results in a particularly fraught engagement with symbolism as a possible structuring device and index of psychological states.

Georg Lukàcs had foreseen the possibility of novels in which the psychology of the individual subject would become so central that

> the outside world which comes into contact with such an interiority has to be completely atomised or amorphous, and in any case must be entirely devoid of meaning. It is a world entirely dominated by convention [...]; a quintessence of meaningless laws in which no relation to the soul can be found.[19]

Lukàcs's description is suggestive in relation to *The Trick is to Keep Breathing* because it shows that such alienation may stem not from the depiction of reality but from an inner tendency of the novel as a literary form: the celebration of the rich interior life of the individual risks becoming a solipsistic bracketing of the social. But as Patricia Waugh has suggested, novels in this line have

---

18   This has been taken to be Galloway's significance by literary historians. For Duncan Petrie, Galloway is part of a 'broadening of the cultural franchise' beyond working-class masculinity, a 'vibrant new female presence in Scottish writing', *Contemporary Scottish Fictions: Film, Television and the Novel* (Edinburgh: Edinburgh University Press, 2004), p. 66. For a similar assessment see Robert Crawford, *Scotland's Books: The Penguin History of Scottish Literature* (London: Penguin Books, 2007), p. 702.

19   Georg Lukàcs, *Theory of the Novel*, trans. by Anna Bostock (London: Merlin, 1971), p. 113.

become increasingly less confident of the value-laden distinction between the fullness of lyrical interiority and the conformism and convention of the social world:

> [T]hroughout the twentieth century, and particularly in its later decades, writers have been driven to depict modern secular life as one of inner void or the emptied-out self. There has been a proliferation of minimal-ist, solipsistic interiors, and impersonalized external landscapes of com-mercial exchange. Often the intellectual challenge for the author or reader of such texts is to discover latently or invent performatively some morality which can connect these spheres.[20]

Taken together, these are helpful guides to the challenges of *The Trick is to Keep Breathing*, a novel of the most profound alienation, manifest not only in psychological and social but also in artistic terms.

Waugh's comment in particular highlights two of the significant departures of the new Scottish fiction, exemplified in Galloway. Whereas earlier twentieth-century Scottish novelists had repeatedly focused on the psychological indi-viduation of central characters – often authorial surrogates – whose flourishing depends on separation from and in some cases reconciliation with commu-nity, Galloway's novel offers us no concrete natural or social environment, but a circular entrapment in which the domestic interior reflects Joy's conscious-ness of isolation back at her. Dissociation is internal – 'I watch myself from the corner of the room' – and the systematic confusion in deictic references makes it impossible to tell which self is watching, and which being observed.[21] The description and vocabulary is flat, unemotional and matter of fact, as through-out the novel. The result is that the few uses of metaphor stand out distinctly: 'Streetlight gets in and makes the furniture glow at the edges, like bits of sunk ship rising out of the wash of green'.[22] Galloway draws a marine vocabulary from the novel's seaboard setting – it is specifically situated around Irvine. But there is something queasy about this image, as if the light, coming not from a natural source but from the planned social environment, cannot bring the spiritual aid we expect from poetry. The liquid imagery introduced here is also recurrent through the novel, providing structure through repetition in the absence of clear narrative development. The final pages of the novel also find

20   Patricia Waugh, *Harvest of the Sixties: English Literature and Its Background, 1960 to 1990* (Oxford: Oxford University Press, 1995), p. 67.

21   Janice Galloway, *The Trick is to Keep Breathing*, 2nd edn (London: Minerva, 1991), p. 7.

22   Galloway, *The Trick is to Keep Breathing*, p. 7.

Joy sitting on the floor of her living room; but this time it is Christmas tree lights that effect the transformation, as she imagines swimming, breasting the ocean that in the first scene resonates only with a sense of shipwreck, sea-wrack, or even drowning. While most critics have seen the closing pages of the novel as promising steps on the path to recovery, at least as striking is the degree to which there is only continuity within this repetition, making Joy's small positive advances seem precarious at best.

Not only are there no moments of lyrical epiphany in *The Trick is to Keep Breathing* but the novel repeatedly challenges the cultural script that connects cultivation of imagination to individual flourishing. This is signalled formally. Not only is Joy's consciousness saturated in the language and judgements of the mass circulation magazines of which she is an apparently sceptical yet voracious reader, but the text of the novel is presented as including cuttings or quotations from these magazines. This breakdown of the boundary between literary and mass culture could be seen as a symptom of social degeneration, or of the individual failure to make significant value judgements. Yet the novel's ambivalence seems to extend towards this distinction itself. In a list of her reading material, Joy equates literature with the miscellaneous texts of mass culture:

> I read *The Prophet*, Gide, Kafka and Ivor Cutler. *Gone with the Wind, Fat is a Feminist Issue*, Norman MacCaig and Byron. *Lanark*, Muriel Spark, *How to cope with your Nerves/Loneliness/Anxiety*, Antonia White and Adrian Mole. *The Francis Gay Friendship Book* and James Kelman. ee cummings. *Unexplained Mysteries* and *Life After Death*. I read magazines, newspapers, billboards, government health warnings, advertising leaf-lets, saucebottles, cans of beans, Scottish Folk Tales and The Bible. They reveal glimpses of things just beyond the reach of understanding, but never the whole truth. I fall into a recurring loop every morning after[23]

Marking Joy as an informed reader of contemporary Scottish writing, this list also suggests her knowledge of the classics of modern literary alienation. Each item promises some kind of ethical guidance, but the list as a whole fails to establish a hierarchy between them. The 'truths' each type of text promises – about life on Earth or life after death, religion or mysticism, politics or friendship – all become equivalent ways of making sense of the world. This implies a cultural condition in which no set of texts has a higher degree of

---

23   Galloway, *The Trick is to Keep Breathing*, pp. 195–96.

authority than any other, indicative perhaps that the novel is concerned with a societal crisis of significance transcending Joy's personal crisis.

The novel is equivocal as to whether the fault lies more largely with Joy's failure to adapt to the social world, or the social world that has failed to provide her with adequate resources to sustain her existence. While centred on Joy's perceptions, thoughts and feelings, the disorientation of her mental world is so great as to significantly obstruct readers' access to any external point by which to explain or understand her interior state. Indeed, for much of the novel, the narrative is so subjectively focused that changing surroundings suggest merely an indifferent interchange of equally hostile backgrounds. One plausible response to the novel is to see it as an exploration of the distinctive social situation of the West of Scotland in the period. Galloway depicts the Bourtreehill estate (part of Irvine, last of the Scottish New Towns to be developed) as isolated and inaccessible; people keep themselves to themselves, roaming children appear threatening and hostile, racist graffiti appears every morning on an Asian shopkeeper's door, while the school is repeatedly vandalised.[24] But another possibility is perhaps more disturbing. As Alison Smith suggested in a perceptive early discussion, the novel 'strips back the everyday surface of life to reveal sheer chaos, to demonstrate that what we call "reality" is merely the flotsam of a deeper, darker place by far'.[25] Although he sees the novel as finally recuperative, Nicholas Royle also recognises in it an exploration not merely of social deprivation, but of more disturbing psychological impulses.[26] For Smith and Royle the novel raises the possibility that Joy's alienation is not symptomatic of social breakdown but a more radical repudiation of the sustaining myths of community in the face of daemonic psychic drives.

These alternatives are hard to reconcile, but perhaps they are also hard to distinguish. By showing us the world from within the perspective of Joy's alienated subjectivity, it becomes impossible to judge whether it is her response to the world, or the world itself, which is at fault. This is a challenge that readers of Kelman frequently face: Simon Kövesi argues that in *The Busconductor Hines* 'the hell that Hines crosses and recrosses is not Glasgow, but his own apocalyptic mind which can set the most mundane of scenes alight'.[27] In this case, Joy has internalised social norms but finds she cannot live by them. She judges her own actions in terms of function and efficiency: her role in the workplace

---

24   Galloway, *The Trick is to Keep Breathing*, pp. 13–14, 26, 133.
25   Alison Smith, 'Four Success Stories', *Chapman*, 74–5 (1993), 177–92 (p. 177).
26   Nicholas Royle, 'Manifestations of Insanity: *Hunger* and contemporary fiction', in *The Uncanny* (Manchester: Manchester University Press, 1993), pp. 213–18.
27   Simon Kövesi, *James Kelman* (Manchester: Manchester University Press, 2007), p. 47.

'tells me what I am'; she worries that she is a burden on the state, a cost to society.[28] This is not simply because of the medical attention she receives, but more broadly that she seems not to be functioning successfully in a world in which '**good** =' both '**productive/hardworking**' and '**value for money**'. This failure marks her as 'unProtestant', an exile from both Scottish tradition and capitalist modernity.[29] But while the novel sketches the destructive pressure of these norms within Joy's sense of self, it provides no basis on which to judge whether their excessive pressure and the intrusion of economic values into the individual lifeworld are failures inherent to the norms themselves, or to Joy's failure to successfully navigate them. Moreover, these kinds of judgements are precisely those that are being assumed when Joy is expected to translate the hard truth of Michael's death into a story that will allow her to overcome the fact of that loss through its successful reintegration of the events into her own self-narration.

Formally, the novel interlaces two sequences of fragments, the majority of which are set in roman type and form a chronological series, albeit extended backwards into earlier events in Joy's life through analeptic retrospection. Some sections focus on a single, relatively discrete, event; others contain a sequence of disconnected scenes, events or action whose relationship the reader has to establish. Most often this relationship is either blankly sequential – one thing happens after another, but the fact of temporal succession is not itself worth commenting on, so the reader is left to fill this in. The roman sections are interspersed with sections set in italics whose status is less clear: some seem to be memories of the events surrounding Michael's drowning, while others appear to be less solidly founded in reality. These images suggest a symbolic complement to the general sense of foreboding and imminent threat which characterises Joy's psychic life and seem to operate by a dream logic of condensation, combining elements from memory with more abstract symbols. Despite its fragmentation, however, the text invites the reader to engage with it as essentially a conventional novel, and thus to seek to reconstruct plot, character and significant patterns. The novel challenges the reader to find or impose such form. At its very beginning, initially disorienting because found on the verso rather than the recto of the first page spread, the first of the italic fragments tells us both '*I can't remember the last week with any clarity*' but also '*Now I remember everything all the time*'.[30] To remember everything is to fail to establish sequential relations between different points in time, and to

---

28   Galloway, *The Trick is to Keep Breathing*, p. 11.
29   Galloway, *The Trick is to Keep Breathing*, p. 81. Emphasis in original.
30   Galloway, *The Trick is to Keep Breathing*, p. 6.

allow the past to overflow into the present. Taken together these comments invite the reader to seek the clarity that the novel lacks, and to restore a form of order to the sequence of impressions by imposing a degree of linearity, hence achieving a differentiation between past and present. This diagnostic reading re-establishes a more traditional relationship between plot and character: grasping the sequence of events that befall Joy can lead us to understand her own failure to do so. But this is also a redemptive reading. Seeking to restore order to what we encounter as broken, the reader becomes aligned with the normative ethical framework with which Joy is in conflict.

The italic sections become the test of this form of reading. Those which refer most directly to events in Spain can be treated as incomplete or partial memories of a specific traumatic moment which continues to disrupt Joy's psychological interiority in the later timeline followed in the roman sections. But as the novel develops, these events are also consciously recalled in the roman section, suggesting that the novel cannot be understood simply in terms of the working through of traumatic experience, or of psychic reintegration. Indeed, the more we learn about Joy's life, the more it seems that Michael's death is less the cause of her present mental disturbance, than merely the latest in a series of events to have confirmed her prior sense that she is being continually punished for some unknown transgression. The novel repeatedly troubles our desire to attribute a causal relationship between events, since to do so would be to claim an illegitimate external authority over Joy's understanding of her own experience from a vantage point unavailable to her. But there are strong hints that her problems in forming healthy relationships are rooted in an abusive childhood. Both the fact that the italic sequence initiates the novel, and the systematic confusion of deictic reference, suggest that the italic passages cannot be fully enclosed within the 'present' timeline established within the roman sections. The 'present' time of the novel cannot subsume or control its 'past'.

This leads to a series of problems caused not so much by Joy's unreliability as a witness to, or reporter of, her own experience but by the deliberate reflexivity of the novel. Looking at the phrases already quoted above, it is impossible to establish with any certainty exactly *when* the novel begins. Either the '*now*' of the second sentence is not the same now as the first or 'everything' must mean everything except the last week. If the '*last week*' seems most likely to relate to the week in Spain whose events are – at first – only told in the italic sequence, it could equally refer to the first few weeks of the main chronological line, in which Joy repeatedly awakens with no memory of the night before, and has to leave herself reminders of medical appointments. If the italic sequence is not so much a description of a trauma to be overcome, but a preconscious condition of subjectivity, then it would also hold that the *'now'* belongs equally to the time of writing. Nor can we discount its reference to the time of reading, as the novel specifically charges the reader with moral responsibilities. If the invitation to recompose experience imposes on the reader something of the dilemma faced by the medical professionals who work with Joy, in weighing her autonomy against her illness, the construction of the novel subjects the reader to the same elisions and misdirection that characterise Joy's accounting to her doctors when she hides her starvation, her drinking or her squirrelling away of painkillers. While there are sections in which the reader can supply information that Joy may lack at a particular point in time, there are many others in which the roles are reversed, and in which it appears that she deliberately suppresses elements of her narration of events, as if choosing to temporarily withdraw from the intimate revelation of self implied by the highly personal narrative form. On the first Sunday night of the main section, for example, Joy leaves the house with a man, who has not been identified to us, and the narrative stops, resuming again the next morning.[31] This makes the novel a defiantly *composed* text: collaged, in part, from what seem to be contemporaneous letters, diaries and reading material. This reminds us that the fragmentary mode relates not to the novelistic *representation* of psychological disturbance, but to deliberate choices made by Joy as herself the author of her account.

Joy's failure in relation to the paradigm of productive social participation might be taken as metonymic of the novel's resistance to being put to work in the service of politically-inflected criticism. While there has been marked disagreement over the exact terms, it has been widely assumed that through its depiction of alienation, the novel becomes the expression, or the critical diagnosis, of larger social problems. An early reviewer felt it showed 'the wounds inflicted by the damage of late-capitalist life in Scotland'.[32] Cairns Craig argues that the novel can be understood as a reflection of 'a society only aware of itself as an absence'.[33] Feminist critics in particular have argued that 'it is too easy [...] to see Joy as representative of any particular kind of Scottishness, or Scotland'; as Carole Jones suggests, Craig's assessment of the novel in terms of a 'masculinist allegory of national crisis' specifically occludes the novel's

---

31   Galloway, *The Trick is to Keep Breathing*, p. 48.

32   Pat Kane, cited by Margery Metzstein, 'Of Myths and Men: Aspects of Gender in the Fiction of Janice Galloway', in *The Scottish Novel Since the Seventies*, pp. 136–46 (p. 139).

33   Cairns Craig, *The Modern Scottish Novel: Narrative and the National Imagination* (Edinburgh: Edinburgh University Press, 1999), p. 199.

concerns with gender.[34] All three responses – anti-capitalist, nationalist and feminist – depend on seeing Joy as in some sense a representative of a larger identity category, whether by allegory or synecdoche, and the novel as a study of characteristic alienation, implicating larger social structures of social or political domination. But through the exploration of its protagonist's claim to autonomy, the novel dramatises its own, and in doing so poses a challenge to the legitimacy of representation in general; while its refusal of judgement demands modes of reading that suspend symptomatic interpretation.

This suspension of diagnostic reading generates part of the ambivalence of the novel's handling of the political question of community. The novel can, for example, be connected to the question of adequate housing. Its symbolic connection both to the perceived failure of municipal planning in the Labour Scotland of the 1950s and 1960s and to the Thatcherite emphasis on home ownership, had made housing by the late 1980s a critical marker in Scottish political discourse. The novel persistently stresses that the rented Housing Authority property is cold, draughty and inadequately furnished; the walls are so thin that she can hear the family next door argue: but Joy is herself a home-owner, forced into rented accommodation by the dry rot spreading through the cottage she has bought after her break-up with Paul. The novel hints that Joy's current predicament represents the failure of her attempt to live 'independent and free', related perhaps to her effort to build a newly 'liberated' type of relationship with Michael – 'he needn't feel he owed me anything. New woman, new man. No jealousies, no possessiveness, no demands' – causing her episodes of distress for which she cannot account.[35] Joy seems to have been ill-served by changing cultural modes, seen as a forgetting of the priority of social relations from which springs the complex interweaving of obligation and debt that characterises moral existence. Joy's need for extreme control over her emotions – reflected in her suspicion of telephones, as well as in the distance she maintains from Ellen, David and other friends – suggests this desire for independence. But it also connects to her longing to be free from guilt, and hence her fantasy of a form of life in which she would not owe anyone anything.

---

34   Glenda Norquay, 'Janice Galloway's Novels: Fraudulent Mooching', in *Contemporary Scottish Women Writers*, ed. by Aileen Christianson and Alison Lumsden (Edinburgh: Edinburgh University Press, 2000), pp. 131–43 (p. 141). Carole Jones, 'Burying the Man that was: Janice Galloway and Gender Disorientation', in *The Edinburgh Companion to Contemporary Scottish Literature*, ed. by Berthold Schoene (Edinburgh: Edinburgh University Press, 2007), pp. 210–18 (p. 214).

35   Galloway, *The Trick is to Keep Breathing*, pp. 192, 195.

Joy's sense of guilt and her desire for autonomy also dominate her interaction with the medical profession; the difficulty of evaluating the consequences further blurs the novel's relationship to social critique. Most critics have taken the presentation of these stilted conversations in a dialogue form as a sign of Joy's estrangement from social services, treating this as an indictment of bureaucratic indifference. Mary McGlynn goes so far as to suggest that Joy's interactions with the medical profession might be a 'pertinent critique' of state-funded welfare provision in general.[36] But there are those who criticise in order to improve such provision, and those who wish to abolish it, and the difference is significant. While their presentation as a dramatic script might suggest that her doctors are merely going through the motions, it also signals Joy's need to rehearse encounters in which her sense of self-preservation and desire for control requires her to deliberately suppress information about her anorexia. Moreover, reality can exceed her expectations: she imagines Dr Stead refusing her a referral but in fact she is on the list.[37] As Galloway herself has stressed, everyone in the novel is at least trying to help: 'even [Tony]'s making an effort with her. I don't think anybody is being lousy to Joy'.[38]

The apparent nihilism of *The Trick is to Keep Breathing* is most starkly illuminated in the scene in which Joy contemplates suicide. The date alone should be significant: it is her birthday, but also exactly one year to the day since Michael's wife has discovered their affair. As elsewhere in the novel, Galloway focuses on the rituals through which Joy establishes some sense of order in her life, and she prepares her means of self-destruction with a certain degree of relish: lining up the contents of a bottle of paracetamol; filling a glass to the brim with gin. Reviewing her situation, she is led outward to explore a series of more metaphysical problems. What is the 'point'? Joy's term embraces the complex interweaving of narrative, design, purpose and destiny that characterises all teleological questions. But if she has not found any reason to persist in existence, nor has she found any more persuasive reason not to do so; and when someone comes to the window, she finds herself compelled to respond: 'If I answer I have to accept what it says about me. That I don't want to die. That I don't want to live very much but I don't want to die'.[39]

---

36   Mary McGlynn, '"I Didn't Need to Eat": Janice Galloway's Anorexic Text and the National Body', *Critique*, 49 (2008), 221–36 (p. 226).

37   Galloway, *The Trick is to Keep Breathing*, pp. 51–53.

38   Isobel Murray, Interview with Janice Galloway, in *Scottish Writers Talking 3* (Edinburgh: Birlinn, 2006), pp. 1–58 (p. 29).

39   Galloway, *The Trick is to Keep Breathing*, p. 203.

There is a sceptical irony in the novel's handling of Joy's half-hearted failure to commit to either death or life, a sardonic wit matching Joy's own. But the scene is powerful because of the contrast between Joy's determination both to take decisive steps and to give good grounds for doing so, and her apparent inability to establish a physical connection between her reasoning and her actions. As often in the novel, she finds herself a witness to, rather than the subject of, her own volition. She is fully conscious of being lost within the circling thought patterns of the depressive, but refuses to resign herself to this, seeing the admission of sickness as abdication of responsibility. In continuing to demand of herself this responsibility – manifest subjectively as the experience of guilt – her thoughts acquire a larger significance. 'Knowing too much at the same time as knowing nothing at all' signals her total awareness of her own situation, as well as her inability to establish sequence, hierarchy or dependence amongst all the things that she knows, and hence to give her experience narratable form.[40] Yet Joy's choice of words also suggests that this may be not so much an individual failing as an unbearable insight (knowing too much) into the (ungrounded, unknowable) conditions of human existence. This is to experience being itself as radically in question, as a set of demands for meaning posed to us: 'They're always there, accusing me of having no answers yet. If there are no answers there is no point: a terror of absurdity'.[41] What kind of a vision of the world is this, the novel asks: blindness or insight, sickness or health?

Posing these questions, the novel follows an existentialist tradition, which finds both a precedent and an opponent in the figure of Descartes. Descartes's arguments in his *Meditations* have long been received as an inaugural attempt to find some kind of fundamental ground for understanding human existence once we rule out God as a transcendental guarantor. But existentialism is defined by its opposition to what it takes to be the Cartesian solution, the re-foundation of certainty in the transparency of the subject as a rational and self-grounding being. Joy's predicament expresses this ambivalent relation throughout the book – her isolation and interiority suggesting a parody of the Cartesian desire not to rely on any external basis for certainty, while continually rehearsing the limits to finding an alternative starting-point in knowledge or reasoning. Here her language – **'There is no point, ergo'** – specifically invokes not merely the attempt to ground existence in logic, but the most famous phrase in Descartes.[42]

---

40   Galloway, *The Trick is to Keep Breathing*, p. 195.
41   Galloway, *The Trick is to Keep Breathing*, p. 195.
42   Galloway, *The Trick is to Keep Breathing*, p. 198. Emphasis in original.

There is a suggestive contrast here to McIlvanney's profession of existential-ist faith in *The Kiln*. Docherty invokes both Descartes and Pascal: 'Right enough, Blaise or René, whichever of you said it':

> This is the most human bet that you can make. Firstly, because to be human is to admit that there is no way you can *know* that anything is there. Secondly, because if there is nothing there, it makes your moral behaviour all the more real, all the more an expression of you. It has no basis but yourself. You replace religious cynicism with human idealism. You exist dramatically in an empty universe.[43]

Galloway offers us the possible nightmarish consequence of accepting McIlvanney's humanist transformation of the Pascalian wager by undercutting our reliance on the reality of the self. The universe of *The Trick is to Keep Breathing* is every bit as empty as that of *The Kiln*, with the billboards outside churches equally as meaningless – or meaningful – as the branding of a super-market. But the flooding of Joy's consciousness by commodity culture, reiterat-ing the message that her actions are an expression of her self, and that as a result her goodness depends on her successful performance of individuality in accordance with the expectations of the society around her, suggests less con-fidence that idealism can be distinguished from heteronomy and conformism. This is a perspective defined by its suspicion, in which community is the name not for the humanistic ideal, but for completed accommodation to social demands.

Joy's problem is not that she is unable to assure herself of her own existence through reason, but instead that the existence of the world provides her with no logical reasons to continue her own existence. The novel presents this as a disjunction between Joy's knowledge that existence is absurd – cannot be justified on the basis of logic – and her refusal to simply accept this absurdity as a condition. She challenges herself on this:

> [T]he defendant refuses to see the Point or to accept what must be accepted whilst being fully apprised of the facts. She knows, ladies and gentlemen, yet the knowing and the knowing making a difference to the conduct is another matter entirely.[44]

---

43   McIlvanney, *The Kiln*, p. 207. Italics in original.
44   Galloway, *The Trick is to Keep Breathing*, p. 200.

The issue is joining up pointlessness and the need to accept this, but Joy is unable to find a logical means to connect these two. Not only might there be no logical basis from which to argue for existence, but the demand for such a basis may be a category mistake. As she contemplates suicide, Joy crashes repetitively back into the repetition:

> The logic of the thing is
> the logic of the thing is
> the logic of the thing[45]

Ultimately the novel suggests that this cannot be connected logically – only action, a decision in favour of continued existence, can break the repetitive cycle. So although she is dissociated from her decision – 'my hands choose' – Joy finds herself going to the window to meet David.[46] As she tells herself the next day, preparing to go to her Saturday job at the bookies: 'the trick is not to think. Just act dammit'.[47]

The echo of the novel's title links this scene to its larger concerns. Insofar as the novel can be said to hold a lesson, it is explicitly announced in the title, and repeated throughout in advice given to Joy by her friends and colleagues, by the medical profession, and in the pamphlets and magazines that she reads. Indeed, she knows it herself from the beginning – 'it was just a matter of getting by and letting time pass' – but as we have seen above, the passage from knowing to being able to act on that knowledge is fraught.[48] Mere endurance, the brute fact of the continuation of bodily processes, the repetitive passage of the breath across the threshold of the body, is enough. For Joy, there is no coming to terms with loss, which the novel presents as a fate into which she has been born. Despite the drama of interpretation that the novel seems to offer, promising a redemptive reintegration of lost experience into the continuity of narrative structure, its more fundamental, fragmentary impulse is towards a serial and repetitive reminder of the failure of any narrative to do justice to our experience of ethical relation. Joy is horrified at the thought that she will forget Michael, but her effort to remember him is what locks her into self-destructive patterns. The novel is not structured in terms of moments of revelation or reversal, but by the filling out of the empty circle of daily existence. It shows us

---

45   Galloway, *The Trick is to Keep Breathing*, pp. 200–01.
46   Galloway, *The Trick is to Keep Breathing*, p. 203.
47   Galloway, *The Trick is to Keep Breathing*, p. 205.
48   Galloway, *The Trick is to Keep Breathing*, p. 15.

that 'persistence is the only thing that works', and that the work involved in this is hard: 'Sometimes things get worse before they get better. Sometimes they just get worse. Sometimes all that happens is passing time'.[49] The deliberate banality of this lesson may suggest the novel's concern not to be drawn into either a didactic moralism or a redemptive aestheticism. It may also underscore a wider reservation about the hierarchical attribution of a saving power to literature at the expense of mass culture. Galloway certainly shares what Michael Wood describes as an 'interest in the life of the commonplace [...] the hunch that we find in Garcia Marquez, Carter and Ishiguro, that clichés could get us out of trouble too'.[50] This deflationary caution, characteristic of the novel's concern with the difficulty of merely passing time, complements its refusal of the cultural expectation that modern literature will elevate everyday existence and found community, whose continued currency is demonstrated by the example of William McIlvanney. This challenges not only the social and economic framework of modern capitalism, but what Leo Bersani has called the 'culture of redemption' that comes to characterise the production and circulation of art under these conditions, a discursive assumption that 'fundamentally meaningless culture [...] ennobles gravely damaged experience. Or to put this in other terms, art redeems the catastrophe of history'.[51]

Juxtaposition of *The Trick is to Keep Breathing* with *The Kiln* suggests that the debate over the nihilistic current in contemporary Scottish fiction hangs on competing conceptions of the role of the literary artwork in social and political life. Where McIlvanney professes his faith in art as an expression of the same imaginative power which can integrate merely social relations into the fuller symbolic bonds that modern tradition has attributed to community, Galloway refuses to assent to such circular recognition. Her novel challenges the explicit humanism of McIlvanney's vision, which, despite its similar recognition of the all-too-human failures of communal life, and of the constitutive tensions between individual and social environment, continues to figure community as the reproduction of a larger communal subject through time. To see the challenges posed by the new Scottish fiction as simply nihilistic is to assume in advance that literature is given over to, and hence vitiated by, the demand for social adaptation whose violence Galloway's novel explores so powerfully.

---

49   Galloway, *The Trick is to Keep Breathing*, pp. 173, 216, 221.

50   Michael Wood, *Children of Silence: Studies in Contemporary Fiction* (London: Pimlico, 1998), p. 189.

51   Leo Bersani, *The Culture of Redemption* (Cambridge, MA: Harvard University Press, 1990), p. 22.

CHAPTER 9

From Subtext to Gaytext? Scottish Fiction's Queer Communities

Carole Jones

Abstract

This chapter examines representations of queer groups in Scottish fiction to investigate whether the concept of community engaged with in these texts succeeds in producing a radical imagining of what Iris Marion Young calls an 'openness to unassimilated otherness' that resists the emerging homonormativity of gay identity.

Keywords

Queer – homosexuality – gay – community – Scottish fiction – drag queen – identity – homonormativity – Ali Smith – Luke Sutherland

This chapter explores the presence of gay communities in Scottish fiction. Though a relatively recent phenomenon, these representations are ambivalent towards closed or strictly bounded social groupings and identities, and illustrate uncertainties for queer people arising from the concept of community. In the early days of gay liberation, community delineated a liberatory alternative space to counter the often violent exclusions enacted by family, kinship, nation and other social formations. However, the interpellation to identity of such communities inevitably produces its own constraints and limitations, constructing closures as well as opportunities for relations. This tension between the individual and community has vivid moments of expression in Scottish gay fictional representation as we move from the subterfuge of the queer-inflected characters in the early twentieth century, through the closeted mid-century, to a gradual but sometimes playfully carnivalesque coming out in the last few decades. The envisioning of queer communities remains ambivalent, presenting rebellious resistance to the heteronormative mainstream as well as what we can term a homonormative embrace of mainstream values. This chapter surveys selected queer Scottish fiction texts with regard to these tensions and examines the evidence they provide for a radical imagining or queering of gay communities to set against an emerging Western conservative homonationalist agenda.[1] I will begin by investigating the queer Scottish context and the significance of community as it emerges in gay rights discourses. I will then turn to the literary contexts, beginning by highlighting some of the queering characters of early twentieth-century Scottish fiction and moving on to examine contrasting representations of gay community in contemporary texts, concluding with readings of two innovative narratives, Luke Sutherland's *Venus as a Boy* and Ali Smith's *Girl Meets Boy*.

Christopher Whyte's 1998 novel *The Gay Decameron* references the parameters for a nationalist debate. At its close a group of gay men, who have just spent the evening, and the novel, having dinner together, speculate on their place in the wider community:

> 'You know, I was listening to a programme on the radio this morning – yesterday morning, I mean – about gay adoption, and a woman actually used the phrase "host community"'.
> 'As if we were immigrants, and could be deported', said Andrew.
> 'Where do they think we arrived from?' Nicol said.
> 'That's the dream, isn't it?' said Ramon. 'A world without homosexuals'.
> 'A country without jessies', said Andrew. 'A denellified Scotland'.[2]

This notion of homosexuals as outsiders, parasites, and alien to the nation's story presents a familiar attitude, until fairly recently, of the wider community, but also of queer individuals themselves. Scottish queers have frequently expressed not feeling part of that national narrative, in their memoirs as well as in their fiction, a consciousness they associate with homosexuality but also specifically with the Scottish context. As Bob Cant has expressed it, '[t]he difficulty there is in Scotland about words [...;] there weren't words that you could use to talk about your sexuality'.[3]

---

1   See Jasbir K. Puar on the emergence of national homosexuality or homonationalism in relation to the post 9/11 US context: 'some homosexual subjects are complicit with heterosexual nationalist formations rather than inherently or automatically excluded from or opposed to them [...;] the war on terror has rehabilitated some – clearly not all or most – lesbians, gays, and queers to U.S. national citizenship within a spatial-temporal domain I am invoking as "homonationalism"'. *Terrorist Assemblages: Homonationalism in Queer Times* (Durham and London: Duke University Press, 2007), pp. 4, 38. These political tendencies can also be seen in Right and Far-right European politics, for example in the figure of Pym Fortuyn in the Netherlands, assassinated in 2002.

2   Christopher Whyte, *The Gay Decameron* (London: Victor Gollancz, 1998), p. 344.

3   Bob Cant, contributor to the *Remember When* oral history project, quoted in *Rainbow City: Stories from Lesbian, Gay, Bisexual and Transgender Edinburgh*, ed. by Ellen Galford and Ken Wilson (Edinburgh: Word Power, 2006), p. 19.

Reference to the lack of words or language with which to talk about sexuality is common, especially in the case of women. Moreover, the enabling of such expression has not been easily facilitated in Scotland. Delaying the decriminalisation of homosexuality until 1980 (passed in England and Wales in 1967) is just one indication of Scottish anxiety around, and repression of, issues of sexuality. Again, Bob Cant, referring to the 1960s in a memoir piece titled 'An Exile's Tale', recalls 'the fact that all the camp men I encountered were invariably English helped me to perceive homosexuality as foreign, as Other. To be both Scottish and queer must surely be an impossibility'.[4] Implicit here, of course, is the association of male homosexuality with effeminacy, and, in relation to the Scottish mainstream, the horror and rejection of femininity in the business of being a man, the Scottish hard man being a common cultural reference, made infamous in texts ranging from Tom McGrath and Jimmy Boyle's notorious 1977 play *The Hard Man* to Irvine Welsh's *Trainspotting* (1993) and the violent Begbie. Even in 1995 Christopher Whyte was moved to write, in reference to Irvine Welsh's representations of homosexual relations, '[t]o be gay and to be Scottish, it would seem, are still mutually exclusive conditions'.[5] Iona McGregor, another activist, concurs with these observations and assessments:

> In the 1940s it was impossible to define myself as homosexual and my friends as heterosexual. Although I knew the words, they were not available as social labels to describe my own experience. They were still only technical terms to be found in medical dictionaries.

She adds, significantly, '[t]here was no place or community for us in Scotland'.[6]

A common plaint in Scottish writing, even in the 1990s, is that for gay people there are no role models or sympathetic community, but rather a sense of having to choose between being Scottish and being gay. The question arises, then, of how to encounter a gay community when gay people are invisible to themselves, as well as to each other. Is it possible to use the term 'community' for a group structured by subterfuge, secrecy and invisibility? As John Maley

---

4 Bob Cant, 'An Exile's Tale', in *The Crazy Jig: Gay and Lesbian Writing from Scotland 2*, ed. by Joanne Winning (Edinburgh: Polygon, 1992), pp. 86–95 (p. 88).
5 Christopher Whyte, 'Introduction', in *Gendering the Nation: Studies in Modern Scottish Literature*, ed. by Christopher Whyte (Edinburgh: Edinburgh University Press, 1995), p. xv.
6 Iona McGregor, 'Visibility Eighties Rising', in *And Thus Will I Freely Sing: An Anthology of Gay and Lesbian Writing from Scotland*, ed. by Toni Davidson (Edinburgh: Polygon, 1989), pp. 15–28 (pp. 20, 28).

writes, introducing his novel/short story cycle *Delilah's: Stories from the Closet till Closing Time*:

> Glasgow is full of invisible lovers. They don't hold hands in the street or walk arm-in-arm in the park. They don't kiss in public places. These invisible Glasgow lovers could pass for friends or strangers. Their unions aren't blessed. They fade into family backgrounds, feign eccentricity, their lips and fates sealed by countless small dangers. Glasgow's invisible lovers are jealous of their reputations, want to keep their jobs [...]. Some of them feel they could breathe more easily and be more at home on the moon.[7]

This strong statement of alienation is a common expression of homosexuality in Scottish writing. I presume here that fiction is useful in discovering how a community is able to develop and sustain itself under such conditions, and to this end it will be informative to consider some of the issues arising from the concept of 'gay community', and the ambivalent consequences of its institutionalisation.

As a marginalised and, in the past, often ostracised group, the word community has been frequently and popularly deployed by gay people in the post-war period of identity politics and activism as a comforting term, describing a useful and indeed necessary group concept. Its necessity relates to the need for a sense of belonging for homosexuals excluded from mainstream society, as well as the need for gay people to recognise each other in safe meeting places. Group identification brings visibility, and potentially political identity and solidarity, prompting the emergence of specific communal institutions such as 'gay and lesbian centres' as well as other significant places like specific bars, clubs and cafes. However, the concept and the word itself raise particular issues. Kath Weston in her study *Families We Choose: Lesbians, Gays, Kinship* points out that the term 'community' only came into popular gay usage with the rise of the gay civil rights movement; it is therefore an anachronism to apply it to the pre-Stonewall (1969) period. In this context it has associations with the radical politics of that period, that is, with the struggle to eliminate oppression, not just for gays but for all oppressed people, in line with the thought and activism of groups such as the Gay Liberation Front. A radical discourse connects this group with the women's movement, the black civil rights movement in the US, and other anti-colonial organisations of the time such as the anti-war movement. This had implications for the approach to sexuality itself, as Weston points out:

---

7   John Maley, *Delilah's: Stories from the Closet till Closing Time* (Glasgow: 11:9, 2002), p. xi.

During the 1970s the concept of community came to embody practical wisdom emerging from the bars, friendship networks, and a spate of new gay organizations; the knowledge that lesbians and gay men, joining together on the basis of sexual identity, could create enduring social ties. In the process, sexuality was reconstituted as a ground of common experience rather than a quintessential personal domain.[8]

Here sexuality begins to be seen as a social and group phenomenon, not only private but public, and not simply an essential individual trait.

This entails a necessary defining of 'community' as non-territorial, as not defined by spatial and geographic boundaries, but resting more specifically, as Weston says, on 'a sense of belonging with one's "own kind" [...]. Founded on the premise of a shared sexual identity, gay community remained, like friendship, an egalitarian and fundamentally nonerotic concept'.[9] In fact, gay community came to be defined 'in terms of a discourse of ethnicity-and-rights', a move which Alan Sinfield argues 'lets the sex-gender system off the hook. It encourages the inference that an out-group needs concessions, rather than the mainstream needing correction', this latter a reference to the radical political approach which resisted gay assimilation into that mainstream.[10] Moreover, Weston points out:

> The paradigm that casts lesbians and gay men in the part of a minority (or subculture) interposes community between 'the individual' and 'society'. In this context, it becomes relatively easy to move from a view of community as a comfortable home or unified interest group to a picture of community as a mini-enforcer, mediator of all the conformity and oppression attributed to Society with a capital 'S'.[11]

This important point has a strong resonance for queer people, where the concept of 'queer' denotes a stance against the closure and fixity of identities. This resistance echoes a feminist critique such as that of philosopher Iris Marion Young, who writes: 'the ideal of community exhibits a totalizing impulse and denies difference'; it privileges 'unity over difference' and 'sympathy over

---

8   Kath Weston, *Families We Choose: Lesbians, Gays, Kinship* (New York: Columbia University Press, 1991), p. 123.

9   Weston, *Families We Choose*, p. 126.

10   Alan Sinfield, *Gay and After* (London: Serpent's Tail, 1998), pp. 19, 20.

11   Weston, *Families We Choose*, p. 128.

recognition of the limits of one's understanding of others from their point of view. Community is an understandable dream'.[12]

The notion of community in itself, then, has oppressive consequences, with rules of inclusion and policed boundaries of normativity. This model of group formation is reproduced in the gay context where *homonormativity* has wider implications than its own policing and stands accused of being complicit with oppressive regulation in 'its inhabitation and reproduction of heteronormative norms', the promotion of gay marriage being just one obvious example.[13] Lisa Duggan draws out the full implications of this when she defines homonormativity as 'a new neo-liberal sexual politics' of a 'depoliticized gay culture anchored in domesticity and consumption'.[14] Robert Caserio also links the developing emancipation of gay identity to the neoliberal context:

> [A]t the very moment of this gay and lesbian bid for a public world, the public world itself began to disappear: The advent of Thatcherism in 1979 signalled an end of collective-minded progressive values that might have offered homosexual men and women full standing as citizens. Privatization – of everything from state industry to personal 'choice' of sexual orientation – became the order of the day. [...] Accordingly, it was not only a meaningful public world that had eroded at the moment gay and lesbians thought they might enter it. Their assumed identity had also begun to dissolve, even as booksellers and readers – and scholars too – were busily constructing it as a market niche.[15]

The turn to homonormativity in 'the pursuit of legitimation rather than social change' from the late 1970s in many ways relied on consumerism and the construction of a gay market;[16] gay community as a set of lifestyle trends produces

---

12   Iris Marion Young, 'The Ideal of Community and the Politics of Difference', in *Feminism/ Postmodernism*, ed. by Linda J. Nicholson (London and New York: Routledge, 1990), pp. 300–23 (pp. 305, 300).

13   Puar, *Terrorist Assemblages*, p. 9.

14   Lisa Duggan, 'The New Homonormativity: The Sexual Politics of Neoliberalism', in *Materializing Democracy: Towards a Revitalized Cultural Politics*, ed. by Russ Castronovo and Dana Nelson (Durham, NC: Duke University Press, 2002), pp. 175–94 (p. 179).

15   Robert L. Caserio, 'Queer Friction: The Ambiguous Emergence of a Genre', in *A Concise Companion to Contemporary British Fiction*, ed. by James F. English (Oxford: Blackwell, 2006), pp. 209–28 (pp. 210, 211). This account echoes the feminist critique of the poststructuralist deconstruction of the subject at the moment when women were gaining social status.

16   Amy Gluckman and Betsy Reed, *Homo Economics: Capitalism, Community, and Lesbian and Gay Life* (London: Routledge, 1997), p. xiv.

the stereotypes of the affluent gay, the 'velvet mafia' or 'muffia', defined this time by popular culture and advertisers. Always inauthentic in the eyes of the heteroculture of the mainstream, gay community often seemed little more than a marketing opportunity, a glib assessment which dumbs down the serious charge that such a gay politics 'does not contest dominant heteronormative forms but upholds and sustains them'.[17] As Leo Bersani caustically remarks,

> Never before in the history of minority groups struggling for recognition and equal treatment has there been an analogous attempt, on the part of any such group, to make itself unidentifiable even as it demands to be recognised [...;] gays have been de-gaying themselves in the very process of making themselves visible.[18]

If, at the other extreme, Bersani envisages 'an anticommunal mode of connectedness we might all share', there have also been other challenges to the assimilationist impulses of gay community.[19] Sinfield for one has always preferred the word 'subculture': 'I envisage it as retaining a strong sense of diversity, of provisionality, of constructedness'.[20] Also deliberately avoiding the evocation of the cosy sense of community as similarity and identification, Iris Marion Young argues that we can understand community as an 'openness toward unassimilated otherness'.[21] This approach resists the more 'totalistic' conceptions of social relations, the sealing of conceptual boundaries, which she challenges in her writing, evoking Judith Butler's desire to expand the definition of the human when she writes: 'We must learn to live and to embrace the destruction and rearticulation of the human in the name of a more capacious and, finally, less violent world, not knowing in advance what precise form our humanness does and will take'.[22] Such an incitement to diversity and openness enables an imaginative queering of community; rather than defining the boundaries of gay identity, such a community would offer a constitutive critical mobility in conceptualising the relationship between the individual and the group that could be radical in its inferences and implications. Taking this as a starting point, we can investigate whether we can find this *openness* in Scottish fiction, and if depictions of gay people approach such a queer

17   Duggan, 'The New Homonormativity: The Sexual Politics of Neoliberalism', p. 179.

18   Leo Bersani, *Homos* (Cambridge, MA: Harvard University Press, 1996), p. 31.

19   Bersani, *Homos*, p. 9.

20   Sinfield, *Gay and After*, p. 43.

21   Young, 'The Ideal of Community and the Politics of Difference', p. 320.

22   Judith Butler, *Undoing Gender* (Abingdon: Routledge, 2004), p. 35.

representation. How has Scottish writing envisioned Scottish identity beyond heterosexism?

In illustrating a lack of community, the sense of individual isolation in an earlier period is mournfully expressed by some anecdotally reported graffiti in the men's toilets of the Cramond Inn in the 1960s which entreated, 'Is no one else queer in Cramond?' In early twentieth-century Scottish fiction we have what can be construed as queer-inflected characters existing in the wider community. For instance, in Nan Shepherd's *The Quarry Wood* (1928), Martha Ironside is empowered to 'create herself' as Alison Smith describes it: '[i]n the end, Martha can even "get" a child for herself *by* herself (completely without the participation of a man)', therefore subverting heterosexual romantic closure.[23] She refuses to marry even under pressure from the uncharitable community who believe the child she has adopted is her own illegitimate child. Willa Muir's *Imagined Corners* (1931) has a central female character leaving her stifling life and marriage when her sister-in-law Elise 'carries her off like Lochinvar' and thinks of her as a 'brand-new daughter, or sister, or wife, or whatever it was'.[24] Such indeterminacy and the passionate relationship between these two women demands a queer interpretation. Jean Brodie, the central character of Muriel Spark's famous Edinburgh novel from 1961, has been the subject of some controversial lesbian readings and speculations.[25] Whether the 'real' lesbian is Jean Brodie or Sandy Stranger, there are several instances of queering conjecture in relation to Brodie culminating in Sandy's charge that she is 'an unconscious Lesbian'.[26] This subversive conclusion is suggestive of something hidden, a repressed state of being, unknown to the conscious self.

It is not the case that a gay community was unimaginable at this time, as demonstrated by Compton Mackenzie's *Extraordinary Women* (1928), his novel set in the bohemian artist community resident on the Isle of Capri in the early twentieth century. This was a notoriously homosexual community which included celebrated individuals such as Romaine Brooks, and Radclyffe Hall was a visitor. The novel is a comedy informed by MacKenzie's own experience of the place, but it treats lesbianism as a given and completely normal in that

23   Alison Smith, 'And Woman Created Woman: Carswell, Shepherd, Muir, and the Self-Made Woman', in *Gendering the Nation*, pp. 25–48 (p. 35). Italics in original.

24   Willa Muir, *Imagined Selves* (Edinburgh: Canongate, 1996), p. 279.

25   See Christopher Whyte, 'Queer Readings, Gay Texts: From *Redgauntlet* to *The Prime of Miss Jean Brodie*', in *Scotland in Theory: Reflections on Culture and Literature*, ed. by Eleanor Bell and Gavin Miller (Amsterdam: Rodopi, 2004), pp. 147–65.

26   Muriel Spark, *The Prime of Miss Jean Brodie* (London: Penguin, 2000), p. 105.

context. This in itself is refreshing when Hall's *The Well of Loneliness* was pros-
ecuted and banned in the same year, and presents a tortured examination of
the existence of the invert. *Extraordinary Women* certainly is not a playful
parody in the manner of Virginia Woolf's *Orlando*, also published in 1928, but
it is an interesting addition to the characterisation of an incredible period
through the eyes of an author who greatly identified with Scotland. Mackenzie
later published *Thin Ice* (1956), a sympathetic novel about a closeted politician,
again emphasising the issues of secrecy and repression which became a fore-
grounded characteristic of homosexual identity and culture in the post-World
War Two period.

   The idea of a gay community in Scottish fiction begins to emerge with self-
consciously gay writing, by which I mean texts by gay people, and/or those
focusing on gay characters. Gay Scots have more recently moved from the sub-
textual margins to occupy the centre of their own narratives, beginning with
two significant texts published on the cusp of the 1990s. In this period gay
rights campaigns were galvanised into action and strengthened by the notorious Section 2A, otherwise known as 'Clause 28' of the Local Government Act
1988, which banned the promotion of homosexuality by local authorities and
the teaching of the acceptability of homosexuality as a 'pretended' family relationship.[27] The effect of this legal censure, coming as it did at the height of the
crisis caused by HIV and AIDS, reinstituted a demonisation of gay people. In
this atmosphere two significant anthologies were published by Polygon: *And
Thus Will I Freely Sing* (1989), edited by Toni Davidson, and a follow-up, *The
Crazy Jig* (1992), edited by Joanne Winning.[28]

   Both texts present us with formally diverse illustrations of the particular
possibilities of being Scottish and gay, incorporating memoir, fiction and poetry
from both new and more established authors. Winning herself has described
these collections as 'irrevocably marked by the effort of defining and concretis-
ing a notion of Scottish lesbian and gay identities, and therefore many of the
writings they contain focus on issues of self-determination, self-declaration,
and the psychic effects of being hidden from national life'.[29] Certainly, they are

---

27   See Local Government Act, 1988, Section 28, which can be accessed at: <http://www
     .legislation.gov.uk/ukpga/1988/9/section/28>.
28   *And Thus Will I Freely Sing: An Anthology of Gay and Lesbian Writing from Scotland*,
     ed. by Toni Davidson (Edinburgh: Polygon, 1989); *The Crazy Jig*, ed. by Joanne Winning
     (Edinburgh: Polygon, 1992).
29   Joanne Winning, 'Crossing the Borderline: Post-devolution Scottish Lesbian and Gay
     Writing', in *The Edinburgh Companion to Contemporary Scottish Literature*, ed. by Berthold
     Schoene (Edinburgh: Edinburgh University Press, 2007), pp. 283–91 (p. 284).

fixed on the individual and give little sense of a gay culture or community. Moreover, in contrast to highlighting and emphasising *connection* they focus on issues that hinder connection, which in the past have stopped it in its tracks and consequently stifled the visibility on which connection can be promoted, such as homophobia, prejudice, violence, and AIDS. There is little evidence in either anthology of any *organised* resistance or protest at these crucial oppressive aspects of gay life, of the kind of radical politics associated with the beginning of the gay rights movement; neither is there an indication of the civil institutions which started to appear even in Scotland from the 1970s, such as gay and lesbian centres. These collections of short texts are not particularly detailed documents of gay civil life.

However, it is possible to conceptualise these two books as in themselves presenting us with a Scottish gay community; within them and between them there is a collective of gay individuals, writers and characters that exist together in a Scottish context. This sense of a community is heightened by the presence of some writers in both volumes; Iona McGregor, for instance, contributes a memoir piece to the first and writes the introduction for the second. If this gives an impression of a small and limited community and sense of communality, this is dispelled to some extent by a further anthology published in 2001 titled *Borderline*, edited by Joseph Mills.[30] This collection includes extracts from non-homosexual identified writers, such as James Kelman, Irvine Welsh, and Janice Galloway, and there is also an extract from the film script of *My Way Home* (1978) by Bill Douglas, therefore establishing a connection and continuity with a wider, more mainstream community (appropriately enough, the subtitle of the anthology is 'the mainstream book of Scottish gay writing' after the publisher). Is it possible, then, to conceptualise this publication as a queering moment for Scottish society after devolution? Or, alternatively, does it represent assimilation, a 'mainstreaming' of gay culture, and therefore a 'de-gaying' of homosexuals, in Bersani's words, producing a dilution of radical homo-ness? These questions encapsulate ongoing political debates, and this evolving textual community succeeds in capturing a sense of change in relation to queer representation in Scottish writing, which, as well as being related to the national context, also reflects the wider influence of international and border-crossing equal rights campaigns.

In looking at the detail of this queering representation, it becomes apparent that if Scottish writing does not delineate an engagement with political or civil institutions in its evocation of gay communality, there is one location common

---

30   *Borderline: The Mainstream Book of Scottish Gay Writing*, ed. by Joseph Mills (Edinburgh: Mainstream, 2001).

to most Western queer writing which has provided an important locus for queer culture throughout the ages, and in this Scottish fiction is no exception; that location is the bar and bar culture. In the words of John D'Emilio in reference to the United States, 'the bars filled a unique role in the evolution of a group consciousness among gay[s]'.[31] The bar can also stand for 'the contradictions of identity and solidarity/solitariness' and this ambivalence is certainly present in Scottish texts.[32] Though pubs and bars can be sites of solidarity they are also presented as sites of anxiety, for example in Peter Robinson's story from *And Thus Will I Freely Sing*:

> The wind snapped at his ankles as the dark carnivorous mouth of the pub closed smoked-glass lips behind him. [...] Driving up the motorway, David thought about the pub. Its dimly lit corners where couples sat cocooned in false privacy under the eyes of sad, voyeuristic old men. He thought of the pillars from where the hunters selected and then stalked their prey.[33]

This is a vivid description of the pub as hell-hole, harbouring a predatory society miserable with its own submerged and animalistic nature. However, only a few pages later, Robinson writes of the gay bar that 'just the experience of being in a place where everyone was like him; where the men loved men, and the women only women, gave him strength'.[34] The pub as a site for potential liberation and escape from a dour *straightgeist* is equally vivid in Ellen Galford's *The Fires of Bride* (1986) when protagonist Maggie has a disorientating experience in a Glasgow pub:

> She walks into a brown room full of tiny old men in flat caps and raincoats, each with a pint of beer in one hand and a glass of whiskey in the other. She wonders if her informant has been away from Scotland too long, or if she's written down the wrong name altogether. But the barmaid catches her eye, winks, and points her to a stained-glass door

---

31   John D'Emilio, *Sexual Politics, Sexual Communities: The Making of a Homosexual Minority in the United States 1940–1970* (Chicago: University of Chicago Press, 1983), p. 99.

32   Katie King, 'Audre Lorde's Lacquered Layerings: The Lesbian Bar as a Site of Literary Production', in *The New Lesbian Criticism*, ed. by Sally Munt (Hemel Hempstead: Harvester Wheatsheaf, 1992), pp. 51–74 (p. 55).

33   Peter D. Robinson, 'The Wabe', in *And Thus Will I Freely Sing*, pp. 29–36 (p. 29).

34   Robinson, 'The Wabe', p. 31.

(a Victorian mosaic of purple grapes and green garlands) in the corner beyond the cigarette machine.

She climbs a stone staircase and enters a paradise of purple dralon, flocked wallpaper, suburban curry-house meets New Orleans whore-house in a fantasia of fringed lampshades and chandeliers. Even the bobbles on the heavy fuschia draperies are rocking and rolling to the thumping disco beat, and the little square of dance floor shines like satin.[35]

All the margins of Scottish life are here, from the 'curry house to the whore-house', an exotic, foreign, fringed playpen existing right above the heads of the more usual locals.

The gay bar provides an opportunity to escape dominant roles and models, most obviously apprehended in the fair number of drag queens to be found in more recent Scottish writing. Signalling a preoccupation with crossing and transgressing boundaries, these are, of course, the highly visible and performa-tive part of gay culture. John Maley's *Delilah's* (2002), for instance, is a series of stories set in a bar called Delilah's run by a drag queen with the heart of gold, Joanie. An array of recurring characters is presented moving in and out of the separate mini-narratives which go to make up the whole. This provides an opportunity for episodic, fluid and impressionistic storytelling, re-creating the texture of the everyday, its mundane nature punctuated with significant moments. Itself defying categorisation, the text highlights the transgression of boundaries with moments of a carnivalesque appropriation of heterosexual culture, including a lesbian wedding complete with family photographs taken in Kelvingrove Park, and a drag party night ending when 'torpedo-titted Madonna and marvellous Marilyn Monroe were winching each other to safety and Karl Marx was finally getting her beard felt, trembling in Bill Clinton's clutches'.[36]

The concept of carnival, though transgressive in its overturning of social hierarchies, can be understood as a permitted transgression within a desig-nated time and space. However, this is not fully liberatory, when the dominant culture is left intact, and the carnival becomes a safety valve for the preserva-tion of that mainstream. Certainly in Russell Barr's monologue *Sisters, Such Devoted Sisters* (2004) the setting of the drag bar becomes an environment in which the violent exclusions and hierarchies of mainstream culture are reiter-ated and reproduced. This is signalled by the kinship relation emphasised in

35   Ellen Galford, *The Fires of Bride* (London: The Women's Press, 1986), p. 27.
36   Maley, *Delilah's*, p. 124.

the title which, as it turns out, constructs its cast of drag queens in the light of the excluding principle of family and bloodlines rather than the more open solidarity of 'sisterhood' developed in the Women's Movement, for instance. Ironically, group identity is ultimately based on a stance of anti-femininity, a revulsion of the feminine demonstrated by a vicious attack by the drag queens on a local male-to-female transsexual at the end of the play. The show closes after the scene of the attack related by the narrator, Bernice:

> Ross gets up to leave and Gerry followed. And for me to join the other boys I had to walk past the transsexual's body and she was unrecognisable. And I went and joined the other boys. I didn't go back and see if she needed any help. I'm absolutely sure Ross and Gerry beat her to death.[37]

Here the limits of this drag queen community are established by the body and a determination to maintain its physical boundaries, imposing a limit on the drag queens' own cultural crossing beyond which they will not go. This may signal their reluctance to give up phallic male power, characterised by the penis, the physical sign of masculinity; they opt for a performance of hysterical violence which aligns them with many literary Scottish hard men, most obviously *Trainspotting*'s Begbie. Moreover, this is not uncommon in the representation of drag queens; it is also an image found in Irvine Welsh's novella 'A Smart Cunt' (1994) where we are told Denise, a close friend of the narrator/protagonist is 'in a state of transformation from one queen stereotype into another', though his embracing of a camp feminised style does not detract from his ability to play the hard man role effectively.[38] Similarly, in Louise Welsh's *The Cutting Room* (2002) the transvestite Leslie is, at one point, looking for his baseball bat to rough up 'some wee nyaff' who owes him money.[39] Feminine attire does not exclude the subject from the traditional hard man role.

In these particular narratives queer communities emerge riven by divisions, exclusions and violently maintained hierarchies which suggest a problematic relationship with the boundaries of identity. Russell Barr's characters, for instance, experience crisis at the point of a radical dissolution of the boundary of sex and gender, as illustrated by the transsexual, and they react in a violent manner; this suggests a desire for a certain fixity in their identities and the resulting power relations entrenched in these communities. Such depictions raise the question of whether there is any queer escape from these violently

37   Russell Barr, *Sisters, Such Devoted Sisters* (London: Oberon, 2005), p. 64.

38   Irvine Welsh, 'A Smart Cunt', *The Acid House* (London: Vintage, 1995), p. 241.

39   Louise Welsh, *The Cutting Room* (Edinburgh: Canongate, 2002), p. 165.

maintained power structures or a possibility of Iris Marion Young's 'openness to unassimilated otherness' in recent Scottish writing.

For such an escape it is necessary, perhaps, to evade the constrictions of realism, as illustrated in two flamboyantly outlandish narratives which appear to go further in their explorations of radical otherness and the implications for community. The first of these, Luke Sutherland's *Venus as a Boy* (2004), tells the story of Désirée, also known as Cupid, a boy born and brought up in Orkney and later a sex worker in London. Désirée has a gift: when he has sex with people they have visions of heaven, and the more he allows himself to feel, the stronger the images he experiences: 'tunnels of light, orchards, and angels, always angels'; 'spreading love brought me visions of Heaven', he says.[40] It is life-changing when he realises that, unusually, he finds it easy to see the good in almost everyone; 'that unjudgemental quality I have is maybe the greatest gift of all'.[41] This openness gives Désirée a special connection with people, characterised as queer and anti-normative: 'As for my sexual orientation', he says, 'I hadn't any [...;] my inclination would do this yo-yo thing that I never questioned [...]. So what?'[42] Yet this gift and this connection does not facilitate queer community; quite the contrary, as Désirée attracts and is attracted to those who are particularly violent in their dealings with others: nazis and skinheads, racists and homophobes. This begins on the island; as a youngster his best friend Finola is attacked and raped, 'ruined' as he says, by a gang of boys led by a biker called Dove. A few years later Désirée finds himself taking part in the racist bullying of the only black boy on the island:

> Next thing Dove's pulled up beside me, revving his engine. Having him so close, after what he'd done to Finola...it was like...flying a plane for the first time. [...] Dove took me under his wing after that [...]. *Poof! Wi me!* he'd shout, with a thumbs up to the two-faced who'd fall about laughing. I'd hop on to the back of his bike, ride with him to the Pier or to the top of the School Brae and back. Some nights he'd drive me the six miles home.
>
> Maybe that sounds strange after everything that'd happened, but I found I couldn't stay angry at folk for long. Even my dad. I still can't. I've always been ready to forgive and forget. And besides, Finola had been gone three years by then and I can't deny I was giddy at the thought of becoming one of the gang.[43]

---

40   Luke Sutherland, *Venus as a Boy* (London: Bloomsbury. 2004), pp. 50, 75.

41   Sutherland, *Venus as a Boy*, p. 69.

42   Sutherland, *Venus as a Boy*, p. 90.

43   Sutherland, *Venus as a Boy*, pp. 32–35. Italics in original.

This is an embrace of destructive outsiderness, a gang not a community, and it is an erotic embrace in a novel where sex is always associated with flying.

Désirée ends up in London in what he calls a modern-day Molly House run by the pimp Radu. Ruthlessly exploited and trapped, Radu, intending to make more money out of him, forces Désirée to take female hormones with the aim of transforming him into a transsexual woman. Desperately unhappy with this situation, Désirée explains, 'I was there in mind but not in body, because my body wasn't my own anymore [...] the last straw was my first tit [...] I became this man with an unwanted woman's body'.[44] After an overdose of his hormone pills Désirée begins literally to turn into gold – a fatal process:

> My teeth are golden, my nails, the *irises* of my eyes. My arms and legs have got all stiff [...] I'm going to die soon, no doubt. The gold'll get to my lungs or my heart or whatever and that'll be it.[45]

Worth his weight in gold, he becomes an embodiment of his exchange value in a corrupted world; the fixing of his fluidity is his death sentence. Though proceeding from an optimistic moment of connection and interrelationality, this conclusion does not evoke in its journey the possibility of gay community. In her sexual liaisons, Désirée offers a vision of heaven, a moment of transcending the material world, of escaping the Earth-bound social scene. This is a very personal and individual moment which leaves the recipient in a trance, in their own opened out world, and, as with other images of salvation, the individual is alone in this moment. 'For those I've touched', Désirée says at the end, 'knowledge of me is knowledge of the divine. [...] All I've ever been is a messenger – a gateway to good news'.[46] This pronouncement suggests a revelation not a revolution, faith not politics, words instead of action. As Alice Ferrebe points out, '[d]espite its plea for forgiveness, Désirée's narrative ultimately denies the possibility of empathising with the experience of another person, instead formulating the racial and sexual outrages it catalogues as essentially formative of individual identity and intensely private'.[47]

In contrast, the most joyful image of community in recent Scottish fiction comes from the second potentially radical text, Ali Smith's *Girl Meets Boy* (2007). This also has classical mythical connections but betrays no qualms

---

44   Sutherland, *Venus as a Boy*, p. 6.
45   Sutherland, *Venus as a Boy*, pp. 4, 7. Italics in original.
46   Sutherland, *Venus as a Boy*, p. 145.
47   Alice Ferrebe, 'Between Camps: Masculinity, Race and Nation in Post-devolution Scotland', in *The Edinburgh Companion to Contemporary Scottish Literature*, pp. 275–82 (p. 282).

regarding bodily crossing and transformation, as can be seen in the opening line: 'Let me tell you about when I was a girl, our grandfather says'.[48] In this novella, Smith rewrites the story of Ovid's Iphis where, through the power of love, a girl brought up as a boy is turned into a boy so she can marry the girl she loves. In Smith's narrative Anthea Gunn falls in love with Robin, a girl dressed as a boy who spends her time daubing their home town of Inverness with anti-capitalist, feminist graffiti. In the final section of the book, called 'all together now', Smith presents us with a vision of community togetherness on the occasion of Anthea and Robin's marriage:

> Reader, I married him/her [...].
> We'd thought we were alone, Robin and I. We'd thought it was just us, under the trees outside the cathedral. But as soon as we'd made our vows there was a great whoop of joy behind us, and when we turned round we saw all the people, there must have been hundreds, they were clapping and cheering, they were throwing confetti, they waved and they roared celebration.[49]

This crowd is made up of their families, people from work, and the whole of the Provost's office. A message arrives from the Loch Ness Monster, along with a half gold-edged, half black-edged telegram-poem from John Knox. Various deities are standing by the drinks table, and 'a goddess so regal she must have been Isis spent the whole reception making fine new guests out of clay'.[50] Even Iphis and Ianthe from the original myth turn up; in a truly carnivalesque climax Smith brings the gods down to earth, mixes the divine with the mortal in a joyfully queer communal togetherness where all boundaries – bodily and historical and heavenly – are crossed and broken down.

At the end of this queer tableau, Anthea admits, 'Uh-huh. Okay. I know. In my dreams', before saying:

> What I mean is that we stood on the bank of the river under the trees, the pair of us, and we promised the nothing that was there, the nothing that made us, the nothing that was listening, that we truly desired to go beyond ourselves. And that's the message. That's it. That's all.[51]

---

48   Ali Smith, *Girl Meets Boy* (Edinburgh: Canongate, 2007), p. 3.
49   Smith, *Girl Meets Boy*, pp. 150–51.
50   Smith, *Girl Meets Boy*, p. 155.
51   Smith, *Girl Meets Boy*, p. 159.

'Going beyond yourself' breaches the boundaries of the autonomous self in acknowledging the other and existing in relations which highlight the vulnerability inherent in holding the self open to relationality – surely the basis of an 'understandable dream' of community. The anti-capitalist activism of Anthea and Robin in support of global justice further opens the concept of community to encompass the world, an 'understandable dream' emanating directly from Butler's vision of an expanded sense of the human. Smith's imaginative breaching of the boundaries of existence through her queer narrative demands a different conception of community, radically unclogged of its narrow identifications and desires.

Scottish fiction has struggled with the task of representing queer community. On the one hand, it presents homosexual groups, marginalised both socially and in civic structures, groups founded on hierarchy and existing in violently maintained power structures, a subculture which, in this Scottish literary context, does little to help us think of the concept of community more openly or queerly. On the other hand, a turn to myth is a way to engage such queerness, enabling a clarity that comes when, as Smith puts it, 'a story from then meets a story from now'.[52] This break away from realism fits comfortably into a Scottish literary tradition famous for its 'escape from reality into romance', particularly in the nineteenth century heyday of fiction.[53] Where this has heretofore often been characterised as a symptom of the inferiority of a culture that lacked national organic continuity and unity, Cairns Craig argues forcefully that this is 'in fact an indication that the realist tradition could not answer the questions which Scottish culture posed to its authors'.[54] Realism, and the progressive model of history it unproblematically claims to reflect, is challenged 'with what it had left out [....,] what it had excluded'.[55] Against such assertions of cultural autonomy, Craig promotes a model that is inherently relational: '[Culture] is a site of dialogue, it is a dialectic, a dialect. It is being between'.[56] This suggestive 'going beyond ourselves' common to the Scottish literary tradition can be appropriated as an evocative invocation of a queering impulse persuasively exemplified in Smith's narrative. Embracing the openness in Scottish literary culture enables an aspiration to more queering representation and queer readings that productively challenge the boundaries of our notions of community, identity and the human.

---

52   Smith, *Girl Meets Boy*, p. 160.
53   Cairns Craig, *Out of History: Narrative Paradigms in Scottish and British Culture* (Edinburgh: Polygon, 1996), p. 46.
54   Craig, *Out of History*, p. 65.
55   Craig, *Out of History*, p. 46.
56   Craig, *Out of History*, p. 206.

CHAPTER 10

'Maybe Singing into Yourself': James Kelman, Inner Speech and Vocal Communion

Scott Hames

Abstract

The achievement of James Kelman is often linked to the recovery of communal voice and representative power. (This is particularly the case in Scottish critical contexts.) On the contrary, the social value of Kelman's fiction lies in its wary resistance to 'voice' as a medium for the display of pre-given community and identity. His art subtly repudiates the ardent singing of readymade peoplehood, which often figures as a threat to the self-emancipation of the individual. This chapter explores a range of Kelman's recent (post-2008) novels and stories in this light, with particular attention to the central importance – and the complex sociality – of un-expressed 'inner speech'. Detailed close readings trace the unraveling of vocal solidarities premised on a bad or empty *withness*, and – from another angle – the pulling inward, and partial redemption, of the lyric subject's fretful relation to external groupness and the illusion of consensus. Key insights of V.N. Volosinov ('inner speech'), Benedict Anderson ('unisonance'), and Étienne Balibar (on individual/collective emancipation) help to frame these explorations, which offer a new approach to Kelman's politics of voice.

Keywords

James Kelman – voice – inner speech – solidarity – interiority – vernacular – Étienne Balibar – V.N. Volosinov

James Kelman is the pivotal figure in the emergence of *vocal democracy* as a key motif of Scottish literary debate since 1979. His writing and influence are most often discussed with reference to demands and techniques for vernacular self-representation, and nearly all Kelman criticism (rightly) takes its bearings from the wider relationship between language, community, and conflict.[1] So strong is Kelman's association with this terrain, we can easily lose

---

1 See Cairns Craig, *The Modern Scottish Novel: Narrative and the National Imagination* (Edinburgh: Edinburgh University Press, 1999), pp. 99–106.

sight of how frequently his writing runs counter to the politics and aesthetics of demotic togetherness. While Kelman's essays are animated by a range of generous solidarities – his 2002 collection *"And the Judges Said..."* is prefaced 'Unity chops elephants. *old African proverb*' – his fiction is overwhelmingly centred on individual struggle and self-experience. Not only does his fiction generally eschew moments of collective identification, it goes out of its way to scramble and corrode them, pulling at their internal torsions and modelling a wary detachment from pre-given modes of 'community' and voice. We should resist the temptation to explain away the radical individualism of Kelman's art, and take seriously the refusal of his writing to affirm the register of vernacular we-ness commonly associated with his influence. On the contrary, Kelman's writing can be seen to puncture and repudiate the forms of readymade people-hood evoked by the assertion of 'identity'. This chapter examines scenes of vocal combination and communion in Kelman's recent fiction, with special attention to the introjection of the communal cry and the lyric-social function of 'inner speech'.

An agonistic relation between individual and society is the norm in Kelman's fiction, and though central to his ethical stance – 'I wanted to write and remain a member of my own community' – the means and experience of collectivity are notoriously difficult to recognise in his art.[2] Critics sympathetic to Kelman's socialist politics have often worried that the strong introversion of his prose flirts with endorsing, even exalting, the bogus universality of the bourgeois subject. Kelman prefers to locate his work in an existential tradition 'that asserted the primacy of the world as perceived and experienced by individual human beings' – a 'primacy' which often seems close to solipsism, before gradually revealing a more layered and dynamic relation between inside and outside.[3]

Take the following passage from Kelman's 2012 novel *Mo said she was quirky*. The narrator, Helen, is recalling her daughter's precocious infancy.

> Sophie had been fourteen months when she started walking and even then, when she looked at you, it was as though she saw into you, and was asking, Who are you? Are you my mother? But these questions were

---

2   James Kelman, 'The Importance of Glasgow in My Work', *Some Recent Attacks: Essays Cultural and Political* (Stirling: AK Press, 1992), pp. 78–84 (p. 81). See Willy Maley, 'Denizens, citizens, tourists and others: marginality and mobility in the writings of James Kelman and Irvine Welsh', in *City Visions*, ed. by David Bell and Azzedine Haddour (Harlow: Prentice Hall, 2000), pp. 60–72.

3   James Kelman, 'And the judges said...', *"And the Judges Said...": Essays* (London: Secker & Warburg, 2002), pp. 37–56 (p. 39).

within herself and the answers came from within herself. Are you my
mother? Sophie asked the question and gave the answer, Yes, you are. It
is you, you are my mother.[4]

Here the very foundation of the social is in the gift of an autarkic toddler. The
process of 'primary attachment', far from constituting the infant ego, is managed and narrated by a fully fledged rational subject, within her own perimeter
and by her own lights. And yet, we gradually register, this passage is the *mother's* speculative view of the toddler's perception – it is Helen who voices the
crisp questions and answers suggested by the look of Sophie, Helen who is
the sovereign 'you' affirming her own imagined recognition. The speaking
gaze projected onto the daughter by the mother, 'as though she saw into [her]',
is a means by which the narrator seizes the controls of the piercing, closed-
circuit look which seems to deny her own input.

Kelman excels in subtle and protracted shifts of this kind, dragging inner
speech from one space or mind to another. Helen and Sophie look intensely
into one another without ever inhabiting the same perceptual moment; the
intimate wonderings of the mother concerning the unfathomable mental
process of the child bring their inner worlds into a delicate tangle, but of a
purely ideational and speculative character. And yet these intricate second-
guessings are the very real ground of Helen's loving attachment, the solid sub-
stance of her worry and hope. In Kelman's hands these conjectures acquire
the dramatic force of events, episodes in an immanent emotional process
'involving' both characters but never on the plane of inter-subjective experience. It seems that Kelman's artistry is increasingly focused on this shifting and
reframing of immersive subjectivity, so that we double back to notice the stark
non-connection it harbours within and against itself.

As we consider the political implications of such effects it becomes apparent that Kelman's fiction, and its treatment of 'voice', is marked by a paradox of
modern individualism. In the précis of Étienne Balibar, post-Enlightenment
citizenship becomes identified with 'the task of self-emancipation from every
domination and subjection by means of a collective and universal access to
politics'.[5] The 'humanity of human individuals becomes determined by the
inalienable character of their "rights"' – rights 'always *attributed to individuals*
in the last instance' but 'achieved and won *collectively*, i.e. politically'.[6] A key

---

4   James Kelman, *Mo said she was quirky* (London: Hamish Hamilton, 2012), p. 140.

5   Étienne Balibar, 'Subjection and Subjectivation', in *Supposing the Subject*, ed. by Joan Copjec
    (London and New York: Verso, 1994), pp. 1–15 (p. 12).

6   Balibar, 'Subjection and Subjectivation', p. 12. Italics in original.

'ethical proposition' emerges in this claim to a universal dignity and equality: 'the value of human agency arises from the fact that no one can be liberated or emancipated *by others*, although no one can liberate himself *without others*'.[7]

The first part of this formula – 'no one can be emancipated by others' – nicely condenses the dominant note in Kelman's fiction, and his primary investments in anarchist-existential thought. Think of Sammy Samuels refusing the help of his would-be lawyer in *How late it was, how late* (1994) – 'He had nay intention of using a rep [...]. Nay cunt was gony get him out of trouble; nay cunt except himself' – or the titular hero at the climax of *The Busconductor Hines* (1984): 'to be perfectly fucking honest with yous all, I dont want anybody going on strike on my behalf. I want to do it on my tod'.[8] This is a joke, but also not. In Kelman's fiction, personal integrity can never survive its mediation by representative regimes (such as parliament, political parties or trade unions), and the pursuit of justice or solidarity via institutions (the law, state bureaucracies) raises, at best, a derisive smile.

This uncompromising demand for ethical autonomy snags on the second part of Balibar's formula, which is my main focus here. How can the Kelman hero achieve emancipation 'with' others while scorning all the conventional structures of political association and joint action? The problem is made more acute by Kelman's politics of form, since these characters move in a fictive universe expressly designed to abolish that bulwark of imagined community, 'the shareable space of realist reportage in a standardised language'.[9] As Aaron Kelly observes, Kelman's literary practice seeks to negate 'the foundational ground of realism – an overarching consensus through which the social totality becomes visible', and declares war on the universalist narrative space where selves and interests may be discursively reconciled or set in their 'proper' places.[10] In this respect Kelman has no truck with the Habermasian public sphere conceived as the 'intersubjectively shared space of a speech situation', a stance which severely limits the role of consociation and reciprocity in his writing.[11] This is not to argue that Kelman's work advocates a withdrawal from the arena of social contestation, or retreats to a 'sovereign' interiority beyond

---

7   Balibar, 'Subjection and Subjectivation', p. 12. Italics in original.

8   James Kelman, *How late it was, how late* (London: Secker & Warburg, 1994), p. 245; *The Busconductor Hines* (Edinburgh: Polygon/Birlinn, 2007), p. 244.

9   Michael Silverstein, 'Whorfianism and the Linguistic Imagination of Nationality', in *Regimes of Language: Ideologies, Polities and Identities*, ed. by Paul V. Kroskrity (Santa Fe, NM: School of American Research Press, 2000), pp. 85–138 (p. 126).

10   Aaron Kelly, *James Kelman: Politics and Aesthetics* (London: Peter Lang, 2013), p. 152.

11   Jürgen Habermas, *Between Facts and Norms*, trans. by William Rehg (Cambridge: Cambridge University Press, 1996), p. 361.

the reach of hegemonic power. My approach here is guided by V.N. Volosinov's insistence on the full interpenetration of private consciousness and the determinations of social reality:

> There is no such thing as thinking outside orientation toward possible expression and, hence, outside the social orientation of that expression and of the thinking involved. Thus the personality of the speaker, taken from within, so to speak, turns out to be wholly a product of social interrelations. Not only its outward expression but also its inner experience are social territory.[12]

The inner speech of Kelman's narrators is washed through with voices not their own, palpably formed by 'external' discourse and conflict, while nonetheless embodying the lyric particularity of unique – and uniquely social – individuals. Mitch Miller and Johnny Rodger note that

> Kelman's characters, through language and their own internal commentaries on their surroundings, seize the right to redefine and reconstruct the world according to their own perceptions, yet do so in social spaces and interstices that insist upon their relationship to others, their close connections with class and kin, and of mutual dependence on each other.[13]

I would further emphasise the effective *internalisation* of these social interstices, their incorporation into the space of subjective reflection and speculation. Kelman's 'interiorizing bastards', in the self-description of the protagonist of *You Have to be Careful in the Land of the Free* (2004), gain an inner toehold of resistance to objective unfreedoms, but via narrative forms which register the hard limits and social contouring of their scope for liberation.[14] These narrators materialise an inner territory partly emancipated from the public world of withness, but profoundly marked by its interpellative pressures.

I want now to examine several striking moments of vocal communion (and its unraveling) in Kelman's recent fiction, highlighting its resistant posture

---

12   V.N. Volosinov, *Marxism and the Philosophy of Language*, trans. by Ladislav Matejka and I.R. Titunik (London: Harvard University Press, 1986), p. 90.

13   Mitch Miller and Johnny Rodger, *The Red Cockatoo: James Kelman and the Art of Commitment* (Dingwall: Sandstone Press, 2011), p. 68.

14   James Kelman, *You Have to be Careful in the Land of the Free* (London: Hamish Hamilton, 2004), p. 178.

toward reified groupness and the collective utterance. I will suggest that *with-ness*, in Kelman, can only be realised in the domain of inner speech, the socioscape dragged inward to be re-figured in the space of lyric *witness*, empathy and self-experience.

All People Were with Us: *Kieron Smith, boy*

Peter Boxall observes that Kelman's post-2000 novels modulate singular experience into 'untensed' continuities that stretch feeling and narration beyond the living moment and the restricted self; this writing 'does not suggest a community to which Kelman's writing strives to give a voice. Indeed the forms of collectivity that are imagined in these works are closely, intimately entwined with a sundering, a cloven alienation between narrator and narrated'.[15] *Kieron Smith, boy* (2008) contains the most sustained example of this effect, in scenes marking an exception to the absence of massified communal affect from Kelman's fiction.

The description of a football match early in the novel finds young Kieron swept up in thrilling mass experience. To a boy of five or six, the force and grandeur of the Rangers crowd is spellbinding:

> People all were singing now, more and more, and shouting, Oh oh oh and all what they were singing, all the words and ye just felt the best ever ye could feel and with them all being there, just everybody, crowds and crowds, all different and all the boys too, or just it was everybody, that was what ye felt, it was just the greatest of all.[16]

It is the noise and not the lyrics that prove seductive here, a contact with intense social energies scarcely containable in speech. 'Oh oh oh' can be heard as a wordless chant, Kieron reproducing the indistinct roar of the crowd, or as the exclamatory kick-starting of Kieron's breathless narration, as he sets about describing what he is almost too excited to relate. The 'allness' of this sound and feeling is vastly potent, and as the passage continues we hear Kieron eagerly knitting himself into the vehement being-in-common of the Rangers crowd. (His enthusiasm may have something to do with his 'Pape's name', the Irish-sounding Kieron, and the doubts it raises about his true place

---

15   Peter Boxall, 'Kelman's Later Novels', in *The Edinburgh Companion to James Kelman*, ed. by Scott Hames (Edinburgh: Edinburgh University Press, 2010), pp. 31–41 (p. 40).

16   James Kelman, *Kieron Smith, boy* (London: Hamish Hamilton, 2008), p. 53.

and identity.[17]) As he gradually picks up the words our attention turns from the expressive force to the verbal 'content' of this defiant togetherness, the group utterance Kieron struggles to make his own:

> [I]f that other team wanted a fight well we would give them it, anytime, anyplace we would fight them fight them fight them, oooohhhhhh till the day is done we would and just fight them and never never surrender, we would never do that if it was dirty Fenian b★★★★★ds, well it was just them and if they wanted their go we would give them it till the day is done, we would just follow on and never surrender if it was up to our knees and that was their blood we never ever would surrender if we were ever cowards, we would never be, never ever.[18]

The boyish hunger of Kieron's emotional investment in these songs yields an extravagant identification with the 'we' and its traditional grievances. But the very excess of this passion erodes its own supposed basis in common feeling. We hear Kieron rushing to internalise the freighted icons of this groupness, but as undigested tokens of a tribalism he can manifest only as borrowed affect – something put on rather than let out. A thick slurry of unearned bile floats on the surface of Kieron's words, and the canned fervour of the 'we' cannot be smoothly incorporated into his own self-narration.

The resulting friction allows the reader to perceive the dubiety and violence of Kieron's 'subjectivation' – his internalising of group norms and codes – without recourse to any supervening layer of narrative commentary or normative judgment. Without an 'objective' point of orientation to Kieron's inner speech, we become highly attuned to its internal dissonance and tonal movement (the chief technique of characterisation in the novel). As we hear Kieron coaxing himself to feel the lurid passions he recites, his inner speech cannot meet the historic-fabular scene evoked by the songs ('It was for our hearts and shields, we would never surrender') on the plane of his own experience (his faltering confidence in being a 'best fighter' on the school playground).[19] The result is an awkwardly jointed voice intended to bridge an anxious gap between the 'we' and the 'I', but in fact stretching zealous attachment to the point of falsity:

> It just made ye angry, if they thought that, if we would be cowards oh we would never be cowards, and it was just everybody, oh who wants to fight

---

17   Kelman, *Kieron Smith, boy*, p. 43.

18   Kelman, *Kieron Smith, boy*, pp. 53–54.

19   Kelman, *Kieron Smith, boy*, p. 54.

us because ye shall die, we will kill yez all we will never give in, never, never never, never shall there be one to give in. We would die first and all people were with us if it was big boys and men and who else just if they were there, and everybody if it was the wee boys it was just everybody there and all helping and you would be beside them all and yer pals too if they were there and it was for King Billy too and if it was for the Gracious Queen oh against the Rebels if we are, oh we are, if we are, oh we are. So what is the cry? a man was shouting, Oh and we were all shouting back, The cry is No Surrender, No Surrender or ye will die.[20]

Rather than supplying ethno-religious anchorage for his own lived fraternities, the colourful plate-glass realm of King Billy and the Rebels feels all the more unreal when placed in proximity with the domain of 'big boys' and 'yer pals'. The more directly and urgently they are invoked, the more violently alien and thing-like do these shibboleths resound, clotting the fluid energies of Kieron's giddy chatter. Gradually the excitement of the scene sours: as Kieron parrots the reified affect of the chants, their collectivising function is reversed. We hear not the ecstasy of unifying song but the staged and wilful quality of its constituent vocal props. Kieron's living experience of elation – of being swept up into the surging social body – is slowly but completely displaced by pre-given codes of group allegiance and antipathy.

In a celebrated passage from *Imagined Communities*, Benedict Anderson writes of

> a special kind of contemporaneous community which language alone suggests – above all in the form of poetry and songs. Take national anthems, for example, sung on national holidays. No matter how banal the words and mediocre the tunes, there is in this singing an experience of simultaneity. At precisely such moments, people wholly unknown to each other utter the same verses to the same melody. The image: unisonance. Singing the Marseillaise, Waltzing Matilda, and Indonesia Raya provide occasions for unisonality, for the echoed physical realization of the imagined community.[21]

But what we hear in these passages, I would argue, is not the voicing of a latent unity. Any sense of 'simultaneity' in Anderson's sense – of occupying

---

20   Kelman, *Kieron Smith, boy*, p. 54.
21   Benedict Anderson, *Imagined Communities: Reflections on the Origin and Spread of Nationalism* (London and New York: Verso, 1991), p. 145.

a communal moment – is drowned out by the much louder echo, in Kieron's mouth, of words palpably not his own, and the false quality of a communion effected purely by means of its internal ritual coherence (as a coded order of ethno-historic references). This 'bad' unisonance inducts its vocal bearers into a fixed, iterative groupness which destroys the spontaneous fraternity it seemed to herald:

> A man beside me was smoking and it was going in my face. He was smok-
> ing it fast and laughing and what he said, Follow follow, and a man beside
> him was just looking and he said it, Follow follow, and then he spat down
> on the ground and did not watch for people's feet.[22]

Instead of a dormant inner unity being released in affirming song, we hear the serial reproduction of tribal verities, their singers reduced to mere carriers of an 'identity' which floats free of the social moment. It is different with Kieron. The very immediacy of his narration – its ardent 'following' – grants the boy a saving ironic distance from what he keenly absorbs. Ingested wholesale, the vocal emblems of we-ness – the constellation of in-group references, songs and slogans – 'stick out' the more faithfully they are incorporated. In Kieron's inner speech, clogged with public cries it cannot dissolve but with which it fails to coincide (see his inner censoring of 'bastards'), Kelman establishes a space of vocal agency defined by non-identity with the group utterance.

Just as Good as Anyone: 'justice for one'

A more recent story explores this theme overtly. We might almost read 'justice for one', from Kelman's 2010 collection *If it is your life*, as a dramatisation of Balibar's dictum 'no one can liberate himself *without others*'. The story begins *in medias res*, with the adult protagonist struggling to find his place at a large protest march:

> They were marching already when I fought my way to the meeting point
> up the hill. Now there were voices all around, and of every kind. I was
> blundering about not understanding what I was to do. How did they
> know and I did not? [...] On all sides folk were walking past. They moved
> quickly. Some were coming so close I felt a draught from their body, going

---

22   Kelman, *Kieron Smith, boy*, p. 55.

to bang into me. Somebody said, The army are there and they are waiting for us.

> I shouted, I beg your pardon![23]

An 'I' who experiences the rhetorical 'us' as an invasive 'they', this character is immersed in the social body but set apart from its constitutive motion, equally unable to dissolve into the group or to escape its aggregative pull. Warned that the army are 'coming in our direction', he cannot process the withness of his position in spatial terms ('Did you say our direction? I said'), and fails to orient his own voice and agency within that of the disparate crowd.[24] Confusion and indifference reign until the assembly gains focus and coherence through a kind of song:

> Then the chanting began:
> Justice for one justice for all.
> I looked for the woman but she too had gone.
> So many people, they just started chanting, and these slogans. There was nothing wrong with these slogans. I tried to say the words aloud and succeeded. I was pleased. I said the words again. I was laughing, just how I could say them, just as good as anyone.
> We all were marching. Armed forces march and so do people. We marched over the brow of the hill. I knew the terrain.
> I listened to the slogans and knew them as fair. These were good words, except the way I said them they sounded different, they sounded as though different, as if in some way singular, they became words to actually decipher, as opposed to a slogan, the sort that one marches to. I tried to pick up that latter rhythm, the way everyone else had it. Justice for one justice for all. Great rhythms, great slogans but could I do it? Or was I only emulating the passion of these other people?[25]

Denise Riley notes that 'one precondition [...] for effective solidarity may well be that critique of an identity which rises from within it'.[26] This faltering assembly and its insipid demand for justice recall, with Balibar, that rights are

---

23   James Kelman, 'justice for one', *If it is your life* (London: Hamish Hamilton, 2010), pp. 249–50.

24   Kelman, *If it is your life*, p. 250.

25   Kelman, *If it is your life*, pp. 253–54.

26   Denise Riley, *The Words of Selves: Identification, Solidarity, Irony* (Stanford, CA: Stanford University Press, 2000), pp. 8–9.

achieved and won collectively but exercised by individuals. Enervated by the social vacuum between 'one' and 'all', this character's self-emancipation proceeds according to a logic and motivation figured as self-given, but arising from the negotiation of collective political demands made in the name of the universal. '[W]ords to actually decipher, as opposed to a slogan': here is the condition Kelman's writing constantly presses for, alongside and despite its mobilisation of vernacular forms which seem to affix to every utterance a defiant claim to cultural self-representation.

In the march, something like the opposite occurs: the collective shout rings both peculiar and trite, a cry of dissent indistinguishable from the smooth self-justifications of power. To demand 'justice for one justice for all' is to re-describe the abstract rights and ideals already baked into modern citizenship. This cry empties into a forceless rehearsal of its own premises, issued as a demand for recognition rather than disruptive action. Rather than disturbing the way of the world, this slogan seeks 'identity' between the operation of power and its pious claims to legitimacy – and to form a collective subject eligible for reciprocal speech 'with' the powers that be. This utterance collapses the rhetorical distance between 'one' and 'all' to a civic space rinsed clean of social contestation, leaving no traction for genuine commitment or solidarity. As the army moves into view, it is left to the 'singular' individual to realise the friction and non-identity necessary to dissent:

> But what does it all mean? I said. I never ever work it out, I was never able to.
>   What did you say? The woman seemed irritated.
>   Dont take it too seriously, I said.
>   A couple of younger fellows rushed past now, arms laden with stones. That meant the army right enough, there would be a pitched battle. That was how it went. History showed us this. It did not require demonstration upon demonstration and does not entail actual changes in how we live our life. I had to go with them, I shouted and ran ahead.[27]

Here the story ends. The banality of these gestures, and their indifferent meaning and motivation, contain a judgement on the communal political project as well as its theatrical objectification. Grand moral demands are decoupled from 'how we live our life' – though it remains tentatively 'ours'. We find Kelman's writing 'flouting the regime of identification by which subjects agree their

---

27   Kelman, *If it is your life*, p. 255.

expression', as Kelly puts it, but clinging to the prospect of togetherness.[28] The central character acknowledges his place (and ultimately accepts his duty to act) *within* but not *with* the group, moving for and against the collectivity whose interpellation he resists. The hero seems to accept the last-ditch claims of a groupness in which he neither belongs nor believes, but refigured as his *own* principle of action and necessity: 'I had to go with them, I shouted and ran ahead'.

Maybe Singing into Yourself: 'If it is your life'

Thus far we have examined the assembly of vocal solidarities premised on a bad or empty withness. I want now to explore the reverse pattern: not the self-falsifying expression of readymade collectivity, but the pulling inward, and partial redemption, of the individual's fretful positionality within and against 'community'.

The long title story of Kelman's *If it is your life* explores vocal communion in a context divorced from mass identification. The central character is a student returning home to Glasgow from his English university. His sense of vocal affiliation with his fellow bus passengers is all the more powerful for its latent and incidental character:

> But what was striking about the Glasgow bus home, right at that minute in time, and you noticed it immediately, and you could not help but notice, that everybody, every last person on the entire bus, each single solitary one was Scottish, they all had accents and were ordinary accents; none was posh. The woman next to me as well, she did not smile or even look at me but I knew. I did not find it relaxing; I do not think I did. I was the same as them but on the other hand was I? Maybe I was not. And what if there were others in a similar situation? It was like we were each one of us disconnected, each one of us, until we were on the bus home, and starting to become Scottish again, Scottish working class. My father would have said that, never to forget it, because they would never allow it.[29]

This association, and its political import, gradually crystallise out of common experience. It is the cheap bus fares and not the accents that assemble this group, and their mode of connection is not staged as a pre-given script. The

28   Kelly, *James Kelman*, p. 93.
29   Kelman, 'If it is your life', *If it is your life*, p. 128.

homely voice, here, is something overheard and silently recognised, an ambient noise marking out a living social envelope the passengers cohabit (but largely apart). In these conditions the protagonist feels comfortable in his own voice – unlike at university, where he must constantly negotiate the expectations and prejudices of others. Asked by his girlfriend Celia to take part in a dramatic reading of Ibsen, his identity is reduced to vocal performance and national stereotype:

> I knew it was the Scottish accent, 'rough and ready'. [...] I nearly did go but then no. I could appreciate the play and it was a laugh doing it. I did the English accent and got it quite good. But why did it have to be the English accent if it was Norwegian, why not Scottish? 'I am sorry Mrs Hedda, but fear I must dispel an amiable illusion'.
> People would smile when I said it. But why? If it is Norwegian it is Norwegian, so it should be any language.
> Because I was the only Scottish person.
> That was not much of an argument.[30]

His own difference and otherness, in this context, exert a twin pressure to assimilate (to adopt the English voice he is surrounded by, and which is valorised in literary culture) and to reify his natural speaking voice, rendering it up as a vocal 'role' he can put on and take off, advantageous to deploy in some theatrical settings but marking his own lack of place in others.

In these conditions the character becomes preoccupied with *not* speaking, and the denial of those codes and hierarchies which attend vocal 'identity', rendered up for the empirical ear. Indeed, this long story is an extended meditation on the inward versus the outward voice. The central character is acutely embarrassed by the antics of a friend who sings in public:

> If you were singing you were not listening. Maybe singing into yourself. Not out loud. A lot of people did that. They walked along the road singing away to themselves. Eric Semple was the worst, an old pal of mine. He sang out loud. It was like he was on stage. You would not have minded if it was walking along the street but he did it at other times too, like on the bus. People could hear him. Talk about embarrassing. That really was. I thought so anyway. He did not. Him and Celia were the same there. It was only me. I was the one that worried.

---

30   Kelman, *If it is your life*, pp. 140–41.

> Why? Why worry about other people. It was not a pleasant trait and
> I wished I did not have it. People should be allowed to get on with their
> own lives without others butting in. Ones like me.[31]

It seems impossible for this character to co-occupy the public world and
remain true to his own nature and perception. These reflections trace a circle
by which social sensitivity is always already a damning sign of personal odd-
ness and egocentrism; where what connects one individual to another is the
shame we feel on the other's behalf – a shame to which we have no rightful
claim. His 'worries about other people' anchor and authenticate this character's relationships, but also mark the limits of his ethical autonomy, where my
scrupulous listening impinges on your scope for free expression. This fretting
over his right to feel embarrassed about the self-realisation of others expands
into a wider reflection on how we orient the separateness of our inner lives to
the universal 'right' to truth and freedom:

> It might sound daft but maybe doing philosophy worked against me.
> I was aware of myself too much and what I thought: what did it matter
> what I thought; but it did, and in the world too, how my thought mattered
> in the world; how it mattered to other human beings, and the one source
> of truth and the absolute base, that was all humanity, and I was part of it
> and of course Celia herself, what we two thought as separate human
> beings. She was so honest but if she said something and it was not what
> I thought I had to say it or else just not talk, better not to talk, so it was
> better I did not talk.[32]

This character's thoughts 'matter in the world' only in an abstract and general
sense, vis-à-vis his 'humanity', but shifting to the more tangible and emotionally resonant plane of his romance with Celia, these 'separate human beings'
can only be grasped in their intransigent difference. It seems impossible, here,
to maintain a relation to 'the world' which sustains the meaning (or mattering)
of one's thought as mediated by the social, as though even this couple's intimate, small-scale commonality can and must be posited (at the level of philosophical verities), but can never be realised as inter-subjective experience. The
unspeech of this character – his suppressed utterance – becomes the means of
orienting his personal truth to 'the world' while resisting its determinations.

---

31   Kelman, *If it is your life*, p. 121.
32   Kelman, *If it is your life*, p. 142.

But the medium of this apparent autonomy is, in fact, thoroughly permeated by the demands of the social. In the words of Volosinov, 'the expression of an experience may be realized or it may be held back, inhibited', but 'even in the original, vague form of glimmering thought and experience, it had already constituted a social event on a small scale and was not an inner act on the part of the individual'.[33] The very evasions (of stereotype, of romantic discord) which affect this character 'from the outside' inscribe the pressure of the social on his inner speech: 'it is a matter *not so much of expression accommodating itself to our inner world but rather of our inner world accommodating itself to the potentialities of our expression, its possible routes and directions*'.[34]

As the story reaches its conclusion, the question of how to behave with others becomes a meditation on the outward traces of self-experience:

> Not only did I appreciate her [Celia's] own lack of self-consciousness I began noticing it in others. Those that had it seemed satisfied with themselves. Not in a bad way. I did not see them as 'smug'. They were content with themselves, or *within* themselves. Maybe it was an illusion. I saw them out and about and their lips were moving. They were not phoning, not texting. Some had earphones and actively engaged with the music, whether singing along or performing actions with their limbs. Others sang on their own account. They were not listening to anything except out their own head. Or in their own head, inside it. From inside it. Inside within it. You listened to things inside your own head, from inside. Or did you? Did people listen inside or from outside?[35]

As though taunting critics of his individualism, Kelman positions this mascot of technological atomism, sealed 'inside' by earphones, as the model for healthy social presence. The search for inner freedom, and the total escape from social anxiety, concludes in a tableau of Cartesian *listening*, an inward digging for that kernel of total self-presence anterior to the traffic noise of inner speech, though occupying the same lyric-perceptual locus. Is our inward singing heard 'with' or 'within' its point of origin? For Volosinov, the answer must be 'with': even our self-audiencing trades in material signs absorbed from the outside. It would be easy to emphasise the 'decentred' quality of this subject, and the (half-conceded) illusory nature of its existential self-presence,

---

33   Volosinov, *Marxism and the Philosophy of Language*, p. 90.

34   Volosinov, *Marxism and the Philosophy of Language*, p. 91. Italics in original.

35   Kelman, *If it is your life*, p. 120. Italics in original.

where the mighty truths available 'from inside' reduce outward expression to absurd, puppet-like behaviour ('performing actions with their limbs'). But pause to notice the character's (and, I would suggest, Kelman's) sincere investment in this figure, and the appeal of its singing on its own account. A genuine and unironic emancipation is to be sought 'inside within' – beyond all experience of withness.

Conclusion: Ones Like Me

I have elsewhere argued that 'voice' acquires a special representative valence within the context of Scottish devolution, the core logic of which is neatly summarised by Alex Law and Gerry Mooney: 'symbolic legitimacy for the devolved state in Scotland derives from a trans-class people-nation'.[36] Rhetorics of vocal difference, suppression and communion are central to the construction and institutionalisation of this people-nation, and in this domain it seems Scottish literary politics really have participated in the refashioning of Scottish political community.[37] There is no doubt that Kelman's writing and influence played a key role in these developments, but we badly misread his art when fitting it to the literary-political narrative traced *through* these developments, which presents Kelman's achievement as the recovery of communal 'voice' and representative power. On the contrary, the social value of Kelman's fiction lies in its wary resistance to 'voice' as a medium for the authentic display of pre-given 'identity', and its undercutting of the collective utterance that symbolically reconciles 'one' and 'all'.

For Adorno, 'the subject forms itself to collective experience all the more intimately the more it hardens itself against linguistically reified expression'.[38] Kelman's singing into yourself achieves a vocal communion marked and mediated by the social, but realised in the space of personal truth and being. At the Rangers match we hear Kieron parrot the tribe into himself, as the direct incorporation of violent codes of belonging premised on what rather than who he is. Self-falsifying, the fraternal roar stiffens in his mouth, bloody pledges of 'identity' sounding as dead ciphers. The unassimilated hero of 'justice

---

36   Alex Law and Gerry Mooney, 'Devolution in a "Stateless Nation": Nation-Building and Social Policy in Scotland', *Social Policy & Administration*, 46.2 (April 2012), 161–77 (p. 172).

37   See Scott Hames, 'On Vernacular Scottishness and its Limits: Devolution and the Spectacle of "Voice"', *Studies in Scottish Literature*, 39.1 (Autumn 2013), 203–24.

38   Theodor Adorno, *Aesthetic Theory*, trans. by Robert Hullot-Kentor (London: Continuum, 2004), pp. 220–21.

for one' unravels the collective subject and its universal rights and entitlements. Injustice will not be overcome by piously rehearsing power's own self-justifications, or by mirroring its claims to totality in evacuating the terrain of lived struggle and solidarity. The collective utterance of this 'we' sealed into a circuit of affirmation, it is left to the individual – 'as though different, as if in some way singular' – to generate the friction and difference necessary to dissent, acting faithfully 'within' while confuting the claims of withness. The hero of 'If it is your life' shrinks from self-performance and the agonies of interlocution, seeking freedom in silence and the depths of self-experience. Seeking, like Kieron, to orient his inner truths to a space of witness in which they are capable of mattering, he sings the problem of withness into himself in a medium both socially constituted and lyrically expressive.

'The narrow path of emancipation', writes Jacques Rancière, 'passes between an acceptance of separate worlds and the illusion of consensus'.[39] This is very much the terrain of Kelman's art: particularising the individual subject on terms which scorn the irenic public sphere and that liberal realism 'that continues to build and render unto Caesar this miraculous world in all its empirical and verifiable splendour', in the words of Jerry in *You Have to be Careful in the Land of the Free*.[40] The point of resisting this objectification is clear; but what is the positive value of the unexpressed utterance, this singing into yourself? Kelman's profoundly Romantic art aims for the lyric 'stretching' of inner space to engulf and remake, as true and free, the bad determinate world outside.[41] True and free, that is, as reflective *experience*, judged by standards of authenticity crystallised out of its own witnessing.

The redemptive potential of inward expression becomes clear later in *Kieron Smith, boy*, as the adolescent hero strives for communion of a more traditional and transcendent kind:

> I said prayers into myself but it was just not good. God would not know. He could not hear everything in the world. If it was inside yer head, He could not hear it. Because if ye were not speaking it, just thinking it, then if ye were not and it was just there.

---

39   Jacques Rancière, *On the Shores of Politics*, trans. by Liz Heron (London and New York: Verso, 1995), p. 50.

40   Kelman, *You Have to be Careful in the Land of the Free*, p. 178.

41   See also Scott Hames, 'The New Scottish Renaissance?', in *The Oxford History of the Novel in English*, ed. by Peter Boxall and Bryan Cheyette (Oxford: Oxford University Press, 2016), pp. 494–511.

How could he hear things in yer head if they were just there and ye were not thinking them? Maybe He did but maybe He did not, maybe He did not.[42]

Even the ultimate witness cannot meet thought unaddressed to any listener in the space of withness and communion. Prayer that falls short of interlocution is not prayer, but an inert collection of 'stuff in yer head' waiting to be spectated (and reified) by an all-hearing Caesar. No reciprocal speech is possible with the only possible audience for this swallowed supplication; even at the spiritual level there is no prospect of do-it-yourself communion. Glossing Volosinov, Jean-Jacques Lecercle writes that 'conciousness is not irreducible individuality but an in-between, an effect of the sociality of interlocution'.[43] To refuse, with Kieron, the public character and reality of 'inner speech' is to erase the lyric agency of the subject, reducing the small 'social event' of consciousness to unmotivated ideation that 'was just there', residues of mental behaviour with no prospect of mattering in the world.

---

42 Kelman, *Kieron Smith, boy*, p. 289.
43 Jean-Jacques Lecercle, *A Marxist Philosophy of Language*, trans. by Gregory Elliot (Chicago, IL: Haymarket, 2009), p. 109.

CHAPTER 11

The New Scots: Migration and Diaspora in Scottish South Asian Poetry

Bashabi Fraser

Abstract

This chapter examines the poetry of Scottish South Asians, the 'New Scots', who bring a whole history of displacement, dislocation and relocation with them, as their memory of the 'elsewhere' enters their writing. Their voices are significant as they embody multicultural Scotland with postcolonial dialectics that signify an encounter in the Third Space where they are affected by and affect the 'host' community. This chapter will question whether the writing of 'New Scots' has added more than just 'colour' to Scottish poetry, as it traces the recent migrant history and analyses the lives and 'voices' of diasporic communities as evident in their poetry. The objective is to assess how the new 'voices' have blended in, expanded and/or challenged the boundaries of what defines Scottish poetry, and determine whether they form a 'community' of poets distinguished by the complexity of their regional allegiances, both past and present.

Keywords

South Asian poetry – New Scots – migration – diaspora – culture – identity – transnational – multicultural – global – postcolonial – displacement – Third Space

In a critical consideration of writers with two worlds, I would like to begin with a reference to Pearl S. Buck, the American writer who was awarded the Nobel Prize for Literature in 1938. She spent the first eighteen years of her life in China where her parents were missionaries. Buck later worked alongside her first husband, John Lossing Buck, an American agriculturist adviser employed first by the American mission in China and then by Nanking University. Hilary Spurling's biography quotes Buck explaining how she coped with her dual existence of living in two worlds:

> When I was in the Chinese World, I was Chinese. I spoke Chinese and behaved as a Chinese and ate as a Chinese did, and I shared their

thoughts and feelings. When I was in the American world, I shut the door between.[1]

Buck also says, 'I became mentally bifocal, and so I learned early to understand there is no such condition in human affairs as absolute truth', recognising that there are many 'truths'.[2] Buck went on to write several biographical and auto-biographical works, but perhaps the title of her autobiography most aptly endorses her ability to feel at home in what she calls *My Several Worlds*.[3] Yet feeling at home in one world, once the door in between had been shut, was a survival tactic learned early on at a time when Buck's compatriots in America were not interested in her life in China, while in China her several worlds remained uncomfortably separate. Buck lived through the times of the 1900 Boxer Rebellion, followed by the humiliating treaties that kept the Chinese out of foreign settlements in their own country and allowed missionary proselytis-ing across a vast and varied country that few understood or cared to under-stand. And then, of course, there was the long drawn out undercover people's war against Japanese occupation, the struggle between the Kuomintang and the Communists, the memorable Long March and the establishment of the Red Star over China, which, along with Soviet Russia, led to a divided world, of the communist world on the one hand and the 'free' capitalist world on the other, Buck's 'several worlds', between which the door would have to remain firmly closed for decades.[4]

Today we are looking at a different world, where the earlier globalised world market, managed and dominated by imperial powers, has been replaced by a freer market dominated by rising economies, led, this time, by China and new players in India, Russia and Brazil, the so called BRIC countries, which are big landmasses and have sizeable populations, where the economic growth has proved phenomenal until very recently, while Europe was hit by recession which began in 2005. There is no Iron Curtain in this 'open' competitive world and much investment now moves from East to West, from former colonies to the developed world. This is a world of connectivity, where the worldwide web (unless controlled by totalitarian regimes), makes closed doors an impossibil-ity, when many people cross borders between nations with ease born of the knowledge of a transnationalism that is no longer the exclusive hallmark of the European or the American, but comes from the reality of belonging to dual

---

1   Hilary Spurling, *Burying the Bones: Pearl Buck in China* (London: Profile Books, 2010), p. 57.
2   Spurling, *Burying the Bones*, p. 56.
3   Pearl S. Buck, *My Several Worlds: A Personal Record* (New York: John Day, 1954).
4   See Edgar Snow, *Red Star Over China* (Harmondsworth: Penguin, 1972).

or several worlds. This is a fresh modernism involving the intellectual émigré, albeit some of whom are the second or third generation of migrant parents and grandparents. Such people who have moved worlds, been born in one and have claimed another, or have entered this 'other' world by right of birth, are, by the very nature of their dual heritage, bifocal. Some are varifocal, given their multiple worlds, having moved across more than two continents. They no longer have to shut the door of one world in order to experience another. Their transculturalism is the brand that marks their writing. The focus of this chapter is on poetry, the work of contemporary South Asian poets who live and write in Scotland. The door remains open between their worlds, as they journey back and forth, carrying the 'elsewhere' to the 'somewhere' they inhabit, as they cross and re-cross boundaries as transnational poets. They continue living between their two worlds, as the title of a poem of mine indicates, 'Between My Two Worlds', and like Buck they have the wisdom of knowing there are many 'truths', as evident in their verse.[5]

The reality of transnationalism comes with multiple experiences of migrating populations and the resultant diasporic groups. Steven Vertovec's description of transnationalism today may be taken as a premise for this study:

> Transnationalism describes a condition in which, despite great distances and notwithstanding the presence of international borders [...] certain kinds of relationships have been globally intensified and now take place paradoxically in a planet-spanning yet common – however virtual – arena of activity.[6]

Vertovec goes on to summarise the 'hallmarks of diaspora as a social form', which is marked by

> a 'triadic relationship' between (a) globally dispersed yet collectively self-identified ethnic groups; (b) the territorial states and contexts where such groups reside; and (c) the homeland states and contexts whence they or their forebears came.[7]

The question is: how active are Scottish South Asian poets in maintaining this planet-spanning relationship in a globally intensified context? Also, how is the 'triadic relationship' signified in the writing of these poets (i) as an ethnic

---

5   Bashabi Fraser, *Tartan & Turban* (Edinburgh: Luath Press, 2004), p. 91.

6   Steven Vertovec, *Transnationalism* (London and New York: Routledge, 2009), p. 3.

7   Vertovec, *Transnationalism*, p. 4.

group, (ii) in their relation to Scotland where they reside and write, and (iii) in their links (real or imaginary) with the land of their familial origin? This chapter will explore the sense of identity these poets have and share, and consider whether they represent a segment of society or whether they make up a distinctive community in Scotland. The poets I will be looking at include Nalini Paul, whose parents moved to Vancouver from the Punjab in India. Paul lives and writes in Glasgow and was for a year George Mackay Brown Writing Fellow in Orkney, so Canada, India, the Scottish mainland and island experience enter Paul's work. Irfan Merchant's father is from Mumbai and his mother is English, and he grew up in Ayr; he lived in Edinburgh and London before moving back to his 'home' territory in Ayrshire. Tariq Latif is born of parents who came from near Lahore to Manchester; he studied in Sheffield then moved to Fife with his British wife. Hamid Shami was born in Pakistan and brought up in Glasgow. Gerry Singh has an Indian father and a Scottish mother, and was born and grew up in Glasgow; he has lived and taught English literature in Perthshire. Shampa Ray moved with her Bengali parents as a little girl from India to Scotland and lives and writes in Edinburgh. Suhayl Saadi came as a boy with his parents from Pakistan to Yorkshire and later to Scotland, where he lives and writes in Glasgow. Raman Mundair's family came to Britain from Ludhiana, and she has lived in Leicester and London and now lives in Shetland. I have lived in Kolkata, Darjeeling and London and now live and write in Edinburgh. Paul has pamphlets of her own. Poems by Shami, Singh, Merchant, Ray, Saadi and Fraser were gathered with images of the poets by artists in a Scottish multicultural anthology, *Wish I Was Here*.[8] Merchant and Singh have been included in *The Redbeck Anthology of British South Asian Poetry*.[9] Shami, Merchant and Fraser have been anthologised in *Scotlands: Poets and the Nation*.[10] Some of these poets appear in the Bloodaxe anthology *Out of Bounds*, which maps Black and Asian poetry in Britain.[11] However, a definitive anthology of Scottish South Asian poetry is still waiting to be gathered into one volume.

When one thinks of diaspora, the violence of cataclysmic events come to mind as in the case of Jewish, Armenian and Irish populations as a result of

---

8   *Wish I Was Here: A Scottish Multicultural Anthology*, ed. by Kevin MacNeil and Alec Finlay (Edinburgh: Canongate, 2000).

9   *The Redbeck Anthology of British South Asian Poetry*, ed. by Debjani Chatterjee (Bradford: The Redbeck Press, 2000).

10   *Scotlands: Poets and the Nation*, ed. by Douglas Gifford and Alan Riach (Manchester: Carcanet, 2004).

11   *Out of Bounds: British Black and Asian Poets* , ed. by Jackie Kay, James Procter and Gemma Robinson (Newcastle: Bloodaxe Books, 2012).

ethnic cleansing or natural calamities, resulting in enforced migrations. The sense of rupture that accompanies such coercive situations that leave no other options open but that of dislocation, leads to a sense of displacement as whole communities are flung across borders and continents in an experience that is fraught with trauma as they are uprooted and relocated.[12] A hiatus is created as images of the 'elsewhere' are evoked through nostalgia, and recall and memory become a repository of a community bound by an irretrievable place which it can only remember and often never return to. As Derek Walcott says:

> [T]his is the exact process of [the] making of poetry, or what should be called not its 'making' but its remaking, the fragmented memory, the armature that frames the god, even the rite that surrenders it to a funeral pyre; the god assembled cane by cane, reed by weaving reed, line by plaited line, as the artisans of felicity would erect his holy echo.[13]

Transnational poets who belong to a diaspora capture a fragmented memory of a nation which they weave into the fabric of their lines, echoing a reality that they or their parents have left behind. So while a new nation is embraced, the nation of origin is the invisible bond that knits diasporic communities together in a sense of togetherness with a shared history of not just the place they left behind, but of the place they have grown new roots in, where their children will stay and find fresh opportunities, in their adopted land which has offered them sanctuary.

Scotland is a nation whose largest export has been its people. Scots in settler colonies and the empire left their homeland for the opportunities that Scotland did not or could not offer. The journeys continued from the seventeenth to the middle of the twentieth century. Apart from the Highland Clearances, there was no evidence of sustained violence prompting the journeys Scots made across the waters; as T.M. Devine notes, 'the Highland factor did loom large in the eighteenth-century movements and in the decades up to the 1850s [...]. [H]owever the Highland share of overall Scottish emigration became minimal. [T]he Highland Clearances [...] cannot explain, either directly or indirectly,

---

12   See Robin Cohen, *Global Diasporas: An Introduction* (London and New York: Routledge, 2008).

13   From Derek Walcott's Nobel Lecture in 1992, quoted in Satendra Nandan, 'The Diasporic Consciousness: From Biswas to Biswaghat', in *Interrogating Post-colonialism: Theory, Text and Context*, ed. by Harish Trivedi and Meenakshi Mukherjee (Shimla: Indian Institute of Advanced Study, 1996), pp. 49–66 (p. 49).

mass Scottish emigration after c.1860'.[14] Scots' colonial encounters with South Asians on the Indian sub-continent meant that the people they 'ruled', worked or traded with as part of the imperial administrative and business fabric led to an association that would culminate in journeys made to the Scottish nation on a reverse track by South Asians. Like the Scots who returned to Scotland, the 'New Scots', as Bashir Maan calls them, bring an 'elsewhere' with them of shared memories from the same region, and they are 'here' because the Scots were once 'there'.[15]

However, to think that the new South Asian Scots are 'here' seeking economic betterment only is to bypass the reality of the events around decolonisation as it was accompanied by the traumatic experience of the Partition of India in 1947, which caused an estimated fourteen million people to be displaced by a whimsical border that they had neither 'desired nor drawn'.[16] When many of these people found themselves on the 'wrong' side of the border, the post-Partition struggle meant that they had to pick up their shattered lives and begin anew elsewhere. However, many found it difficult in the next few decades to reshape their lives after they had lost the familiarity of their ancestral roots. Some of the displaced people from Lahore, Calcutta or Dhaka in divided Punjab or Bengal, people from communally divided Mumbai or Delhi, made the decision to leave when their homeland changed around them from the familiar hospitable spaces to unfamiliar hostile territories, which forced populations to scramble across borders, abandoning their property or seeing it change hands. This is where the journey of many South Asians begins. So do the South Asian poets in Scotland voice a fractured identity reflective of their communities? Vijay Mishra, writing on Indian diasporic writers, argues:

> All diasporas are unhappy, but every diaspora is unhappy in its own way. Diasporas refer to people who do not feel comfortable with their own non-hyphenated identities as indicated on their passport. Diasporas are people who would want to explore the meaning of the hyphen,

14   T.M. Devine, *To the Ends of the Earth: Scotland's Global Diaspora* (London: Allen Lane, 2011), p. 98.

15   Bashir Mann, *The New Scots: The Story of Asians in Scotland* (Edinburgh: John Donald, 1992). See Louis Kushnick, '"We're Here Because You Were There": Britain's Black Population', *Trotter Review*, 7.2 (1993), A Special Issue of the Political and Social Relations between Communities of Colour, Article 7.

16   Mushirul Hasan, *India Partitioned: The Other Face of Freedom* (New Delhi: Roli Books, 1997), p. 28.

but perhaps not press the hyphen too far for fear that this would lead to massive communal schizophrenia. They are precariously lodged within an episteme of real or imagined displacements, self-imposed sense of exile; they are haunted by spectres, by ghosts arising from within that encourage irredentist or separatist movements. Diasporas are both celebrated (by late/post-modernity) and maligned (by early modernity).[17]

'New Scots' bring a whole history of displacement, dislocation and relocation with them. As post-midnight children, they do not have the first-hand experience of the pangs of Partition that their parents or grandparents witnessed.[18] Rather, their memory of the 'elsewhere' enters their writing, which asserts a cultural identity that is constantly being shaped and formed by the Scotland they live in and the links they may or may not maintain with their 'homeland'. However, the reality of Partition is part of their 'postmemory', gleaned from the stories of trauma and violence they have heard from an older generation, and it often forms the subliminal theme of their work even when they write from within the Scottish context of their lived experience.[19] Their voices remain significant inasmuch as they embody multi-cultural Scotland with postcolonial dialectics that signify an encounter in what Homi Bhabha calls the Third Space, where they are affected by and affect the host community.[20] Their presence and writing bring home the reality that the very shores that Scots landed on 'elsewhere' and the people they encountered, are the lands from which the new fabric of today's Scottish community has been woven.

Fredric Jameson's controversial article 'Third-World Literature in the Era of Multinational Capitalism' confidently proposes that:

All third-world texts are necessarily [...] allegorical, and in a very specific way: they are to be read as what I will call *national allegories*, even when,

---

17   Vijay Mishra, *The Literature of the Indian Diaspora: Theorising the Diasporic Imaginary* (London and New York: Routledge, 2007), p. 3.

18   Pakistan was formed on 14 August 1947. India regained her identity as a nation on the stroke of midnight on 15 August 1947. Children born in independent India are known as 'post-midnight children' after the title of Salman Rushdie's seminal magic realist novel, *Midnight's Children* (1981).

19   See Eva Hoffman, *After Such Knowledge: Memory, History and the Legacy of the Holocaust* (New York: Public Affairs, 2004), and Marianne Hirsch, 'The Generation of Postmemory', *Poetics Today*, 29.1 (Spring 2008), 103–28.

20   Homi K. Bhabha, *The Location of Culture* (London and New York: Routledge, 2004), pp. 53–56.

or [...] particularly when their forms develop out of predominantly western machineries of representation.[21]

It is true that Jameson here is referring particularly to the novel and not to
poetry; however, poetic forms for South Asian writers in English do emanate
largely from the established Anglophone rubric of poetry. For Jameson,

> one of the determinants of capitalist culture [...] is a radical split between
> the private and the public, between the poetic and the political, between
> what we have come to think of as the domain of sexuality and the uncon-
> scious and that of the public world of classes, of the economic, and of the
> secular political power: in other words, Freud versus Marx.

He expands on this idea:

> Third-world texts, even those which are seemingly private and invested
> with a properly libidinal dynamic – necessarily project a political dimen-
> sion in the form of national allegory: *the story of the private individual
> destiny is always an allegory of the embattled situation of the public third-
> world culture and society.*[22]

Jameson's sweeping statements have invited a surge of counter criticism from
many shocked postcolonial critics and one of them, Aijaz Ahmed, is horrified
by the generalisation '[a]ll third-world texts' and the firm conviction embodied
in 'necessarily' as he reflects: 'I was born in India and I write poetry in Urdu, a
language not commonly understood among us intellectuals' such as Jameson.[23]
Yet Ahmed's conclusion regarding his positioning *vis-à-vis* critics like Jameson
has a disturbing finality about it:

> [T]he further I read, the more I realised, with no little chagrin, that the
> man whom I had for so long, so affectionately, albeit from a physical dis-
> tance, taken as a comrade was, in his own opinion, my civilizational
> Other. It was not a good feeling.[24]

---

21   Fredric Jameson, 'Third-World Literature in the Era of Multinational Capitalism', *Social
      Text*, 15 (Autumn, 1986), 65–88 (p. 69). Italics in original.
22   Jameson, 'Third-World Literature in the Era of Multinational Capitalism', p. 69. Italics in
      original.
23   Aijaz Ahmed, *In Theory: Classes, Nations, Literatures* (New York: Verso, 2007), p. 96.
24   Ahmed, *In Theory*, p. 96.

Neil Lazarus reflects on the significance of Ahmed's response as the latter's realisation of the reality of more than a physical distance existing between him and Jameson, but rather an 'ideological distance [...] specifically, the "distance" or, better, the yawning divide between incompatible optics deriving ultimately from the colonial encounter'.[25]

My first response to the debate round Jameson's statement is to question the continuing use of the term Third World, especially when the Second World of the Soviet bloc disappeared after December 1992. How valid can First and Third worlds be when there is the missing aporia of a whole reality in between? Then there is a second question. If we continue to use Third World in relation to writing by or from writers originating in once colonised countries, where do writers from these places, now located in the so-called First World of Jameson's definition, fit in? Do they continue to be categorised as Third World and, in this case, migrant (or modernist émigrés) forever writing national allegories, incapable of escaping the political dimension of expressing their 'third-world culture and society' in their work? Or do they, by virtue of living and writing from within a former colonial metropolitan space, experience an intellectual and cultural slippage, as they become indistinguishable from First World writers? The reality of globalisation further problematises the notion of First World countries being capitalist with Third World countries remaining outside this purview, as global capitalism has inevitably brought all worlds – East and West, North and South – together into the insidious web of commercial exchange and connectivity through networks facilitated by the worldwide web. In my consideration of Scottish South Asian poets, the question that will need to be explored is whether these poets, to borrow Ahmed's phrase, remain the 'civilizational Other', perpetually on the margins of the Scottish literary mainstream? Or rather, to return to Vijay Mishra's analysis of diasporic communities, will these poets remain forever uncomfortable with their non-hyphenated passport identities, and weave the hyphen back into their work unconsciously, or consciously and even defiantly?

This consideration of identity and belonging brings me to my next consideration. Do these diasporic writers carry a dual identity? Hamid Shami writes of his cousin's dilemma:

> Father was Scottish,
> Mother Pakistani...

---

25   Neil Lazarus, *The Postcolonial Unconscious* (Cambridge: Cambridge University Press, 2011), p. 94.

Father wanted him brought up
A Catholic; mother wanted a Muslim.[26]

After a 'confused childhood' he heads for the Himalayas, where 'God's sure to find him'.[27] In 'Mother Tongue' Shami concedes that he speaks fluent Urdu, but his language of dreams and curses is the Queen's English.[28] Most bilingual speakers have their own version of their 'mother tongue' poems. In mine I muse on the choice of my daughter's name, Rupsha, lifted from the river that flows over the border from where my family were rudely dislocated by a historic midnight declaration:

naming my daughter
Has captured a haunting melody,
Retrieved the memory of a lost land
And subsumed the magic of poetry.[29]

Shampa Ray can recover her language in an image of India:

This Ikea lucky bamboo only 99p
Durga announces from her hallway
I smile and close my door
Seal a distant railway sound
And in this silent Scotland
I hear a language all my own.[30]

The internalisation of Scottish and Subcontinental, an experience of living between two worlds, means poets like Gerry Singh can feel disoriented, as in 'India Gate' where the noon sun lights up Delhi and the M8 at the same time and he sees a Lama at Shimla while 'Looking towards the Lomonds'.[31] The reference to the Raj here is echoed in my poem in 'The Same Moon from Edinburgh to Calcutta', where shifting images of places are evoked through the refracted lens of a transfiguring vision which might allow continents to merge:

---

26 *Wish I Was Here*, p. 23.

27 *Wish I Was Here*, p. 23.

28 *Wish I Was Here*, p. 67.

29 Bashabi Fraser, 'Rupsha', *Letters to My Mother and Other Mothers* (Edinburgh: Luath Press, 2015), p. 102.

30 *Out of Bounds*, p. 66.

31 *Wish I Was Here*, p. 36.

Could such a meeting build an arch
Across the Hoogly – stall the dam
That rose between it and the ramparts

Of Empire?[32]

In a poem such as 'Sea Sound', there is the haunting question: 'Why I wonder/
Are my two worlds/So different?'

A cold sea under a light sky
And a warm sea under a night sky –
One stops me at its brink
The other lets me dive and sink.

Absentmindedly I pick
Up a shell and for
A moment lose track
Of where I am
On which shore?[33]

Images from the old and the new worlds collide in Gerry Singh's 'Ladhar Bheinn':

For ruler and ruled alike
The rock waits.
The path is clear,
Dry and dusty as an Asian mouth
Where colour, birth or better
Cannot fashion a sari from a fetter
Or lock horns with the king of the deer
Who waits for you to move.[34]

The initial encounter with the place of relocation continues in my 'An Intimate
City':

The hazy glow of yellow festooned lights
Above the edge of the gentle slope

32   Fraser, *Tartan & Turban*, p. 70.
33   Fraser, *Tartan & Turban*, pp. 55–56.
34   *Out of Bounds*, p. 59.

> Of Bruntsfield Links, flanked by the stately
> Steeple of what is no longer a church,
> Was my first glimpse of Edinburgh.[35]

But in 'There will always be…' there is also a self-imposed assurance that wants to believe that 'There will always be/Paddy green for me/Though the floods come every year/And flow relentlessly', thus reinforcing that insidious hyphen which can creep in with its dual suggestiveness.[36]

Words from another world seep into these poems, the 'elsewhere' which lurks beneath the surface of consciousness, finding a voice in a vision that is, time and again, bifocal. Nalini Paul refers to that other world in *Burra mummy*, *ayahs*, *chapattis*, *chai* and *khana* – that *acha* 'all right' world, which she knew as a girl and can journey back to in 'All of the Above', or where Burra mummy is vulnerably small and out of place as in 'Not Quite Flying'.[37] Both these poems were written in Scotland but hark back to Canada, that second land where Paul spent formative years before finding her writer's stop in Scotland. Memory is like a whiff that follows the poet, as in Shampa Ray's 'Scent of Memory', where a stone overturned reveals that:

> Dampness lived in the hollow
> Where stories are told, so
> Quietly to themselves, we miss them
> memories that
> …scatter
> Away like the darts of memory.[38]

Memories may be elusive, but are also unsettling and always there, like the moss that gathers under an undisturbed stone where it lies after its own tumultuous journeys, waiting to be disturbed and uncovered, or even recovered.

Going back in time, the journey made by a South Asian in colonial times across the Black Water is evoked by Suhayl Saadi in 'Slave': 'A boat departing slowly over black water/The town, shrinking/I, nothing'.[39] This captures the disturbing image of an enforced journey that reduces the one who sees the

---

35   Fraser, *Tartan & Turban*, p. 78.
36   Fraser, *Tartan & Turban*, p. 66.
37   Nalini Paul, *Slokt By Sea* (Scotland: Red Squirrel Press, 2009), pp. 24–25, 265.
38   *Wish I Was Here*, p. 119.
39   *Wish I Was Here*, p. 93.

town of another continent diminishing with time and distance. In Paul's 'Memory Piece', memories are evoked in the vision of

> A moth in a gutter
> in Scotland, gathered in moments which
> [...] are framed
> Behind bars,
> Peek-a-boo gaps,
> Pieces of memories trying to escape
> Like the baseball batted
> At the neighbour's window.[40]

This memory of 'elsewhere' is transported to lend meaning to a current reality in Saadi's 'Bhangra', where 'Electrical Punjabis' meet 'Boys with boys/Girls with girls' dancing to music 'Lewd [and] Loud as Hell' from the Punjab:

> Reds and yellows
> Blues and greens
> A psychotic rainbow
> Painted in Hell.
> And brought to earth
> On the back of the Beast.[41]

There is a strong undercurrent of the sense of a journey accomplished, which binds the past to the present of a community celebrating with the confidence of the second generation at a college fest. The rhythms of that other world can reverberate through the poetry of this group of poets, as in my 'Come Play with Me, it's Holi!'

> Tell me you won't play
> and I'll pelt you anyway
> with colours that will stay
> with you all day, for today
> is Holi![42]

---

40   *Hidden City*, volume 5, ed. by Rachel Jury (Glasgow: Dancing Rabbit Productions, 2009),
      p. 36.
41   *Wish I Was Here*, pp. 145, 144.
42   *Wish I Was Here*, pp. 20–21.

The two worlds, the 'here' and the 'there', merge as 'guests' are welcomed to 'our homes' and invited to contribute to the pattern of a universal garden expressed in a carpet of variegated colour in Saadi's 'Glasgow: Mantle of the Green Hollow':

> we began the weaving of an endless carpet, one
> which can be added to by every guest who passes through our homes,
> each traveller may leave their mark,
> their vision of the garden, become heart,
> upon the green earth of our place
> until eventually
> the carpet will spread out and cover
> the mountains, the lochs, the world....[43]

The world in the familial home is where the 'elsewhere' stays alive, nurtured in the cuisine, smells and tastes of South Asia. Raman Mundair's 'Osmosis' recalls a moment of intimacy and awakening with her mother:

> My head
> resting on her
> shalwared thighs
> feeling warmth
> oozing through her
> skin to skin....
> My mother
> Cross-legged on the floor,
> A *parat* of fresh *methay*
> In front of her.[44]

In Latif's 'The Chucky', the picture of the grandmother is vividly caught in a similar nurturing role, in another world as 'She funnels/A handful of maize into the hole/Then she turns the upper slab/Clockwise, just as her mother used to'.[45] Yet now, in the 'somewhere' where Latif has arrived, he notes the difference in his several worlds:

---

43   *Out of Bounds*, p. 55.

44   Raman Mundair, *Lovers, Liars, Conjurers and Thieves* (Leeds: Peepal Tree, 2003), pp. 14–15. Italics in original.

45   Tariq Latif, *The Minister's Garden* (Todmorden: Arc Publications, 1996), p. 8.

My mother
Has a Philips grinder and my sister
Knows how to change the fuse.

And when they make maize rotti
We always have it with spinach
And lots of butter.[46]

Tastes of South Asia are savoured beyond the familial domain in the public arena as Irfan Merchant addresses in Burnsian fashion, not the haggis, but chicken tikka masala:

Fair fa' the nation's favourite dish
fulfilling everybody's wish,
great chieftain, O so very Scottish,
    the spice of life
ye came and conquered the English
    curing the strife.

He traces the journey of the dish on a reverse track too:

Noo we export tae India
oor national dish, making it clear
that Scotland is a warld leader
    in aa ther airts
fir chicken tikka masala
    ye've won oor hairts.[47]

Here the acceptance of the 'nation', where Merchant's father had arrived some decades ago, is complete, imbued with a sense of proud ownership expressed in the language of the adopted nation that Merchant has made his own.

The past becomes part of the present, a past beyond one's living memory, gathered through time's relentless passage, yet etched and retrievable, however brittle, in the present circumstances. In Shampa Ray's 'Scent of Memory', a stone, 'strewn with moss and dirt', reveals when turned over a hollow 'where stories are told, so/quietly to themselves, we miss them', scattered 'myths' that

---

46   Latif, *The Minister's Garden*, p. 8.
47   *Out of Bounds*, pp. 55–56.

'are like darts of memory', a 'print of gathered past'.[48] The tension between the familial and the social, the private and the public, the microcosm and the macrocosm of life in the community and within the mainstream, respectively, is a felt experience as expressed by these poets. A home scene unfolds in Latif's 'Here to Stay', as the parents are

> reflected in the window [...]
> Almost out of my reach, as now
> They bow before Allah [...].
>   In the kitchen
> The fans hum as Usma places cutlery
> Around the table. Upstairs Khalid listens
> To the Stone Roses. Qasim looks bleakly
> At his future among GCSE options.
> Soon Lubna will be home from Hull University
> And we shall say Bismillah-i-Rah-man-ir-Raheem
> Over allo goshte and pillau rice.[49]

Inside homes, cultural identities are played out with humour, as news of political boundaries that have led to protracted displacements are recalled. Merchant recounts being the only brown boy at school in Ayrshire to play in the football team, while in the second part of 'National Colours' another set of loyalties is depicted:

> At home football was not just cricket;
> My dad wanted me to bat for India
> Or England, depending who was beating Pakistan.[50]

Outside the safety of familial walls, the transnational Scottish South Asian poet can experience the reality of being 'precariously lodged within an episteme of real or imagined displacements', depending on how she or he is perceived in the 'somewhere'.[51] Merchant wonders if he hears *'Earwig, Irvine, Fanny-Face; or/Paki-Bastard, Shoe-shine Boy, Get Back Home'* on the football pitch, 'the mysterious dervish name from Persia/whirled on the thick-set

---

48   *Wish I Was Here*, p. 119.
49   *Wish I Was Here*, p. 37.
50   *Wish I Was Here*, p. 148.
51   Mishra, *The Literature of the Indian Diaspora*, p. 3.

tongue of Ayrshire'.[52] He sees a message on a bus saying "'If this is a paki, a darkie and a chinky, you're a racist'", and muses in 'I'm a Racist':

> I saw a paki
> On the side of a bus.
>
> I'm a paki.
>
> I thought to myself:
>
> How nice.
> On the side of a bus.[53]

Hamid Shami's 'Animal Impersonations' lists a string of identifiable calls, echoing the sense of marginalisation that minority communities experience in public spaces:

> Dog –
> woof woof
>
> Cow –
> Moo
>
> Skinhead –
> fuckin' – black – bastard.[54]

These poetic reflections, where the poet is, in Ahmed's terms, the 'civilizational Other', place the writers in non-spaces of unbelonging, a feeling or realisation that has been reiterated in the work of Kamala Markandaya who lived and wrote her novels (the first published in 1954 and the last posthumously in 2008) in Britain. She captures the diasporic Indian experience of marginalised protagonists remaining on the peripheral consciousness of mainstream citizens in spite of decades spent at the metropolitan centre. Srinivas in Markandaya's *The Nowhere Man* (1972) embodies this unavoidable truth as he realises that since he is not wanted here, he should leave, but where can he go to? Is there such a place?

---

52   *Wish I Was Here*, p. 147. Italics in original.
53   *Wish I Was Here*, p. 153.
54   *Wish I Was Here*, p. 66.

[H]e (Srinivas) is not wanted in the country he considers his own, because, as he realises that leaving implies that there is a place to go. He, however, has nowhere to go. As he says to himself, he is 'a nowhere man', a man searching for a 'nowhere city'.[55]

Have the Scottish South Asian poets, writing at the turn of the millennium and in the twenty-first century, moved on from Srininvas's self-definition of the 'Nowhere Man' looking for a 'nowhere city' or nation?

Previously in this chapter, I used Vertovec's transnational framework to explore the 'triadic relationship' that Scottish South Asian poets might maintain within their 'ethnic' group, with their adopted nation of residence, and with the 'homeland' of their forebears. In *Transnational Migration*, Thomas Faist, Margit Fauser and Eveline Reisenauer explain a transnational perspective:

[M]igration is not an irrevocable process but may entail repeated movements and, above all, continued transactions – bounded communication between actors – between migrants and non-migrants across the borders of states. Cross-border migration inherently generates cross-border ties and practices: letters, phone calls, visits, family remittances and economic investments in migrants' communities of origin yield feedback spurring additional departures and manifold changes in the regions where they and their significant others live.[56]

The New Scots belong to the new diasporas that, unlike the old diasporic communities, are not in a position where they cannot travel back to the land of their forebears. Their parents and they retain cross-border connections through travel and technological connectivity. They have overstepped multiple boundaries, a reality that can be paralleled by Faist, Fauser and Reisenauer's critique of the 2007 film *The Edge of Heaven* by the German-Turkish director Fatih Akin. Faist, Fauser and Reisenauer consider the trajectory of the German and Turkish protagonists of this narrative, who cross and re-cross borders of nations with affiliations, contacts and sympathies that defy nation-state

---

55   Hena Ahmed, 'Kamala Markandaya and the Indian Immigrant Experience in Britain', in *Reworlding: The Literature of the Indian Diaspora*, ed. by Emmanuel S. Nelson (Westport, CT: Greenwood Press, 1992), p. 143.

56   Thomas Faist, Margit Fauser and Eveline Reisenauer, *Transnational Migration* (Cambridge: Polity Press, 2013), p. 1.

boundaries. They scrutinise the encounter between Suzanne (German) and Nejat, a successful professor in Germany, born of a migrant Turkish father:

> [These] two figures stand not for different cultures but for persons with similar life stories who happen to meet, suggesting that it is not a fixed or even a hyphenated identity which occupies the foreground. Rather, what is at stake are the connectivities and ties between people and across generations, families, religions and states.[57]

However, over a decade after 'National Colours', 'I am a Racist' and 'Animal Impersonations' were published, the responses to the Scottish homeland have taken on a new aura. With the economic burgeoning that marks old colonies that now invest in Britain, thus giving a new boost to an economy staggering from a harsh recession, these poets are infused with a sense of confidence as they juggle with their dual worlds. Migrant communities have the self-assurance that comes from having contributed substantially to the economy and culture of their adopted country, with whom their bond is no longer as tenuous as was the case with their parents' and grandparents' generation, who experienced dislocation with a poignancy that this new generation no longer shares. Scottish South Asian poets write with their identity boldly carved in Bhabha's interstitial space, marked by a meaningful enunciation. Thus Raman Mundair can write about her adopted homeland in 'Sheep Hill, Fair Isle': holding a sheep for shearing, 'I sooth/with lullaby;/you settle'.[58] In 'Stories fae da Shoormal', 'da Artic tundra/shivers, readjusts hits spines,/sends secret messages idda dialect/tae hits nerve-endins in Shetlan'.[59] Nalini Paul is fascinated by the birdlife in Orkney in closely observed nature poems. In 'Sea Words':

> A heron glides
> A crow fans fingered wings
> An oyster catcher flits sea-wards
> An eider bobs like a decoy.[60]

Here, in her adopted third continent, Paul has spotted Douglas fir and Sitka spruce from her second continent of North America, at home with cedar and pine with trees like maple, Pacific willow and Western yew in 'Skirlags'. This

---

57   Faist, Fauser and Reisenauer, *Transnational Migration*, p. 4.
58   *Out of Bounds*, p. 31.
59   *Out of Bounds*, p. 29.
60   Nalini Paul, *Skirlags* (Scotland: Red Squirrel Press, 2009), p. 34.

establishes a continuity that resonates with her own journeys as a poet, as she walks along the shore in the present:

> Rain stretches like washing on the line
> From Hoy to the Black Craig [...]
> until country roads darken
> and lapwings take flight.

She remains, 'a martyr, of sorts', walking in 'Blustering'.[61] The old world continues to seep through the current one as images from the elsewhere are lifted to describe the immediate environs in 'Shetland Muse' by Raman Mundair:

> Outside dark molasses
> absorbs the last juice
> from a misshapen tangerine
> and pours thick across the vale.
> The wind furious at being
> ignored whips the ocean in a roar.[62]

After the multiple border-crossings, today's Scottish South Asian poets can confront the reader with an acceptance of their dual and multiple identities, content to move between their several worlds with the confidence of belonging, not limited to writing national allegories, their voices resonant with confidence that is not overtly or covertly political.

To mark Scotland's 2009 Year of the Homecoming, Scottish PEN commissioned writers to contribute to a CD whose very title, *Departures and Arrivals*, encapsulates the journeys writers from Scotland have made. In this compilation of recordings, there are two extracts from longer works by South Asian poets in Scotland: from 'Rylock' by Raman Mundair, and 'The Homing Bird' by Bashabi Fraser. In my collection *Ragas & Reels* I have worked with the photographer Herman Rodrigues, who has captured images which reflect the journeys Scots made to the Subcontinent and brought back the 'there' to their shores in sculptures, place names, and brand names and names of homes, public buildings and institutions.[63] The collection has photographs of South Asians in Scotland who have made the journey in the footsteps of the transcultural

---

61   Paul, *Slokt by Sea*, p. 11.

62   *Out of Bounds*, p. 28.

63   Bashabi Fraser, *Ragas & Reels: Visual and Poetic Stories of Migration and Diaspora*, with photographs by Herman Rodrigues (Edinburgh: Luath Press, 2012).

Scot, keeping the door open between their two worlds, accepting the multiple truths of their multicultural heritage, comfortable at last to drop the hyphen in their postcolonial present, and retain it in what they see as the end of their post-Partition journey.

All the poets in this chapter have been through their own personal journeys in their role as Scottish South Asian writers, never consenting to the door being shut between their two or multiple worlds, accepting and affirming that there are many truths which they voice in their work. The poets discussed here all continue to live and write in Scotland. While in much of their early work they have recorded and evoked colours, tastes and images of their own and their ancestral past, and recorded the difference between life inside their homes in Scotland and outside in Scottish society, they have, with time, embraced the Scottish landscape and Scotland's social arena, giving voice to their own experience as individuals, not just as South Asian writers. These New Scots are transcultural writers who can move across boundaries of nation and write with a deep consciousness of a global reality of interconnectedness. So the early poems on racism are followed by poems about environmental awareness and urban living, which they write about as established writers who are at home in Scotland. They are all, like most writers, elitist in their privileged positions that higher education ensures. They do not represent a homogenous Scottish South Asian community, but they do, through their work, assert and affirm that they do not need to write about ethnicity or possess exclusive regional community allegiances as they are, like most writers, moved by the local and affected by the global. And so they can, like their Scottish counterparts, act local while they think global. They are, as the title of one of Tariq Latif's poems says, 'Here to Stay'.

CHAPTER 12

Community Spirit? Haunting Secrets and Displaced Selves in Contemporary Scottish Fiction

Monica Germanà

Abstract

Framed by the disquieting coalescence of the unfamiliar within the familiar, described by Sigmund Freud in his study of the 'uncanny', and later developed by Homi K. Bhabha and Julia Kristeva with specific references to the 'strangers' of our communities, this chapter deploys this theoretical basis to highlight the problematic representation of community within contemporary Scottish writing. What emerges in the two representative works that this chapter analyses in detail – Louise Welsh's *The Cutting Room* (2002) and John Burnside's *The Devil's Footprints* (2007) – is a deep interrogation of the self/other binary opposition with regard to the construction of identity and community. Rather than the collective knowledge of shared values and traditions, what binds these 'imagined communities' is a spectral web of secrets and the shared awareness of human corruption.

Keywords

Scottish Gothic – contemporary Scottish fiction – the uncanny – imagined communities – John Burnside – Louise Welsh

Although community and common values may be seen to have traditionally underpinned Scottish politics and culture, in the twenty-first century, when 'glocal' has replaced global, community has developed into an increasingly problematic political concept.[1] In fact, at the end of the twentieth century, community was already looked upon with a degree of suspicion, with Anthony Cohen suggesting that "'[c]ommunity" is one of those words – like "culture", "myth", "ritual", "symbol" – bandied around in ordinary, everyday speech, apparently readily intelligible to speaker and listener, which, when imported into the

---

1　See Sally M. Miller, *Recapitalizing America: Alternatives to the Corporate Distortion of National Policy* (Boston: Routledge and Kegan Paul, 1981), p. 180.

discourse of social science [...] causes immense difficulty'.[2] That the postmodern demise of grand narratives registered in the second half of the twentieth century may have exacerbated the notions of disorientation and dislocation that characterise the politics of postcolonial/postmodern identity seems hardly surprising. As Jonathan Rutherford notes, too, there is a sense in which '[i]n this postmodern, "wide-open" world our bodies are bereft of those spatial and temporal co-ordinates essential for historicity, for a consciousness of our own collective and personal past', and that '[o]ur struggles for identity and a sense of personal coherence and intelligibility are centred on this *threshold* between interior and exterior, between *self* and *other*'.[3] What both Rutherford and Cohen draw attention to is the positioning of demarcating lines, 'thresholds' or 'boundaries', which serve to define those who belong in communities in the name of their intrinsic homogeneity, or sameness, *vis-à-vis* the others, those who, by virtue of their difference, do not belong to such communities. Yet, as Cohen further illustrates, the nature of such boundaries is largely symbolic, and, in turn, communities are the by-product of the complex intersection of emotional, political and social factors. Discussing the case of Scottish devolution, and, in particular, the first referendum campaign in the late 1970s, Cohen claims that the political conversation went beyond the pros and cons of devolution, to interrogate the foundations of Scottish national identity in much more fundamental terms.

> The question became not simply, 'Are the Scots different from the English?', but, 'How different am I, as a particular Scot, from him, another particular Scot?' In other words, is the boundary dividing Scotland from England more meaningful to the highlander than those which distinguish him from the lowlander, the Glaswegian from the Edinburghian; the Shetlander from the Orcadian; the inhabitants of one Shetland island from those of another; the members of one township of a Shetland island from the members of another.[4]

What Cohen's influential study emphasises is the interrelationship between community and identity particularly in reference to the individual desire to

---

2   Anthony P. Cohen, *The Symbolic Construction of Community* (London and New York: Routledge, 1985), p. 11.

3   Jonathan Rutherford, 'A Place Called Home: Identity and the Cultural Politics of Difference', in *Identity: Community, Culture, Difference*, ed. by Jonathan Rutherford (London: Lawrence & Wishart, 1990), pp. 9–27 (p. 24). Emphasis added.

4   Cohen, *The Symbolic Construction of Community*, p. 13.

belong to a collective group. As Gerard Delanty suggests, following Cohen, 'the term *community* does in fact designate both an idea about belonging and a particular social phenomenon, such as expressions of longing for community, the search for meaning and solidarity, and collective identities'.[5] The slipperiness of the term, and especially the relationship between community and identity, become increasingly harder to pin down in the twenty-first century cosmopolitan context of globalised markets and postcolonial diasporic migrations, where the concept of community remains ambiguous. As Delanty argues:

> Lying at the heart of the idea of community is an ambivalence. On the one side, it expresses locality and particularness – the domain of immediate social relations, the familiar, proximity – and, on the other, it refers to the universal community in which all human beings participate.[6]

This chapter explores the problematic representation of community in two examples of post-devolution Scottish fiction: Louise Welsh's *The Cutting Room* (2002) and John Burnside's *The Devil's Footprints* (2007). The investigation highlights the challenging exposure of the clash between collective identity and individual desire, resulting in the representation of uncanny communities simultaneously haunted by the presence of troubling secrets and the apparent threat of outsiders. This is a theme already foreshadowed in the late-twentieth-century literary production of the so-called second Scottish Renaissance: the societies represented in the works of James Kelman (such as *The Busconductor Hines* [1984] and *A Chancer* [1985]), Iain Banks (*The Wasp Factory* [1984]), Janice Galloway (*The Trick is To Keep Breathing* [1989] and *Blood* [1992]), A.L. Kennedy (*Looking for the Possible Dance* [1993] and *So I Am Glad* [1995]), as well as in the (post)apocalyptic fictions of Alasdair Gray's *Lanark* (1981), Margaret Elphinstone's *The Incomer* (1987) and *A Sparrow's Flight* (1989), and Alan Warner's *These Demented Lands* (1997) display a distinct lack of coherent community. The winning of devolution in 1997 and the establishment of the Scottish Parliament in 1999 would not appear to have assuaged the inner tensions of Scottish communities. What in fact emerges in the more recent works which this chapter analyses is an intense interrogation of the self/other, us/them binaries, pointing to wider questions about the so-called 'community spirit' against the glocal context in which these novels are situated.

---

5   Gerard Delanty, *Community* (London and New York: Routledge, 2003), p. 3. Italics in original.
6   Delanty, *Community*, p. 12.

What binds together these 'imagined communities', then, rather than the collective knowledge of shared values and traditions, is the spectral web of secrets that may undermine any stable reading of 'community spirit'. For Benedict Anderson, the nation 'is an imagined political community – and imagined as both inherently limited and sovereign', and he argues that '[i]t is *imagined* because the members of even the smallest nation will never know most of their fellow-members, meet them, or even hear of them, yet in the minds of each lives the image of their communion'.[7] There are several problems with Anderson's conceptualisation of 'imagined community', and many subsequent critics have offered critical rejoinders to Anderson's study. Homi Bhabha responds to Anderson's theory, emphasising the liminal quality of the 'image' conjured up by Anderson's 'imagined community'.[8] Bhabha's argument reads the nation not in the terms of cultural uniformity and shared consensus implied in Anderson's argument, but rather as the complex and composite site of the tensions and dissonances generated by a nation's 'conceptual indeterminacy':

> If the ambivalent figure of the nation is a problem of its transitional history, its conceptual indeterminacy, its wavering between vocabularies, then what effect does this have on narratives and discourses that signify a sense of 'nationness': the *heimlich* pleasures of the hearth, the *unheimlich* terror of the space or race of the Other; the comfort of social belonging, the hidden injuries of class; the customs of taste, the powers of political affiliation; the sense of social order, the sensibility of sexuality; the blindness of bureaucracy, the straight insight of institutions; the quality of justice, the common sense of injustice; the *langue* of the law and the *parole* of the people.[9]

In his juxtaposition of 'the *heimlich* pleasures of the hearth' with 'the *unheimlich* terror of the space or race of the Other', it is significant that Bhabha uses the language of the Gothic uncanny to challenge the monologic coherence of nation as 'imagined community'. Sigmund Freud famously drew attention to the ambiguous semantics of *unheimlich* (uncanny), pointing to the coalescence of the familiar and the unfamiliar within the same term. Repeating the words

---

7 Benedict Anderson, *Imagined Communities: Reflections on the Origin and Spread of Nationalism* (London and New York: Verso, 1991), p. 6. Italics in original.

8 Homi K. Bhabha, 'Introduction: Narrating the Nation', in *Nation and Narration*, ed. by Homi K. Bhabha (London: Routledge, 1990), pp. 1–7 (p. 1).

9 Bhabha, *Nation and Narration*, p. 2.

of Schelling, Freud claims that 'the term "uncanny" [...] applies to everything that was intended to remain secret, hidden away, and has come into the open'.[10] Thus uncanny refers to that which is homely, known and familiar, and simultaneously, foreign, mysterious and unfamiliar. As David Punter comments, '[t]his remains the crucial point in the definition of the uncanny: namely, that it represents a feeling which relates to a dialectic between that which is *known* and which is *unknown*'.[11] It is, however, the notion of 'familiarity' that, implicit as it is in the notion of the uncanny, raises questions about familiar bonds and kinship. As Andrew Bennett and Nicholas Royle rightly suggest:

> The uncanny is not just a matter of the weird or spooky, but has to do more specifically with a disturbance of the familiar. Such a disturbance might be hinted at by way of the word 'familiar' itself. 'Familiar' goes back to the Latin *familia*, a family: we all have some sense of how odd families can seem (whether or not one is 'part of the family'). The idea of 'keeping things in the family' or of something that 'runs in the family', for instance, is at once familiar and potentially secretive or strange.[12]

In using the term *unheimlich* to refer to the threat of the other, Bhabha unveils the darker side of what we might call community. Haunting a collective of people with seemingly shared values and interests at heart is the unhomely side of the uncanny: that which does not sit comfortably within the boundaries set by the community; that which deviates from the norm; that which cannot be understood or even spoken about.

It is this 'mysterious' quality of community that Zygmunt Bauman relates to in his response to Anderson's theorisation of community. Moving away from its original association with the nation, and focusing instead on the definition of community itself, Bauman reflects on the inexplicable bonds within a community of strangers:

> Benedict Anderson coined the term 'imagined community' to account for the mystery of self-identification with a large category of unknown

---

10   See Sigmund Freud, *The Uncanny* [1919], ed. by Hugh Haughton, trans. by David McLintock (London: Penguin, 2003), p. 132.

11   David Punter, 'The Uncanny', in *The Routledge Companion to Gothic*, ed. by Catherine Spooner and Emma McEvoy (London and New York: Routledge, 2007), pp. 129–36 (p. 130). Italics in original.

12   Andrew Bennett and Nicholas Royle, *An Introduction to Literature, Criticism and Theory* (Harlow: Pearson, 2004), p. 34.

strangers with whom one believes oneself to share something important enough to make one speak of them as 'we' of which I, the speaker,
am a part.[13]

Bauman finds the roots of Anderson's argument in 'the disintegration of impersonal ties and bonds' which had defined the culture of the late-twentieth century in terms of the 'closeness, intimacy, "sincerity", "turning oneself inside
out", holding no secrets, compulsive and compulsory confessing [that] were
fast becoming the sole human defences against loneliness and the sole yarn
available to weave the craved-for togetherness'.[14] Within this open, transpar-
ent community framework, 'sameness' becomes erroneously associated with
'identity', and, consequently, an arguably misguided sense of belonging.

The two novels analysed in this chapter interrogate the notion of community, emphasising the coexistence of the 'unhomely', 'unfamiliar', and 'deviant'
next to the 'homely', 'familiar', and 'normal'. In this way, the novels revolve
around the strange stories buried under the surface of apparently familiar settings, and unveil the unsettling geographies of uncanny communities. What
links the collective groups of Welsh's *The Cutting Room* and Burnside's *The
Devil's Footprints* is not a set of shared values and beliefs, nor the 'easy' sense of
belonging within the imagined thresholds of each community; rather, what
distinguishes the uncanny communities of the two novels is the presence
of secretive knowledge which haunts the individual members of the community. Such secrets, whilst creating a profound sense of division, and distrust of
the other(s), also, paradoxically, bind the community together, hinting at a
less manifest, but nevertheless, 'real' community spirit based on an increased
empathy towards the other.

Set in Glasgow, *The Cutting Room* is a literary crime novel plotted around a
collection of disturbing pornographic images found by Rilke, an auctioneer, as
part of the estate of the recently deceased Roddy McKindless. The images –
part of a set of a sadistic snuff photo-shoot at the end of which the female
model is apparently murdered – send Rilke on a trail for clues about their
authenticity, a disturbing treasure hunt partly motivated by Rilke's untold troubled past. As Lesley McDowell notes in her review of the novel: 'The girl in the
pictures has perplexed and frightened him. His ramshackle investigation into
her decades-old murder is an attempt to make amends; Rilke feels implicated

---

13   Zygmunt Bauman, *Liquid Love: On the Frailty of Human Love* (Cambridge: Polity, 2003),
        p. 32.
14   Bauman, *Liquid Love*, p. 32.

somehow in the world that exploited and wasted the girl'.[15] The implied reference to Rilke's past echoes the overarching use of Gothic conventions which make *The Cutting Room* a hybrid crime novel; while exposing Glasgow's *demi-monde*, Welsh self-consciously deploys many of Glasgow's Gothic settings – the University cloisters, the Royal Infirmary, and the Necropolis, 'Glasgow's first "hygienic cemetery", established in the early nineteenth century, designed to avoid the spread of cholera and a slippage of corpses from ill-dug graves, which had become a city scandal'.[16] Links to the Gothic exist also in the form of important literary references to Scottish Gothic texts such as James Hogg's *The Private Memoirs and Confessions of a Justified Sinner* (1824) – we are told, for instance, that pub owner Victor Gilmartin is a 'man under whose tarmacadamed roads are reputed to lie not a few bodies' – and Robert Louis Stevenson's *Strange Case of Dr Jekyll and Mr Hyde* (1886), which is referenced in one of the novel's epigraphs and in the name of Steenie (Steven) Stevenson.[17] With these canonical *doppelgänger* narratives *The Cutting Room* also shares the duality which pervades the novel's main characters: first and foremost, the villain, Roddy McKindless, is presented as the perfect legacy of Dr Jekyll and Mr Hyde, a distinguished gentleman with a dark fetish for voyeurism and torture. But beside him, the remaining characters all partake in the moral ambiguities of Hogg's and Stevenson's anti-heroes: as part of their business, both Rilke and his employer, Rose Bowery, are enmeshed in the corrupt world of antique dealing; even the integrity of Anderson, the policeman, is tainted by virtue of his friendship with Rilke and, most importantly, his liaison with Rose: 'She'll get me into trouble', he admits towards the end of the novel, 'if I'm not careful'.[18] Welsh's deliberate flirtations with these Scottish Gothic predecessors function to establish a sense of endemic corruption: just as in Stevenson's novella, where all the main characters are in some way linked to Hyde, so do all the characters in *The Cutting Room* share a network of relationships, which make them all complicit in the endemic corruption that qualifies Glasgow as a community.

Damaged to the core, Glasgow is a city haunted by its own past. Driving through the city, Rilke wonders, for instance, 'if any suicides were buried beneath these crossroads. [...] I tried to conjure them in my mind's eye. The

---

15   Lesley McDowell, '*The Cutting Room* by Louise Welsh: The Literary Beauty of a Glaswegian Beast', *The Independent*, 9 August 2002 <http://www.independent.co.uk/arts-entertainment/books/reviews/the-cutting-room-by-louise-welsh-639353.html> [accessed 17 September 2014].

16   Louise Welsh, *The Cutting Room* (Edinburgh: Canongate, 2002), p. 196.

17   Welsh, *The Cutting Room*, pp. 134, 167.

18   Welsh, *The Cutting Room*, p. 249.

waltzing ghosts of the dead meeting the afternoon passers-by'.[19] Although, as Paul Magrs observes in his review of the novel, 'Glasgow is a place awash with its own perverse delights', it is also true that the city is presented in much darker terms, pointing to the uneasy relationship Rilke has with the city.[20] On visiting Hyndland, where McKindless used to live with his sister, his feelings reveal a strong sense of the city's Jekyll and Hyde complex: 'I hate Hyndland. You'll find its like in any large city. Green leafy suburbs, two cars, children at public school and boredom, boredom, boredom. Petty respectability up front, intricate cruelties behind closed doors'.[21] In hindsight, Rilke's observations foreshadow the past crimes he will set out to resolve. But similar observations about the city's lack of community ethics return when Rilke walks through the city centre.

> The industrial age had given way to a white-collar revolution and the sons and daughters of shipyard toilers now tapped keyboards and answered telephones in wipe-clean sweatshops. They shuffled invisible paper and sped communications through electronic magic. [...] Elevator buildings that inspired the Chicago skyline disgorged men and women crumpled by the day, some barely a step from the door before they lit their first fag of freedom, sucking long and hard, deep inhalations that revealed their cheekbones, smoke curling from their nostrils, working for a hit. And all around me mobile phones. People talk, talk, talking to a distant party while the world marched by.[22]

The scene captures some important changes in the social and economic structure of the city. Glasgow's evolution from shipyard to service industry has signalled the erasure of a 'tangible' economy in favour of the simulacral commerce of 'invisible paper' and 'electronic magic'. Technological revolution also affects interpersonal social interaction: in place of face-to-face meetings, mobile phone conversations are the preferred mode of communication. In this context, the concept of 'community' becomes not only vague, but also, as Bauman argues, redundant:

---

19   Welsh, *The Cutting Room*, p. 190.
20   Paul Magrs, 'More Tease, Less Strip', *The Guardian*, 31 August 2002 <http://www.theguardian .com/books/2002/aug/31/featuresreviews.guardianreview18> [accessed 17 September 2014].
21   Welsh, *The Cutting Room*, p. 2.
22   Welsh, *The Cutting Room*, p. 65.

'[C]ommunity', as a way of referring to the totality of the population inhabiting the sovereign territory of the state, sounds increasingly hollow. Interhuman bonds, once woven into a security net worthy of a large and continuous investment of time and effort, and worth the sacrifice of immediate individual interests (or what might be seen as being in an individual's interest), become increasingly frail and admitted to be temporary.[23]

The reasons behind the failure of community to survive within the current cultural context are primarily associated with the economic and political changes dictated by capitalism and globalisation, according to Bauman:

Individual exposure to the vagaries of commodity-and-labour markets inspires and promotes division, not unity [...]. 'Society' is increasingly viewed and treated as a 'network' rather than a 'structure' (let alone a solid 'totality'): it is perceived and treated as a matrix of random connections and disconnections and of an essentially infinite volume of possible permutations.[24]

Behind the façade of efficient modernity and affluence, however, the sad reality of social injustice remains, as the plot of *The Cutting Room* unfolds as a story of systematic exploitation of the outsiders. The apparent prosperity has widened the gaps between rich and poor, both financially and morally. When Rilke gives a 'bruised boy with the face of a prophet' a coin, 'a beefy man, sweating in his grey pinstripe', grumbles '[y]ou'll only encourage him'.[25]

The duality of Glasgow is reflected also in the queer subtext of the novel. Although Welsh does not make this the primary theme in *The Cutting Room*, Rilke's sexuality, and his insider's outlook on the lesbian, gay, bisexual, and transgender community in Glasgow adds complexity to the novel's treatment of identity politics. Queer sexuality is another source of duality and sectarianism in Glasgow: Rilke's resistance to commitment and his casual sexual affairs suggest a reading of his queer sexuality as anti-normative. This is also further emphasised by Rilke's observations about the transgendered community, whose secrets remain protected within the walls of the Chelsea Lounge club:

---

23   Zygmunt Bauman, *Liquid Times: Living in an Age of Uncertainty* (Cambridge: Polity, 2007), p. 3.

24   Bauman, *Liquid Times*, p. 3.

25   Welsh, *The Cutting Room*, p. 66.

Somewhere on the journey, they may pull into a lay-by, or perhaps a deserted alleyway, remove their wig, ease out of their carefully selected frock, the satin slip, so nice to the touch, the constricting nylons, brassiere swollen with silicon mounds and bought mail order, the package collected from a PO Box hired for the purpose and opened with quick anticipation [...]. Last of all, they open the glove compartment, remove a moist wipe and, in the dim glow of the car's interior light, clean away the face they put on for a night. But while they are in the Chelsea Lounge, dressed with care, they are the girls.[26]

Sexual deviancy and the ambiguity of sexual desire constitute the thematic centre of *The Cutting Room*. While Rilke's hunt for clues to solve the mystery behind McKindless's snuff photographs puts him in contact with Glasgow's darker side, the novel deliberately erodes the boundaries between good and evil, honesty and crime, legitimate and illicit pleasures. This is particularly evident when Anne-Marie, the actress-model who once posed for McKindless, recalls the disturbing effect that his demands for sadistic shots had on her mind, when she admits to feeling 'strange', '[c]harged', 'hyper-sensitive' and ultimately 'aroused'.[27] Her response to McKindless's degeneracy is highly reminiscent, in its abject quality, to Henry Jekyll's description of the doctor's sensations at the time of his first transformation into his alter-ego – 'There was something strange in my sensations, something indescribably new and its very novelty, incredibly sweet', – underpinning the psychological fragmentation caused by the insurgence of desire.[28] Anne-Marie's admission foreshadows the more disturbing aspects of the sexual desires and practices of the wider community of Glasgow. Her vulnerable position and alleged collusion with McKindless's games for personal gain is mirrored in the network of sex-slavery and trafficking which Anderson unveils towards the end of the novel. As well as detailing the horrific experience shared by many Eastern European women lured to Britain under the false pretences of professional career prospects, 'The Transcript of Evidence Given by Adia Kovalyova' casts a sinister light on Glasgow and its people:

We were not allowed out, but I would peer through the frosted windows and see people walking by, normal people. Then I began to think, in a

---

26   Welsh, *The Cutting Room*, p. 102.

27   Welsh, *The Cutting Room*, p. 219.

28   Robert Louis Stevenson, *Strange Case of Dr Jekyll and Mr Hyde* (New York: Norton, 2003), p. 50.

world where such evil exists, are there normal people? Who were the
men that used us? Did they go home and kiss their wives, cuddle their
daughters, with the smell of our abuse on their fingers?[29]

Placed towards the end of the novel, the statement is yet another demonstration of the city's inherent corruption. The 'frosted windows', concealing the
sins committed behind closed doors, endorse the community boundaries –
leaving the 'others' out – and, simultaneously, embody the ultimate erosion of
the community's moral boundaries, where the notion of normality is no longer
relevant.

   Set against the backdrop of a society where 'normal' people's sadistic desires
result in the secretive exploitation of the 'others', and particularly the objectification of female bodies for the pleasures of the male gaze, *The Cutting Room's*
queer subtext serves the purpose of, perhaps, showing a glimmer of hope, or at
least an alternative perspective. Significantly, Rilke's viewpoint establishes a
counter perspective to the exploitative male gaze of pornographers such as
McKindless and Trapp. That Rilke's gaze constitutes a force antithetical to that
of the novel's villains is made obvious by his reaction when, at the Chelsea
Lounge, he discovers a cameraman secretly shooting a video portrait of a
transvestite: 'He took people and killed them with a lens', he explains to justify
his violent reaction to the event.[30] Towards the end, too, Rilke, whose sexuality
is still chastised in Glasgow by hypocrites such as Steenie Stevenson, feels
empathy towards all the victims of sexual abuse:

> And I found I wasn't crying for the girl in the photograph. I was crying for
> other victims, present and future. I looked once more at the images, then
> took out my lighter, touched flame to paper, dropped it on the earth floor,
> watch it curl into ash, then stamped on the embers. I sat for a moment
> longer, wishing there was someone to pray to, then wiped my face and
> went back to the bar.[31]

Although the ritualistic destruction of the evidence of crimes from the past
may be a cathartic gesture for Rilke, the awareness remains that the city he will
be returning to after a short break in Paris will continue to operate under the
burden of its past crimes and, sadly, towards a less than bright future.

---

29   Welsh, *The Cutting Room*, p. 282.
30   Welsh, *The Cutting Room*, p. 114.
31   Welsh, *The Cutting Room*, p. 293.

John Burnside's *The Devil's Footprints* shares with *The Cutting Room* the exploration of the human capacity for evil and the network of dark secrets around which a community exists. At the centre of the novel is the mystery of the suicide of Moira Birnie (née Kennedy), who kills herself and two of her children by setting fire to her car. Amidst the suspicion that Moira might have been the victim of an abusive marriage, the plot revolves around the strange relationship between her surviving daughter, Hazel, and the narrator, Michael Gardiner, who used to date Moira as a youth. But the novel differs from *The Cutting Room* primarily in terms of its location: in place of the urban setting of Welsh's novel, Burnside's novel is set in the rural community of Coldhaven, 'a fictional fishing town on the east coast of Scotland that is quite as bad as its name'.[32] Like Welsh's Glasgow, however, the village community of Coldhaven is presented in Gothic terms, as a place haunted by its own mysterious past:

> Long ago, in Coldhaven, a small fishing town on the east coast of Scotland, the people woke in the darkness of a mid-December morning to find, not only that their homes were buried in one of those deep, dreamlike snowfalls that only happen once or twice in a generation, but also that something strange had happened while they slept, something they could only account for in rumours and stories that, being good, church-going folk, they were ashamed to repeat, stories that grudgingly allowed for some unseen force in the world that, most of the time, they preferred to ignore.[33]

Significantly, the moral boundaries of the community, which on the surface would appear to be conventionally religious, are instead challenged by the persistence of the ancestors' 'superstitions and terrors' casting an uncanny shadow on the symbolic borderlines of the community, which sits in the liminal position between old and new, known and unknown, homely and unhomely.[34] In its isolated position, too, Coldhaven becomes a deviant kind of place, echoing Michel Foucault's definition of 'other places' as those locations and situations which diverge from the norm; in Foucault's words, 'counter-sites [...] in which

32   Claudia Fitzherbert, 'Derangement, Deaths and Devils', *The Telegraph*, 11 March 2007 <http://www.telegraph.co.uk/culture/books/3663693/Derangement-deaths-and-devils .html> [accessed 19 September 2014].

33   John Burnside, *The Devil's Footprints* (London: Vintage, 2007), p. 1.

34   Burnside, *The Devil's Footprints*, p. 1.

the real sites [...] are simultaneously represented, contested and inverted'.[35] Thus Michael's 'accidental' killing of the village bully, Malcolm Kennedy, Moira's brother, becomes part of the village lore because

> It was an event that happened in the shadows, back in the far corner of an old farm building, and it was an event for which nobody could be held responsible because, in that shadow place, the usual laws did not apply.[36]

Michael is not the only victim of bullying. When Michael's parents – 'an unsuspecting incomer with a strange accent and an American wife who was somewhat younger than himself' – choose to move to Coldhaven, their arrival marks the outsider's intrusion within the dysfunctional community of the village.[37] As Michael explains,

> My parents' offence, of course, was to be who they were. [...] They both wanted to belong to the place, but to my father belonging had nothing to do with blood or birth, nothing to do with community or kinship, it was all about the land and the sea, it was all about imagination, about choice. He belonged here because this was his sky, this was his light, his stretch of sea.[38]

Michael's parents seek a different kind of belonging, a sense of community that relates more to the place itself, its elemental beauty and topography, rather than its people. The sense of impossible belonging evoked in Burnside's novel can be read in line with Bauman's critique of the 'utopian' aspect of community; '[t]he communion of inner selves grounded in mutually encouraged self-disclosure may be the nucleus of the love relationship', Bauman admits, but the same template does not apply to extended kinds of communal bonds:

> The tools of the I-Thou togetherness, however perfectly mastered and impeccably wielded, will prove helpless in the face of the variance, disparity and discord that separate the multitudes of those that are a potential 'Thou' from each other and keep them on a war footing: in a shooting, rather than talking mood.[39]

---

35 See Michel Foucault, 'Of Other Spaces', trans. by Jay Miskowiec, *Diacritics*, 16.1 (Spring, 1986), 22–27 (p. 24).

36 Burnside, *The Devil's Footprints*, p. 78.

37 Burnside, *The Devil's Footprints*, p. 79.

38 Burnside, *The Devil's Footprints*, pp. 80–81.

39 Bauman, *Liquid Love*, p. 33.

Ostracised by the community's hostility towards them, the Gardiners' move to Whitland, on the outskirts of Coldhaven, reinforces Michael's sense of their inability to belong in the community: 'my parents didn't belong to Coldhaven. They belong to the land and the sky and the light and, maybe, they belonged to an idea that had become untenable even before I was born'.[40]

The move also complicates the definition of home, highlighting the Gardiners' unexpressed individualisms, 'each of them taking for granted that the other knew exactly what they meant by the word *home*'.[41] For Michael, however, the new house represents a different way of belonging, expressed significantly in the Gothic haunting that his new bedroom accommodates:

> [It] seemed haunted by the history of that place, a history of summer warmth seeping up through the pipes and the sweet vapour of milk rising from the kitchen, a good haunting, a warm presence, like the heat that still remains in the embers of a fire long after it burns out.[42]

David Ratmoko notes that to 'haunt' means to 'provide with a home'.[43] In its haunted status – belonging both to the community's past and the Gardiners' present – the house represents the contested site of identities within the community. As Michael's father explains to his friend John:

> Imagine you have been set down in a strange place, amongst strange people, people who resemble you, superficially, physically [...] – but in an odd, inconclusive way, as if there was nothing really to be said, other than nonsense or mild pleasantries. And, of course, you are new in their territory, you are a stranger.[44]

Community cannot be defined in the simple terms of kinship and shared values. A group of human beings who choose – for disparate reasons – to share the same residence does not necessarily support the foundations of community. The insider/outsider opposition is here determined not by 'foreignness' of nationality, ethnicity, or religion, but by the outsiders' different sets of knowledge, which disrupt the community: 'you are a stranger with new maps, maps

---

40   Burnside, *The Devil's Footprints*, p. 89.

41   Burnside, *The Devil's Footprints*, p. 83. Italics in original.

42   Burnside, *The Devil's Footprints*, p. 90.

43   David Ratmoko, *On Spectrality: Fantasies of Redemption in the Western Canon* (New York: Peter Lang, 2006), p. 1.

44   Burnside, *The Devil's Footprints*, p. 82.

they have never seen before, and they think you have come to tell them that their maps are *wrong*'.[45]

The significance of partaking in the knowledge – and the secrets – of Coldhaven persists when Michael, as an adult, perceives his home as 'a sensitive membrane, a register, where every shift in the atmosphere – weather and gossip and the most subtle demographics – was brought to my awareness in real time, as it happened'.[46] An important channel of information is Michael's cleaner, Mrs K, who 'was born at the western end of Coldhaven, just where the devil is supposed to have emerged from the sea, that winter's morning, long ago'.[47] Mrs K's own peripheral position in the community makes her the receptacle of the important knowledge Michael also craves: 'like many internal exiles, [she] was an expert in gossip and it wasn't long before she became my main source of information'.[48] Such gossip includes the story about the disappearance of one of the village women, Angela, who allegedly drowned herself following the birth of her abnormal child: 'a woman in Coldhaven [...] had given birth to a baby with two heads. One of the heads was perfectly formed, quite beautiful, in fact; the other was a hideous mass of noses and ears, with tiny pinpricks for the eyes'.[49] Although to begin with the narrator believes that Angela, who 'had turned into some kind of mental ghost' after the birth, had drowned herself, he later finds out that she is still alive.[50] The story is indicative of the secretive knowledge that binds the community of Coldhaven together, while, simultaneously, its lack of veracity points to the bogus foundations upon which the community is based:

> The whole story was shrouded in mystery, a matter of hearsay and conjecture, and nobody could agree about anything other than the plain fact that this woman, dead or alive, mad or sane, had been in love with Frank Collings, and that he was the father of her baby.[51]

After eloping with Hazel, only to find out that her real intention was to use him to get what she wanted, which is to run away from home and be with her boyfriend, Michael embarks on a long journey 'home' on foot. The novel's circular

---

45   Burnside, *The Devil's Footprints*, p. 82. Italics in original.
46   Burnside, *The Devil's Footprints*, p. 109.
47   Burnside, *The Devil's Footprints*, p. 11.
48   Burnside, *The Devil's Footprints*, p. 15.
49   Burnside, *The Devil's Footprints*, p. 29.
50   Burnside, *The Devil's Footprints*, p. 29.
51   Burnside, *The Devil's Footprints*, p. 30.

structure retraces the 'devil's footprints' of the title, pointing to the uncanny
repetitions that haunt the community's past and present:

> The town was asleep, as it had been on that night a hundred years before,
> when the devil came up from the sea and walked from street to street,
> leaving hard, black, feral marks in the snow. [...] It should have been pain-
> fully *familiar*, but I was coming back to it now, as a *stranger* – and I was
> seeing it all as if for the first time.[52]

Michael's *déjà-vu* is indeed an uncanny manifestation as he experiences his
return to the 'familiar' sight 'as a stranger'. Yet it is precisely the uncanniness of
this experience that creates enough distance for Michael to see the community
for what it is: 'The fishing was almost gone now, but it had been replaced by
pleasure craft, bright, clean boats with names like *Arcturus*, and *Khayyam* and
Braveheart'.[53] Significantly, while the community appears to have moved away
from its rural past and embraced a kind of global modernity (as reflected in the
names of the boats), there is a sense in which its supernatural association with
the devil is still an issue. This is not because Michael believes in the devil's
footprints, but because he realises there is a seamless continuity between the
ordinary world of Coldhaven and the hell of the ancient belief:

> But there wasn't a separate world, there was only this: the air, the sky, the
> snow, these strange marks, the water, the odd gust of wind finding me as
> I followed the tracks to where they stopped, all of a sudden, at exactly the
> point where my path diverged from the road.[54]

With no neat borders demarcating the moral boundaries of Coldhaven, the
narrative suggests that the legend originates from the human awareness that
we are our own devils; we are the only source of evil:

> Because *they* were the ones who were afraid of being possessed, they
> were the ones who thought that the day might come when a decent citi-
> zen was going about his ordinary business, walking his fields or steering
> his boat through the harbour mouth, and the devil would come and

---

52 Burnside, *The Devil's Footprints*, p. 198. Emphasis added.
53 Burnside, *The Devil's Footprints*, p. 199.
54 Burnside, *The Devil's Footprints*, p. 201.

touch him on the shoulder, singling him out and taking him aside so he could see and hear and smell his own true self.[55]

As previously seen in the intertextual structure of *The Cutting Room*, in engaging with the question of human duality *The Devil's Footprints* displays the influence of classic Scottish Gothic texts such as Hogg's *Confessions of a Justified Sinner* and Stevenson's *Dr Jekyll and Mr Hyde*, but also their twentieth-century legacy, from Muriel Spark's *The Ballad of Peckham Rye* (1960) to James Robertson's *The Testament of Gideon Mack* (2006). With these texts, Burnside's novel shares the preoccupation with psychological fragmentation and a concern with the location of evil. As noted by Claudia Fitzherbert:

> The folk tale about the devil's footprints points both to the existence of evil in the town and the difficulty of locating it. [...] And yet there is no doubt that evil has been done in Coldhaven, and will continue. We may mistake men for devils, but the footprints are real. Or are they?[56]

Central to Michael's narrative, then, is the tension between the narrator's solipsistic drive and his desire – and failure – to connect with other human beings. On witnessing a car accident two weeks after Moira's death, for instance, Michael recognises the track playing from one of the car stereos – Alanis Morissette's 'Mercy' – and has 'an odd sensation, to think that whoever it was who had been driving the car was someone who liked the same music I did'.[57] It is arguably the same desire that lets him believe that there might be a bond between himself and Hazel, even after he realises that she could not be his own daughter as previously conjectured. Yet, he feels 'connected to her, if not by blood, then by circumstance. My life was entwined with hers, one way or another'.[58] Significantly, what really links his fate with Hazel's is Michael's secret knowledge about the death of Malcolm, 'the uncle Hazel never got to meet'.[59] In spite of these isolated episodes, Michael remains acutely aware of the solipsistic duality of the human condition, the notion that 'we are

---

55   Burnside, *The Devil's Footprints*, p. 203. Italics in original.

56   Claudia Fitzherbert, 'Derangement, Deaths and Devils', *The Telegraph*, 11 March 2007 <http://www.telegraph.co.uk/culture/books/3663693/Derangement-deaths-and-devils .html> [accessed 19 September 2014]. See also Anne Enright, 'The Devil Inside', *The Guardian*, 17 March 2007 <http://www.theguardian.com/books/2007/mar/17/featuresre views.guardianreview17>.

57   Burnside, *The Devil's Footprints*, p. 58.

58   Burnside, *The Devil's Footprints*, p. 126.

59   Burnside, *The Devil's Footprints*, p. 126.

essentially alone, the idea that we never see ourselves as we seem to others, the realisation that we lie, to ourselves mostly, in a vain attempt to cheat time, to cheat death'.[60]

The tension between these opposite forces opens a split, fragments Michael's psyche, so that the insider/outsider crack within the community is also reflected in the divided self of the narrator. In a moment of lucidity, after eloping with Hazel, Michael asks himself: 'Was all this some elaborate ruse to distract myself from some deep, secret, utterly horrific perversion that I'd been nurturing for years?'[61] After the elopement his narrative disintegrates, replacing the rational balance of the first part of the story with the Gothic chaos of nightmares and hallucinations, which increasingly intrude in his narrative, pointing to his progressive psychological breakdown. Echoing Stevenson's Jekyll and Hyde, nevertheless, there is a sense in which, away from the normative constrains of his community, his alter-ego can exist in elemental communion with the wilderness:

> All at once, I was aware of a chill, animal pleasure, a continuity between my own flesh and the shadows in the bushes; yet the fear, the apprehension, was still there, and I realised that these two sensations were inseparable, fear and pleasure, apprehension and the tentative joy of being there, alive.[62]

Such epiphanic awareness of one's own darker side points here to the possibility of a different kind of common ground, based not on the illusion of shared values but on the secretive awareness of shared flaws and mistakes. The notion that Moira's husband, Tom, might be the devil, rumoured to be behind Moira's suicide, is in the end overtly rejected: 'It turns out he wasn't the devil after all; he was just a man', says Michael, towards the end of the story.[63] This affirmation is, in turn, followed by a hint of empathy, the suggestion that a different kind of understanding might after all exist between the two men, who have in different ways been ostracised by their community: 'I feel sorry for him, I suppose. I never speak to him, or give out any signal that I know who he is, but there are times when I want to take him out to the point and show him the birds'.[64]

---

60   Burnside, *The Devil's Footprints*, p. 91.
61   Burnside, *The Devil's Footprints*, p. 138.
62   Burnside, *The Devil's Footprints*, p. 135.
63   Burnside, *The Devil's Footprints*, p. 216.
64   Burnside, *The Devil's Footprints*, p. 217.

Looking at the Scottish literary production of the last decade, it is hardly surprising that twenty-first-century Scottish fiction has challenged Anderson's reading of 'imagined communities'. Significantly, the failure to translate the abstract notion of shared values into the incongruous, sectarian, fragmented communities which form the background of *The Cutting Room* and *The Devil's Footprints* also emerges in novels as diverse as Michel Faber's *Under the Skin* (2000), Zoë Strachan's *Spin Cycle* (2004), and Luke Sutherland's *Venus as a Boy* (2004). Dealing with the problematic clash between insiders and outsiders, post-devolution Scottish fiction would appear to be deeply concerned with the fixed boundaries and definitions of its communities. What these novels propose, in different ways, is to map out new kinds of communities rooted not within the contained boundaries of shared knowledge, but gravitating around the liminal spaces of secretive disjunctures.

Reworking Freud's theory of the uncanny, Julia Kristeva has argued for an ethical understanding of the coalescence of familiar and unfamiliar within ourselves and our communities:

> With Freud indeed, foreignness, an uncanny one, creeps into the tranquillity of reason itself, and without being restricted to madness, beauty, or faith anymore than to ethnicity or race, irrigates our very speakingbeing, estranged by other logics, including the heterogeneity of biology.... Henceforth, we know that we are foreigners to ourselves, and it is with the help of that sole support that we can attempt to live with others.[65]

It is precisely in line with these principles that the novels analysed in this chapter reflect on the paradoxes of the communal values and shared geographies we associate with the narrative of community. Both novels expose communities as, on the one hand, the ambiguous sites of familiarity, comfort, and understanding, and on the other, strangeness, disturbance, and conflict. Haunting the narratives, therefore, is an uncanny community spirit, a web of secretive knowledge around which the community revolves. Perhaps the most unsettling secret, implied in both narratives, points to the inherently divided structure of the human self as that which is responsible for the predicament of uncanny communities. In other words, behind these uncanny communities are uncanny individual selves. In Kristeva's words: 'Uncanny, foreignness is within us: we are our own foreigners, we are divided'.[66]

---

65   Julia Kristeva, *Strangers to Ourselves* (London: Harvester Wheatsheaf, 1991), p. 170.
66   Kristeva, *Strangers to Ourselves*, p. 181.

Bibliography

Adorno, Theodor, *Aesthetic Theory* [first published in German 1970], trans. by Robert Hullot-Kentor (London: Continuum, 2004).

Ahmed, Aijaz, *In Theory* (New York: Verso, 2007).

Ahmed, Hena, 'Kamala Markandaya and the Indian Immigrant Experience in Britain', in *Reworlding: The Literature of the Indian Diaspora*, ed. by Emmanuel S. Nelson (Westport, CT: Greenwood Press, 1992).

Anderson, Benedict, *Imagined Communities: Reflections on the Origin and Spread of Nationalism* [1983] (London and New York: Verso, 1991).

Anonymous, 'Men Should Weep', *The Scotsman*, 31 January 1947, p. 6.

Appadurai, Arjun, *Modernity At Large: Cultural Dimensions of Globalization* (Minneapolis: University of Minnesota Press, 1996).

Archibald, David, 'History in Contemporary Scottish Theatre', in *The Edinburgh Companion to Scottish Drama*, ed. by Ian Brown (Edinburgh: Edinburgh University Press, 2011), pp. 85–94.

Arnold, Matthew, 'Dover Beach', in *Selected Poems*, ed. by Timothy Peltason (London: Penguin, 1994).

Arnott, Peter, 'Joe Corrie: *In Time O' Strife* and Me', *Staging the Nation: A Conversation about Theatre*, 2011 <http://stagingthenation.com/peter-arnott-joe-corrie-in-time-o'-strife-and-me/>.

Ascherson, Neal, 'MacDiarmid and Politics', in *The Age of MacDiarmid: Essays on Hugh MacDiarmid and his influence on contemporary Scotland*, ed. by P.H. Scott and A.C. Davis (Edinburgh: Mainstream, 1980), pp. 224–37.

Avery, Charles, *The Islanders: An Introduction* (London: Parasol unit/Koenig Books, 2010).

Baker, Timothy C., *George Mackay Brown and the Philosophy of Community* (Edinburgh: Edinburgh University Press, 2009).

Balibar, Étienne, 'Subjection and Subjectivation', in *Supposing the Subject*, ed. by Joan Copjec (London and New York: Verso, 1994), pp. 1–15.

Balso, Judith, 'To Present Oneself to the Present. The Communist Hypothesis: A Possible Hypothesis for Philosophy, an Impossible Name for Politics?', in *The Idea of Communism*, ed. by Costas Douzinas and Slavoj Žižek (London and New York: Verso, 2010), pp. 15–32.

Barke, James, *The World His Pillow* (London: Collins, 1933).

———, 'Lewis Grassic Gibbon', *Left Review*, 2.5. (1936), 220–25.

———, *Major Operation* (London: Collins, 1936).

Barr, Russell, *Sisters, Such Devoted Sisters* (London: Oberon, 2005).

Barthes, Roland, 'The Death of the Author' [1967], in Roland Barthes, *Image Music Text* (London: Collins, 1977), pp. 142–48.

————, *Mythologies* [1957], trans. by Annette Lavers (London: Vintage, 2000).

Bartie, Angela, *The Edinburgh Festivals: Culture and Society in Post-war Britain* (Edinburgh: Edinburgh University Press, 2013).

Bateman, Meg, *Soirbheas / Fair Wind* (Edinburgh: Polygon, 2007).

Bauman, Zygmunt, *Liquid Love: On the Frailty of Human Love* (Cambridge: Polity, 2003).

————, *Liquid Times: Living in an Age of Uncertainty* (Cambridge: Polity, 2007).

————, *Community: Seeking Safety in an Insecure World* (Cambridge: Polity, 2012).

————, *Culture in a Liquid Modern World*, trans. by Lydia Bauman (Cambridge: Polity, 2012).

————, *Liquid Modernity* (Cambridge: Polity, 2012).

Beer, Gillian, 'Discourses of the Island', in *Literature and Science as Modes of Exploration*, ed. by Fredrick Amrine (Dordrecht: Kluwer Academic Publishers, 1989), pp. 1–27.

————, 'The Island and the Aeroplane: The Case of Virginia Woolf', in *Nation and Narration*, ed. by Homi K. Bhabha (London and New York: Routledge, 1990), pp. 265–90.

Bell, Eleanor, *Questioning Scotland: Literature, Nationalism, Postmodernism* (Basingstoke: Palgrave Macmillan, 2004).

————, and Linda Gunn, eds, *The Scottish Sixties: Reading, Rebellion, Revolution?* (Amsterdam and New York: Rodopi, 2013).

Bennett, Andrew, and Nicholas Royle, *An Introduction to Literature, Criticism and Theory* (Harlow: Pearson, 2004).

Bersani, Leo, *The Culture of Redemption* (Cambridge, MA: Harvard University Press, 1990).

————, *Homos* (Cambridge, MA: Harvard University Press, 1996).

Beveridge, Craig, and Ronald Turnbull, *The Eclipse of Scottish Culture: Inferiorism and the Intellectuals* (Edinburgh: Polygon, 1989).

Bhabha, Homi K., ed., *Nation and Narration* (London: Routledge, 1990).

————, *The Location of Culture* [1991] (London and New York: Routledge, 2004).

Bissett, Alan, 'The "New Weegies": The Glasgow Novel in the Twenty-first Century', in *The Edinburgh Companion to Contemporary Scottish Literature*, ed. by Berthold Schoene (Edinburgh: Edinburgh University Press, 2007), pp. 59–67.

Black, Ronald, ed., *An Tuil: Anthology of Twentieth-Century Scottish Gaelic Verse* (Edinburgh: Polygon, 1999).

Blake, George, *Barrie and the Kailyard School* (London: Arthur Barker, 1951).

Blanchot, Maurice, *The Unavowable Community* [first published in French 1983], trans. by Pierre Joris (Barrytown: Station Hill, 1988).

Bold, Alan, *MacDiarmid: Christopher Murray Grieve: A Critical Biography* (London: John Murray, 1998).

Bowd, Gavin, *'The Outsiders': Alexander Trocchi and Kenneth White, An Essay* (London: Akros, 1998).

Boxall, Peter, 'Kelman's Later Novels', in *The Edinburgh Companion to James Kelman*, ed. by Scott Hames (Edinburgh: Edinburgh University Press, 2010), pp. 31–41.

Braidotti, Rosi, *Nomadic Subjects: Embodiment and Sexual Difference in Contemporary Feminist Theory* (New York: Columbia University Press, 1994).

Braidwood, Alistair, 'Iain Banks, James Kelman and the Art of Engagement: An Application of Jean-Paul Sartre's Theories of Literature and Existentialism to Two Modern Scottish Novelists' (unpublished doctoral thesis, University of Glasgow, 2011).

Braudel, Fernand, *The Mediterranean and the Mediterranean World in the Age of Philip II*, trans. by Sian Reynolds, 2 vols (London: Collins, 1972–73).

Brenkman, John, 'Innovation: Notes on Nihilism and the Aesthetics of the Novel', in *The Novel, Volume 2: Forms and Themes*, ed. by Franco Moretti (Princeton: Princeton University Press, 2006), pp. 808–38.

Brennan, Mary, '*Rantin*', Cottiers Theatre, Glasgow', *The Herald*, 19 April 2013, p. 12.

Breslauer, George W., in *The Soviet Polity in the Modern Era*, ed. by Erik P. Hoffmann and Robbin Frederick Laird (New York: Aldine de Gruyter, 1984), p. 23.

Brown, George Douglas, *The House with the Green Shutters* [1901] (Edinburgh: Polygon, 2005).

Brown, George Mackay, *Three Plays: The Loom of Light, The Well* and *The Voyage of Saint Brandon* (London: Chatto & Windus, 1984).

Brown, Ian, 'Plugged into History', in *Scottish Theatre Since the Seventies*, ed. by Randall Stevenson and Gavin Wallace (Edinburgh: Edinburgh University Press, 1996), pp. 84–99.

Brown, Ian, and John Ramage, 'Referendum to Referendum and Beyond: Political Vitality and Scottish Theatre', *The Irish Review*, 18 (2001), 46–57.

Brown, Mark, 'True Test of Girl Power', *The Herald*, 4 November 2012, p. 17.

Brown, Timothy, and Lorena Anton, 'Introduction', in *Between the Avant-garde and the Everyday: Subversive Politics in Europe from 1957 to the Present*, ed. by Timothy Brown and Lorena Anton (New York: Berghahn, 2011), pp. 1–10.

Buchan, John, *The Island of Sheep* (London: Hodder and Stoughton, 1936).

Buck, Pearl S., *My Several Worlds: A Personal Record* (New York: John Day, 1954).

Burgess, Moira, and Hamish Whyte, 'Gaitens, Edward (1897–1966)', *Oxford Dictionary of National Biography*, vol. 25 (Oxford: Oxford University Press, 2004), pp. 285–86.

Burke, Gregory, *The National Theatre of Scotland's Black Watch* (London: Faber and Faber, 2007).

Burnside, John, *The Devil's Footprints* (London: Vintage, 2007).

Butler, Judith, *Undoing Gender* (Abingdon: Routledge, 2004).

Butler, Neil, *The Roost* (Edinburgh: Thirsty Books, 2011).

Byrne, Michel, and Dorothy McMillan, eds, *Modern Scottish Women Poets* (Edinburgh: Canongate, 2003).

Calder, John, *Garden of Eros: The Story of the Paris Expatriates and the Post-War Literary Scene* (Richmond: Alma, 2014).

Campbell, Allan, and Tim Niel, eds, *A Life In Pieces: Reflections on Alexander Trocchi* (Edinburgh: Rebel Inc., 1997).

Campbell, Angus Peter, *Invisible Islands* (Glasgow: Otago, 2006).

———, *Archie and the North Wind* (Edinburgh: Luath, 2010).

———, *Aibisidh* (Edinburgh: Polygon, 2011).

———, *The Girl on the Ferryboat* (Edinburgh: Luath, 2013).

Campbell, Ian, *Kailyard: A New Assessment* (Edinburgh: The Ramsay Head Press, 1981).

Campbell, James, 'Introduction' to Edward Gaitens, *Dance of the Apprentices* (Edinburgh: Canongate, 1990), pp. v–viii.

Campbell, James, *Syncopations: Beats, New Yorkers, and Writers in the Dark* (Berkeley: University of California, 2008).

Camus, Albert, *The Rebel* [1951] (London: Penguin, 2000).

Cant, Bob, 'An Exile's Tale', in *The Crazy Jig: Gay and Lesbian Writing from Scotland 2*, ed. by Joanne Winning (Edinburgh: Polygon, 1992), pp. 86–95.

Carmichael, Alexander, 'Grazing and Agrestic Customs of the Outer Hebrides', in *Report of Her Majesty's Commissioners of Inquiry into the Conditions of the Crofters and Cottars in the Highlands and Islands of Scotland* (Edinburgh, 1884), pp. 451–82.

———, *Carmina Gadelica: hymns and incantations with illustrative notes on words, rites, and customs, dying and obsolete*, Vol. 1 (Edinburgh: T. and A. Constable, 1900).

Carruthers, Gerard, *Scottish Literature* (Edinburgh: Edinburgh University Press, 2009).

Caserio, Robert L., 'Queer Friction: The Ambiguous Emergence of a Genre', in *A Concise Companion to Contemporary British Fiction*, ed. by James F. English (Oxford: Blackwell, 2006), pp. 209–28.

Caute, David, 'Introduction', in Jean-Paul Sartre, *'What is Literature?' And Other Essays* (Cambridge: Harvard College, 1998), pp. vii–xxi.

Chatterjee, Debjani, ed., *The Redbeck Anthology of British South Asian Poetry* (Bradford: The Redbeck Press, 2000).

Claeys, Gregory, *Searching for Utopia: The History of an Idea* (London: Thames & Hudson, 2011).

Clastres, Pierre, *Society against the State* (Oxford: Basil Blackwell, 1977).

Cohen, Anthony P., *The Symbolic Construction of Community* (London and New York: Routledge, 1985).

Cohen, Robin, *Global Diasporas: An Introduction* (London and New York: Routledge, 2008).

Collins, Patricia Hill, 'The New Politics of Community', *American Sociological Review*, 75.1 (2010), 7–30.

Conrad, Peter, *Islands: A Trip through Time and Space* (London: Thames and Hudson, 2009).

Corrie, Joe, *Black Earth* (London: Routledge, 1939).

Coverley, Merlin, *Psychogeography* (London: Pocket Essentials, 2010).

Cowan, Edward J., ed., *The People's Past: Scottish Folk, Scottish History* (Edinburgh: Polygon, 1980).

Craig, Cairns, 'Going Down to Hell is Easy: *Lanark*, Realism and the Limits of the Imagination', in *The Arts of Alasdair Gray*, ed. by Robert Crawford and Thom Nairn (Edinburgh: Edinburgh University Press, 1991), pp. 90–107.

——, *Out of History: Narrative Paradigms in Scottish and British Culture* (Edinburgh: Polygon, 1996).

——, *The Modern Scottish Novel: Narrative and the National Imagination* (Edinburgh: Edinburgh University Press, 1999).

——, 'Beyond Reason – Hume, Seth, Macmurray and Scotland's Postmodernity', in *Scotland in Theory: Reflections on Culture and Theory*, ed. by Eleanor Bell and Gavin Miller (Amsterdam and New York: Rodopi, 2004), pp. 249–83.

——, 'Devolving the Scottish Novel', in *A Concise Companion to Contemporary British Fiction*, ed. by James F. English (Oxford: Blackwell, 2006), pp. 121–40.

Cranston, Maurice, *Sartre* (Edinburgh: Oliver and Boyd, 1970).

Crawford, Robert, *Scotland's Books: The Penguin History of Scottish Literature* (London: Penguin, 2007).

Crawford, Thomas, 'Introduction', *A Scots Quair* (Edinburgh: Canongate, 2008), pp. vii–xii.

Crockett, S.R., *The Lilac Sunbonnet: A Love Story* (New York: D. Appleton and Company, 1894).

D'Emilio, John, *Sexual Politics, Sexual Communities: The Making of a Homosexual Minority in the United States 1940–1970* (Chicago: University of Chicago Press, 1983).

Davidson, Toni, ed., *And Thus Will I Freely Sing: An Anthology of Gay and Lesbian Writing from Scotland* (Edinburgh: Polygon, 1989).

De Luca, Christine, *North End of Eden* (Edinburgh: Luath, 2010).

Debord, Guy, 'Report on the Construction of Situations and on the International Situationist Tendency's Conditions of Organisation and Action', *Bureau of Public Secrets* (1957), <http://www.bopsecrets.org/SI/report.htm>.

——, Letter to Alexander Trocchi, 12 October 1964, <http://www.notbored.org/debord-12October1964.html>.

——, *Panegyric* (London and New York: Verso, 2009).

Delanty, Gerard, *Community*, 2nd edn (Abingdon: Routledge, 2010).

Deleuze, Gilles, *Desert Islands and Other Texts, 1953–1974*, ed. by David Lapoujade, trans. by Michael Taormina (Los Angeles and New York: Semiotext(e), 2004).

Deleuze, Gilles, and Félix Guattari, *A Thousand Plateaus: Capitalism and Schizophrenia* (London: Athlone, 1988).

Derrida, Jacques, *The Beast and the Sovereign: Volume II*, ed. by Michel Lisse, Marie-Louise Mallet, and Ginette Michaud, trans. by Geoffrey Bennington (Chicago and London: University of Chicago Press, 2011).

Devine, T.M., *The Scottish Nation 1700–2000* (Harmondsworth: Penguin, 2000).

———, *To the Ends of the Earth: Scotland's Global Diaspora* (London: Allen Lane, 2011).

Dolan, Jill, *Utopia in Performance: Finding Hope at the Theater* (Michigan: The University of Michigan Press, 2005).

Donnelly, Mark, *Sixties Britain: Culture, Society and Politics* (London: Routledge, 2013).

Duggan, Lisa, 'The New Homonormativity: The Sexual Politics of Neoliberalism', in *Materializing Democracy: Towards a Revitalized Cultural Politics*, ed. by Russ Castronovo and Dana Nelson (Durham, NC: Duke University Press, 2002), pp. 175–94.

Dunn, Douglas, 'Divergent Scottishness: William Boyd, Allan Massie, Ronald Frame', in *The Scottish Novel Since the Seventies: New Visions, Old Dreams*, ed. by Gavin Wallace and Randall Stevenson (Edinburgh: Edinburgh University Press, 1993), pp. 149–69.

Eliot, T.S., 'Was There a Scottish Literature?', *Athenaeum*, 1 August 1919, 680–81.

———, *Notes towards the Definition of Culture* (London: Faber and Faber, 1948).

English, James F., 'Introduction', in *A Concise Companion to Contemporary British Fiction*, ed. by James F. English (Oxford: Blackwell, 2006), pp. 1–15.

Entwistle, W.J., *European Balladry* (Oxford: Clarendon, 1939).

Esposito, Roberto, *Communitas: The Origin and Destiny of Community*, trans. by Timothy Campbell (Stanford: Stanford University Press, 2010).

Faist, Thomas, Margit Fauser and Eveline Reisenauer, *Transnational Migration* (Cambridge: Polity Press, 2013).

Ferrebe, Alice, 'Between Camps: Masculinity, Race and Nation in Post-devolution Scotland', in *The Edinburgh Companion to Contemporary Scottish Literature*, ed. by Berthold Schoene (Edinburgh: Edinburgh University Press, 2007), pp. 275–82.

Ferry, Anne, 'Anonymity: The Literary History of a Word', *New Literary History*, 33 (2002), 193–214.

Fitzherbert, Claudia, 'Derangement, Deaths and Devils', *The Telegraph*, 11 March 2007 <http://www.telegraph.co.uk/culture/books/3663693/Derangement-deaths-and-d evils.html>.

Forster, E.M., *Anonymity: An Enquiry* (London: Hogarth, 1925).

Foucault, Michel, 'Of Other Spaces', trans. by Jay Miskowiec, *Diacritics*, 16.1 (Spring, 1986), 22–27.

Fraser, Bashabi, *Tartan & Turban* (Edinburgh: Luath Press, 2004).

———, *Ragas & Reels*: Poems on Migration and Diaspora with photographs by Herman Rodrigues (Edinburgh: Luath Press, 2012).

———, *Letters to My Mother and Other Mothers* (Edinburgh: Luath Press, 2015).

Freud, Sigmund, *The Uncanny* [first published in German 1919], ed. by Hugh Haughton, trans. by David McLintock (London: Penguin, 2003).

Frost, William Goodell, 'Our Contemporary Ancestors in the Southern Mountains', *Atlantic Monthly*, 83 (March 1899), 311–19.

Gaitens, Edward, *Dance of the Apprentices* [1948] (Edinburgh: Canongate, 1990).

——, *Growing Up* (Glasgow: McLellan, 1942).

Galford, Ellen, *The Fires of Bride* (London: The Women's Press, 1986).

Galford, Ellen, and Ken Wilson, eds, *Rainbow City: Stories from Lesbian, Gay, Bisexual and Transgender Edinburgh* (Edinburgh: Word Power, 2006).

Galloway, Janice, *The Trick is to Keep Breathing*, 2nd edn (London: Minerva, 1991).

Gardiner, Michael, *Time and Action in the Scottish Independence Referendum* (Basingstoke: Palgrave Macmillan, 2015).

Gardner, Lyn, 'Theatre Review: *The Last Witch*', *The Guardian*, 25 August 2009, p. 8.

Gibbon, Lewis Grassic, *Sunset Song* [1932] (Edinburgh: Canongate, 2008).

——, 'Glasgow', in Lewis Grassic Gibbon and Hugh MacDiarmid, *Scottish Scene, or The Intelligent Man's Guide to Albyn* [1934] (London and Melbourne: Hutchinson, n.d.), pp. 114–25.

——, *Grey Granite* [1934] (London: Pan, 1973).

——, *A Scots Quair* [1946] (Edinburgh: Canongate, 1995).

Gibson, Corey, *The Voice of the People: Hamish Henderson and Scottish Cultural Politics* (Edinburgh: Edinburgh University Press, 2015).

Gifford, Douglas, and Alan Riach, eds, *Scotlands: Poets and the Nation* (Manchester Carcanet, 2004).

Gifford, Douglas, and others, eds, *Scottish Literature in English and Scots* (Edinburgh: Edinburgh University Press, 2002).

Gillies, Anne Lorne, ed., *Songs of Gaelic Scotland* (Edinburgh: Birlinn, 2005).

Gitlin, Todd, *The Sixties: Years of Hope, Days of Rage* (London: Bantam, 1993).

Gluckman, Amy, and Betsy Reed, *Homo Economics: Capitalism, Community, and Lesbian and Gay Life* (London: Routledge, 1997).

Goldie, David, 'Hugh MacDiarmid: The Impossible Persona', in *The Edinburgh Companion to Hugh MacDiarmid*, ed. by Scott Lyall and Margery Palmer McCulloch (Edinburgh: Edinburgh University Press, 2011), pp. 123–35.

Gray, Alasdair, *Lanark: A Life in 4 Books* [1981] (London: Picador, 1991).

——, *Of Me and Others* (Glasgow: Cargo Publishing, 2014).

Greig, David, *Selected Plays 1999–2009* (London: Faber and Faber, 2010).

Greig, Gavin, and Alexander Keith, eds, *Last Leaves of Traditional Ballads and Ballad Airs* (Aberdeen: Aberdeen University Press, 1925).

Greig, Gavin, *Folk-Song in Buchan and Folk-Song of the North-East*, 2 vols (Hatboro: Folklore Associates, 1963).

Habermas, Jürgen, 'The Public Sphere: An Encyclopedia Article', *New German Critique*, 3 (1974), 49–55.

——, *Between Facts and Norms*, trans. by William Rehg (Cambridge: Cambridge University Press, 1996).

Hadfield, Jen, *Nigh-No-Place* (Tarset: Bloodaxe, 2008).

Hames, Scott, ed., *Unstated: Writers on Scottish Independence* (Edinburgh: Word Power, 2012).

——, 'On Vernacular Scottishness and its Limits: Devolution and the Spectacle of "Voice"', *Studies in Scottish Literature*, 39.1 (Autumn 2013), 203–24.

——, 'The New Scottish Renaissance?', in *The Oxford History of the Novel in English, vol. VII: British And Irish Fiction since 1940*, ed. by Peter Boxall and Bryan Cheyette (Oxford: Oxford University Press, 2016), pp. 494–511.

Hamilton, Christine, Consulting, 'Review of the Theatre Sector in Scotland for Creative Scotland', 2012 <www.creativescotland.com/resources/our-publications/sector-reviews/theatre-sector-review>.

Hannan, Chris, *Elizabeth Gordon Quinn*, in *Scot-Free: New Scottish Plays*, ed. by Alasdair Cameron (London: Nick Hern Books, 1990), pp. 105–46.

Hardy, Forsyth, *Scotland in Film* (Edinburgh: Edinburgh University Press, 1990).

Hart, Francis Russell, *The Scottish Novel: From Smollett to Spark* (Cambridge, MA: Harvard University Press, 1978).

Harvey, David, *Spaces of Hope* (Edinburgh: Edinburgh University Press, 2002).

Hasan, Mushirul, *India Partitioned: The Other Face of Freedom* (New Delhi: Roli Books, 1997).

Hay, George Campbell, *Collected Poems and Songs of George Campbell Hay*, ed. by Michel Byrne (Edinburgh: Edinburgh University Press, 2003).

Haywood, Ian, *Working-Class Fiction from Chartism to Trainspotting* (Plymouth: Northcote House, 1997).

Heaney, Seamus, 'An Invocation', *London Review of Books*, 14.15 (August 1992), p. 16.

Henderson, Hamish, 'Freedom Becomes People', *Chapman*, 42 (1985), 1–7.

——, 'The Ballad and Popular Tradition to 1660', in *The History of Scottish Literature, Volume 1: Origins to 1660*, ed. by R.D.S. Jack, 4 vols. (Aberdeen: Aberdeen University Press, 1988), pp. 263–83.

——, *The Armstrong Nose: Selected Letters of Hamish Henderson* (Edinburgh: Polygon, 1996).

——, *Alias MacAlias: Writings on Songs, Folk and Literature* [1992] (Edinburgh: Polygon, 2004).

Hendry, Joy, 'The Scottish Accent of the Mind', in *Borne on the Carrying Stream: The Legacy of Hamish Henderson*, ed. by Eberhard Bort (Ochtertyre: Grace Note, 2010), pp. 195–203.

Herbert, W.N., *To Circumjack MacDiarmid: The Poetry and Prose of Hugh MacDiarmid* (Oxford: Clarendon Press, 1992).

Herd, David, *Ancient and Modern Scottish Songs, Heroic Ballads, etc.* [1769] (Edinburgh: Scottish Academic Press, 1973).

Heslop, Harold, *The Gate of a Strange Field* (London: Brentano's, 1929).

Hill, John, 'Towards a Scottish People's Theatre: The Rise and Fall of Glasgow Unity', *Theatre Quarterly*, 7.27 (1977), 61–70.

Hirsch, Marianne, 'The Generation of Postmemory', in *Poetics Today*, 29.1 (Spring, 2008), 103–28.

Hobsbawm, Eric, *The Age of Extremes: The Short Twentieth Century, 1914–1991* (London: Abacus, 1995).

——, *The Age of Revolution, 1789–1848* [1962] (London: Abacus, 2014).

Hoffman, Eva, *After Such Knowledge: Memory, History and the Legacy of the Holocaust* (New York: Public Affairs, 2004).

Holdsworth, Nadine, 'Case Study: Ena Lamont Stewart's *Men Should Weep*, 1947', in *The Cambridge History of British Theatre: Volume 3 from 1895*, ed. by Baz Kershaw (Cambridge: Cambridge University Press, 2004), pp. 228–41.

——, ed., *Theatre and National Identity: Re-imagining Conceptions of Nation* (New York: Routledge, 2014).

Hunter, Edward, *The Road the Men Came Home* (London: National Labour Press, 1920).

——, *The Dream of Toil* (Glasgow: The Author, 1922).

——, 'The Underworld', *Labour Leader*, 26 April 1929.

——, *When Sleeps the Tide: Pictures – Music – Songs and Poems* (Glasgow: The Author, 1943).

Innes, Bill, 'Poetry of the Oral Tradition: How Relevant Is It to Gaelic in the 21st Century?', *Transactions of the Gaelic Society of Inverness*, 62 (2004), 79–109.

Innes, Kirstin, 'Mark Renton's Bairns: Identity and Language in the Post-*Trainspotting* Novel', in *The Edinburgh Companion to Contemporary Scottish Literature*, ed. by Berthold Schoene (Edinburgh: Edinburgh University Press, 2007), pp. 301–09.

Jaeggi, Rahel, *Alienation*, trans. by Frederick Neuhouser and Alan E. Smith (New York: Columbia University Press, 2014).

Jameson, Fredric, 'Third-World Literature in the Era of Multinational Capitalism', *Social Text*, 15 (Autumn, 1986), 65–88.

——, *Archaeologies of the Future: The Desire Called Utopia and Other Science Fictions* (London and New York: Verso, 2005).

Jamieson, John, *Jamieson's Dictionary of the Scottish Language* [1808] (Paisley: A. Gardner, 1912).

Jones, Carole, 'Burying the Man that was: Janice Galloway and Gender Disorientation', in *The Edinburgh Companion to Contemporary Scottish Literature*, ed. by Berthold Schoene (Edinburgh: Edinburgh University Press, 2007), pp. 210–18.

Joyce, James, *Ulysses* [1922] (Harmondsworth: Penguin, 1992).

Jury, Rachel, ed., *Hidden City 5* (Glasgow: Dancing Rabbit Productions, 2009).

Kay, Jackie, James Procter and Gemma Robinson, eds, *Out of Bounds: British Black and Asian Poets* (Newcastle: Bloodaxe Books, 2012).

Kelly, Aaron, *James Kelman: Politics and Aesthetics* (London: Peter Lang, 2013).

Kelman, James, *Some Recent Attacks: Essays Cultural and Political* (Stirling: AK Press, 1992).

———, *How late it was, how late* (London: Secker & Warburg, 1994).

———, *"And the Judges Said...": Essays* (London: Secker & Warburg, 2002).

———, *You Have to be Careful in the Land of the Free* (London: Hamish Hamilton, 2004).

———, *The Busconductor Hines* [1984] (Edinburgh: Polygon/Birlinn, 2007).

———, *Kieron Smith, boy* (London: Hamish Hamilton, 2008).

———, *If it is your life* (London: Hamish Hamilton, 2010).

———, *Mo said she was quirky* (London: Hamish Hamilton, 2012).

Kertzer, David I., 'Generation as a Sociological Problem', *Annual Review of Sociology*, 9 (1983), 125–49.

King, Katie, 'Audre Lorde's Lacquered Layerings: The Lesbian Bar as a Site of Literary Production', in *The New Lesbian Criticism*, ed. by Sally Munt (Hemel Hempstead: Harvester Wheatsheaf, 1992), pp. 51–74.

Klaus, H. Gustav, *The Literature of Labour: Two Hundred Years of Working-Class Writing* (Brighton: Harvester, 1985).

———, 'James C. Welsh: Major Miner Novelist', *Scottish Literary Journal*, 13.2 (1986), 65–86.

———, 'James Barke: A Great-Hearted Writer, a Hater of Oppression, a True Scot', in *A Weapon in the Struggle: The Cultural History of the Communist Party*, ed. by Andy Croft (London: Pluto, 1998), pp. 7–27.

Kövesi, Simon, *James Kelman* (Manchester: Manchester University Press, 2007).

Kristeva, Julia, *Strangers to Ourselves* (London: Harvester Wheatsheaf, 1991).

Kushnick, Louis, '"We're Here Because You Were There": Britain's Black Population', *Trotter Review*, 7.2 (1993), A Special Issue of the Political and Social Relations between Communities of Colour, Article 7.

Latif, Tariq, *The Minister's Garden* (Todmorden: Arc Publications, 1996).

Law, Alex, and Gerry Mooney, 'Devolution in a "Stateless Nation": Nation-Building and Social Policy in Scotland', *Social Policy & Administration*, 46.2 (April 2012), 161–77.

Lawson, Henry, *While the Billy Boils* (Sydney: Angus and Robertson, 1907).

Lazarus, Neil, *The Postcolonial Unconscious* (Cambridge: Cambridge University Press, 2011).

Lebel, Jean-Jacques, 'On the Necessity of Violation', *The Drama Review*, 13 (1968), 89–105.

Lecercle, Jean-Jacques, *A Marxist Philosophy of Language*, trans. by Gregory Elliot (Chicago, IL: Haymarket, 2009).

Leneman, Leah, *A Guid Cause: The Women's Suffrage Movement in Scotland*, 2nd rev. edn (Edinburgh: Mercat Press, 1995).

Letters from Sorley MacLean to Douglas Young, Acc 6419 Box 38b, National Library of Scotland.

Lindsay, Maurice, *The Scottish Renaissance* (Edinburgh: Serif, 1948).

Lingis, Alphonso, *The Community of Those Who Have Nothing in Common* (Bloomington and Indianapolis: Indiana University Press, 1994).

Lorca, Federico García, *Deep Song and Other Prose*, ed. and trans. by Christopher Maurer (London: Boyars, 1980).

Lukàcs, Georg, *Theory of the Novel* [first published in book form 1920], trans. by Anna Bostock (London: Merlin, 1971).

Lyall, Scott, *Hugh MacDiarmid's Poetry and Politics of Place: Imagining a Scottish Republic* (Edinburgh: Edinburgh University Press, 2006).

———, '"That Ancient Self": Scottish Modernism's Counter-Renaissance', *European Journal of English Studies*, 18.1 (2014), 73–85.

———, 'The Kailyard's Ghost: Community in Modern Scottish Fiction', in *Roots and Fruits of Scottish Culture: Scottish Identities, History and Contemporary Literature*, ed. by Ian Brown and Jean Berton (Glasgow: Scottish Literature International, 2014), pp. 82–96.

Maan, Bashir, *The New Scots: The Story of Asians in Scotland* (Edinburgh: John Donald Publishers, 1992).

MacCaig, Norman, 'Hugh MacDiarmid (1)', in *Poems Addressed to Hugh MacDiarmid and Presented to him on his Seventy-Fifth Birthday* (Preston: Akros, 1967).

MacColla, Fionn, *At the Sign of the Clenched Fist* (Edinburgh: M. MacDonald, 1967).

MacDiarmid, Hugh, *The Islands of Scotland: Hebrides, Orkneys, and Shetlands* (London: B.T. Batsford, 1939).

———, ed., *The Golden Treasury of Scottish Poetry* [1940] (London: Macmillan, 1941).

———, *Selected Prose*, ed. by Alan Riach (Manchester: Carcanet, 1992).

———, *Scottish Eccentrics* [1936], ed. by Alan Riach (Manchester: Carcanet, 1993).

———, *Complete Poems, Volume I*, ed. by Michael Grieve and W.R. Aitken (Manchester: Carcanet, 1993).

———, *Complete Poems, Volume II*, ed. by Michael Grieve and W.R. Aitken (Manchester: Carcanet, 1994).

———, *Lucky Poet: A Self-Study in Literature and Political Ideas, Being the Autobiography of MacDiarmidHugh (Christopher Murray Grieve)* [1943], ed. by Alan Riach (Manchester: Carcanet, 1994).

———, *Contemporary Scottish Studies* [1926], ed. by Alan Riach (Manchester: Carcanet, 1995).

———, *Albyn: Shorter Books and Monographs*, ed. by Alan Riach (Manchester: Carcanet, 1996).

———, *The Raucle Tongue: Hitherto Uncollected Prose, Volume I: 1911–1926*, ed. by Angus Calder, Glen Murray and Alan Riach (Manchester: Carcanet, 1996).

——, *The Raucle Tongue: Hitherto Uncollected Prose, Volume II: 1927–1936*, ed. by Angus Calder, Glen Murray and Alan Riach (Manchester: Carcanet, 1997).

——, *The Raucle Tongue: Hitherto Uncollected Prose, Volume III: 1937–1978*, ed. by Angus Calder, Glen Murray and Alan Riach (Manchester: Carcanet, 1998).

——, *New Selected Letters*, ed. by Dorian Grieve, O.D. Edwards and Alan Riach (Manchester: Carcanet, 2001).

——, *The Revolutionary Art of the Future: Rediscovered Poems of Hugh MacDiarmid*, ed. by John Manson, Dorian Grieve and Alan Riach (Manchester: Carcanet, 2003).

MacInnes, John, 'Gaelic Poetry in the Nineteenth Century', in *Dùthchas Nan Gàidheal: Selected Essays of John MacInnes*, ed. by Michael Newton (Edinburgh: Birlinn, 2006), pp. 357–79.

MacLean, Sorley [Somhairle MacGill-Eain], 'My Relationship with the Muse', in *Ris a' Bhruthaich: The Criticism and Prose Writings of Sorley MacLean*, ed. by William Gillies (Stornoway: Acair, 1985), pp. 6–14.

——, *From Wood to Ridge / O Choille gu Bearradh* (Manchester and Edinburgh: Carcanet / Birlinn, 1999).

——, *Caoir Gheal Leumraich / White Leaping Flame. Sorley MacLean: Collected Poems*, ed. by Christopher Whyte and Emma Dymock (Edinburgh: Polygon, 2011).

MacMillan, James, 'Scottish independence essay: arts and the referendum', *The Scotsman*, 30 April 2014 <www.scotsman.com/what-s-on/theatre-comedy-dance/scottish-independence-essay-arts-and-the-referendum-1-3393306>.

MacNeil, Kevin, ed., *These Islands, We Sing: An Anthology of Scottish Islands Poetry* (Edinburgh: Polygon, 2011).

MacNeil, Kevin, and Alec Finlay, eds, *Wish I Was Here: A Scottish Multicultural Anthology* (Edinburgh: Canongate, 2000).

Macwhirter, Iain, *Democracy in the Dark: The Decline of the Scottish Press and How to Keep the Lights On* (Edinburgh: Saltire, 2014).

——, *Disunited Kingdom: How Westminster Won a Referendum but Lost Scotland* (Glasgow: Cargo Publishing, 2014).

Magrs, Paul, 'More Tease, Less Strip', *The Guardian*, 31 August 2002 <http://www.theguardian.com/books/2002/aug/31/featuresreviews.guardianreview18>.

Malcolm, William K., *A Blasphemer & Reformer: A Study of James Leslie Mitchell / Lewis Grassic Gibbon* (Aberdeen: Aberdeen University Press, 1984).

Maley, John, *Delilah's: Stories from the Closet till Closing Time* (Glasgow: 11:9, 2002).

Maley, Willy, 'Denizens, citizens, tourists and others: marginality and mobility in the writings of James Kelman and Irvine Welsh', in *City Visions*, ed. by David Bell and Azzedine Haddour (Harlow: Prentice Hall, 2000), pp. 60–72.

Maloney, Paul, 'Twentieth-Century Popular Theatre', in *The Edinburgh Companion to Scottish Drama*, ed. by Ian Brown (Edinburgh: Edinburgh University Press, 2011), pp. 60–72.

Marr, Andrew, *Andrew Marr's Great Scots: The Writers Who Shaped a Nation*, BBC2, first broadcast 30 August 2014.

Marx, Karl, and Friedrich Engels, *The Communist Manifesto* [1848] (London: Vintage, 2010).

Maxwell, Stephen, *The Case for Left Wing Nationalism: Essays and Articles* (Edinburgh: Luath Press, 2013).

McCrone, David, *Understanding Scotland: The Sociology of a Nation*, 2nd edn (London and New York: Routledge, 2001).

McCulloch, Margery Palmer, and Kirsten Matthews, 'Transcending the Thistle in *A Drunk Man* and *Cencrastus*', in *The Edinburgh Companion to Hugh MacDiarmid*, ed. by Scott Lyall and Margery Palmer McCulloch (Edinburgh: Edinburgh University Press, 2011), pp. 58–67.

McDowell, Lesley, '*The Cutting Room* by Louise Welsh: The literary beauty of a Glaswegian beast', *The Independent*, 9 August 2002 <http://www.independent.co.uk/arts-entertainment/books/reviews/the-cutting-room-by-louise-welsh-639353.html>.

McGlynn, Mary, '"I Didn't Need to Eat": Janice Galloway's Anorexic Text and the National Body', *Critique,* 49 (2008), 221–36.

McGrath, Tom, 'Remembering Alex Trocchi', *Edinburgh Review*, 70 (1985), 36–47.

McGregor, Iona, 'Visibility Eighties Rising', in *And Thus Will I Freely Sing: An Anthology of Gay and Lesbian Writing from Scotland*, ed. by Toni Davidson (Edinburgh: Polygon, 1989), pp. 15–28.

McIlvanney, Liam, 'The Politics of Narrative in the Post-War Scottish Novel', in *On Modern British Fiction*, ed. by Zachary Leader (Oxford: Oxford University Press, 2002), pp. 181–208.

McIlvanney, William, *The Kiln* (London: Sceptre, 1996).

McLaren, Moray, 'MacAliases', *New Statesman*, 12 March 1960, p. 360.

McMillan, Joyce, 'Theatre Review: *In Time O' Strife*', *The Scotsman*, 7 October 2013, p. 17.

McNeil, Kirsty, 'Interview with James Kelman', *Chapman*, 59 (1989), 1–9.

Meek, Donald, ed., *Caran an t-Saoghal: Anthology of Nineteenth-Century Scottish Gaelic Verse* (Edinburgh: Birlinn, 2003).

Metzstein, Margery, 'Of Myths and Men: Aspects of Gender in the Fiction of Janice Galloway', in *The Scottish Novel Since the Seventies*, ed. by Gavin Wallace and Randall Stevenson (Edinburgh: Edinburgh University Press, 1993), pp. 136–46.

Miller, Gavin, *Alasdair Gray: The Fiction of Communion* (Amsterdam and New York, Rodopi, 2005).

Miller, Mitch, and Johnny Rodger, *The Red Cockatoo: James Kelman and the Art of Commitment* (Dingwall: Sandstone Press, 2011).

Miller, Sally M., *Recapitalizing America: Alternatives to the Corporate Distortion of National Policy* (Boston: Routledge and Kegan Paul, 1981).

Mills, Joseph, ed., *Borderline: The Mainstream Book of Scottish Gay Writing* (Edinburgh: Mainstream, 2001).

Mishra, Vijay, *The Literature of the Indian Diaspora: Theorising the Diasporic Imaginary* (London and New York: Routledge, 2007).

Mitchell, Jack, 'The Struggle for the Working-Class Novel in Scotland', *Zeitschrift für Anglistik und Amerikanistik*, 21.4 (1973), 384–413.

Mitchell, Robert, 'Interview with Robert Mitchell', *Scottish Theatre Archive*, 1967, Glasgow, University of Glasgow, Tape 60.

Morgan, J.O., *Natural Mechanical* (London: CB Editions, 2009).

Morrison, Ewan, *Tales from the Mall* (Glasgow: Cargo Publishing, 2012).

Moss, Sarah, *Night Waking* (London: Granta, 2011).

Muir, Edwin, *The Story and the Fable: An Autobiography* (London: George Harrap, 1940).

———, *The Voyage and Other Poems* (London: Faber and Faber, 1946).

———, *Scott and Scotland: The Predicament of the Scottish Writer* [1936] (Edinburgh: Polygon, 1982).

———, *An Autobiography* [1954] (Minnesota: Graywolf Press, 1990).

———, *Scottish Journey* [1935] (Edinburgh and London: Mainstream, 1999).

Muir, Willa, *Living with Ballads* (London: Hogarth, 1965).

———, *Imagined Corners* [1931], in *Imagined Selves*, ed. by Kirsty Allen (Edinburgh: Canongate, 1996).

Mullan, John, *Anonymity: A Secret History of English Literature* (London: Faber and Faber, 2007).

Müller, Anja, and Clare Wallace, eds, *Cosmopotia: Transnational Identities in David Greig's Theatre* (Prague: Univerzita Karlova, 2011).

Mundair, Raman, *Lovers, Liars, Conjurers and Thieves* (Leeds: Peepal Tree, 2003).

Murray, Isobel, Interview with Janice Galloway, in *Scottish Writers Talking 3* (Edinburgh: Birlinn, 2006), pp. 1–58.

Nairn, Tom, *The Break-Up of Britain: Crisis and Neo-Nationalism* (London: NLB, 1977).

Nancy, Jean-Luc, 'Of Being-in-Common', in *Community at Loose Ends*, ed. by the Miami Theory Collective (Minneapolis and Oxford: University of Minnesota Press, 1991), pp. 1–12.

———, *The Inoperative Community*, trans. by Peter Connor et al. [1991] (Minneapolis and London: University of Minnesota Press, 2008).

———, 'Communism, the Word', in *The Idea of Communism*, ed. by Costas Douzinas and Slavoj Žižek (London and New York: Verso, 2010), pp. 145–53.

———, *Adoration: The Deconstruction of Christianity II*, trans. by John McKeane (New York: Fordham University Press, 2013).

Nandan, Satendra, 'The Diasporic Consciousness: From Biswas to Biswaghat', in *Interrogating Post-colonialism: Theory, Text and Context*, ed. by Harish Trivedi and Meenakshi Mukherjee (Shimla: Indian Institute of Advanced Study, 1996).

Nash, Andrew, *Kailyard and Scottish Literature* (Amsterdam and New York: Rodopi, 2007).

———, 'Introduction', Ian Maclaren, *Beside the Bonnie Brier Bush* (Glasgow: Kennedy & Boyd, 2009), pp. ix–xvi.

Neat, Timothy, *The Summer Walkers: Travelling People and Pearl-Fishers in the Highlands of Scotland* (Edinburgh: Canongate, 1996).

———, 'The Unknown Soldier', *Scotland on Sunday*, 11 November 2007.

———, *Poetry becomes People (1952–2002)* Vol. 2, *Hamish Henderson: A Biography* (Edinburgh: Polygon/Birlinn, 2009).

Newton, Michael, *Warriors of the Word: The World of the Scottish Highlanders* (Edinburgh: Birlinn, 2009).

Nisbet, Robert, *The Quest for Community: A Study in the Ethics of Order and Freedom* [1953] (Wilmington, Del: ISI Books, 2010).

Norquay, Glenda, 'Janice Galloway's Novels: Fraudulent Mooching', in *Contemporary Scottish Women Writers*, ed. by Aileen Christianson and Alison Lumsden (Edinburgh: Edinburgh University Press, 2000), pp. 131–43.

Nuttall, Jeff, *Bomb Culture* (London: Paladin, 1968).

Owen, Robert, *A New View of Society And Other Writings* (Harmondsworth: Penguin, 1991).

Paul, Nalini, *Skirlags* (Scotland: Red Squirrel Press, 2009).

———, *Slokt by Sea* (Scotland: Red Squirrel Press, 2009).

Petrie, Duncan, *Contemporary Scottish Fictions: Film, Television and the Novel* (Edinburgh: Edinburgh University Press, 2004).

Pocock, J.G.A., *The Discovery of Islands: Essays in British History* (Cambridge: Cambridge University Press, 2005).

Puar, Jasbir K., *Terrorist Assemblages: Homonationalism in Queer Times* (Durham and London: Duke University Press, 2007).

Punter, David, 'The Uncanny', in *The Routledge Companion to Gothic*, ed. by Catherine Spooner and Emma McEvoy (London and New York: Routledge, 2007), pp. 129–36.

Purdie, Bob, *Hugh MacDiarmid: Black, Green, Red and Tartan* (Cardiff: Welsh Academic Press, 2012).

Rancière, Jacques, *On the Shores of Politics*, trans. by Liz Heron (London and New York: Verso, 1995).

———, *The Flesh of Words: The Politics of Writing*, trans. by Charlotte Mandell (Stanford: Stanford University Press, 2004).

Ratmoko, David, *On Spectrality: Fantasies of Redemption in the Western Canon* (New York: Peter Lang, 2006).

Rebellato, Dan, 'Introduction', in David Greig, *Plays: One* (London: Methuen, 2002), pp. ix–xxiii.

Redfield, Robert, *The Little Community*, in *The Little Community* and *Peasant Society and Culture* (Chicago and London: Phoenix Books, 1963).

Reid, Trish, *Theatre and Scotland* (Basingstoke: Palgrave Macmillan, 2013).

———, 'Staging Scotland: National Theatre of Scotland and Shifting Conceptions of Scottish Identity', in *The Media in Europe's Small Nations*, ed. by Huw David Jones (Newcastle: Cambridge Scholars Press, 2014), pp. 105–20.

Riley, Denise, *The Words of Selves: Identification, Solidarity, Irony* (Stanford, CA: Stanford University Press, 2000).

Robinson, Peter D., 'The Wabe', in *And Thus Will I Freely Sing*, ed. by Toni Davidson (Edinburgh: Polygon, 1989), pp. 29–36.

Rose, Gillian, *The Broken Middle: Out of Our Ancient Society* (Oxford: Blackwell, 1992).

Rousseau, Jean-Jacques, *Reveries of the Solitary Walker* [1782], trans. by Peter France (London: Penguin, 2004).

Royle, Nicholas, 'Manifestations of Insanity: *Hunger* and contemporary fiction', *The Uncanny* (Manchester: Manchester University Press, 1993), pp. 213–18.

Rutherford, Jonathan, 'A Place Called Home: Identity and the Cultural Politics of Difference', in *Identity: Community, Culture, Difference*, ed. by Jonathan Rutherford (London: Lawrence & Wishart, 1990), pp. 9–27.

Sartre, Jean-Paul, *Existentialism and Human Emotions* [1957] (New York: Citadel, 1994).

———, *'What Is Literature?' And Other Essays* (Cambridge: Harvard, 1998).

Schalansky, Judith, *Atlas of Remote Islands*, trans. by Christine Lo (London: Particular Books, 2010).

Scott, Andrew Murray, *Alexander Trocchi: The Making of the Monster* (Edinburgh: Polygon, 1991).

Scottish Arts Council, *Scottish National Theatre: Final Report of the Independent Working Group*, 2001 <http://www.sac.org.uk/nonhtdocs/single-page-pdf>.

Scullion, Adrienne, 'Glasgow Unity Theatre: The Necessary Contradictions of Scottish Political Theatre', *Twentieth Century British History*, 13.3 (2002), 215–52.

Shelley, Percy Bysshe, *A Defence of Poetry* [1840], in *The Major Works*, ed. by Zachary Leader and Michael O'Neill (Oxford: Oxford University Press, 2003), pp. 674–701.

Shepherd, Gillian, 'The Kailyard', in *The History of Scottish Literature, Vol. 3: Nineteenth Century*, ed. by Douglas Gifford, 4 vols (Aberdeen: Aberdeen University Press, 1989), pp. 309–18.

Sierz, Aleks, *In-Yer-Face Theatre: British Drama Today* (London: Methuen, 2001).

Silver, Christopher, 'Lewis Grassic Gibbon and Scottish Nationalism', in *The International Companion to Lewis Grassic Gibbon*, ed. by Scott Lyall (Glasgow: Scottish Literature International, 2015), pp. 105–18.

Silver, Naomi E., 'The Politics of Sacrifice', in *The Politics of Community*, ed. by Michael Strysick (Aurora, CO: The Davies Group, 2002), pp. 201–19.

Silverstein, Michael, 'Whorfianism and the Linguistic Imagination of Nationality', in *Regimes of Language: Ideologies, Polities and Identities*, ed. by Paul V. Kroskrity (Santa Fe, NM: School of American Research Press, 2000), pp. 85–138.

Sinfield, Alan, *Gay and After* (London: Serpent's Tail, 1998).

———, *Literature, Politics and Culture in Postwar Britain* (London: Continuum, 2004).

Smith, Ali, *Girl Meets Boy* (Edinburgh: Canongate, 2007).

Smith, Alison, 'Four Success Stories', *Chapman*, 74–5 (1993), 177–92.

———, 'And Woman Created Woman: Carswell, Shepherd and Muir, and the Self-made Woman', in *Gendering the Nation: Studies in Modern Scottish Literature*, ed. by Christopher Whyte (Edinburgh: Edinburgh University Press, 1995), pp. 25–48.

Smith, Donald, 'The Mid-Century Dramatists', in *The Edinburgh Companion to Scottish Drama*, ed. by Ian Brown (Edinburgh: Edinburgh University Press, 2011), pp. 118–29.

Smith, Iain Crichton, 'Real People in a Real Place', in *Towards the Human: Selected Essays* (Edinburgh: MacDonald Publishers, 1986), pp. 37–38.

———, *Collected Poems* (Manchester: Carcanet, 1992).

———, *The Red Door: The Complete English Stories 1949–76*, ed. by Kevin MacNeil (Edinburgh: Birlinn, 2001).

Smith, Mark Ryan, *The Literature of Shetland* (Lerwick: The Shetland Times Ltd., 2014).

Smith, Stephen P., 'Hugh MacDiarmid's *Lucky Poet*: Autobiography and the Art of Attack', in *Hugh MacDiarmid: Man and Poet*, ed. by Nancy K. Gish (Edinburgh: Edinburgh University Press, 1992), pp. 275–94.

Snow, Edgar, *Red Star Over China* [1938] (Harmondsworth: Penguin, 1972).

Spark, Muriel, *The Prime of Miss Jean Brodie* [1961] (London: Penguin, 2000).

Spurling, Hilary, *Burying the Bones: Pearl Buck in China* (London: Profile Books, 2010).

Steven, Kenneth C., 'The Nihilism of the New', *The Herald*, 1 June 1996, p. 23.

Stevenson, Randall, 'Drama, Language and Revival', in *The Edinburgh Companion to Scottish Drama*, ed. by Ian Brown (Edinburgh: Edinburgh University Press, 2011), pp. 73–84.

Stevenson, Robert Louis, *Strange Case of Dr Jekyll and Mr Hyde* [1886] (New York: Norton, 2003).

Strysick, Michael, 'The End of Community and the Politics of Grammar', in *The Politics of Community*, ed. by Michael Strysick (Aurora, CO: The Davies Group, 2002), pp. 45–64.

Sutherland, Luke, *Venus as a Boy* (London: Bloomsbury, 2004).

Tange, Hanne, 'Language, Class and Social Power in *A Scots Quair*', in *The International Companion to Lewis Grassic Gibbon*, ed. by Scott Lyall (Glasgow: Scottish Literature International, 2015), pp. 22–32.

Thatcher, Margaret, 'Aids, education and the year 2000!' ['There is no such thing as society'], interview for *Woman's Own*, 31 October 1987, pp. 8–10 <http://www.margaretthatcher.org/speeches/displaydocument.asp?docid=106689>.

Thomson, Alex, '"You can't get there from here": Devolution and Scottish literary history', *International Journal of Scottish Literature*, 3 (2007).

Thomson, Derick S. [Ruaraidh MacThomais], *Creachadh na Clarsaiach: Cruinneachadh de Bhardachd, 1940–1980 / Plundering the Harp: Collected Poems, 1940–1980* (Edinburgh: MacDonald, 1982).

Tobar an Dualchais / Kist o Riches, Digital Archives from the School of Scottish Studies (University of Edinburgh), BBC Scotland, and the National Trust for Scotland's Canna Collection <http://www.tobarandualchais.co.uk>.

Tönnies, Ferdinand, *Community and Association* [first published in German 1887], trans. by Charles P. Loomis (London: Routledge & Kegan Paul, 1974).

Trengove, Graham, 'Who is you? Grammar and Grassic Gibbon', *Scottish Literary Journal* 2.2 (1975), 47–62.

Trocchi, Alexander, 'Editorial', *Merlin Collection*, 2.1 (1952).

———, 'Editorial', *Merlin Collection*, 3.1 (1952–53).

———, 'Words and War', *Merlin*, 3.2 (1954), 141–43 and 209–27.

———, 'Potlach', *Sigma Portfolio*, 4 (1964).

———, 'Sigma: General Informations "Third Impression"', *Sigma Portfolio*, 5 (1964).

———, 'Subscription Form', *Sigma Portfolio*, 12 (1964).

———, 'Sigma: A Tactical Blueprint', in *Invisible Insurrection of a Million Minds: A Trocchi Reader*, ed. by Andrew Murray Scott (Edinburgh: Polygon, 1991), pp. 192–203.

———, 'The Invisible Insurrection of a Million Minds', in *Invisible Insurrection of a Million Minds: A Trocchi Reader*, ed. by Andrew Murray Scott (Edinburgh: Polygon, 1991), pp. 177–91.

———, *Cain's Book* [1960] (London: Calder, 1992).

———, *Young Adam* [1954] (Oxford: Oneworld, 2003).

Trocchi, Alexander, and Phillip Green, 'project sigma: Cultural Engineering', in *A Life in Pieces: Reflections on Alexander Trocchi*, ed. by Allan Campbell and Tim Niel (Edinburgh: Rebel Inc., 1997), pp. 189–93.

Veitch, James, *George Douglas Brown* (London: Herbert Jenkins, 1952).

Vertovec, Steven, *Transnationalism* (London and New York: Routledge, 2009).

Volosinov, V.N., *Marxism and the Philosophy of Language*, trans. by Ladislav Matejka and I.R. Titunik (London: Harvard University Press, 1986).

Wallace, Gavin, 'Introduction', in *The Scottish Novel Since the Seventies*, ed. by Gavin Wallace and Randall Stevenson (Edinburgh: Edinburgh University Press, 1993), pp. 1–7.

———, 'Voices in Empty Houses: The Novel of Damaged Identity', in *The Scottish Novel Since the Seventies*, ed. by Gavin Wallace and Randall Stevenson (Edinburgh: Edinburgh University Press, 1993), pp. 217–31.

Waugh, Patricia, *Harvest of the Sixties: English Literature and Its Background, 1960 to 1990* (Oxford: Oxford University Press, 1995).

Welsh, Irvine, 'A Smart Cunt', in *The Acid House* (London: Vintage, 1995).

———, *Trainspotting* [1993] (London: Vintage, 2004).

Welsh, James C., *Songs of a Miner* (London: Herbert Jenkins, 1917).

———, *The Underworld: The Story of Robert Sinclair, Miner* (London: Herbert Jenkins, 1923).

Welsh, Louise, *The Cutting Room* (Edinburgh: Canongate, 2002).

———, *Naming the Bones* (Edinburgh: Canongate, 2010).

Weston, Kath, *Families We Choose: Lesbians, Gays, Kinship* (New York: Columbia University Press, 1991).

Whyte, Betsy, *The Yellow on the Broom* (Edinburgh: Chambers, 1979).

———, *Red Rowans and Wild Honey* (Edinburgh: Canongate, 1990).

Whyte, Christopher, ed., *Gendering the Nation: Studies in Modern Scottish Literature* (Edinburgh: Edinburgh University Press, 1995).

———, *The Gay Decameron* (London: Victor Gollancz, 1998).

———, *Bho Leabhar-Latha Maria Malibran / From the Diary of Maria Malibran*, Gaelic poems with English versions by Michel Byrne, Sally Evans, W.N. Herbert, Ian MacDonald, Niall O'Gallagher and the author (Stornoway: Acair, 2009).

Williams, Raymond, *The English Novel from Dickens to Lawrence* (London: Chatto and Windus, 1973).

Winning, Joanne, ed., *The Crazy Jig* (Edinburgh: Polygon, 1992).

———, 'Crossing the Borderline: Post-devolution Scottish Lesbian and Gay Writing', in *The Edinburgh Companion to Contemporary Scottish Literature*, ed. by Berthold Schoene (Edinburgh: Edinburgh University Press, 2007), pp. 283–91.

Wood, Michael, *Children of Silence: Studies in Contemporary Fiction* (London: Pimlico, 1998).

Young, Iris Marion, 'The Ideal of Community and the Politics of Difference', in *Feminism / Postmodernism*, ed. by Linda J. Nicholson (London and New York: Routledge, 1990), pp. 300–23.

Yule, Eleanor, and David Manderson, *The Glass Half Full: Moving Beyond Scottish Miserabilism* (Edinburgh: Luath, 2014).

Zerdy, Joanne, 'Fashioning a Scottish Operative: *Black Watch* and Banal Theatrical Nationalism on Tour in the US', *Theatre Research International*, 38.3 (2013), 181–95.

Index